VISIT US AT

D1484643

www.syngress.com

Syngress is committed to publishing high-quality books for IT Professionals and delivering those books in media and formats that fit the demands of our customers. We are also committed to extending the utility of the book you purchase via additional materials available from our Web site.

SOLUTIONS WEB SITE

To register your book, visit www.syngress.com/solutions. Once registered, you can access our solutions@syngress.com Web pages. There you may find an assortment of value-added features such as free e-books related to the topic of this book, URLs of related Web sites, FAQs from the book, corrections, and any updates from the author(s).

ULTIMATE CDs

Our Ultimate CD product line offers our readers budget-conscious compilations of some of our best-selling backlist titles in Adobe PDF form. These CDs are the perfect way to extend your reference library on key topics pertaining to your area of expertise, including Cisco Engineering, Microsoft Windows System Administration, CyberCrime Investigation, Open Source Security, and Firewall Configuration, to name a few.

DOWNLOADABLE E-BOOKS

For readers who can't wait for hard copy, we offer most of our titles in downloadable Adobe PDF form. These e-books are often available weeks before hard copies, and are priced affordably.

SYNGRESS OUTLET

Our outlet store at syngress.com features overstocked, out-of-print, or slightly hurt books at significant savings.

SITE LICENSING

Syngress has a well-established program for site licensing our e-books onto servers in corporations, educational institutions, and large organizations. Contact us at sales@syngress.com for more information.

CUSTOM PUBLISHING

Many organizations welcome the ability to combine parts of multiple Syngress books, as well as their own content, into a single volume for their own internal use. Contact us at sales@syngress.com for more information.

SYNGRESS®

Google Hacking

FOR PENETRATION TESTERS
VOLUME 2

Johnny Long

KEY	SERIAL NUMBER
001	HJIRTCV764
002	PO9873D5FG
003	829KM8NJH2
004	TYK428MML8
005	CVPLQ6WQ23
006	VBP965T5T5
007	HJJJ863WD3E
008	2987GVTWMK
009	629MP5SDJT
010	IMWQ295T6T

PUBLISHED BY
Syngress Publishing, Inc.
Elsevier, Inc.
30 Corporate Drive
Burlington, MA 01803

Google Hacking for Penetration Testers, Volume 2

Printed in the United States of America
1 2 3 4 5 6 7 8 9 0
ISBN 13: 978-1-59749-176-1

Publisher: Amorette Pedersen
Acquisitions Editor: Andrew Williams
Cover Designer: Michael Kavish
Page Layout and Art: Patricia Lupien
Copy Editor: Judy Eby
Indexer: J. Edmund Rush

For information on rights, translations, and bulk sales, contact Matt Pedersen, Commercial Sales Director and Rights, at Syngress Publishing; email m.pedersen@elsevier.com.

Acknowledgments

There are many people to thank this time around, and I won't get to them all. But I'll give it my best shot. First and foremost, thanks to God for the many blessings in my life. Christ for the Living example, and the Spirit of God that encourages me to live each day with real purpose. Thanks to my wife and three wonderful children. Words can't express how much you mean to me. Thanks for putting up with the "real" j0hnny.

Thanks to the book team: CP, Seth Fogie, Jeffball55, L0om, pdp, Roelof Temmingh, Rar, Zanthas. Thanks to my friends Nathan, Mike "Corn" Chaney, Seth Fogie, Arun, @tlas and Apu. Thanks to my many confidants and supporters in the Shmoo group, the ihackcharities volunteers and supporters, Malcolm Mead and Pat, The Predestined (David, Em, Isaac, Josh, Steve, Vanessa), The Tushabe family, Dennis and all of the AOET family.

I would also like to take this opportunity to thank the members of the Google Hacking Community. The following have made the book and the movement of Google Hacking what it is. They are listed below, sorted by number of contributions to the GHDB.

Jimmy Neutron (107), rgod (104), murfie (74), golfo (54), Klouw (52), CP (48), L0om (32), stonersavant (32), cybercide (27), jeffball55 (23), Fr0zen (22), wolveso (22), yeseins (22), Rar (21), ThePsyko (20), MacUk (18), crash_monkey (17), MILKMAN (17), zoro25 (15), digital.revolution (15), Cesar (15), sfd (14), hermes (13), mlynch (13), Renegade334 (12), urban (12), deadlink (11), Butt-Pipe (11), FiZiX (10), webby_guy (10), jeffball55+CP (8), James (7), Z!nCh (7), xlockex (6), ShadowSpoof (6), noAcces (5), vipsta (5), injection33 (5), Fr0zen+MacUK (5), john (5), Peefy (4), sac (4), sylex (4), dtire (4), Deakster (4), jorokin (4), Fr0zen rgod (4), zurik6am (4), brasileiro (4), miss.Handle (4), golfo42 (3), romosapien (3), klouw (3), MERLiiN (3), Darksun (3), Deeper (3), jeffball55+klouw (3), ComSec (3), Wasabi (3), THX (3), putsCTO (3)

The following made two additions to the GHDB: HaVoC88, ToFu, Digital_Spirit, CP and golfo, ceasar2, namenone, youmolo, MacUK / CP / Klouw, 242, golfo, CP and jeff, golfo and CP, Solereaper cp, nuc, bigwreck_3705, ericf, ximum, /iachilles, MacUK

/ CP, golfo and jeffball55, hevnsnt, PiG_DoG, GIGO, Tox1cFaith, strace, dave@cirt.net, murk, klouw & sylex, NRoberts, X-Ravin, ZyMoTiCo, dc0, Fr0zen jeffball55, Rar CP, rgod jeffball55, vs1400, pitt2k, John Farr, Kartik, QuadsteR, server1, rar klouw, Steve Campbell

The following made one addition to the GHDB: Richie Wolk, baxter_jb, D3ADLiN3, accesspwd1, darkwalk, bungerScorpio, Liqdfire, pmedinua, WarriorClown, murfie & webbyguy, stonersavant, klouw, thereallinuxinit, arrested, Milkman & Vipsta, Jamuse and Wolveso, FiZiX and c0wz, spreafd, blaqueworm, HackerBlaster, FiZiX and klouw, Capboy118, Mac & CP, philY, CP and MacUK, rye, jeffball55 MacUK CP9, rgod + CP, maveric, rar, CP, rgod + jeffball55, norocosul_alex R00t, Solereaper, Daniel Bates, Kevin LAcroix, ThrowedOff, Apoc, mastakillah, juventini, plaztic, Abder, hevensnt, yeseins & klouw, bsdman & klouw & mil, digital.ronin, harry-aac, none90810, donjoe145, toxic-snipe, shadowsliv, golfo and klouw, MacUK / Klouw, Carnage, pulverized, Demogorgo, guardian, golfo, macuk, klouw,, Cylos, nihil2006, anonymous, murfie and rgod, D. Garcia, offset, average joe, sebastian, mikem, Andrew A. Vladimirov, bullmoose, effexca, kammo, burhansk, cybercide cybercide, Meohaw, ponds, blackasinc, mr.smoot, digital_revolution, freeeak, zawa, rolf, cykyc, golfo wolveso, sfd wolveso, shellcoder, Jether, jochem, MacUK / df, tikbalang, mysteryman0122, irn-bru, blue_matrix, dopefish, muts, filbert, adsl3000, FiNaLBeTa, draino, bARDO, Z!nCh & vs1400, abinidi, klouw & murfie, wwooww, stonersavant, jimmyn, linuxinit, url, dragg, pedro#, jon335, sfd cseven, russ, kg1, greenflame, vyom, EviL_Phreak, golfo, CP, klouw,, rar murfie, Golem, rgod +murfie, Madness!, de Mephisteau, gEnTi, murfie & wolveso, DxM, l0om wolveso, olviTar, digitus, stamhaney, serenh, NaAcces, Kai, good-virus, barabas, fasullo, ghooli, digitalanimal, Ophidian, MacUK / CP / Jeffb, NightHacker, BinaryGenius, Mindframe, TechStep, rgod +jeffball55 +cp, Fusion, Phil Carmody, johnny, laughing_clown, joenorris, peefy & joenorris, bugged, xxC0BRAxx, Klouw & Renegade334, Front242, Klouw & digital.revo, yomero, Siress, wolves, DonnyC, toadflax, mojo.jojo, cseven, mamba n★p, mynewuser, Ringo, Mac / CP, MacUK / golfo, trinkett, jazzy786, paulfaz, Ronald MacDonald, .-DioXin-., jerry c, robertserr, norbert.schuler, zoro25 / golfo, cyber_, PhatKahr4u2c, hyp3r, offtopic, jJimmyNeutron, Counterhack, ziggy1621, Demonic_Angel, XTCA2S, m00d, marco-media, codehunter007, AnArmyOfNone, MegaHz, Maerim, xyberpix, D-jump Fizix, D-jump, Flight Lieutenant Co, windsor_rob, Mac, TPSMC, Navaho Gunleg, EviL Phreak, sfusion, paulfaz, Jeffball55, rgod + cp clean +, stokaz, Revan-th, Don, xewan, Blackdata, wifimuthafucka, chadom, ujen, bunker, Klouw & Jimmy Neutro, JimmyNeutron & murfi, amafui, battletux, lester, rippa, hexsus, jounin, Stealth05,

WarChylde, demonio, plazmo, golfo42 & deeper, jeffball55 with cle, MacUK / CP / Klou, Staplerkid, firefalconx, ffenix, hypetech, ARollingStone, kicktd, Solereaper Rar, rgod + webby_guy, googler.

Lastly, I would like to reiterate my thanks to everyone mentioned in the first edition, all of which are still relevant to me:

Thanks to Mom and Dad for letting me stay up all hours as I fed my digital addiction. Thanks to the book team, Alrik "Murf" van Eijkelenborg, James Foster, Steve, Matt, Pete and Roelof. Mr. Cooper, Mrs. Elliott, Athy C, Vince Ritts, Jim Chapple, Topher H, Mike Schiffman, Dominique Brezinski and rain.forest.puppy all stopped what they were doing to help shape my future. I couldn't make it without the help of close friends to help me through life: Nathan B, Sujay S, Stephen S. Thanks to Mark Norman for keeping it real. The Google Masters from the Google Hacking forums made many contributions to the forums and the GHDB, and I'm honored to list them here in descending post total order: murfie, jimmyneutron, klouw, l0om, ThePsyko, MILKMAN, cybercide, stonersavant, Deadlink, crash_monkey, zoro25, Renegade334, wasabi, urban, mlynch, digital.revolution, Peefy, brasileiro, john, Z!nCh, ComSec, yeseins, sfd, sylex, wolveso, xlockex, injection33, Murk. A special thanks to Murf for keeping the site afloat while I wrote this book, and also to mod team: ThePsyko, l0om, wasabi, and jimmyneutron.

The StrikeForce was always hard to describe, but it encompassed a large part of my life, and I'm very thankful that I was able to play even a small part: Jason A, Brian A, Jim C, Roger C, Carter, Carey, Czup, Ross D, Fritz, Jeff G, Kevin H, Micha H, Troy H, Patrick J, Kristy, Dave Klug, Logan L, Laura, Don M, Chris Mclelland, Murray, Deb N, Paige, Roberta, Ron S, Matty T, Chuck T, Katie W, Tim W, Mike W.

Thanks to CSC and the many awesome bosses I've had. You rule: "FunkSoul", Chris S, Matt B, Jason E, and Al E. Thanks to the 'TIP crew for making life fun and interesting five days out of seven. You're too many to list, but some I remember I've worked with more than others: Anthony, Brian, Chris, Christy, Don, Heidi, Joe, Kevan, The 'Mikes', "O", Preston, Richard, Rob, Ron H, Ron D, Steve, Torpedo, Thane.

It took a lot of music to drown out the noise so I could churn out this book. Thanks to P.O.D. (thanks Sonny for the words), Pillar, Project 86, Avalon O2 remix, D.J. Lex, Yoshinori Sunahara, Hashim and SubSeven (great name!). (Updated for second edition: Green Sector, Pat C., Andy Hunter, Matisyahu, Bono and U2). Shouts to securitytribe, Joe Grand, Russ Rogers, Roelof Temmingh, Seth Fogie, Chris Hurley, Bruce Potter, Jeff, Ping, Eli, Grifter at Blackhat, and the whole Syngress family of authors. I'm honored to be a part of the group, although you all keep me humble! Thanks to Andrew and Jaime. You guys rule!

Thanks to Apple Computer, Inc for making an awesome laptop (and OS).

—Johnny Long

Lead Author

"I'm Johnny. I Hack Stuff."

Have you ever had a hobby that changed your life? This Google Hacking thing began as a hobby, but sometime in 2004 it transformed into an unexpected gift. In that year, the high point of my professional career was a speaking gig I landed at Defcon. I was on top of the world that year and I let it get to my head—I really was an egotistical little turd. I presented my Google Hacking talk, making sure to emulate the rock-star speakers I admired. The talk went well, securing rave reviews and hinting at a rock-star speaking career of my own. The outlook was very promising, but the weekend left me feeling empty.

In the span of two days a series of unfortunate events flung me from the mountaintop of success and slammed me mercilessly onto the craggy rocks of the valley of despair. Overdone? A bit, but that's how it felt for me—and I didn't even get a Balroc carcass out of the deal. I'm not sure what caused me to do it, but I threw up my hands and gave up all my professional spoils—my career, my five hundred user website and my fledgling speaking career—to God.

At the time, I didn't exactly understand what that meant, but I was serious about the need for drastic change and the inexplicable desire to live with a higher purpose. For the first time in my life, I saw the shallowness and self-centeredness of my life, and it horrified me. I wanted something more, and I asked for it in a real way. The funny thing is, I got so much more than I asked for.

Syngress approached and asked if I would write a book on *Google Hacking,* the first edition of the book you're holding. Desperately hoping I could mask my inexperience and distaste for writing, I accepted what I would come to call the "original gift." *Google Hacking* is now a best seller.

My website grew from 500 to nearly 80,000 users. The Google book project led to ten or so additional book projects. The media tidal wave was impressive—first came Slashdot, followed quickly by the online, print, TV and cable outlets. I quickly earned my world traveler credentials as conference bookings started pouring in. The community I wanted so much to be a part of—the hacking community—embraced me unconditionally, despite my newly conservative outlook. They bought books through my website, generating income for charity, and eventually they fully funded my wife and me on our mission's trip to Uganda, Africa. That series of events changed my life and set the stage for ihackcharities.com, an organization aimed at connecting the skills of the hacking community with charities that need those skills. My "real" life is transformed as well—my relationship with my wife and kids is better than it ever has been.

So as you can see, this is so much more than just a book to me. This really was the original gift, and I took the task of updating it very seriously. I've personally scrutinized every single word and photo—especially the ones I've written—to make sure it's done right. I'm proud of this second edition, and I'm grateful to you, the reader, for supporting the efforts of the many that have poured themselves into this project. Thank you.

Thank you for visiting us at **http://johnny.ihackstuff.com** and for getting the word out. Thank you for supporting and linking to the Google Hacking Database. Thank you for clicking through our Amazon links to fund charities. Thank you for giving us a platform to affect real change, not only in the security community but also in the world at large. I am truly humbled by your support.

—*Johnny Long*
October 2007

Contributing Authors

Roelof Temmingh Born in South Africa, Roelof studied at the University of Pretoria and completed his Electronic Engineering degree in 1995. His passion for computer security had by then caught up with him and manifested itself in various forms. He worked as developer, and later as a system architect at an information security engineering firm from 1995 to 2000. In early 2000 he founded the security assessment and consulting firm SensePost along with some of the leading thinkers in the field. During his time at SensePost he was the Technical Director in charge of the assessment team and later headed the Innovation Centre for the company. Roelof has spoken at various international conferences such as Blackhat, Defcon, Cansecwest, RSA, Ruxcon, and FIRST. He has contributed to books such as *Stealing the Network: How to Own a Continent, Penetration Tester's Open*

Source Toolkit, and was one of the lead trainers in the "Hacking by Numbers" training course. Roelof has authored several well known security testing applications like Wikto, Crowbar, BiDiBLAH and Suru. At the start of 2007 he founded Paterva in order to pursue R&D in his own capacity. At Paterva Roelof developed an application called Evolution (now called Maltego) that has shown tremendous promise in the field of information collection and correlation.

Petko "pdp" D. Petkov is a senior IT security consultant based in London, United Kingdom. His day-to-day work involves identifying vulnerabilities, building attack strategies and creating attack tools and penetration testing infrastructures. Petko is known in the underground circles as pdp or architect but his name is well known in the IT security industry for his strong technical background and creative thinking. He has been working for some of the world's top companies, providing consultancy on the latest security vulnerabilities and attack technologies.

His latest project, GNUCITIZEN (gnucitizen.org), is one of the leading web application security resources on-line where part of his work is disclosed for the benefit of the public. Petko defines himself as a cool hunter in the security circles.

He lives with his lovely girlfriend Ivana, without whom his contribution to this book would not have been possible.

CP is a moderator of the GHDB and forums at http://johnny.ihackstuff.com, a Developer of many open source tools including Advanced Dork: and Google Site Indexer, Co-Founder of http://tankedgenius.com , a freelance security consultant, and an active member of DC949 http://dc949.org in which he takes part in developing and running an annual hacking contest Known as Amateur/Open Capture the Flag as well as various research projects.

"I am many things, but most importantly, a hacker." – CP

Jeff Stewart, Jeffball55, currently attends East Stroudsburg University where he's majoring in Computer Science, Computer Security, and Applied Mathematics. He actively participates on johnny.ihackstuff.com forums, where he often writes programs and Firefox extensions that interact with Google's services. All of his current projects can be found on http://www.tankedgenius.com. More recently he has taken a job with FD Software Enterprise, to help produce an Incident Management System for several hospitals.

Ryan Langley is a California native who is currently residing in Los Angeles. A part time programmer and security evaluator Ryan is constantly exploring and learning about IT security, and new evaluation techniques. Ryan has five years of system repair and administration experience. He can often be found working on a project with either CP or Jeffball.

Contents

## Chapter 1

Google Searching Basics

Solutions in this chapter:

- Exploring Google's Web-based Interface
- Building Google Queries
- Working With Google URLs

☑ Summary

☑ Solutions Fast Track

☑ Frequently Asked Questions

Introduction

Google's Web interface is unmistakable. Its "look and feel" is copyright-protected, and for good reason. It is clean and simple. What most people fail to realize is that the interface is also extremely powerful. Throughout this book, we will see how you can use Google to uncover truly amazing things. However, as in most things in life, before you can run, you must learn to walk.

This chapter takes a look at the basics of Google searching. We begin by exploring the powerful Web-based interface that has made Google a household word. Even the most advanced Google users still rely on the Web-based interface for the majority of their day-to-day queries. Once we understand how to navigate and interpret the results from the various interfaces, we will explore basic search techniques.

Understanding basic search techniques will help us build a firm foundation on which to base more advanced queries. You will learn how to properly use the Boolean operators (*AND*, *NOT*, and *OR*) as well as exploring the power and flexibility of grouping searches. We will also learn Google's unique implementation of several different wildcard characters.

Finally, you will learn the syntax of Google's Uniform Resource Locator (URL) structure. Learning the ins and outs of the Google URL will give you access to greater speed and flexibility when submitting a series of related Google searches. We will see that the Google URL structure provides an excellent "shorthand" for exchanging interesting searches with friends and colleagues.

Exploring Google's Web-based Interface

Google's Web Search Page

The main Google Web page, shown in Figure 1.1, can be found at www.google.com. The interface is known for its clean lines, pleasingly uncluttered feel, and friendly interface. Although the interface might seem relatively featureless at first glance, we will see that many different search functions can be performed right from this first page.

As shown in Figure 1.1, there's only one place to type. This is the *search field*. In order to ask Google a question or query, you simply type what you're looking for and either press **Enter** (if your browser supports it) or click the **Google Search** button to be taken to the results page for your query.

Figure 1.1 The Main Google Web Page

The links at the top of the screen (Web, Images, Video, and so on) open the other search areas shown in Table 1.1. The basic search functionality of each section is the same: each search area of the Google Web interface has different capabilities and accepts different search operators, as we will see in Chapter 2. For example, the *author* operator works well in Google Groups, but may fail in other search areas. Table 1.1 outlines the functionality of each distinct area of the main Google Web page.

Table 1.1 The Links and Functions of Google's Main Page

Interface Section	Description
The Google toolbar	The browser I am using has a Google "toolbar" installed and presented next to the address bar. We will take a look at various Google toolbars in the next section.
Web, Images, Video, News, Maps, Gmail and more tabs	These tabs allow you to search Web pages, photographs, message group postings, Google maps, and Google Mail, respectively. If you are a first-time Google user, understand that these tabs are not always a replacement for the Submit Search button. These tabs simply whisk you away to other Google search applications.
iGoogle	This link takes you to your personal Google home page.

Continued

Table 1.1 The Links and Functions of Google's Main Page

Interface Section	Description
Sign in	This link allows you to sign in to access additional functionality by logging in to your Google Account.
Search term input field	Located directly below the alternate search tabs, this text field allows you to enter a Google search term. We will discuss the syntax of Google searching throughout this book.
Google Search button	This button submits your search term. In many browsers, simply pressing the Enter/Return key after typing a search term will activate this button.
I'm Feeling Lucky button	Instead of presenting a list of search results, this button will forward you to the highest-ranked page for the entered search term. Often this page is the most relevant page for the entered search term.
Advanced Search	This link takes you to the Advanced Search page as shown. We will look at these advanced search options in Chapter 2.
Preferences	This link allows you to select several options (which are stored in cookies on your machine for later retrieval). Available options include language selection, parental filters, number of results per page, and window options.
Language tools	This link allows you to set many different language options and translate text to and from various languages.

Google Web Results Page

After it processes a search query, Google displays a results page. The results page, shown in Figure 1.2, lists the results of your search and provides links to the Web pages that contain your search text.

The top part of the search result page mimics the main Web search page. Notice the Images, Video, News, Maps, and Gmail links at the top of the page. By clicking these links from a search page, you automatically resubmit your search as another type of search, without having to retype your query.

Figure 1.2 A Typical Web Search Results Page

The results line shows which results are displayed (1–10, in this case), the approximate total number of matches (here, over eight million), the search query itself (including links to dictionary lookups of individual words), and the amount of time the query took to execute. The speed of the query is often overlooked, but it is quite impressive. Even large queries resulting in millions of hits are returned within a fraction of a second!

For each entry on the results page, Google lists the name of the site, a summary of the site (usually the first few lines of content), the URL of the page that matched, the size and date the page was last crawled, a cached link that shows the page as it appeared when Google last crawled it, and a link to pages with similar content. If the result page is written in a language other than your native language and Google supports the translation from that language into yours (set in the preferences screen), a link titled *Translate this page* will appear, allowing you to read an approximation of that page in your own language (see Figure 1.3).

Figure 1.3 Google Translation

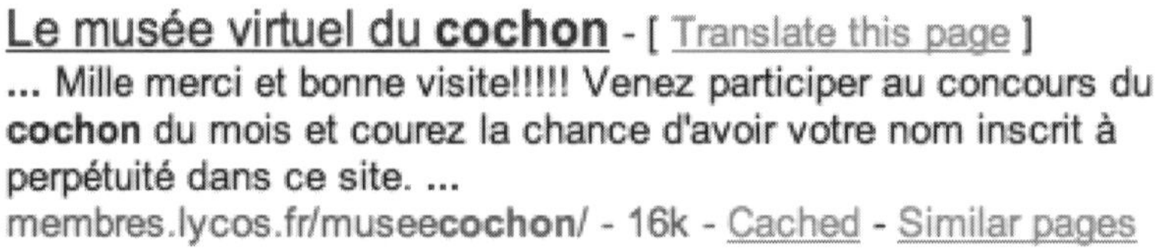

<u>Le musée virtuel du **cochon**</u> - [<u>Translate this page</u>]
... Mille merci et bonne visite!!!!! Venez participer au concours du
cochon du mois et courez la chance d'avoir votre nom inscrit à
perpétuité dans ce site. ...
membres.lycos.fr/musee**cochon**/ - 16k - <u>Cached</u> - <u>Similar pages</u>

Underground Googling...

Translation Proxies

It's possible to use Google as a transparent proxy server via the translation service. When you click a *Translate this page* link, you are taken to a translated copy of that page hosted on Google's servers. This serves as a sort of proxy server, fetching the page on your behalf. If the page you want to view requires no translation, you can still use the translation service as a proxy server by modifying the *hl* variable in the URL to match the native language of the page. Bear in mind that images are not proxied in this manner.

Google Groups

Due to the surge in popularity of Web-based discussion forums, blogs, mailing lists, and instant-messaging technologies, USENET newsgroups, the oldest of public discussion forums, have become an overlooked form of online public discussion. Thousands of users still post to USENET on a daily basis. A thorough discussion about what USENET encompasses can be found at www.faqs.org/faqs/usenet/what-is/part1/. DejaNews (www.deja.com) was once considered the authoritative collection point for all past and present newsgroup messages until Google acquired deja.com in February 2001 (see www.google.com/press/pressrel/pressrelease48.html). This acquisition gave users the ability to search the entire archive of USENET messages posted since 1995 via the simple, straightforward Google search interface. Google refers to USENET groups as Google Groups. Today, Internet users around the globe turn to Google Groups for general discussion and problem solving. It is very common for Information Technology (IT) practitioners to turn to Google's Groups section for answers to all sorts of technology-related issues. The old USENET community still thrives and flourishes behind the sleek interface of the Google Groups search engine.

The Google Groups search can be accessed by clicking the **Groups** tab of the main Google Web page or by surfing to http://groups.google.com. The search interface (shown in

Figure 1.4) looks quite a bit different from other Google search pages, yet the search capabilities operate in much the same way. The major difference between the Groups search page and the Web search page lies in the newsgroup browsing links.

Figure 1.4 The Google Groups Search Page

Entering a search term into the entry field and clicking the Search button whisks you away to the Groups search results page, which is very similar to the Web search results page.

Google Image Search

The Google Image search feature allows you to search (at the time of this writing) over a billion graphic files that match your search criteria. Google will attempt to locate your search terms in the image filename, in the image caption, in the text surrounding the image, and in other undisclosed locations, to return a somewhat "de-duplicated" list of images that match your search criteria. The Google Image search operates identically to the Web search, with the exception of a few of the advanced search terms, which we will discuss in the next chapter. The search results page is also slightly different, as you can see in Figure 1.5.

Figure 1.5 The Google Images Search Results Page

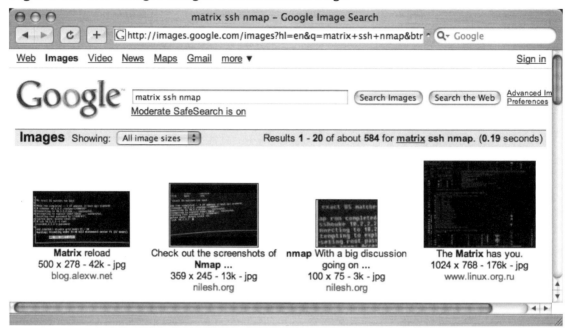

The page header looks familiar, but contains a few additions unique to the search results page. The *Moderate SafeSearch* link below the search field allows you to enable or disable images that may be sexually explicit. The *Showing* dropdown box (located in the *Results* line) allows you to narrow image results by size. Below the header, each matching image is shown in a thumbnail view with the original resolution and size followed by the name of the site that hosts the image.

Google Preferences

You can access the Preferences page by clicking the **Preferences** link from any Google search page or by browsing to www.google.com/preferences. These options primarily pertain to language and locality settings, as shown in Figure 1.6.

The Interface Language option describes the language that Google will use when printing tips and informational messages. In addition, this setting controls the language of text printed on Google's navigation items, such as buttons and links. Google assumes that the language you select here is your native language and will "speak" to you in this language whenever possible. Setting this option is not the same as using the translation features of Google (discussed in the following section). Web pages written in French will still appear in French, regardless of what you select here.

Figure 1.6 The Google Preferences Screen

To get an idea of how Google's Web pages would be altered by a change in the interface language, take a look at Figure 1.7 to see Google's main page rendered in "hacker speak." In addition to changing this setting on the preferences screen, you can access all the language-specific Google interfaces directly from the Language Tools screen at www.google.com/language_tools.

Figure 1.7 The Main Google Page Rendered in "Hacker Speak"

Even though the main Google Web page is now rendered in "hacker speak," Google is still searching for Web pages written in any language. If you are interested in locating Web pages that are written in a particular language, modify the Search Language setting on the Google preferences page. By default, Google will always try to locate Web pages written in any language.

Underground Googling...

Proxy Server Language Hijinks

As we will see in later chapters, proxy servers can be used to help hide your location and identity while you're surfing the Web. Depending on the geographical location of a proxy server, the language settings of the main Google page may change to match the language of the country where the proxy server is located. If your language settings change inexplicably, be sure to check your proxy server settings. Even experienced proxy users can lose track of when a proxy is enabled and when it's not. As we will see later, language settings can be modified directly via the URL.

The preferences screen also allows you to modify other search parameters, as shown in Figure 1.8.

Figure 1.8 Additional Preference Settings

SafeSearch Filtering blocks explicit sexual content from appearing in Web searches. Although this is a welcome option for day-to-day Web searching, this option should be disabled when you're performing searches as part of a vulnerability assessment. If sexually explicit content exists on a Web site whose primary content is not sexual in nature, the existence of this material may be of interest to the site owner.

The Number of Results setting describes how many results are displayed on each search result page. This option is highly subjective, based on your tastes and Internet connection speed. However, you may quickly discover that the default setting of 10 hits per page is simply not enough. If you're on a relatively fast connection, you should consider setting this to 100, the maximum number of results per page.

When checked, the Results Window setting opens search results in a new browser window. This setting is subjective based on your personal tastes. Checking or unchecking this option should have no ill effects unless your browser (or other software) detects the new window as a pop-up advertisement and blocks it. If you notice that your Google results pages are not displaying after you click the Search button, you might want to uncheck this setting in your Google preferences.

As noted at the bottom of this page, these changes won't stick unless you have enabled cookies in your browser.

Language Tools

The Language Tools screen, accessed from the main Google page, offers several different utilities for locating and translating Web pages written in different languages. If you rarely search for Web pages written in other languages, it can become cumbersome to modify your preferences before performing this type of search. The first portion of the Language Tools screen (shown in Figure 1.9) allows you to perform a quick search for documents written in other languages as well as documents located in other countries.

Figure 1.9 Google Language Tools: Search Specific Languages or Countries

The Language Tools screen also includes a utility that performs basic translation services. The translation form (shown in Figure 1.10) allows you to paste a block of text from the clipboard or supply a Web address to a page that Google will translate into a variety of languages.

Figure 1.10 The Google Translation Tool

In addition to the translation options available from this screen, Google integrates translation options into the search results page, as we will see in more detail. The translation options available from the search results page are based on the language options that are set from the Preferences screen shown in Figure 1.6. In other words, if your interface language is set to English and a Web page listed in a search result is French, Google will give you the option to translate that page into your native language, English. The list of available language translations is shown in Figure 1.11.

Underground Googling...

Google Toolbars

Don't get distracted by the allure of Google "helper" programs such as browser toolbars. All the important search features are available right from the main Google search screen. Each toolbar offers minor conveniences such as one-click directory traversals or select-and-search capability, but there are so many different toolbars available, you'll have to decide for yourself which one is right for you and your operating environment. Check the Web links at the end of this section for a list of some popular alternatives.

Figure 1.11 Google's Translation Languages

Arabic to English BETA
Chinese to English BETA
Chinese (Simplified to Traditional) BETA
Chinese (Traditional to Simplified) BETA
English to Arabic BETA
English to Chinese (Simplified) BETA
English to Chinese (Traditional) BETA
English to French
English to German
English to Italian
English to Japanese BETA
English to Korean BETA
English to Portuguese
English to Russian BETA
English to Spanish
French to English
French to German
German to English
German to French
Italian to English
Japanese to English BETA
Korean to English BETA
Portuguese to English
Russian to English BETA
✓ Spanish to English

Building Google Queries

Google query building is a process. There's really no such thing as an incorrect search. It's entirely possible to create an ineffective search, but with the explosive growth of the Internet and the size of Google's cache, a query that's inefficient today may just provide good results tomorrow—or next month or next year. The idea behind effective Google searching is to get a firm grasp on the basic syntax and then to get a good grasp of effective *narrowing* techniques. Learning the Google query syntax is the easy part. Learning to effectively narrow searches can take quite a bit of time and requires a bit of practice. Eventually, you'll get a feel for it, and it will become second nature to find the needle in the haystack.

The Golden Rules of Google Searching

Before we discuss Google searching, we should understand some of the basic ground rules:

- **Google queries are *not* case sensitive.** Google doesn't care if you type your query in lowercase letters (*hackers*), uppercase (*HACKERS*), camel case (*hAcKeR*), or psycho-case (*haCKeR*)—the word is always regarded the same way. This is especially important when you're searching things like source code listings, when the case of the term carries a great deal of meaning for the programmer. The one notable exception is the word *or*. When used as the Boolean operator, *or* must be written in uppercase, as *OR*.

■ **Google wildcards.** Google's concept of wildcards is not the same as a programmer's concept of wildcards. Most consider *wildcards* to be either a symbolic representation of any single letter (UNIX fans may think of the question mark) or any series of letters represented by an asterisk. This type of technique is called *stemming*. Google's wildcard, the asterisk (*), represents nothing more than a single *word* in a search phrase. Using an asterisk at the beginning or end of a word will not provide you any more hits than using the word by itself.

■ **Google reserves the right to ignore you.** Google ignores certain common words, characters, and single digits in a search. These are sometimes called *stop words*. According to Google's basic search document (www.google.com/help/basics.html), these words include *where* and *how*, as shown in Figure 1.12. However, Google does seem to include those words in a search. For example, a search for WHERE 1=1 returns less results than a search for 1=1. This is an indication that the WHERE is being included in the search. A search for where pig returns significantly less results than a simple search for pig, again an indication that Google does in fact include words like how and where. Sometimes Google will silently ignore these stop words. For example, a search for HOW 1 = WHERE 4 returns the same number of results as a query for 1 = WHERE 4. This seems to indicate that the word HOW is irrelevant to the search results, and that Google silently ignored the word. There are no obvious rules for word exclusion, but sometimes when Google ignores a search term, a notification will appear on the results page just below the query box.

Figure 1.12 Ignored Words in a Query

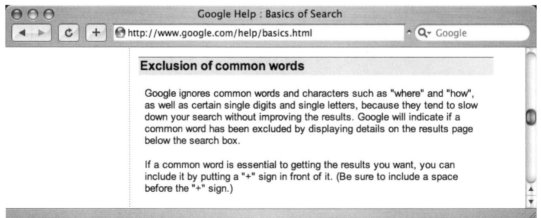

One way to force Google into using common words is to include them in quotes. Doing so submits the search as a phrase, and results will include all the words in the term, regardless of how common they may be. You can also precede the term with a + sign, as in the query +*and*. Submitted without the quotes, taking care not to put a space between the + and the word *and*, this search returns nearly five billion results!

Underground Googling...

Super-Size That Search!

One very interesting search is the search for *of* *. This search produces somewhere in the neighborhood of eighteen billion search results, making it one of the most prolific searches known! Can you top this search?

- **32-word limit**   Google limits searches to 32 words, which is up from the previous limit of ten words. This includes search terms as well as advanced operators, which we'll discuss in a moment. While this is sufficient for most users, there are ways to get beyond that limit. One way is to replace some terms with the wildcard character (*). Google does not count the wildcard character as a search term, allowing you to extend your searches quite a bit. Consider a query for the wording of the beginning of the U.S. Constitution:

```
we the people of the united states in order to form a more perfect union
establish justice
```

This search term is seventeen words long. If we replace some of the words with the asterisk (the wildcard character) and submit it as

```
"we * people * * united states * order * form * more perfect * establish *"
```

including the quotes, Google sees this as a nine-word query (with eight uncounted wildcard characters). We could extend our search even farther, by two more real words and just about any number of wildcards.

Basic Searching

Google searching is a process, the goal of which is to find information about a topic. The process begins with a basic search, which is modified in a variety of ways until only the pages of relevant information are returned. Google's ranking technology helps this process along by placing the highest-ranking pages on the first results page. The details of this ranking system are complex and somewhat speculative, but suffice it to say that for our purposes Google rarely gives us *exactly* what we need following a single search.

The simplest Google query consists of a single word or a combination of individual words typed into the search interface. Some basic word searches could include:

- hacker
- FBI hacker Mitnick
- mad hacker dpak

Slightly more complex than a word search is a *phrase search*. A phrase is a group of words enclosed in double-quote marks. When Google encounters a phrase, it searches for all words in the phrase, in the exact order you provide them. Google does not exclude common words found in a phrase. Phrase searches can include

- "Google hacker"
- "adult humor"
- "Carolina gets pwnt"

Phrase and word searches can be combined and used with advanced operators, as we will see in the next chapter.

Using Boolean Operators and Special Characters

More advanced than basic word searches, phrase searches are still a basic form of a Google query. To perform advanced queries, it is necessary to understand the Boolean operators *AND, OR,* and *NOT.* To properly segment the various parts of an advanced Google query, we must also explore visual grouping techniques that use the parenthesis characters. Finally, we will combine these techniques with certain special characters that may serve as shorthand for certain operators, wildcard characters, or placeholders.

If you have used any other Web search engines, you have probably been exposed to Boolean operators. Boolean operators help specify the results that are returned from a query. If you are already familiar with Boolean operators, take a moment to skim this section to help you understand Google's particular implementation of these operators, since many search engines handle them in different ways. Improper use of these operators could drastically alter the results that are returned.

The most commonly used Boolean operator is *AND.* This operator is used to include multiple terms in a query. For example, a simple query like *hacker* could be expanded with a Boolean operator by querying for *hacker AND cracker.* The latter query would include not only pages that talk about hackers but also sites that talk about hackers and the snacks they might eat. Some search engines require the use of this operator, but Google does not. The term *AND* is redundant to Google. By default, Google automatically searches for *all* the terms you include in your query. In fact, Google will warn you when you have included terms that are obviously redundant, as shown in Figure 1.13.

Figure 1.13 Google's Warnings

```
hot and spicy                                    Search    Advanced Search
                                                            Preferences

The "AND" operator is unnecessary -- we include all search terms by default. [details]
```

NOTE

When first learning the ways of Google-fu, keep an eye on the area below the query box on the Web interface. You'll pick up great pointers to help you improve your query syntax.

The plus symbol (+) forces the inclusion of the word that follows it. There should be no space following the plus symbol. For example, if you were to search for *and*, *justice*, *for*, and *all* as separate, distinct words, Google would warn that several of the words are too common and are excluded from the search. To force Google to search for those common words, preface them with the plus sign. It's okay to go overboard with the plus sign. It has no ill effects if it is used excessively. To perform this search with the inclusion of all words, consider a query such as *+and justice for +all*. In addition, the words could be enclosed in double quotes. This generally will force Google to include all the common words in the phrase. This query presented as a phrase would be *and justice for all*.

Another common Boolean operator is *NOT*. Functionally the opposite of the *AND* operator, the *NOT* operator excludes a word from a search. The best way to use this operator is to preface a search word with the minus sign (−). Be sure to leave no space between the minus sign and the search term. Consider a simple query such as *hacker*. This query is very generic and will return hits for all sorts of occupations, like golfers, woodchoppers, serial killers, and those with chronic bronchitis. With this type of query, you are most likely not interested in each and every form of the word hacker but rather a more specific rendition of the term. To narrow the search, you could include more terms, which Google would automatically *AND* together, or you could start narrowing the search by using *NOT* to remove certain terms from your search. To remove some of the more unsavory characters from your search, consider using queries such as *hacker −golf* or *hacker −phlegm*. This would allow you to get closer to the dastardly wood choppers you're looking for. Or just try a Google Video search for *lumberjack song*. Talk about twisted.

A less common and sometimes more confusing Boolean operator is *OR*. The *OR* operator, represented by the pipe symbol (|)or simply the word *OR* in uppercase letters, instructs Google to locate *either* one term *or* another in a query. Although this seems fairly straightforward when considering a simple query such as *hacker* or *"evil cybercriminal,"* things can get terribly confusing when you string together a bunch of *ANDs* and *ORs* and *NOTs*. To help alleviate this confusion, don't think of the query as anything more than a sentence read from left to right. Forget all that order of operations stuff you learned in high school algebra. For our purposes, an *AND* is weighed equally with an *OR*, which is weighed as equally as an advanced operator. These factors may affect the rank or order in which the search results appear on the page, but have no bearing on how Google handles the search query.

Let's take a look at a very complex example, the exact mechanics of which we will discuss in Chapter 2:

```
intext:password | passcode intext:username | userid | user filetype:csv
```

This example uses advanced operators combined with the *OR* Boolean to create a query that reads like a sentence written as a polite request. The request reads, "Locate all pages that have either *password* or *passcode* in the text of the document. From those pages, show me only the pages that contain either the words *username*, *userid*, or *user* in the text of the document. From those pages, only show me documents that are CSV files." Google doesn't get confused by the fact that technically those *OR* symbols break up the query into all sorts of possible interpretations. Google isn't bothered by the fact that from an algebraic standpoint, your query is syntactically wrong. For the purposes of learning how to create queries, all we need to remember is that Google reads our query from left to right.

Google's cut-and-dried approach to combining Boolean operators is still very confusing to the reader. Fortunately, Google is not offended (or affected by) parenthesis. The previous query can also be submitted as

```
intext:(password | passcode) intext:(username | userid | user) filetype:csv
```

This query is infinitely more readable for us humans, and it produces exactly the same results as the more confusing query that lacked parentheses.

Search Reduction

To achieve the most relevant results, you'll often need to narrow your search by modifying the search query. Although Google tends to provide very relevant results for most basic searches, we will begin looking at fairly complex searches aimed at locating a very narrow subset of Web sites. The vast majority of this book focuses on search reduction techniques and suggestions, but it's important that you at least understand the basics of search reduction.

As a simple example, we'll take a look at GNU Zebra, free software that manages Transmission Control Protocol (TCP)/Internet Protocol (IP)-based routing protocols. GNU Zebra uses a file called *zebra.conf* to store configuration settings, including interface information and passwords. After downloading the latest version of Zebra from the Web, we learn that the included *zebra.conf.sample* file looks like this:

```
! -*- zebra -*-
!
! zebra sample configuration file
!
! $Id: zebra.conf.sample,v 1.14 1999/02/19 17:26:38 developer Exp $
!
hostname Router
password zebra
enable password zebra
!
! Interface's description.
!
!interface lo
! description test of desc.
!
!interface sit0
! multicast

!
! Static default route sample.
!
!ip route 0.0.0.0/0 203.181.89.241
!


!log file zebra.log
```

To attempt to locate these files with Google, we might try a simple search such as:

```
"! Interface's description. "
```

This is considered the *base search*. Base searches should be as unique as possible in order to get as close to our desired results as possible, remembering the old adage "Garbage in, garbage out." Starting with a poor base search completely negates all the hard work you'll put into reduction. Our base search is unique not only because we have focused on the words *Interface's* and *description,* but we have also included the exclamation mark, the spaces, and the period following the phrase as part of our search. This is the exact syntax that the configuration file itself uses, so this seems like a very good place to start. However, Google takes some liberties with this search query, making the results less than adequate, as shown in Figure 1.14.

Figure 1.14 Dealing with a Base Search

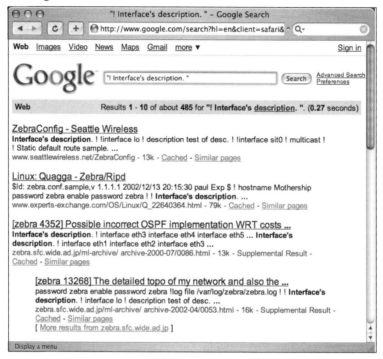

These results aren't bad at all, and the query is relatively simple, but we started out looking for *zebra.conf* files. So let's add this to our search to help narrow the results. This makes our next query:

```
"! Interface's description. " zebra.conf
```

As Figure 1.15 shows, the results are slightly different, but not necessarily better.

For starters, the seattlewireless hit we had in our first search is missing. This was a valid hit, but because the configuration file was not named zebra.conf (it was named ZebraConfig) our "improved" search doesn't see it. This is a great lesson to learn about search reduction: don't reduce your way past valid results.

Figure 1.15 Search Reduction in Action

Notice that the third hit in Figure 1.15 references *zebra.conf.sample*. These sample files may clutter valid results, so we'll add to our existing query, reducing hits that contain this phrase. This makes our new query

```
"! Interface's description. " -"zebra.conf.sample"
```

However, it helps to step into the shoes of the software's users for just a moment. Software installations like this one often ship with a sample configuration file to help guide the process of setting up a custom configuration. Most users will simply edit this file, changing only the settings that need to be changed for their environments, saving the file not as a *.sample* file but as a *.conf* file. In this situation, the user could have a live configuration file with the term *zebra.conf.sample* still in place. Reduction based on this term may remove valid configuration files created in this manner.

There's another reduction angle. Notice that our *zebra.conf.sample* file contained the term *hostname Router*. This is most likely one of the settings that a user will change, although we're making an assumption that his machine is *not* named Router. This is less a gamble than reducing based on *zebra.conf.sample*, however. Adding the reduction term *"hostname Router"* to our query brings our results number down and reduces our hits on potential sample files, all without sacrificing potential live hits.

Although it's certainly possible to keep reducing, often it's enough to make just a few minor reductions that can be validated by eye than to spend too much time coming up with the perfect search reduction. Our final (that's four qualifiers for just one word!) query becomes:

```
"! Interface's description. " -"hostname Router"
```

This is *not* the best query for locating these files, but it's good enough to give you an idea about how search reduction works. As we'll see in Chapter 2, advanced operators will get us even closer to that perfect query!

Underground Googling...

Bad Form on Purpose

In some cases, there's nothing wrong with using poor Google syntax in a search. If Google safely ignores part of a human-friendly query, leave it alone. The human readers will thank you!

Working With Google URLs

Advanced Google users begin testing advanced queries right from the Web interface's search field, refining queries until they are just right. Every Google query can be represented with a URL that points to the results page. Google's results pages are not static pages. They are dynamic and are created "on the fly" when you click the Search button or activate a URL that links to a results page. Submitting a search through the Web interface takes you to a results page that can be represented by a single URL. For example, consider the query *ihack-stuff*. Once you enter this query, you are whisked away to a URL similar to the following:

```
www.google.com/search?q=ihackstuff
```

If you bookmark this URL and return to it later or simply enter the URL into your browser's address bar, Google will reprocess your search for *ihackstuff* and display the results. This URL then becomes not only an active connection to a list of results, it also serves as a nice, compact sort of shorthand for a Google query. Any experienced Google searcher can take a look at this URL and realize the search subject. This URL can also be modified fairly easily. By changing the word *ihackstuff* to *iwritestuff*, the Google query is changed to find the term *iwritestuff*. This simple example illustrates the usefulness of the Google URL for advanced searching. A quick modification of the URL can make changes happen fast!

Underground Googling...

Uncomplicating URL Construction

The only URL parameter that is required in most cases is a query (the q parameter), making the simplest Google URL www.google.com/search?q=google.

URL Syntax

To fully understand the power of the URL, we need to understand the syntax. The first part of the URL, *www.google.com/search*, is the location of Google's search script. I refer to this URL, as well as the question mark that follows it, as the *base*, or starting URL. Browsing to this URL presents you with a nice, blank search page. The question mark after the word *search* indicates that parameters are about to be passed into the search script. Parameters are options that instruct the search script to actually *do* something. Parameters are separated by the ampersand (&) and consist of a *variable* followed by the equal sign (=) followed by the *value* that the variable should be set to. The basic syntax will look something like this:

```
www.google.com/search?variable1=value&variable2=value
```

This URL contains very simple characters. More complex URL's will contain special characters, which must be represented with hex code equivalents. Let's take a second to talk about hex encoding.

Special Characters

Hex encoding is definitely geek stuff, but sooner or later you may need to include a special character in your search URL. When that time comes, it's best to just let your browser help you out. Most modern browsers will adjust a typed URL, replacing special characters and spaces with hex-encoded equivalents. If your browser supports this behavior, your job of URL construction is that much easier. Try this simple test. Type the following URL in your browser's address bar, making sure to use spaces between *i*, *hack*, and *stuff*:

```
www.google.com/search?q="i hack stuff"
```

If your browser supports this auto-correcting feature, after you press Enter in the address bar, the URL should be corrected to www.google.com/search?q="i%20hack%20stuff" or something similar. Notice that the spaces were changed to %20. The percent sign indicates that the next two digits are the hexadecimal value of the space character, 20. Some browsers will take the conversion one step further, changing the double-quotes to %22 as well.

    If your browser refuses to convert those spaces, the query will not work as expected. There may be a setting in your browser to modify this behavior, but if not, do yourself a favor and use a modern browser. Internet Explorer, Firefox, Safari, and Opera are all excellent choices.

Underground Googling...

Quick Hex Conversions

To quickly determine hex codes for a character, you can run an American Standard Code for Information Interchange (ASCII) from a UNIX or Linux machine, or Google for the term "ascii table."

Putting the Pieces Together

Google search URL construction is like putting together Legos. You start with a URL and you modify it as needed to achieve varying search results. Many times your base URL will come from a search you submitted via the Google Web interface. If you need some added parameters, you can add them directly to the base URL in any order. If you need to modify parameters in your search, you can change the value of the parameter and resubmit your search. If you need to remove a parameter, you can delete that entire parameter from the URL and resubmit your search. This process is especially easy if you are modifying the URL directly in your browser's address bar. You simply make changes to the URL and press Enter. The browser will automatically fetch the address and take you to an updated search page. You could achieve similar results by poking around Google's advanced search page (www.google.com/advanced_search, shown in Figure 1.16) and by setting various preferences, as discussed earlier, but ultimately most advanced users find it faster and easier to make quick search adjustments directly through URL modification.

Figure 1.16 Using Google's Advanced Search Page

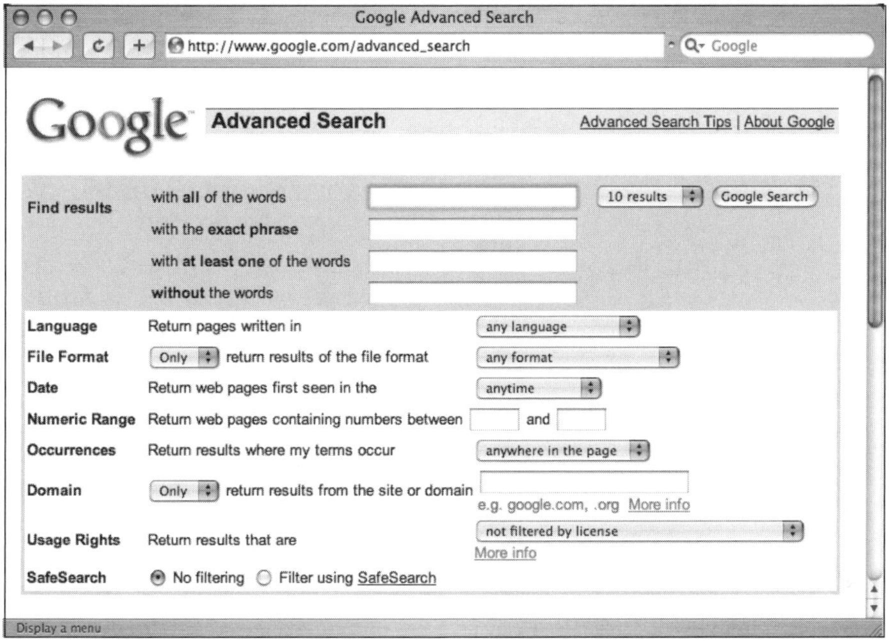

A Google search URL can contain many different parameters. Depending on the options you selected and the search terms you provided, you will see some or all of the variables listed in Table 1.2. These parameters can be added or modified as needed to change your search criteria.

Table 1.2 Google's Search Parameters

Variable	Value	Description
q or as_q	The search query	The search query.
as_eq	A search term	These terms will be excluded from the search.
start	0 to the max number of hits	Used to display pages of results. Result 0 is the first result on the first page of results.
num maxResults	1 to 100	The number of results per page (max 100).
filter	0 or 1	If filter is set to 0, show potentially duplicate results.
restrict	restrict code	Restrict results to a specific country.

Continued

Table 1.2 continued Google's Search Parameters

Variable	Value	Description
hl	language code	This parameter describes the language Google uses when displaying results. This should be set to your native tongue. Located Web pages are not translated.
lr	language code	Language restrict. Only display pages written in this language.
ie	UTF-8	The input encoding of Web searches. Google suggests UTF-8.
oe	UTF-8	The output encoding of Web searches. Google suggests UTF-8.
as_epq	a search phrase	The value is submitted as an exact phrase. This negates the need to surround the phrase with quotes.
as_ft	i = include file type e = exclude file type	Include or exclude the file type indicated by *as_filetype.*
as_filetype	a file extension	Include or exclude this file type as indicated by the value of *as_ft.*
as_qdr	all - all results m3 = 3 months m6 = 6 months y = past year	Locate pages updated within the specified timeframe.
as_nlo	low number	Find numbers between *as_nlo* and *as_nhi.*
as_nhi	high number	Find numbers between *as_nlo* and *as_nhi.*
as_oq	a list of words	Find at least one of these words.
as_occt	any = anywhere title = title of page body = text of page url = in the page URL links = in links to the page	Find search term in a specific location.
as_dt	i = only include site or domain e = exclude site or domain	Include or exclude searches from the domain specified by *as_sitesearch.*
as_sitesearch	domain or site	Include or exclude this domain or site as specified by *as_dt.*

Continued

Table 1.2 continued Google's Search Parameters

Variable	Value	Description
safe	active = enable SafeSearch images = disable SafeSearch	Enable or disable SafeSearch.
as_rq	URL	Locate pages similar to this URL.
as_lq	URL	Locate pages that link to this URL.
rights	cc_*	Locate pages with specific usage rights (public, commercial, non-commercial, and so on)

Some parameters accept a language restrict (*lr*) code as a value. The *lr* value instructs Google to only return pages written in a specific language. For example, *lr=lang_ar* only returns pages written in Arabic. Table 1.3 lists all the values available for the *lr* field:

Table 1.3 Language Restrict Codes

lr Language code	Language
lang_ar	Arabic
lang_hy	Armenian
lang_bg	Bulgarian
lang_ca	Catalan
lang_zh-CN	Chinese (Simplified)
lang_zh-TW	Chinese (Traditional)
lang_hr	Croatian
lang_cs	Czech
lang_da	Danish
lang_nl	Dutch
lang_en	English
lang_eo	Esperanto
lang_et	Estonian
lang_fi	Finnish
lang_fr	French
lang_de	German
lang_el	Greek
lang_iw	Hebrew

Continued

Table 1.3 continued Language Restrict Codes

lr Language code	Language
lang_hu	Hungarian
lang_is	Icelandic
lang_id	Indonesian
lang_it	Italian
lang_ja	Japanese
lang_ko	Korean
lang_lv	Latvian
lang_lt	Lithuanian
lang_no	Norwegian
lang_fa	Persian
lang_pl	Polish
lang_pt	Portuguese
lang_ro	Romanian
lang_ru	Russian
lang_sr	Serbian
lang_sk	Slovak
lang_sl	Slovenian
lang_es	Spanish
lang_sv	Swedish
lang_th	Thai
lang_tr	Turkish
lang_uk	Ukrainian
lang_vi	Vietnamese

The *hl* variable changes the language of Google's messages and links. This is not the same as the *lr* variable, which restricts our results to pages written in a specific language, nor is it like the translation service, which translates a page from one language to another.

Figure 1.17 shows the results of a search for the word *food* with an *hl* variable set to DA (Danish). Notice that Google's *messages and links* are in Danish, whereas the search results are written in English. We have not asked Google to restrict or modify our search in any way.

Figure 1.17 Using the *hl* Variable

To understand the contrast between *hl* and *lr*, consider the *food* search resubmitted as an *lr* search, as shown in Figure 1.18. Notice that our URL is different: There are now far fewer results, the search results are written in Danish, Google added a Search Danish pages button, and Google's messages and links are written in English. Unlike the *hl* option (Table 1.4 lists the values for the *hl* field), the *lr* option changes our search results. We have asked Google to *return only pages written in Danish*.

Figure 1.18 Using Language Restrict

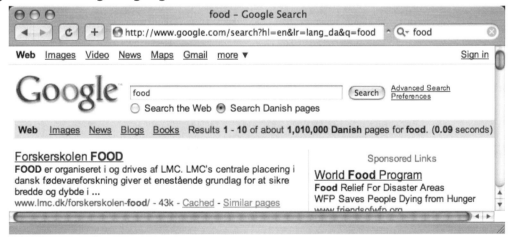

Table 1.4 *h1* Language Field Values

hl Language Code	Language
af	Afrikaans
sq	Albanian
am	Amharic
ar	Arabic
hy	Armenian
az	Azerbaijani
eu	Basque
be	Belarusian
bn	Bengali
bh	Bihari
xx-bork	Bork, bork, bork!
bs	Bosnian
br	Breton
bg	Bulgarian
km	Cambodian
ca	Catalan
zh-CN	Chinese (Simplified)
zh-TW	Chinese (Traditional)
co	Corsican
hr	Croatian
cs	Czech
da	Danish
nl	Dutch
xx-elmer	Elmer Fudd
en selected	English
eo	Esperanto
et	Estonian
fo	Faroese
tl	Filipino
fi	Finnish
fr	French
fy	Frisian

Continued

Table 1.4 continued *h1* Language Field Values

hl Language Code	Language
gl	Galician
ka	Georgian
de	German
el	Greek
gn	Guarani
gu	Gujarati
xx-hacker	Hacker
iw	Hebrew
hi	Hindi
hu	Hungarian
is	Icelandic
id	Indonesian
ia	Interlingua
ga	Irish
it	Italian
ja	Japanese
jw	Javanese
kn	Kannada
kk	Kazakh
xx-klingon	Klingon
ko	Korean
ku	Kurdish
ky	Kyrgyz
lo	Laothian
la	Latin
lv	Latvian
ln	Lingala
lt	Lithuanian
mk	Macedonian
ms	Malay
ml	Malayalam
mt	Maltese

Continued

Table 1.4 continued *h1* Language Field Values

hl Language Code	Language
mr	Marathi
mo	Moldavian
mn	Mongolian
ne	Nepali
no	Norwegian
nn	Norwegian (Nynorsk)
oc	Occitan
or	Oriya
ps	Pashto
fa	Persian
xx-piglatin	Pig Latin
pl	Polish
pt-BR	Portuguese (Brazil)
pt-PT	Portuguese (Portugal)
pa	Punjabi
qu	Quechua
ro	Romanian
rm	Romansh
ru	Russian
gd	Scots Gaelic
sr	Serbian
sh	Serbo-Croatian
st	Sesotho
sn	Shona
sd	Sindhi
si	Sinhalese
sk	Slovak
sl	Slovenian
so	Somali
es	Spanish
su	Sundanese
sw	Swahili

Continued

Table 1.4 continued *h1* Language Field Values

hl Language Code	Language
sv	Swedish
tg	Tajik
ta	Tamil
tt	Tatar
te	Telugu
th	Thai
ti	Tigrinya
to	Tonga
tr	Turkish
tk	Turkmen
tw	Twi
ug	Uighur
uk	Ukrainian
ur	Urdu
uz	Uzbek
vi	Vietnamese
cy	Welsh
xh	Xhosa
yi	Yiddish
yo	Yoruba
zu	Zulu

Underground Googling...

Sticky Subject

The *hl* value is sticky! This means that if you change this value in your URL, it sticks for future searches. The best way to change it back is through Google preferences or by changing the *hl* code directly inside the URL.

The *restrict* variable is easily confused with the *lr* variable, since it restricts your search to a particular language. However, *restrict* has nothing to do with language. This variable gives you the ability to restrict your search results to one or more countries, determined by the top-level domain name (*.us*, for example) and/or by geographic location of the server's IP address. If you think this smells somewhat inexact, you're right. Although inexact, this variable works amazingly well. Consider a search for *people* in which we restrict our results to JP (Japan), as shown in Figure 1.19. Our URL has changed to include the restrict value (shown in Table 1.5), but notice that the second hit is from www.unu.edu, the location of which is unknown. As our sidebar reveals, the host does in fact appear to be located in Japan.

Figure 1.19 Using *restrict* to Narrow Results

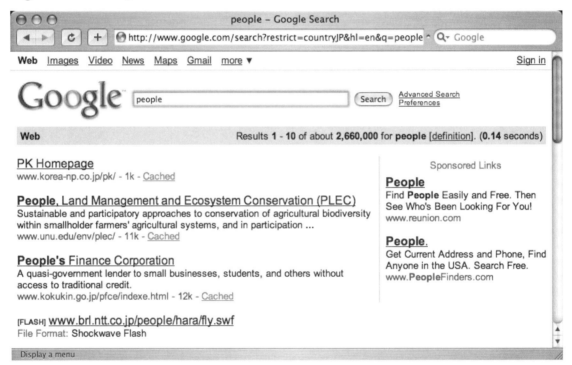

Underground Googling...

How Google Owns the Continents

It's easy to get a relative idea of where a host is located geographically. Here's how *host* and *whois* can be used to figure out where www.unu.edu is located:

```
wh00p:~# host www.unu.edu

www.unu.edu has address 202.253.138.42

wh00p:~# whois 202.253.138.42


role:         Japan Network Information Center
address:      Kokusai-Kougyou-Kanda Bldg 6F, 2-3-4 Uchi-Kanda
address:      Chiyoda-ku, Tokyo 101-0047, Japan
country:      JP
phone:        +81-3-5297-2311
fax-no:       +81-3-5297-2312
```

Table 1.5 *restrict* Field Values

Country	Restrict Code
Andorra	countryAD
United Arab Emirates	countryAE
Afghanistan	countryAF
Antigua and Barbuda	countryAG
Anguilla	countryAI
Albania	countryAL
Armenia	countryAM
Netherlands Antilles	countryAN
Angola	countryAO
Antarctica	countryAQ
Argentina	countryAR
American Samoa	countryAS
Austria	countryAT

Continued

Table 1.5 continued *restrict* Field Values

Country	Restrict Code
Australia	countryAU
Aruba	countryAW
Azerbaijan	countryAZ
Bosnia and Herzegowina	countryBA
Barbados	countryBB
Bangladesh	countryBD
Belgium	countryBE
Burkina Faso	countryBF
Bulgaria	countryBG
Bahrain	countryBH
Burundi	countryBI
Benin	countryBJ
Bermuda	countryBM
Brunei Darussalam	countryBN
Bolivia	countryBO
Brazil	countryBR
Bahamas	countryBS
Bhutan	countryBT
Bouvet Island	countryBV
Botswana	countryBW
Belarus	countryBY
Belize	countryBZ
Canada	countryCA
Cocos (Keeling) Islands	countryCC
Congo, The Democratic Republic of the	countryCD
Central African Republic	countryCF
Congo	countryCG
Burundi	countryBI
Benin	countryBJ
Bermuda	countryBM
Brunei Darussalam	countryBN
Bolivia	countryBO

Table 1.5 continued *restrict* Field Values

Country	Restrict Code
Brazil	countryBR
Bahamas	countryBS
Bhutan	countryBT
Bouvet Island	countryBV
Botswana	countryBW
Belarus	countryBY
Belize	countryBZ
Canada	countryCA
Cocos (Keeling) Islands	countryCC
Congo, The Democratic Republic of the	countryCD
Central African Republic	countryCF
Congo	countryCG
Switzerland	countryCH
Cote D'ivoire	countryCI
Cook Islands	countryCK
Chile	countryCL
Cameroon	countryCM
China	countryCN
Colombia	countryCO
Costa Rica	countryCR
Cuba	countryCU
Cape Verde	countryCV
Christmas Island	countryCX
Cyprus	countryCY
Czech Republic	countryCZ
Germany	countryDE
Djibouti	countryDJ
Denmark	countryDK
Dominica	countryDM
Dominican Republic	countryDO
Algeria	countryDZ
Ecuador	countryEC

Continued

Table 1.5 continued *restrict* Field Values

Country	Restrict Code
Estonia	countryEE
Egypt	countryEG
Western Sahara	countryEH
Eritrea	countryER
Spain	countryES
Ethiopia	countryET
European Union	countryEU
Finland	countryFI
Fiji	countryFJ
Falkland Islands (Malvinas)	countryFK
Micronesia, Federated States of	countryFM
Faroe Islands	countryFO
France	countryFR
France, Metropolitan	countryFX
Gabon	countryGA
United Kingdom	countryUK
Grenada	countryGD
Georgia	countryGE
French Quiana	countryGF
Ghana	countryGH
Gibraltar	countryGI
Greenland	countryGL
Gambia	countryGM
Guinea	countryGN
Guadeloupe	countryGP
Equatorial Guinea	countryGQ
Greece	countryGR
South Georgia and the South Sandwich Islands	countryGS
Guatemala	countryGT
Guam	countryGU
Guinea-Bissau	countryGW

Continued

Table 1.5 continued *restrict* Field Values

Country	Restrict Code
Guyana	countryGY
Hong Kong	countryHK
Heard and Mc Donald Islands	countryHM
Honduras	countryHN
Croatia (local name: Hrvatska)	countryHR
Haiti	countryHT
Hungary	countryHU
Indonesia	countryID
Ireland	countryIE
Israel	countryIL
India	countryIN
British Indian Ocean Territory	countryIO
Iraq	countryIQ
Iran (Islamic Republic of)	countryIR
Iceland	countryIS
Italy	countryIT
Jamaica	countryJM
Jordan	countryJO
Japan	countryJP
Kenya	countryKE
Kyrgyzstan	countryKG
Cambodia	countryKH
Kiribati	countryKI
Comoros	countryKM
Saint Kitts and Nevis	countryKN
Korea, Democratic People's Republic of	countryKP
Korea, Republic of	countryKR
Kuwait	countryKW
Cayman Islands	countryKY
Kazakhstan	countryKZ
Lao People's Democratic Republic	countryLA

Continued

Table 1.5 continued *restrict* Field Values

Country	Restrict Code
Lebanon	countryLB
Saint Lucia	countryLC
Liechtenstein	countryLI
Sri Lanka	countryLK
Liberia	countryLR
Lesotho	countryLS
Lithuania	countryLT
Luxembourg	countryLU
Latvia	countryLV
Libyan Arab Jamahiriya	countryLY
Morocco	countryMA
Monaco	countryMC
Moldova	countryMD
Madagascar	countryMG
Marshall Islands	countryMH
Macedonia, The Former Yugoslav Republic of	countryMK
Mali	countryML
Myanmar	countryMM
Mongolia	countryMN
Macau	countryMO
Northern Mariana Islands	countryMP
Martinique	countryMQ
Mauritania	countryMR
Montserrat	countryMS
Malta	countryMT
Mauritius	countryMU
Maldives	countryMV
Malawi	countryMW
Mexico	countryMX
Malaysia	countryMY
Mozambique	countryMZ

Continued

Table 1.5 continued *restrict* Field Values

Country	Restrict Code
Namibia	countryNA
New Caledonia	countryNC
Niger	countryNE
Norfolk Island	countryNF
Nigeria	countryNG
Nicaragua	countryNI
Netherlands	countryNL
Norway	countryNO
Nepal	countryNP
Nauru	countryNR
Niue	countryNU
New Zealand	countryNZ
Oman	countryOM
Panama	countryPA
Peru	countryPE
French Polynesia	countryPF
Papua New Guinea	countryPG
Philippines	countryPH
Pakistan	countryPK
Poland	countryPL
St. Pierre and Miquelon	countryPM
Pitcairn	countryPN
Puerto Rico	countryPR
Palestine	countryPS
Portugal	countryPT
Palau	countryPW
Paraguay	countryPY
Qatar	countryQA
Reunion	countryRE
Romania	countryRO
Russian Federation	countryRU
Rwanda	countryRW

Continued

Table 1.5 continued *restrict* Field Values

Country	Restrict Code
Saudi Arabia	countrySA
Solomon Islands	countrySB
Seychelles	countrySC
Sudan	countrySD
Sweden	countrySE
Singapore	countrySG
St. Helena	countrySH
Slovenia	countrySI
Svalbard and Jan Mayen Islands	countrySJ
Slovakia (Slovak Republic)	countrySK
Sierra Leone	countrySL
San Marino	countrySM
Senegal	countrySN
Somalia	countrySO
Suriname	countrySR
Sao Tome and Principe	countryST
El Salvador	countrySV
Syria	countrySY
Swaziland	countrySZ
Turks and Caicos Islands	countryTC
Chad	countryTD
French Southern Territories	countryTF
Togo	countryTG
Thailand	countryTH
Tajikistan	countryTJ
Tokelau	countryTK
Turkmenistan	countryTM
Tunisia	countryTN
Tonga	countryTO
East Timor	countryTP
Turkey	countryTR
Trinidad and Tobago	countryTT

Continued

Table 1.5 continued *restrict* Field Values

Country	Restrict Code
Tuvalu	countryTV
Taiwan	countryTW
Tanzania	countryTZ
Ukraine	countryUA
Uganda	countryUG
United States Minor Outlying Islands	countryUM
United States	countryUS
Uruguay	countryUY
Uzbekistan	countryUZ
Holy See (Vatican City State)	countryVA
Saint Vincent and the Grenadines	countryVC
Venezuela	countryVE
Virgin Islands (British)	countryVG
Virgin Islands (U.S.)	countryVI
Vietnam	countryVN
Vanuatu	countryVU
Wallis and Futuna Islands	countryWF
Samoa	countryWS
Yemen	countryYE
Mayotte	countryYT
Yugoslavia	countryYU
South Africa	countryZA
Zambia	countryZM
Zaire	countryZR

Summary

Google is deceptively simple in appearance, but offers many powerful options that provide the groundwork for powerful searches. Many different types of content can be searched, including Web pages, message groups such as USENET, images, video, and more. Beginners to Google searching are encouraged to use the Google-provided forms for searching, paying close attention to the messages and warnings Google provides about syntax. Boolean operators such as *OR* and *NOT* are available through the use of the minus sign and the word *OR* (or the | symbol), respectively, whereas the *AND* operator is ignored, since Google automatically includes all terms in a search. Advanced search options are available through the Advanced Search page, which allows users to narrow search results quickly. Advanced Google users narrow their searches through customized queries and a healthy dose of experience and good old common sense.

Solutions Fast Track

Exploring Google's Web-based Interface

- ☑ There are several distinct Google search areas (including Web, group, video, and image searches), each with distinct searching characteristics and results pages.

- ☑ The Web search page, the heart and soul of Google, is simple, streamlined, and powerful, enabling even the most advanced searches.

- ☑ A Google Groups search allows you to search all past and present newsgroup posts.

- ☑ The Image search feature allows you to search for nearly a billion graphics by keyword.

- ☑ Google's preferences and language tools enable search customization, translation services, language-specific searches, and much more.

Building Google Queries

- ☑ Google query building is a process that includes determining a solid base search and expanding or reducing that search to achieve the desired results.

- ☑ Always remember the "golden rules" of Google searching. These basic premises serve as the foundation for a successful search.

- ☑ Used properly, Boolean operators and special characters help expand or reduce searches. They can also help clarify a search for fellow humans who might read your queries later on.

Working With Google URLs

- ☑ Once a Google query has been submitted, you are whisked away to the Google results page, the URL of which can be used to modify a search or recall it later.

- ☑ Although there are many different variables that can be set in a Google search URL, the only one that is really required is the *q,* or query, variable.

- ☑ Some advanced search options, such as *as_qdr* (date-restricted search by month), cannot be easily set anywhere besides the URL.

Links to Sites

- ☑ www.google.com This is the main Google Web page, the entry point for most searches.

- ☑ http://groups.google.com The Google Groups Web page.

- ☑ http://images.google.com/ Search Google for images and graphics.

- ☑ http://video.google.com Search Google for video files.

- ☑ www.google.com/language_tools Various language and translation options.

- ☑ www.google.com/advanced_search The advanced search form.

- ☑ www.google.com/preferences The Preferences page, which allows you to set options such as interface language, search language, SafeSearch filtering, and number of results per page.

Frequently Asked Questions

The following Frequently Asked Questions, answered by the authors of this book, are designed to both measure your understanding of the concepts presented in this chapter and to assist you with real-life implementation of these concepts. To have your questions about this chapter answered by the author, browse to **www. syngress.com/solutions** and click on the **"Ask the Author"** form.

Q: Some people like using nifty toolbars. Where can I find information about Google tool-bars?

A: Ask Google. Seriously, if you aren't already in the habit of simply asking Google when you have a Google-related question, you should get in that habit. Google can almost always provide an answer if you can figure out the query.

Here's a list of some popular Google search tools:

Platform	Tool	Location
Mac	Google Notifier, Google Desktop, Google Sketchup	www.google.com/mac.html
PC	Google Pack (includes IE & Firefox toolbars, Google Desktop and more)	www.google.com/tools
Mozilla Browser	Googlebar	http://googlebar.mozdev.org/
Firefox, Internet Explorer	Groowe multi-engine Toolbar	www.groowe.com/

Q: Are there any techniques I can use to learn how to build Google URL's?

A: Yes. There are a few ways. First, submit basic queries through the Web interface and look at the URL that's generated when you submit the search. From the search results page, modify the query slightly and look at how the URL changes when you submit it. This boils down to "do it, watch what it does then do it again." The second way involves using "query builder" programs that present a graphical interface, which allows you to select the search options you want, building a Google URL as you navigate through the interface. Keep an eye on the search engine hacking forums at http://johnny.ihackstuff. com, specifically the "coders corner" where users discuss programs that perform this type of functionality.

Q: What's better? Using Google's interface, using toolbars, or writing URL's?

A: It's not fair to claim that any one technique is better than the others. It boils down to personal preference, and many advanced Google users use each of these techniques in different ways. Many lengthy Google sessions begin as a simple query typed into the www.google.com Web interface. Depending on the narrowing process, it may be easier to add or subtract from the query right in the search field. Other times, like in the case of the daterange operator (covered in Chapter 2), it may be easier to add a quick *as_qdr* parameter to the end of the URL. Toolbars excel at providing you quick access to a Google search while you're browsing another page. Most toolbars allow you to select text on a page, right-click on the page and select "Google search" to submit the selected text as a query to Google. Which technique you decide to use ultimately depends on your tastes and the context in which you perform searches.

## Chapter 2

Advanced Operators

Solutions in this chapter:

- Operator Syntax
- Introducing Google's Advanced Operators
- Combining Advanced Operators
- Colliding Operators and Bad Search-Fu
- Links to Sites

☑ Summary

☑ Solutions Fast Track

☑ Frequently Asked Questions

Introduction

Beyond the basic searching techniques explored in the previous chapter, Google offers special terms known as *advanced operators* to help you perform more advanced queries. These operators, used properly, can help you get to exactly the information you're looking for without spending too much time poring over page after page of search results. When advanced operators are not provided in a query, Google will locate your search terms in *any* area of the Web page, including the title, the text, the Uniform Resource Locator (URL), or the like. We take a look at the following advanced operators in this chapter:

- *intitle, allintitle*
- *inurl, allinurl*
- *filetype*
- *allintext*
- *site*
- *link*
- *inanchor*
- *daterange*
- *cache*
- *info*
- *related*
- *phonebook*
- *rphonebook*
- *bphonebook*
- *author*
- *group*
- *msgid*
- *insubject*
- *stocks*
- *define*

Operator Syntax

Advanced operators are additions to a query designed to narrow down the search results. Although they re relatively easy to use, they have a fairly rigid syntax that must be followed. The basic syntax of an advanced operator is *operator:search_term*. When using advanced operators, keep in mind the following:

- There is no space between the operator, the colon, and the search term. Violating this syntax can produce undesired results and will keep Google from understanding what it is you're trying to do. In most cases, Google will treat a syntactically bad advanced operator as just another search term. For example, providing the advanced operator *intitle* without a following colon and search term will cause Google to return pages that contain the word *intitle*.

- The *search term* portion of an operator search follows the syntax discussed in the previous chapter. For example, a search term can be a single word or a phrase surrounded by quotes. If you use a phrase, just make sure there are no spaces between the operator, the colon, and the first quote of the phrase.

- Boolean operators and special characters (such as *OR* and +) can still be applied to advanced operator queries, but be sure they don't get in the way of the separating colon.

- Advanced operators can be combined in a single query as long as you honor both the basic Google query syntax as well as the advanced operator syntax. Some advanced operators combine better than others, and some simply cannot be combined. We will take a look at these limitations later in this chapter.

- The *ALL* operators (the operators beginning with the word *ALL*) are oddballs. They are generally used once per query and cannot be mixed with other operators.

Examples of valid queries that use advanced operators include these:

- ***intitle:Google***   This query will return pages that have the word *Google* in their title.

- ***intitle: "index of"***   This query will return pages that have the phrase *index of* in their title. Remember from the previous chapter that this query could also be given as *intitle:index.of,* since the period serves as any character. This technique also makes it easy to supply a phrase without having to type the spaces and the quotation marks around the phrase.

- ***intitle: "index of" private***   This query will return pages that have the phrase *index of* in their title and also have the word *private* anywhere in the page, including in the URL, the title, the text, and so on. Notice that *intitle* only applies to the phrase *index of* and not the word *private*, since the first unquoted space follows the phrase *index of*. Google interprets that space as the end of your advanced operator search term and continues processing the rest of the query.

■ *intitle: "index of" "backup files"* This query will return pages that have the phrase *index of* in their title and the phrase *backup files* anywhere in the page, including the URL, the title, the text, and so on. Again, notice that *intitle* only applies to the phrase *index of*.

Troubleshooting Your Syntax

Before we jump head first into the advanced operators, let's talk about troubleshooting the inevitable syntax errors you'll run into when using these operators. Google is kind enough to tell you when you've made a mistake, as shown in Figure 2.1.

Figure 2.1 Google's Helpful Error Messages

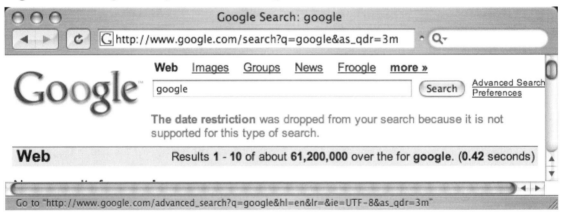

In this example, we tried to give Google an invalid option to the *as_qdr* variable in the URL. (The correct syntax would be *as_qdr=m3,* as we'll see in a moment.) Google's search result page listed right at the top that there was some sort of problem. These messages are often the key to unraveling errors in either your query string or your URL, so keep an eye on the top of the results page. We've found that it's easy to overlook this spot on the results page, since we normally scroll past it to get down to the results.

Sometimes, however, Google is less helpful, returning a blank results page with no error text, as shown in Figure 2.2.

Figure 2.2 Google's Blank Error Message

Fortunately, this type of problem is easy to resolve once you understand what's going on. In this case, we simply abused the *allintitle* operator. Most of the operators that begin with *all* do not mix well with other operators, like the *inurl* operator we provided. This search got Google all confused, and it coughed up a blank page.

Notes from the Underground...

But That's What I Wanted!

As you grom in your Google-Fu, you will undoubtedly want to perform a search that Google's syntax doesn't allow. When this happens, you'll have to find other ways to tackle the problem. For now though, take the easy route and play by Google's rules.

Introducing Google's Advanced Operators

Google's advanced operators are very versatile, but not all operators can be used everywhere, as we saw in the previous example. Some operators can only be used in performing a Web search, and others can only be used in a Groups search. Refer to Table 2.3, which lists these distinctions. If you have trouble remembering these rules, keep an eye on the results line near the top of the page. If Google picks up on your bad syntax, an error message will be displayed, letting you know what you did wrong. Sometimes, however, Google will not pick up on your bad form and will try to perform the search anyway. If this happens, keep an eye on the search results page, specifically the words Google shows in bold within the search results. These are the words Google interpreted as your search terms. If you see the word *intitle* in bold, for example, you've probably made a mistake using the *intitle* operator.

Intitle and *Allintitle*: Search Within the Title of a Page

From a technical standpoint, the title of a page can be described as the text that is found within the *TITLE* tags of a Hypertext Markup Language (HTML) document. The title is displayed at the top of most browsers when viewing a page, as shown in Figure 2.3. In the context of Google groups, *intitle* will find the term in the title of the message post.

Figure 2.3 Web Page Title

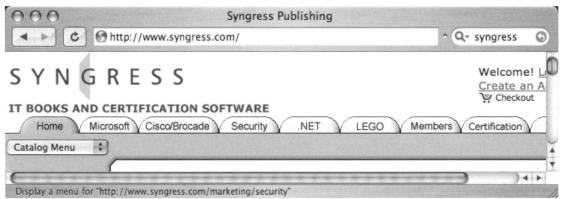

As shown in Figure 2.3, the title of the Web page is "Syngress Publishing." It is important to realize that some Web browsers will insert text into the title of a Web page, under certain circumstances. For example, consider the same page shown in Figure 2.4, this time captured before the page is actually finished loading.

Figure 2.4 Title Elements Injected by Browser

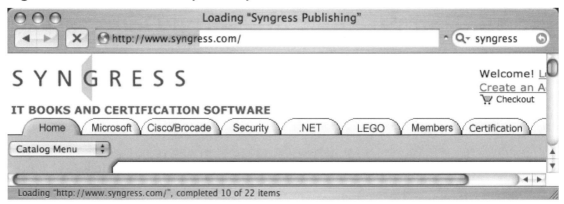

This time, the title of the page is prepended with the word "Loading" and quotation marks, which were inserted by the Safari browser. When using *intitle*, be sure to consider what text is actually from the title and which text might have been inserted by the browser.

Title text is not limited, however, to the *TITLE* HTML tag. A Web page's document can be generated in any number of ways, and in some cases, a Web page might not even have a title at all. The thing to remember is that the title is the text that appears at the top of the Web page, and you can use *intitle* to locate text in that spot.

When using *intitle*, it's important that you pay special attention to the syntax of the search string, since the word or phrase following the word intitle is considered the search phrase. *Allintitle* breaks this rule. *Allintitle* tells Google that every single word or phrase that follows is to be found in the title of the page. For example, we just looked at the *intitle:"index of" "backup files"* query as an example of an *intitle* search. In this query, the term *"backup files"* is found not in the title of the second hit but rather in the text of the document, as shown in Figure 2.5.

Figure 2.5 The *Intitle* Operator

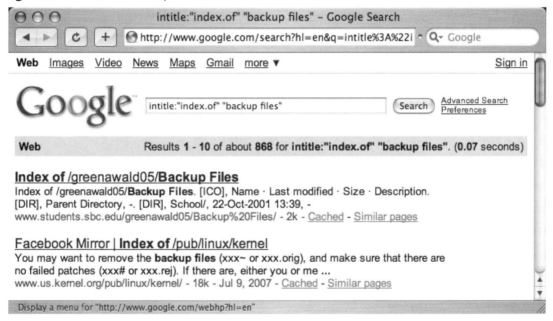

If we were to modify this query to *allintitle:"index of" "backup files"* we would get a different response from Google, as shown in Figure 2.6.

Figure 2.6 *Allintitle* Results Compared

Now, every hit contains both *"index of"* and *"backup files"* in the title of each hit. Notice also that the *allintitle* search is also more restrictive, returning only a fraction of the results as the *intitle* search.

Notes from the Underground…

Google Highlighting

Google highlights search terms using multiple colors when you're viewing the cached version of a page, and uses a bold typeface when displaying search terms on the search results pages. Don't let this confuse you if the term is highlighted in a way that's not consistent with your search syntax. Google highlights your search terms *everywhere* they appear in the search results. You can also use Google's cache as a sort of virtual highlighter. Experiment with modifying a Google cache URL. Locate your search terms in the URL, and add words around your search terms. If you do it correctly and those words are present, Google will highlight those new words on the page.

Be wary of using the *allintitle* operator. It tends to be clumsy when it's used with other advanced operators and tends to break the query entirely, causing it to return no results. It's better to go overboard and use a bunch of *intitle* operators in a query than to screw it up with *allintitle's* funky conventions.

Allintext: Locate a String Within the Text of a Page

The *allintext* operator is perhaps the simplest operator to use since it performs the function that search engines are most known for: locating a term within the text of the page. Although this advanced operator might seem too generic to be of any real use, it is handy when you *know* that the text you're looking for should *only* be found in the text of the page. Using *allintext* can also serve as a type of shorthand for "find this string anywhere *except* in the title, the URL, and links." Since this operator starts with the word *all*, every search term provided after the operator is considered part of the operator's search query.

For this reason, the *allintext* operator should not be mixed with other advanced operators.

Inurl and *Allinurl*: Finding Text in a URL

Having been exposed to the *intitle* operators, it might seem like a fairly simple task to start throwing around the *inurl* operator with reckless abandon. I encourage such flights of searching fancy, but first realize that a URL is a much more complicated beast than a simple page title, and the workings of the *inurl* operator can be equally complex.

First, let's talk about what a URL is. Short for Uniform Resource Locator, a URL is simply the address of a Web page. The beginning of a URL consists of a protocol, followed by ://, like the very common *http://* or *ftp://*. Following the protocol is an address followed by a pathname, all separated by forward slashes (/). Following the pathname comes an optional filename. A common basic URL, like http://www.uriah.com/apple-qt/1984.html, can be seen as several different components. The protocol, *http*, indicates that this is basically a Web server. The server is located at www.uriah.com, and the requested file, 1984.html, is found in the /apple-qt directory on the server. As we saw in the previous chapter, a Google search can be conveyed as a URL, which can look something like http://www.google.com/search?q=ihackstuff.

We've discussed the protocol, server, directory, and file pieces of the URL, but that last part of our example URL, *?q=ihackstuff*, bears a bit more examination. Explained simply, this is a list of parameters that are being passed into the "search" program or file. Without going into much more detail, simply understand that all this "stuff" is considered to be part of the URL, which Google can be instructed to search with the *inurl* and *allinurl* operators.

So far this doesn't seem much more complex than dealing with the *intitle* operator, but there are a few complications. First, Google can't effectively search the protocol portion of the URL—*http://*, for example. Second, there are a ton of special characters sprinkled around the URL, which Google also has trouble weeding through. Attempting to specifically include these special characters in a search could cause unexpected results and might limit your search in undesired ways. Third, and most important, other advanced operators (*site* and *filetype*, for example) can search more specific places *inside* the URL even better than *inurl* can. These factors make *inurl* much trickier to use effectively than an *intitle* search, which is very simple by comparison. Regardless, *inurl* is one of the most indispensable operators for advanced Google users; we'll see it used extensively throughout this book.

As with the *intitle* operator, *inurl* has a companion operator, known as *allinurl*. Consider the *inurl* search results page shown in Figure 2.7.

Figure 2.7 The *Inurl* Search

This search located the word *admin* in the URL of the document and the word *index* anywhere in the document, returning more than two million results. Replacing the *intitle* search with an *allintitle* search, we receive the results page shown in Figure 2.8.

This time, Google was instructed to find the words *admin* and *index* only in the URL of the document, resulting in about a million less hits. Just like the *allintitle* search, *allinurl* tells Google that every single word or phrase that follows is to be found only in the URL of the page. And just like *allintitle*, *allinurl* does not play very well with other queries. If you need to find several words or phrases in a URL, it's better to supply several *inurl* queries than to succumb to the rather unfriendly *allinurl* conventions.

Figure 2.8 *Allinurl* Compared

Site: Narrow Search to Specific Sites

Although technically a part of a URL, the address (or domain name) of a server can best be searched for with the *site* operator. *Site* allows you to search only for pages that are hosted on a specific server or in a specific domain. Although fairly straightforward, proper use of the site operator can take a little bit of getting used to, since Google reads Web server names from right to left, as opposed to the human convention of reading site names from left to right. Consider a common Web server name, www.apple.com. To locate pages that are hosted on blackhat.com, a simple query of *site:blackhat.com* will suffice, as shown in Figure 2.9.

Figure 2.9 Basic Use of the *Site* Operator

Notice that the first two results are from www.blackhat.com and japan.blackhat.com. Both of these servers end in *blackhat.com* and are valid results of our query.

Like many of Google's advanced operators, site can be used in interesting ways. Take, for example, a query for *site:r*, the results of which are shown in Figure 2.10.

Figure 2.10 Improper Use of *Site*

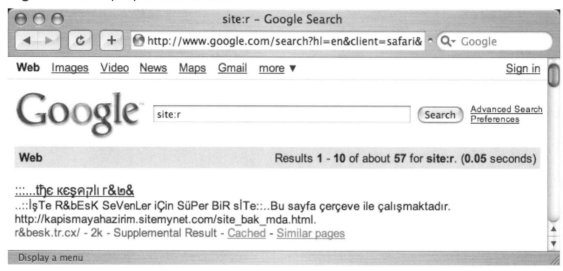

Look very closely at the results of the query and you'll discover that the URL for the first returned result looks a bit odd. Truth be told, this result *is* odd. Google (and the Internet at large) reads server names (really *domain names*) from right to left, not from left to right. So a Google query for *site:r* can never return valid results because there is no *.r* domain name. So why does Google return results? It's hard to be certain, but one thing's for sure: these oddball searches and their associated responses are very interesting to advanced search engine users and fuel the fire for further exploration.

Notes from the Underground...

Googleturds

So, what about that link that Google returned to r&besk.tr.cx? What is that thing? I coined the term *googleturd* to describe what is most likely a typo that was crawled by Google. Depending on certain undisclosed circumstances, oddball links like these are sometimes retained. Googleturds can be useful, as we will see later on.

The *site* operator can be easily combined with other searches and operators, as we'll see later in this chapter.

Filetype: Search for Files of a Specific Type

Google searches more than just Web pages. Google can search many different types of files, including PDF (Adobe Portable Document Format) and Microsoft Office documents. The *filetype* operator can help you search for these types of files. More specifically, *filetype* searches for pages that end in a particular file extension. The file extension is the part of the URL following the last period of the filename but before the question mark that begins the parameter list. Since the file extension can indicate what type of program opens a file, the *filetype* operator can be used to search for specific types of files by searching for a specific file extension. Table 2.1 shows the main file types that Google searches, according to www.google.com/help/faq_filetypes.html#what.

Table 2.1 The Main File Types Google Searches

File Type	File Extension
Adobe Portable Document Format	Pdf
Adobe PostScript	Ps
Lotus 1-2-3	wk1, wk2, wk3, wk4, wk5, wki, wks, wku
Lotus WordPro	Lwp
MacWrite	Mw
Microsoft Excel	Xls
Microsoft PowerPoint	Ppt
Microsoft Word	Doc
Microsoft Works	wks, wps, wdb
Microsoft Write	Wri
Rich Text Format	Rtf
Shockwave Flash	Swf
Text	ans, txt

Table 2.1 does not list every file type that Google will attempt to search. According to http://filext.org, there are thousands of known file extensions. Google has examples of *each and every one* of these extensions in its database! This means that Google will *crawl* any type of page with any kind of extension, but understand that Google might not have the capability to *search* an unknown file type. Table 2.1 listed the *main* file types that Google searches, but you might be wondering which of the thousands of file extensions are the most prevalent on the Web. Table 2.2 lists the top 25 file extensions found on the Web, sorted by the number of hits for that file type.

Tools & Traps...

How'd You Do That?

The data in Table 2.2 came from two sources: filext.org and Google. First, I used lynx to scrape portions of the filext.org Web site in order to compile a list of known file extensions. For example, this line of bash will extract every file extension starting with the letter A, outputting it to a file called *extensions*:

```
lynx -source "http://filext.com/alphalist.php?extstart=%5EA" | grep "<td
width=\"120\"" | awk -F "file-extension/" '{print $2}' | awk -F "\"" '{print
$1}' > extensions
```

Then, each extension is fired through a Google *filext* search, to concentrate on the *Results* line:

```
for ext in `cat extensions`; do lynx -dump
"http://www.google.com/search?q=filetype:$ext" | grep Results | grep "of
about"; done
```

The process took tens of thousands of queries and several hours to run. Google was gracious enough not to blacklist me for the flagrant violation of its Terms of Use!

Table 2.2 Top 25 File Extensions, According to Google

2004		2007	
Extension	Number of Hits (Approx.)	Extension	Number of Hits (Approx.)
HTML	18,100,000	HTML	4,960,000,000
HTM	16,700,000	HTM	1,730,000,000
PHP	16,600,000	PHP	1,050000,000
ASP	15,700,000	ASP	831,000,000
CGI	11,600,000	CFM	481,000,000
PDF	10,900,000	ASPX	442,000,000
CFM	9,880,000	SHTML	310,000,000
SHTML	8,690,000	PDF	260,000,000
JSP	7,350,000	JSP	240,000,000

Table 2.2 continued Top 25 File Extensions, According to Google

2004		2007	
Extension	Number of Hits (Approx.)	Extension	Number of Hits (Approx.)
ASPX	6,020,000	CGI	83,000,000
PL	5,890,000	DO	63,400,000
PHP3	4,420,000	PL	54,500,000
DLL	3,050,000	XML	53,100,000
PHTML	2,770,000	DOC	42,000,000
FCGI	2,550,000	SWF	40,000,000
SWF	2,290,000	PHTML	38,800,000
DOC	2,100,000	PHP3	38,100,000
TXT	1,720,000	FCGI	30,300,000
PHP4	1,460,000	TXT	30,100,000
EXE	1,410,000	STM	29,900,000
MV	1,110,000	FILE	18,400,000
XLS	969,000	EXE	17,000,000
JHTML	968,000	JHTML	16,300,000
SHTM	883,000	XLS	16,100,000
BML	859,000	PPT	13,000,000

So Much has changed in the three years since this process was run for the first edition. Just look at how many more hits Google is reporting! The jump in hits is staggering. If you're unfamiliar with some of these extensions, check out www.filext.com, a great resource for getting detailed information about file extensions, what they are, and what programs they are associated with.

TIP

The *ext* operator can be used in place of filetype. A query for *filetype:xls* is identical to a query for *ext:xls*.

Google converts every document it searches to either HTML or text for online viewing. You can see that Google has searched and converted a file by looking at the results page shown in Figure 2.11.

Figure 2.11 Converted File Types on a Search Page

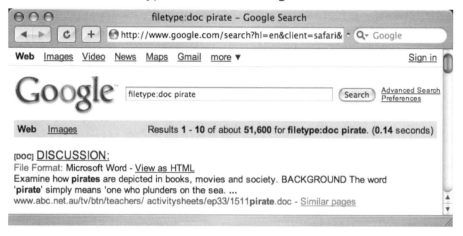

Notice that the first result lists *[DOC]* before the title of the document and a file format of *Microsoft Word*. This indicates that Google recognized the file as a Microsoft Word document. In addition, Google has provided a View as HTML link that when clicked will display an HTML approximation of the file, as shown in Figure 2.12.

Figure 2.12 A Google-converted Word Document

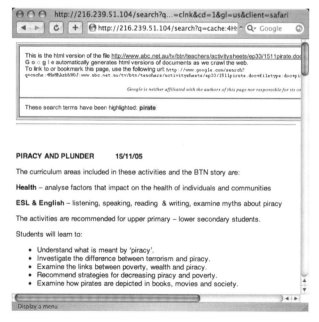

When you click the link for a document that Google has converted, a header is displayed at the top of the page, indicating that you are viewing the HTML version of the page. A link to the original file is also provided. If you think this looks similar to the cached view of a page, you're right. This *is* the cached version of the original page, converted to HTML.

Although these are great features, Google isn't perfect. Keep these things in mind:

- Google doesn't always provide a link to the converted version of a page.

- Google doesn't always properly recognize the file type of even the most common file formats.

- When Google crawls a page that ends in a particular file extension but that file is blank, Google will sometimes provide a valid file type and a link to the converted page. Even the HTML version of a blank Word document is still, well, blank.

This operator flakes out when *OR*ed. As an example, the query *filetype:doc* returns 39 million results. The query *filetype:pdf* returns 255 million results. The query *(filetype:doc | filetype:pdf)* returns 335 million results, which is pretty close to the two individual search results combined. However, when you start adding to this precocious combination with things like *(filetype:doc | filetpye:pdf) (doc | pdf)*, Google flakes out and returns 441 million results: even more than the original, broader query. I've found that Boolean logic applied to this operator is usually flaky, so beware when you start tinkering.

This operator can be mixed with other operators and search terms.

Notes from the Underground...

Google Hacking Tip

We simply can't state this enough: The real hackers play in the gray areas all the time. The *filetype* operator opens up another interesting playground for the true Google hacker. Consider the query *filetype:xls -xls.* This query should return zero results, since XLS have XLS in the URL, right? Wrong. At the time of this writing, this query returns over 7,000 results, all of which are odd in their own right.

Link: Search for Links to a Page

The *link* operator allows you to search for pages that link to other pages. Instead of providing a search term, the *link* operator requires a URL or server name as an argument. Shown in its most basic form, *link* is used with a server name, as shown in Figure 2.13.

Figure 2.13 The *Link* Operator

Each of the search results shown in Figure 2.10 contains HTML links to the http://www.defcon.org Web site. The *link* operator can be extended to include not only basic URLs, but complete URLs that include directory names, filenames, parameters, and the like. Keep in mind that long URLs are much more specific and will return fewer results than their shorter counterparts.

The only place the URL of a link is visible is in the browser's status bar or in the source of the page. For that reason, unlike other cached pages, the cached page for a *link* operator's search result does not highlight the search term, since the search term (the linked Web site) is never really shown in the page. In fact, the cached banner does not make any reference to your search query, as shown in Figure 2.14.

Figure 2.14 A Generic Cache Banner Displayed for a *Link* Search

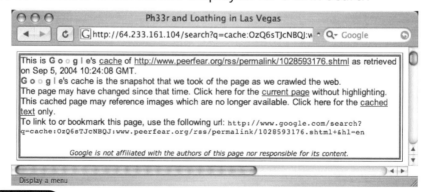

It is a common misconception to think that the *link* operator can actually search for text within a link. The *inanchor* operator performs something similar to this, as we'll see next. To properly use the *link* operator, you must provide a full URL (including protocol, server, directory, and file), a partial URL (including only the protocol and the host), or simply a server name; otherwise, Google could return unpredictable results. As an example, consider a search for *link:linux*, which returns 151,000 results. This search is not the proper syntax for a link search, since the domain name is invalid. The correct syntax for a search like this might be *link:linux.org* (with 317 results) or *link:linux.org* (with *no* results). These numbers don't seem to make sense, and they certainly don't begin to account for the 151,000 hits on the original query. So what exactly is being returned from Google for a search like *link:linux*? Figures 2.15 and 2.16 show the answer to this question.

Figure 2.15 *link:linux* Returns 151,000 Results

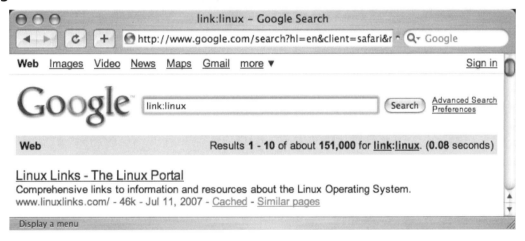

Figure 2.16 *"link linux"* Returns an Identical 151,000 Results

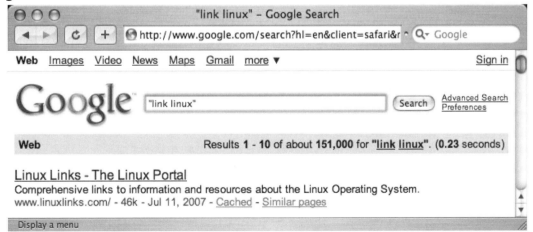

When an invalid *link:* syntax is provided, Google treats the search as a phrase search. Google offers another clue as to how it handles invalid link searches through the cache page. As shown in Figure 2.17, the cached banner for a site found with a *link:linux* search does not resemble a typical link search cached banner, but rather a standard search cache banner with included highlighted terms.

Figure 2.17 An Invalid *Link* Search Page

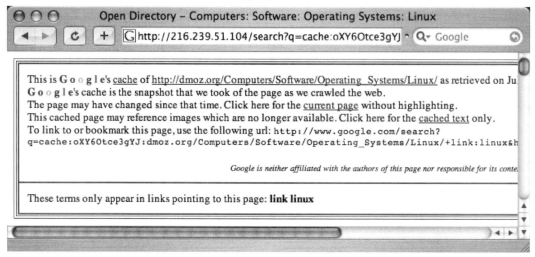

This is an indication that Google did not perform a link search, but instead treated the search as a phrase, with a colon representing a word break.

The *link* operator cannot be used with other operators or search terms.

Inanchor: Locate Text Within Link Text

This operator can be considered a companion to the *link* operator, since they both help search links. The *inanchor* operator, however, searches the text representation of a link, not the actual URL. For example, in Figure 2.17, the Google link to *"current page"* is shown in typical form—as an underlined portion of text. When you click that link, you are taken to the URL http://dmoz.org/Computers/Software/Operating_Systems/Linux. If you were to look at the actual source of that page, you would see something like this:

```
<A HREF="http://dmoz.org/Computers/Software/Operating_Systems/Linux/">current
page</A>
```

The *inanchor* operator helps search the anchor, or the displayed text on the link, which in this case is the phrase "current page". This is not the same as using *inurl* to find this page with a query like *inurl:Computers inurl:Operating_Systems.*

Inanchor accepts a word or phrase as an argument, such as *inanchor:click* or *inanchor:James.Foster.* This search will be handy later, especially when we begin to explore ways of searching for relationships between sites. The *inanchor* operator can be used with other operators and search terms.

Cache: Show the Cached Version of a Page

As we've already discussed, Google keeps snapshots of pages it has crawled that we can access via the cached link on the search results page. If you would like to jump right to the cached version of a page without first performing a Google query to get to the cached link on the results page, you can simply use the *cache* advanced operator in a Google query such as *cache:blackhat.com* or *cache:www.netsec.net/content/index.jsp.* If you don't supply a complete URL or hostname, Google could return unpredictable results. Just as with the *link* operator, passing an invalid hostname or URL as a parameter to *cache* will submit the query as a phrase search. A search for *cache:linux* returns exactly as many results as *"cache linux"*, indicating that Google did indeed treat the cache search as a standard phrase search.

The *cache* operator can be used with other operators and terms, although the results are somewhat unpredictable.

Numrange: Search for a Number

The *numrange* operator requires two parameters, a low number and a high number, separated by a dash. This operator is powerful but dangerous when used by malicious Google hackers. As the name suggests, *numrange* can be used to find numbers within a range. For example, to locate the number 12345, a query such as *numrange:12344-12346* will work just fine. When searching for numbers, Google ignores symbols such as currency markers and commas, making it much easier to search for numbers on a page. A shortened version of this operator exists as well. Instead of supplying the *numrange* operator, you can simply provide two numbers in a query, separated by two periods. The shortened version of the query just mentioned would be *12344..12346*. Notice that the *numrange* operator was left out of the query entirely.

This operator can be used with other operators and search terms.

Notes from the Underground…

Bad Google Hacker!

If Gandalf the Grey were to author this sidebar, he wouldn't be able to resist saying something like "There are fouler things than characters lurking in the dark places of Google's cache." The most grave examples of Google's power lies in the use of the *numrange* operator. It would be extremely irresponsible of me to share these powerful queries with you. Fortunately, the abuse of this operator has been curbed due to the diligence of the hard-working members of the Search Engine Hacking forums at http://johnny.ihackstuff.com. The members of that community have taken the high road time and time again to get the word out about the dangers of Google hackers without spilling the beans and creating even more hackers. This sidebar is dedicated to them!

Daterange: Search for Pages Published Within a Certain Date Range

The *daterange* operator can tend to be a bit clumsy, but it is certainly helpful and worth the effort to understand. You can use this operator to locate pages indexed by Google within a certain date range. Every time Google crawls a page, this date changes. If Google locates some very obscure Web page, it might only crawl it once, never returning to index it again. If you find that your searches are clogged with these types of obscure Web pages, you can remove them from your search (and subsequently get fresher results) through effective use of the *daterange* operator.

The parameters to this operator must always be expressed as a range, two dates separated by a dash. If you only want to locate pages that were indexed on one specific date, you must provide the same date twice, separated by a dash. If this sounds too easy to be true, you're right. It *is* too easy to be true. Both dates passed to this operator must be in the form of two *Julian dates*. The Julian date is the number of days that have passed since January 1, 4713 B.C. For example, the date September 11, 2001, is represented in Julian terms as 2452164. So, to search for pages that were indexed by Google on September 11, 2001, and contained the word *"osama bin laden,"* the query would be *daterange:2452164-2452164 "osama bin laden"*.

Google does not officially support the *daterange* operator, and as such your mileage may vary. Google seems to prefer the date limit used by the advanced search form at www.google.com/advanced_search. As we discussed in the last chapter, this form creates fields in the URL string to perform specific functions. Google designed the *as_qdr* field to help you locate pages that have been *updated* within a certain time frame. For example, to find pages that have been *updated* within the past three months and that contain the word *Google*, use the query *http://www.google.com/search?q=google&as_qdr=m3*.

This might be a better alternative date restrictor than the clumsy *daterange* operator. Just understand that these are very different functions. *Daterange* is not the advanced-operator equivalent for *as_qdr,* and unfortunately, there is no operator equivalent. If you want to find pages that have been updated within the past year or less, you must either use Google advanced search interface or stick *&as_qdr=3m* (or equivalent) on the end of your URL.

The *daterange* operator *must* be used with other search terms or advanced operators. It will not return any results when used by itself.

Info: Show Google's Summary Information

The *info* operator shows the summary information for a site and provides links to other Google searches that might pertain to that site, as shown in Figure 2.18. The parameter to this operator must be a valid URL or site name. You can achieve this same functionality by supplying a site name or URL as a search query.

Figure 2.18 A Google *Info* Query's Output

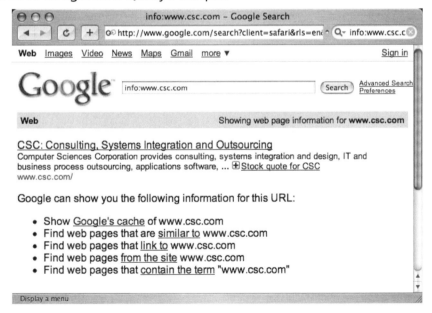

If you don't supply a complete URL or hostname, Google could return unpredictable results. Just as with the *link* and *cache* operators, passing an invalid hostname or URL as a parameter to *info* will submit the query as a phrase search. A search for *info:linux* returns exactly as many results as *"info linux",* indicating that Google did indeed treat the *info* search as a standard phrase search.

The *info* operator cannot be used with other operators or search terms.

Related: Show Related Sites

The *related* operator displays sites that Google has determined are related to a site, as shown in Figure 2.19. The parameter to this operator is a valid site name or URL. You can achieve this same functionality by clicking the "Similar Pages" link from any search results page, or by using the "Find pages similar to the page" portion of the advanced search form (shown in Figure 2.19).

Figure 2.19 Related in Action?

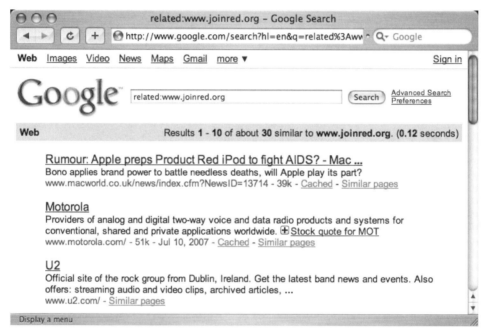

If you don't supply a complete URL or hostname, Google could return unpredictable results. Passing an invalid hostname or URL as a parameter to *related* will submit the query as a phrase search. A search for *related:linux* returns exactly as many results as *"related linux"*, indicating that Google did indeed treat the cache search as a standard phrase search.

The *related* operator cannot be used with other operators or search terms.

Author: Search Groups for an Author of a Newsgroup Post

The *author* operator will allow you to search for the author of a newsgroup post. The parameter to this option consists of a name or an e-mail address. This operator can only be used in conjunction with a Google Groups search. Attempting to use this operator outside a Groups search will result in an error. When you're searching for a simple name , such as *author:Johnny*, the search results will include posts written by anyone with the first, middle, or last name of *Johnny*, as shown in Figure 2.20.

Figure 2.20 A Search for *Author:Johnny*

As you can see, we've got hits for Johnny Lurker, Johnny Walker, Johnny, and Johnny Anderson. Makes you wonder if those are real names, doesn't it? In most cases, these are not real names. This is the nature of the newsgroup beast. Pseudo-anonymity is fairly easy to maintain when anyone can post to newsgroups through Google using nothing more than a free e-mail account as verification.

The *author* operator can be a bit clumsy to use, since it doesn't interpret its parameters in exactly the same way as some of the operators. Simple searches such as *author:Johnny* or *author:Johnny@ihackstuff.com* work just as expected, but things get dicey when we attempt to search for names given in the form of a phrase. Consider a search like *author:"Johnny Long"*, an attempt to search for an author with a full name of Johnny Long. This search fails pretty miserably, as shown in Figure 2.21.

Figure 2.21 Phrase Searching and *Author* Don't Mix

Passing the query of *author:Johnny.long*, however, gets us the results we're expecting: Johnny Long as the posts' author, as shown in Figure 2.22.

Figure 2.22 *Author* Searches Prefer Periods

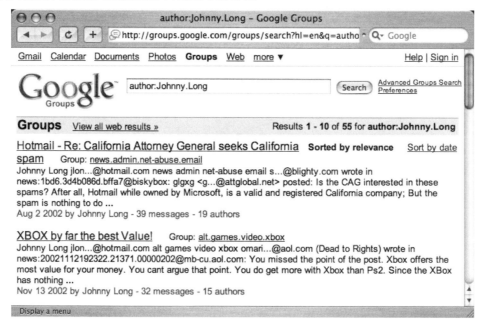

The *author* operator can be used with other valid Groups operators or search terms.

Group: Search Group Titles

This operator allows you to search the title of Google Groups posts for search terms. This operator only works within Google Groups. This is one of the operators that is very compatible with wildcards. For example, to search for groups that end in *forsale*, a search such as *group:*.forsale* works very well. In some cases, Google finds your search term not in the actual name of the group but in the keywords *describing* the group. Consider the search *group:windows*, as shown in Figure 2.23. Not all of the groups returned contain the word *windows*, but all the returned groups discuss Windows topics.

Figure 2.23 The *Group* Search Digs Deeper Than Group Name

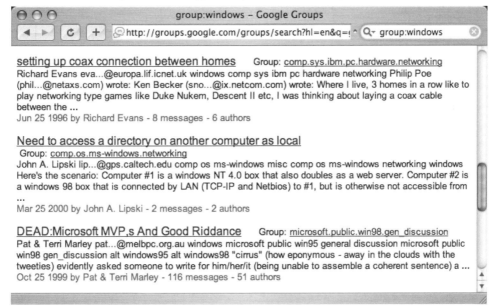

In our experience, the *group* operator does not mix very well with other operators. If you get odd results when throwing *group* into the mix, try using other operators such as *intitle* to compensate.

Insubject: Search Google Groups Subject Lines

The *insubject* operator is effectively the same as the *intitle* search and returns the same results. Searches for *intitle:dragon* and *insubject:dragon* return exactly the same number of results. This is most likely because the subject of a group post is also the title of the post. Subject is (and was, in USENET) the more precise term for a message title, and this operator most likely exists to help ease the mental shift from "deja/USENET searching" to Google searching.

Just like the *intitle* operator, *insubject* can be used with other operators and search terms.

Msgid: Locate a Group Post by Message ID

In the first edition of this book, I presented the *msgid* operator, which displays one specific message in Google Groups. This operator took only one argument, a group message identifier. A message identifier (or message ID) is a unique string that identifies a newsgroup post. The format is something like *xxx@yyy.com*. Things have changed since that printing, and now *msgid* is mostly broken, replaced by the *as_msgid* search URL parameter, now accessible through the advanced groups page at http://groups.google.com/advanced_search. However, we'll discuss Message ID's here to give you an idea of how that functionality worked, just in case the *msgid* parameter is brought back to life.

To view message IDs, you must view the original group post format. When viewing a post (see Figure 2.24), simply click **Show Options** and then follow the **Show original** link. You will be taken to a page that lists the entire content of the group post, as shown in Figure 2.25.

Figure 2.24 A Typical Group Message

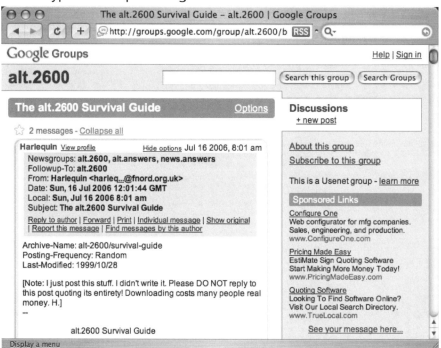

Figure 2.25 The Message ID of a Post Is Visible Only in the Post's Original Format

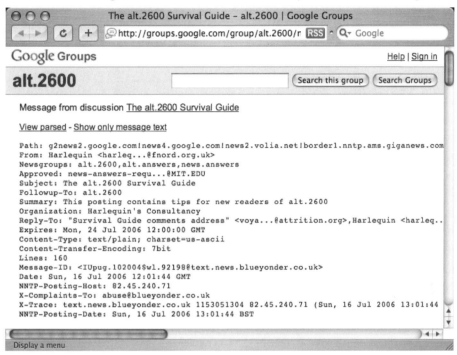

The Message ID of this message (*IUpug.102004$wl.92198@text.news.blueyonder.co.uk*) can be used in the advance search form, with the *as_msgid* URL parameter, or with the *msgid* operator should it make a comeback.

When operational, the *msgid* operator does not mix with other operators or search terms.

Stocks: Search for Stock Information

The *stocks* operator allows you to search for stock market information about a particular company. The parameter to this operator must be a valid stock abbreviation. If you provide an valid stock ticker symbol, you will be taken to a screen that allows further searching for a correct ticker symbol, as shown in Figure 2.26.

Figure 2.26 Searching for a Valid Stock Symbol

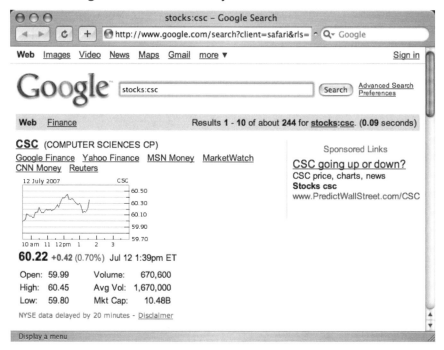

The *stocks* operator cannot be used with other operators or search terms.

Define: Show the Definition of a Term

The *define* operator returns definitions for a search term. Fairly simple, and very straightforward, arguments to this operator may be a word or phrase. Links to the source of the definition are provided, as shown in Figure 2.27.

Figure 2.27 Results of a *Define* Search

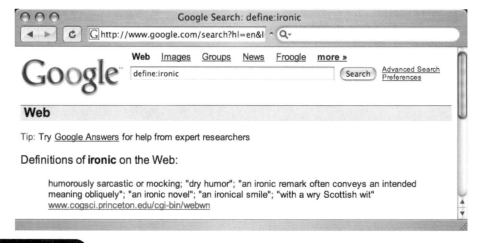

The *define* operator cannot be used with other operators or search terms.

Phonebook: Search Phone Listings

The *phonebook* operator searches for business and residential phone listings. Three operators can be used for the phonebook search: *rphonebook*, *bphonebook*, and *phonebook*, which will search residential listings, business listings, or both, respectively. The parameters to these operators are all the same and usually consist of a series of words describing the listing and location. In many ways, this operator functions like an *allintitle* search, since every word listed after the operator is included in the operator search. A query such as *phonebook:john darling ny* would list both business and residential listings for John Darling in New York. As shown in Figure 2.28, links are provided for popular mapping sites that allow you to view maps of an address or location.

Figure 2.28 The Output of a *Phonebook* Query

To get access to business listings, play around with the *bphonebook* operator. This operator doesn't always work as expected, but for certain queries (like *bphonebook:korean food washington DC*, shown below in Figure 2.29) it works very well, transporting you to a Google Local listing of businesses that match the description.

Figure 2.29 Google's Business Operator: bphonebook

There are other ways to get to this information without the *phonebook* operators. If you supply what looks like an address (including a state) or a name and a state as a standard query, Google will return a link allowing you to map the location in the case of an address or a phone listing in the case of a name and street match.

Notes from the Underground...

Hey, Get Me Outta Here!

If you're concerned about your address information being in Google's databases for the world to see, have no fear. Google makes it possible for you to delete your information so others can't access it via Google. Simply fill out the form at www.google.com/help/pbremoval.html and your information will be removed, usually within 48 hours. This doesn't remove you from the Internet (let us know if you find a link to do that), but the page gives you a decent list of places that list similar information. Oh, and Google is trusting you not to delete other people's information with this form.

The *phonebook* operators do not provide very informative error messages, and it can be fairly difficult to figure out whether or not you have bad syntax. Consider a query for *phone-book:john smith*. This query does not return any results, and the results page looks a lot like a standard "no results" page, as shown in Figure 2.30.

Figure 2.30 *Phonebook* Error Messages Are Very Misleading

To make matters worse, the suggestions for fixing this query are all wrong. In this case, you need to provide *more* information in your query to get hits, not fewer keywords, as Google suggests. Consider *phonebook:john smith ny,* which returns approximately 600 results.

Colliding Operators and Bad Search-Fu

As you start using advanced operators, you'll realize that some combinations work better than others for finding what you're looking for. Just as quickly, you'll begin to realize that some operators just don't mix well at all. Table 2.3 shows which operators can be mixed with others. Operators listed as "No" should not be used in the same query as other operators. Furthermore, these operators will sometimes give funky results if you get too fancy with their syntax, so don't be surprised when it happens.

This table also lists operators that can only be used within specific Google search areas and operators that cannot be used alone. The values in this table bear some explanation. A box marked "Yes" indicates that the operator works as expected in that context. A box marked "No" indicates that the operator does not work in that context, and Google indicates this with a warning message. Any box marked with "Not really" indicates that Google attempts to translate your query when used in that context. True Google hackers love exploring gray areas like the ones found in the "Not really" boxes.

Table 2.3 Mixing Operators

Operator	Mixes with Other Operators?	Can Be Used Alone?	Web?	Images?	Groups?	News?
intitle	Yes	Yes	Yes	Yes	Yes	Yes
allintitle	No	Yes	Yes	Yes	Yes	Yes
inurl	Yes	Yes	Yes	Yes	Not really	Like *intitle*
allinurl	No	Yes	Yes	Yes	Yes	Like *intitle*
filetype	Yes	No	Yes	Yes	No	Not really
allintext	Not really	Yes	Yes	Yes	Yes	Yes
site	Yes	Yes	Yes	Yes	No	Not really
link	No	Yes	Yes	No	No	Not really
inanchor	Yes	Yes	Yes	Yes	Not really	Yes
numrange	Yes	Yes	Yes	No	No	Not really
daterange	Yes	No	Yes	Not really	Not really	Not really
cache	No	Yes	Yes	No	Not really	Not really
info	No	Yes	Yes	Not really	Not really	Not really
related	No	Yes	Yes	No	No	Not really
phonebook, rphonebook, bphonebook	No	Yes	Yes	No	No	Not really
author	Yes	Yes	No	No	Yes	Not really
group	Not really	Yes	No	No	Yes	Not really
insubject	Yes	Yes	Like *intitle*	Like *intitle*	Yes	Like *intitle*
msgid	No	Yes	Not really	Not really	Yes	Not really
stocks intitle	No	Yes	No	No	No	Like
define	No	Yes	Yes	Not really	Not really	Not really

Allintext gives all sorts of crazy results when it is mixed with other operators. For example, a search for *allintext:moo goo gai filetype:pdf* works well for finding Chinese food menus, whereas *allintext:Sum Dum Goy intitle:Dragon* gives you that empty feeling inside—like a year without the 1985 classic *The Last Dragon* (see Figure 2.31).

Figure 2.31 *Allintext* Is Bad Enough to Make You Want to Cry

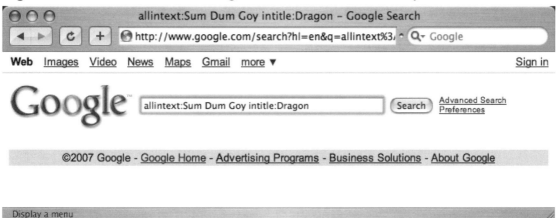

Despite the fact that some operators do combine with others, it's still possible to get less than optimal results by running your operators head-on into each other. This section focuses on pointing out a few of the potential bad collisions that could cause you headaches. We'll start with some of the more obvious ones.

First, consider a query like *something −something*. By asking for something and taking away something, we end up with... nothing, and Google tells you as much. This is an obvious example, but consider *intitle:something −intitle:something*. This query, just like the first, returns nothing, since we've negated our first search with a duplicate *NOT* search. Literally, we're saying "find something in the title and hide all the results with something in the title." Both of these examples clearly illustrate the point that you can't query for something and negate that query, because your results will be zero.

It gets a bit tricky when the advanced operators start overlapping. Consider *site* and *inurl*. The URL *includes* the name of the site. So, extending the "don't contradict yourself" rule, don't include a term with *site* and exclude that term with *inurl* and vice versa and expect sane results. A query like *site:microsoft.com -inurl:microsoft.com* doesn't make much sense at all, and shouldn't work, but as Figure 2.32 shows, it does work.

Figure 2.32 No One Said Hackers Obeyed Reality

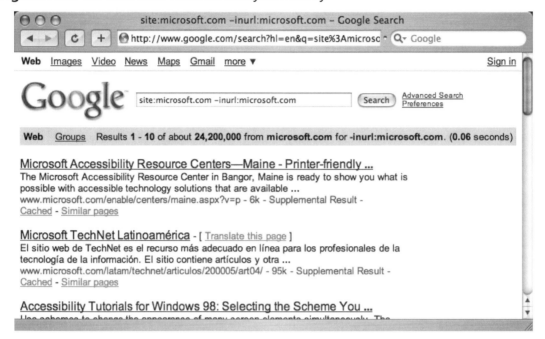

When you're really trying to home in on a topic, keep the "rules" in mind and you'll accelerate toward your target at a much faster pace. Save the rule breaking for your required Google hacking license test!

Here's a quick breakdown of some broken searches and why they're broken:

site:com site:edu A hit can't be both an *edu* and a *com* at the same time. What you're more likely to search for is *(site:edu | site:com)*, which searches for either domain.

inanchor:click −click This is contradictory. Remember, unless you use an advanced operator, your search term can appear *anywhere* on the page, including the title, URL, text, and even *anchors*.

allinurl:pdf allintitle:pdf Operators starting with *all* are notoriously bad at combining. Get out of the habit of combining them before you get *into* the habit of using them! Replace *allinurl* with *inurl*, *allintitle* with *intitle*, and just don't use *allintext*. It's evil.

site:syngress.com allinanchor:syngress publishing This query returns zero results, which seems natural considering the last example and the fact that most *all** searches are nasty to use. However, this query suffers from an ordering problem, a fairly common problem that can really throw off some narrow searches. By changing the query to *allinanchor:syngress publishing site:syngress.com*, which moves the *allinanchor* to the beginning of the query, we can get many more results. This does not at all seem natural, since the *allintitle* operator considers all the following terms to be parameters to the operator, but that's just the way it is.

link:www.microsoft.com linux   This is a nasty search for a beginner because it *appears* to work, finding sites that link to Microsoft and mention the word *linux* on the page. Unfortunately, *link* doesn't mix with other operators, but instead of sending you an error message, Google "fixes" the query for you and provides the exact results as *"link.www.microsoft.com" linux*.

Summary

Google offers plenty of options when it comes to performing advanced searches. URL modification, discussed in Chapter 1, can provide you with lots of options for modifying a previously submitted search, but advanced operators are better used within a query. Easier to remember than the URL modifiers, advance operators are the truest tools of any Google hacker's arsenal. As such, they should be the tools used by the good guys when considering the protection of Web-based information.

Most of the operators can be used in combination, the most notable exceptions being the *allintitle, allinurl, allinanchor,* and *allintext* operators. Advanced Google searchers tend to steer away from these operators, opting to use the *intitle, inurl,* and *link* operators to find strings within the title, URL, or links to pages, respectively. *Allintext,* used to locate all the supplied search terms within the text of a document, is one of the least used and most redundant of the advanced operators. *Filetype* and *site* are very powerful operators that search specific sites or specific file types. The *daterange* operator allows you to search for files that were indexed within a certain time frame, although the URL parameter *as_qdr* seems to be more in vogue. When crawling Web pages, Google generates specific information such as a cached copy of a page, an information snippet about the page, and a list of sites that seem related. This information can be retrieved with the *cache, info,* and *related* operators, respectively. To search for the author of a Google Groups document, use the *author* operator. The *phonebook* series of operators return business or residential phone listings as well as maps to specific addresses. The *stocks* operator returns stock information about a specific ticker symbol, whereas the *define* operator returns the definition of a word or simple phrase.

Solutions Fast Track

Intitle

- Finds strings in the title of a page
- Mixes well with other operators
- Best used with Web, Group, Images, and News searches

Allintitle

- Finds all terms in the title of a page
- Does not mix well with other operators or search terms
- Best used with Web, Group, Images, and News searches

Inurl

- Finds strings in the URL of a page
- Mixes well with other operators
- Best used with Web and Image searches

Allinurl

- Finds all terms in the URL of a page
- Does not mix well with other operators or search terms
- Best used with Web, Group, and Image searches

Filetype

- Finds specific types of files based on file extension
- Synonymous with ext
- Requires an additional search term
- Mixes well with other operators
- Best used with Web and Group searches

Allintext

- Finds all provided terms in the text of a page
- Pure evil—don't use it
- Forget you ever heard about *allintext*

Site

- Restricts a search to a particular site or domain
- Mixes well with other operators
- Can be used alone
- Best used with Web, Groups and Image searches

Link

- Searches for links to a site or URL
- Does not mix with other operators or search terms

■ Best used with Web searches

Inanchor

- Finds text in the descriptive text of links
- Mixes well with other operators and search terms
- Best used for Web, Image, and News searches

Daterange

- Locates pages indexed within a specific date range
- Requires a search term
- Mixes well with other operators and search terms
- Best used with Web searches
- Might be phased out to make way for *as_qdr*.

Numrange

- Finds a number in a particular range
- Mixes well with other operators and search terms
- Best used with Web searches
- Synonymous with *ext*.

Cache

- Displays Google's cached copy of a page
- Does not mix with other operators or search terms
- Best used with Web searches

Info

- Displays summary information about a page
- Does not mix with other operators or search terms
- Best used with Web searches

Related

- Shows sites that are related to provided site or URL
- Does not mix with other operators or search terms
- Best used with Web searches

Phonebook, Rphonebook, /Bphonebook

- Shows residential or business phone listings
- Does not mix with other operators or search terms
- Best used as a Web query

Author

- Searches for the author of a Group post
- Mixes well with other operators and search terms
- Best used as a Group search

Group

- Searches Group names, selects individual Groups
- Mixes well with other operators
- Best used as a Group search

Insubject

- Locates a string in the subject of a Group post
- Mixes well with other operators and search terms
- Best used as a Group search

Msgid

- Locates a Group message by message ID
- Does not mix with other operators or search terms
- Best used as a Group search
- Flaky. Use the advanced search form at *groups.google.com/advanced_search* instead

Stocks

- Shows the Yahoo Finance stock listing for a ticker symbol
- Does not mix with other operators or search terms
- Best provided as a Web query

Define

- Shows various definitions of a provided word or phrase
- Does not mix with other operators or search terms
- Best provided as a Web query

Links to Sites

- The Google filetypes FAQ, www.google.com/help/faq_filetypes.html
- The resource for file extension information, www.filext.com   This site can help you figure out what program a particular extension is associated with.
- http://searchenginewatch.com/searchday/article.php/2160061?? This article discusses some of the issues associated with Google's date restrict search options.
- Very nice online Julian date converters, www.24hourtranslations.co.uk/dates.htm and www.tesre.bo.cnr.it/~mauro/JD/

Frequently Asked Questions

The following Frequently Asked Questions, answered by the authors of this book, are designed to both measure your understanding of the concepts presented in this chapter and to assist you with real-life implementation of these concepts. To have your questions about this chapter answered by the author, browse to **www. syngress.com/solutions** and click on the **"Ask the Author"** form.

Q: Do other search engines provide some form of advanced operator? How do their advanced operators compare to Google's?

A: Yes, most other search engines offer similar operators. Yahoo is the most similar to Google, in my opinion. This might have to do with the fact that Yahoo once relied solely on Google as its search provider. The operators available with Yahoo include *site* (domain search), *hostname* (full server name), *link, url* (show only one document), *inurl*, and *intitle*. The Yahoo advanced search page offers other options and URL modifiers. You can dissect the HTML form at http://search.yahoo.com/search/options to get to the interesting options here. Be prepared for a search page that looks a lot like Google's advanced search page.

AltaVista offers *domain, host, link, title*, and *url* operators. The AltaVista advanced search page can be found at www.altavista.com/web/adv. Of particular interest is the *timeframe* search, which allows more granularity than Google's *as_qdr* URL modifier, allowing you to search either ranges or specific time frames such as the past week, two weeks, or longer.

Q: Where can I get a quick rundown of all the advanced operators?

A: Check out www.google.com/help/operators.html. This page describes various operators and is a good summary of this chapter. It is assumed that new operators are listed on this page when they are released, but keep in mind that some operators enter a beta stage before they are released to the public. Sometimes these operators are discovered by unsuspecting Google users throwing around the colon separator too much. Who knows, maybe you'll be the next person to discover the newest hidden operator!

Q: How can I keep up with new operators as they come out? What about other Google-related news and tips?

A: There are quite a few Web sites that we frequent for news and information about all things Google. The first is http://googleblog.blogspot.com, Google's *official* Weblog. Although not necessarily technical in nature, it's a nice way to gain insight into some of the happenings at Google. Another is Aaron Swartz's *unofficial* Google blog, located at http://google.blogspace.com. Not endorsed or sponsored by Google, this site is often more pointed, and sometimes more insightful. A third site that's a must-bookmark one is the Google Labs page at http://labs.google.com. This is one of the best places to get news about new features and capabilities Google has to offer. Also, to get updates about new Google queries, even if they're not Google related, check out www.google.com/alerts, the main Google Alerts page. Google Alerts sends you e-mail when there are updates to a search term. You could use this tool to uncover new operators by alerting on a search term such as *google advanced operator site:google.com*. Last but not least, watch Google Trends at www.google.com/trends and Google Zeitgeist (www.google.com/press/zeitgeist.html) to keep an eye on what others are searching for. You might just catch a few Google hackers in the wild.

Q: Is the word order in a query significant?

A: Sometimes. If you are interested in the ranking of a site, especially which sites float up to the first few pages, order is very significant. Google will take two adjoining words in a query and try to first find sites that have those words *in the order you specified*. Switching the order of the words still returns the same exact sites (unless you put quotes around the words, *forcing* Google to find the words in that order), regardless of which order you provided the terms in your query. To get an idea of how this works, play around with some basic queries such as *food clothes* and *clothes food*.

Q: Can't you give me any more cool operators?

A: The list could be endless. Google is so hard to keep up with. OK. How about this one: *view*. Throw *view:map* or *view:timeline* on the end of a Web query to view the results in either a map view or a cool timeline view. For something educational, try *"Abraham Lincoln" view:timeline*. To find out where all the hackers in the world are, try *hackers view:map*. To find out if bell bottoms are really making a comeback, try *"bell bottoms" view:timeline*. Here's a spoiler: apparently, they are.

## Chapter 3

Google Hacking Basics

Solutions in this chapter:

- **Using Caches for Anonymity**
- **Directory Listings**
- **Going Out on a Limb: Traversal Techniques**

☑ **Summary**

☑ **Solutions Fast Track**

☑ **Frequently Asked Questions**

Introduction

A fairly large portion of this book is dedicated to the techniques the "bad guys" will use to locate sensitive information. We present this information to help you become better informed about their motives so that you can protect yourself and perhaps your customers. We've already looked at some of the benign basic searching techniques that are foundational for any Google user who wants to break the barrier of the basics and charge through to the next level: the ways of the Google hacker. Now we'll start looking at more nefarious uses of Google that hackers are likely to employ.

First, we'll talk about Google's cache. If you haven't already experimented with the cache, you're missing out. I suggest you at least click a few various *cached links* from the Google search results page before reading further. As any decent Google hacker will tell you, there's a certain anonymity that comes with browsing the cached version of a page. That anonymity only goes so far, and there are some limitations to the coverage it provides. Google can, however, very nicely veil your crawling activities to the point that the target Web site might not even get a single packet of data from you as you cruise the Web site. We'll show you how it's done.

Next, we'll talk about directory listings. These "ugly" Web pages are chock full of information, and their mere existence serves as the basis for some of the more advanced attack searches that we'll discuss in later chapters.

To round things out, we'll take a look at a technique that has come to be known as *traversing*: the expansion of a search to attempt to gather more information. We'll look at directory traversal, number range expansion, and extension trolling, all of which are techniques that should be second nature to any decent hacker—and the good guys that defend against them.

Anonymity with Caches

Google's cache feature is truly an amazing thing. The simple fact is that if Google crawls a page or document, you can almost always count on getting a copy of it, even if the original source has since dried up and blown away. Of course the down side of this is that hackers can get a copy of your sensitive data even if you've pulled the plug on that pesky Web server. Another down side of the cache is that the bad guys can crawl your entire Web site (including the areas you "forgot" about) without even sending a single packet to your server. If your Web server doesn't get so much as a packet, it can't write anything to the log files. (You *are* logging your Web connections, aren't you?) If there's nothing in the log files, you might not have any idea that your sensitive data has been carried away. It's sad that we even have to think in these terms, but untold megabytes, gigabytes, and even terabytes of sensitive data leak from Web servers every day. Understanding how hackers can mount an anonymous attack on your sensitive data via Google's cache is of utmost importance.

Google grabs a copy of *most* Web data that it crawls. There are exceptions, and this behavior is preventable, as we'll discuss later, but the vast majority of the data Google crawls is copied and filed away, accessible via the *cached* link on the search page. We need to examine some subtleties to Google's cached document banner. The banner shown in Figure 3.1 was gathered from www.phrack.org.

Figure 3.1 This Cached Banner Contains a Subtle Warning About Images

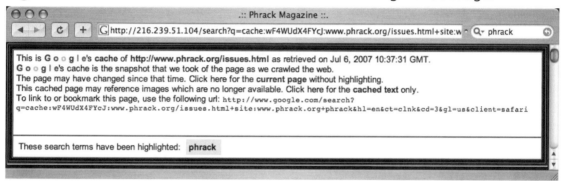

If you've gotten so familiar with the cache banner that you just blow right past it, slow down a bit and actually read it. The cache banner in Figure 3.1 notes, "This cached page may reference images which are no longer available." This message is easy to miss, but it provides an important clue about what Google's doing behind the scenes.

To get a better idea of what's happening, let's take a look at a snippet of *tcpdump* output gathered while browsing this cached page. To capture this data, *tcpdump* is simply run as *tcpdump −n*. Your installation or implementation of *tcpdump* might require you to also set a listening interface with the *−i* switch. The output of the *tcpdump* command is shown in Figure 3.2.

Figure 3.2 *Tcpdump* Output Fragment Gathered While Viewing a Cached Page

```
10.0.1.6.49847 > 200.199.20.162.80:
10.0.1.6.49848 > 200.199.20.162.80:
200.199.20.162.80 > 10.0.1.6.49847:
10.0.1.6.49847 > 200.199.20.162.80:
200.199.20.162.80 > 10.0.1.6.49848:
10.0.1.6.49848 > 200.199.20.162.80:
10.0.1.6.49847 > 200.199.20.162.80:
10.0.1.6.49848 > 200.199.20.162.80:
66.249.83.83.80 > 10.0.1.3.58785:
66.249.83.83.80 > 10.0.1.3.58790:
66.249.83.83.80 > 10.0.1.3.58790:
```

```
66.249.83.83.80 > 10.0.1.3.58790:
66.249.83.83.80 > 10.0.1.3.58790:
66.249.83.83.80 > 10.0.1.3.58790:
```

Let's take apart this output a bit, starting at the bottom. This is a port 80 (Web) conversation between our browser machine (10.0.1.6) and a Google server (66.249.83.83). This is the type of traffic we should expect from any transaction with Google, but the beginning of the capture reveals another port 80 (Web) connection to 200.199.20.162. This is not a Google server, and an *nslookup* of that Internet Protocol (IP) shows that it is the www.phrack.org Web server. The connection to this server can be explained by rerunning *tcpdump* with more options specifically designed to show a few hundred bytes of the data inside the packets as well as the headers. The partial capture shown in Figure 3.3 was gathered by running:

```
tcpdump -Xx -s 500 -n
```

and shift-reloading the cached page. Shift-reloading forces most browsers to contact the Web host again, not relying on any caches the browser might be using.

Figure 3.3 A Partial HTTP Request Showing the *Host* Header Field

```
0x0030:    085c 0661 4745 5420 2f69 6d67 2f70 6872    .\.aGET./img/phr
0x0040:    6163 6b2d 6c6f 676f 2e6a 7067 2048 5454    ack-logo.jpg.HTT
0x0050:    502f 312e 310d 0a41 6363 6570 743a 202a    P/1.1..Accept:.*
0x0060:    2f2a 0d0a 4163 6365 7074 2d4c 616e 6775    /*..Accept-Langu
0x0070:    6167 653a 2065 6e0d 0a41 6363 6570 742d    age:.en..Accept-
0x0080:    456e 636f 6469 6e67 3a20 677a 6970 2c20    Encoding:.gzip,.
0x0090:    6465 666c 6174 650d 0a52 6566 6572 6572    deflate..Referer
0x00a0:    3a20 6874 7470 3a2f 2f32 3136 2e32 3339    :.http://216.239
0x00b0:    2e35 312e 3130 342f 7365 6172 6368 3f71    .51.104/search?q
0x00c0:    3d63 6163 6865 3a77 4634 5755 6458 3446    =cache:wF4WUdX4F
0x00d0:    5963 4a3a 7777 772e 7068 7261 636b 2e6f    YcJ:www.phrack.o
0x00e0:    7267 2f69 7373 7565 732e 6874 6d6c 2b73    rg/issues.html+s

[...]
0x01b0:    6565 702d 616c 6976 650d 0a48 6f73 743a    eep-alive..Host:
0x01c0:    2077 7777 2e70 6872 6163 6b2e 6f72 670d    .www.phrack.org.
```

Lines 0x30 and 0x40 show that we are downloading (via a *GET* request) an image file—specifically, a JPG image from the server. Farther along in the network trace, a *Host* field reveals that we are talking to the www.phrack.org Web server. Because of this *Host* header and the fact that this packet was sent to IP address 200.199.20.162, we can safely assume that the Phrack Web server is virtually hosted on the physical server located at that address. This means that when viewing the cached copy of the Phrack Web page, we are pulling images *directly from* the Phrack server itself. If we were striving for anonymity by viewing the Google cached page, we just blew our cover! Furthermore, line 0x90 shows that the *REFERER* field was passed to the Phrack server, and that field contained a Uniform Resource Locator (URL) reference to Google's cached copy of Phrack's page. This means that not only were we *not* anonymous, but our browser informed the Phrack Web server that we were trying to view a cached version of the page! So much for anonymity.

It's worth noting that most real hackers use proxy servers when browsing a target's Web pages, and even their Google activities are first bounced off a proxy server. If we had used an anonymous proxy server for our testing, the Phrack Web server would have only gotten our proxy server's IP address, not our *actual* IP address.

Notes from the Underground…

Google Hacker's Tip

It's a good idea to use a proxy server if you value your anonymity online. Penetration testers use proxy servers to emulate what a real attacker would do during an actual break-in attempt. Locating working, high-quality proxy servers can be an arduous task, unless of course we use a little Google hacking to do the grunt work for us! To locate proxy servers using Google, try these queries:

```
inurl:"nph-proxy.cgi" "Start browsing"
```

or

```
"cacheserverreport for" "This analysis was produced by calamaris"
```

These queries locate online public proxy servers that can be used for testing purposes. Nothing like Googling for proxy servers! Remember, though, that there are lots of places to obtain proxy servers, such as the *atomintersoft* site or the *samair.ru* proxy site. Try Googling for those!

The cache banner does, however, provide an option to view only the data that Google has captured, without any external references. As you can see in Figure 3.1, a link is available in the header, titled "Click here for the cached text only." Clicking this link produces the *tcdump* output shown in Figure 3.4, captured with *tcpdump −n*.

Figure 3.4 Cached Text Only Captured with *Tcpdump*

```
216.239.51.104.80 > 10.0.1.6.49917:
216.239.51.104.80 > 10.0.1.6.49917:
216.239.51.104.80 > 10.0.1.6.49917:
10.0.1.6.49917 > 216.239.51.104.80:
10.0.1.6.49917 > 216.239.51.104.80:
216.239.51.104.80 > 10.0.1.6.49917:
216.239.51.104.80 > 10.0.1.6.49917:
216.239.51.104.80 > 10.0.1.6.49917:
10.0.1.6.49917 > 216.239.51.104.80
```

Despite the fact that we loaded the same page as before, this time we communicated only with a Google server (at 216.239.51.104), not any external servers. If we were to look at the URL generated by clicking the "cached text only" link in the cached page's header, we would discover that Google appended an interesting parameter, *&strip=1*. This parameter forces a Google *cache* URL to display only cached text, avoiding any external references. This URL parameter only applies to URLs that reference a Google cached page.

Pulling it all together, we can browse a cached page with a fair amount of anonymity without a proxy server, using a quick cut and paste and a URL modification. As an example, consider query for *site:phrack.org*. Instead of clicking the cached link, we will right-click the cached link and copy the URL to the Clipboard, as shown in Figure 3.5. Browsers handle this action differently, so use whichever technique works for you to capture the URL of this link.

Figure 3.5 Anonymous Cache Viewing Via Cut and Paste

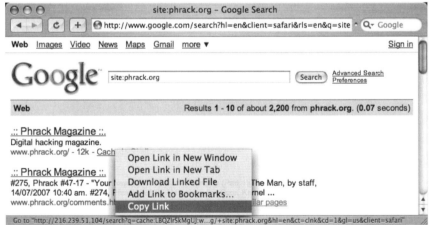

Once the URL is copied to the Clipboard, paste it into the address bar of your browser, and append the *&strip=1* parameter to the end of the URL. The URL should now look something like http://216.239.51.104/search?q=cache:LBQZIrSkMgUJ:www.phrack.org/ +site:phrack.org&hl=en&ct=clnk&cd=1&gl=us&client=safari&strip=1. Press **Enter** after modifying the URL to load the page, and you should be taken to the *stripped version* of the cached page, which has a slightly different banner, as shown in Figure 3.6.

Figure 3.6 A Stripped Cached Page's Header

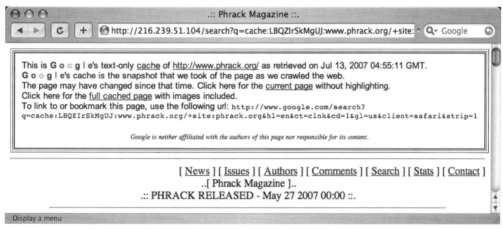

Notice that the stripped cache header reads differently than the standard cache header. Instead of the "This cached page may reference images which are no longer available" line, there is a new line that reads, "Click here for the full cached version with images included." This is an indicator that the current cached page has been stripped of external references. Unfortunately, the stripped page does not include graphics, so the page could look quite different from the original, and in some cases a stripped page might not be legible at all. If this is the case, it never hurts to load up a proxy server and hit the page, but real Google hackers "don't need no steenkin' proxy servers!"

Notes from the Underground...

Google's Highlight Tool

If you've ever scrolled through page after page of a document looking for a particular word or phrase, you probably already know that Google's cached version of the page will highlight search terms for you. What you might not realize is that you can use Google's highlight tool to highlight terms on a cached page that weren't included in

Continued

your original search. This takes a bit of URL mangling, but it's fairly straightforward. For example, if you searched for peeps marshmallows and viewed the second cached page, part of the cached page's URL looks something like www.peepresearch.org/peeps+marshmallows&hl=en. Notice the search terms we used listed after the base page URL. To highlight other terms, simply play around with the area after the base URL, in this case +peeps+marshmallows. Simply add or subtract words and press Enter, and Google will highlight your terms! For example, to include fear and risk to the list of highlighted words, simply add them into the URL, making it read something like www.peepresearch.org/+fear+risk+peeps+marshmallows&hl =en. Did you ever know that Marshmallow Peeps actually feel fear? Don't believe me? Just ask Google.

Directory Listings

A *directory listing* is a type of Web page that lists files and directories that exist on a Web server. Designed to be navigated by clicking directory links, directory listings typically have a title that describes the current directory, a list of files and directories that can be clicked, and often a footer that marks the bottom of the directory listing. Each of these elements is shown in the sample directory listing in Figure 3.7.

Figure 3.7 A Directory Listing Has Several Recognizable Elements

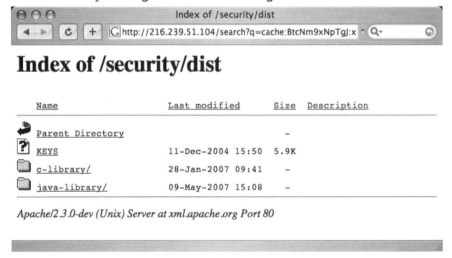

Much like an FTP server, directory listings offer a no-frills, easy-install solution for granting access to files that can be stored in categorized folders. Unfortunately, directory listings have many faults, specifically:

- They are not secure in and of themselves. They do not prevent users from down-loading certain files or accessing certain directories. This task is often left to the protection measures built into the Web server software or third-party scripts, modules, or programs designed specifically for that purpose.

- They can display information that helps an attacker learn specific technical details about the Web server.

- They do not discriminate between files that are meant to be public and those that are meant to remain behind the scenes.

- They are often displayed accidentally, since many Web servers display a directory listing if a top-level index file (*index.htm*, *index.html*, *default.asp*, and so on) is missing or invalid.

All this adds up to a deadly combination.

In this section, we'll take a look at some of the ways Google hackers can take advantage of directory listings.

Locating Directory Listings

The most obvious way an attacker can abuse a directory listing is by simply finding one! Since directory listings offer "parent directory" links and allow browsing through files and folders, even the most basic attacker might soon discover that sensitive data can be found by simply locating the listings and browsing through them.

Locating directory listings with Google is fairly straightforward. Figure 3.11 shows that most directory listings begin with the phrase "Index of," which also shows in the title. An obvious query to find this type of page might be *ntitle:index.of*, which could find pages with the term *index of* in the title of the document. Remember that the period (".") serves as a single-character wildcard in Google. Unfortunately, this query will return a large number of false positives, such as pages with the following titles:

```
Index of Native American Resources on the Internet
LibDex - Worldwide index of library catalogues
Iowa State Entomology Index of Internet Resources
```

Judging from the titles of these documents, it is obvious that not only are these Web pages intentional, they are also not the type of directory listings we are looking for. As Ben Kenobi might say, "This is not the directory listing you're looking for." Several alternate queries provide more accurate results—for example, *intitle:index.of "parent directory"* (shown in Figure 3.8) or *intitle:index.of name size*. These queries indeed reveal directory listings by not only focusing on *index.of* in the title, but on keywords often found inside directory listings, such as *parent directory*, *name*, and *size*. Even judging from the summary on the search results page, you can see that these results are indeed the types of directory listings we're looking for.

Figure 3.8 A Good Search for Directory Listings

Finding Specific Directories

In some cases, it might be beneficial not only to look for directory listings, but to look for directory listings that allow access to a specific directory. This is easily accomplished by adding the name of the directory to the search query. To locate "admin" directories that are accessible from directory listings, queries such as *intitle:index.of.admin* or *intitle:index.of inurl:admin* will work well, as shown in Figure 3.9.

Figure 3.9 Locating Specific Directories in a Directory Listing

Finding Specific Files

Because these types of pages list names of files and directories, it is possible to find very specific files within a directory listing. For example, to find WS_FTP log files, try a search such as *intitle:index.of ws_ftp.log*, as shown in Figure 3.10. This technique can be extended to just about any kind of file by keying in on the *index.of* in the title and the filename in the text of the Web page.

Figure 3.10 Locating Files in a Directory Listing

You can also use *filetype* and *inurl* to search for specific files. To search again for *ws_ftp.log* files, try a query like *filetype:log inurl:ws_ftp.log*. This technique will generally find more results than the somewhat restrictive *index.of* search. We'll be working more with specific file searches throughout the book.

Server Versioning

One piece of information an attacker can use to determine the best method for attacking a Web server is the exact software version. An attacker could retrieve that information by connecting directly to the Web port of that server and issuing a request for the Hypertext Transfer Protocol (HTTP) (Web) headers. It is possible, however, to retrieve similar information from Google without ever connecting to the target server. One method involves using the information provided in a directory listing.

Figure 3.11 shows the bottom portion of a typical directory listing. Notice that some directory listings provide the name of the server software as well as the version number. An adept Web administrator could fake these *server tags*, but most often this information is legitimate and exactly the type of information an attacker will use to refine his attack against the server.

Figure 3.11 This Server Tag Can Be Used to Profile a Web Server

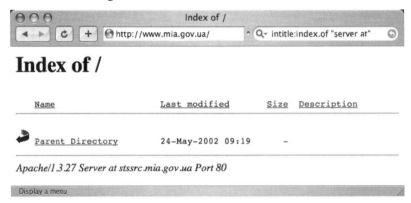

The Google query used to locate servers this way is simply an extension of the *intitle:index.of* query. The listing shown in Figure 3.11 was located with a query of *intitle:index.of "server at"*. This query will locate all directory listings on the Web with *index of* in the title and *server at* anywhere in the text of the page. This might not seem like a very specific search, but the results are very clean and do not require further refinement.

Notes from the Underground…

Server Version? Who Cares?

Although server versioning might seem fairly harmless, realize that there are two ways an attacker might use this type of information. If the attacker has already chosen his target and discovers this information on that target server, he could begin searching for an exploit (which may or may not exist) to use against that specific software version. Inversely, if the attacker already has a working exploit for a very specific version of Web server software, he could perform a Google search for targets that he can compromise with that exploit. An attacker, armed with an exploit and drawn to a potentially vulnerable server, is especially dangerous. Even small information leaks like this can have *big* payoffs for a clever attacker.

To search for a specific server version, the *intitle:index.of* query can be extended even further to something like *intitle:index.of "Apache/1.3.27 Server at"*. This query would find pages like the one listed in Figure 3.11. As shown in Table 3.1, many different servers can be identified through a directory listing.

Table 3.1 Some Specific Servers Locatable Via Directory Listings

Directory Listing of Web Servers

"AnWeb/1.42h" intitle:index.of

"Apache Tomcat/" intitle:index.of

"Apache-AdvancedExtranetServer/" intitle:index.of

"Apache/df-exts" intitle:index.of

"Apache/" intitle:index.of

"Apache/AmEuro" intitle:index.of

"Apache/Blast" intitle:index.of

"Apache/WWW" intitle:index.of

"Apache/df-exts" intitle:index.of

"CERN httpd 3.0B (VAX VMS)" intitle:index.of

"CompySings/2.0.40" intitle:index.of

"Davepache/2.02.003 (Unix)" intitle:index.of

"DinaHTTPd Server/1.15" intitle:index.of

"HP Apache-based Web "Server/1.3.26" intitle:index.of

"HP Apache-based Web "Server/1.3.27 (Unix) mod_ssl/2.8.11 OpenSSL/0.9.6g" intitle:index.of

"HP-UX_Apache-based_Web_Server/2.0.43" intitle:index.of

*"httpd+ssl/kttd" * server at intitle:index.of*

"IBM_HTTP_Server" intitle:index.of

"IBM_HTTP_Server/2.0.42" intitle:index.of

"JRun Web Server" intitle:index.of

"LiteSpeed Web" intitle:index.of

"MCWeb" intitle:index.of

"MaXX/3.1" intitle:index.of

"Microsoft-IIS/ server at" intitle:index.of*

"Microsoft-IIS/4.0" intitle:index.of

"Microsoft-IIS/5.0 server at" intitle:index.of

"Microsoft-IIS/6.0" intitle:index.of

Continued

Table 3.1 continued Some Specific Servers Locatable Via Directory Listings

Directory Listing of Web Servers

"OmniHTTPd/2.10" intitle:index.of
"OpenSA/1.0.4" intitle:index.of
"OpenSSL/0.9.7d" intitle:index.of
"Oracle HTTP Server/1.3.22" intitle:index.of
"Oracle-HTTP-Server/1.3.28" intitle:index.of
"Oracle-HTTP-Server" intitle:index.of
"Oracle HTTP Server Powered by Apache" intitle:index.of
"Patchy/1.3.31" intitle:index.of
"Red Hat Secure/2.0" intitle:index.of
"Red Hat Secure/3.0 server at" intitle:index.of
"Savant/3.1" intitle:index.of
*"SEDWebserver *" "server at" intitle:index.of*
"SEDWebserver/1.3.26" intitle:index.of
"TcNet httpsrv 1.0.10" intitle:index.of
"WebServer/1.3.26" intitle:index.of
"WebTopia/2.1.1a " intitle:index.of
"Yaws 1.65" intitle:index.of
"Zeus/4.3" intitle:index.of

Table 3.2 Directory Listings of Apache Versions

Queries That Locate Apache Versions Through Directory Listings

"Apache/1.0" intitle:index.of
"Apache/1.1" intitle:index.of
"Apache/1.2" intitle:index.of
"Apache/1.2.0 server at" intitle:index.of
"Apache/1.2.4 server at" intitle:index.of
"Apache/1.2.6 server at" intitle:index.of
"Apache/1.3.0 server at" intitle:index.of
"Apache/1.3.2 server at" intitle:index.of
"Apache/1.3.1 server at" intitle:index.of
"Apache/1.3.1.1 server at" intitle:index.of

Continued

Table 3.2 Directory Listings of Apache Versions

Queries That Locate Apache Versions Through Directory Listings

"Apache/1.3.3 server at" intitle:index.of
"Apache/1.3.4 server at" intitle:index.of
"Apache/1.3.6 server at" intitle:index.of
"Apache/1.3.9 server at" intitle:index.of
"Apache/1.3.11 server at" intitle:index.of
"Apache/1.3.12 server at" intitle:index.of
"Apache/1.3.14 server at" intitle:index.of
"Apache/1.3.17 server at" intitle:index.of
"Apache/1.3.19 server at" intitle:index.of
"Apache/1.3.20 server at" intitle:index.of
"Apache/1.3.22 server at" intitle:index.of
"Apache/1.3.23 server at" intitle:index.of
"Apache/1.3.24 server at" intitle:index.of
"Apache/1.3.26 server at" intitle:index.of
"Apache/1.3.27 server at" intitle:index.of
"Apache/1.3.27-fil" intitle:index.of
"Apache/1.3.28 server at" intitle:index.of
"Apache/1.3.29 server at" intitle:index.of
"Apache/1.3.31 server at" intitle:index.of
"Apache/1.3.33 server at" intitle:index.of
"Apache/1.3.34 server at" intitle:index.of
"Apache/1.3.35 server at" intitle:index.of
"Apache/2.0 server at" intitle:index.of
"Apache/2.0.32 server at" intitle:index.of
"Apache/2.0.35 server at" intitle:index.of
"Apache/2.0.36 server at" intitle:index.of
"Apache/2.0.39 server at" intitle:index.of
"Apache/2.0.40 server at" intitle:index.of
"Apache/2.0.42 server at" intitle:index.of
"Apache/2.0.43 server at" intitle:index.of
"Apache/2.0.44 server at" intitle:index.of
"Apache/2.0.45 server at" intitle:index.of

Continued

Table 3.2 continued Directory Listings of Apache Versions

Queries That Locate Apache Versions Through Directory Listings

"Apache/2.0.46 server at" intitle:index.of

"Apache/2.0.47 server at" intitle:index.of

"Apache/2.0.48 server at" intitle:index.of

"Apache/2.0.49 server at" intitle:index.of

"Apache/2.0.49a server at" intitle:index.of

"Apache/2.0.50 server at" intitle:index.of

"Apache/2.0.51 server at" intitle:index.of

"Apache/2.0.52 server at" intitle:index.of

"Apache/2.0.55 server at" intitle:index.of

"Apache/2.0.59 server at" intitle:index.of

In addition to identifying the Web server version, it is also possible to determine the operating system of the server as well as modules and other software that is installed. We'll look at more specific techniques to accomplish this later, but the server versioning technique we've just looked at can be extended by including more details in our query. Table 3.3 shows queries that located extremely esoteric server software combinations, revealed by server tags. These tags list a great deal of information about the servers they were found on and are shining examples proving that even a seemingly small information leak can sometimes explode out of control, revealing more information than expected.

Table 3.3 Locating Specific and Esoteric Server Versions

Queries That Locate Specific and Esoteric Server Versions

"Apache/1.3.12 (Unix) mod_fastcgi/2.2.12 mod_dyntag/1.0 mod_advert/1.12 mod_czech/3.1.1b2" intitle:index.of

"Apache/1.3.12 (Unix) mod_fastcgi/2.2.4 secured_by_Raven/1.5.0" intitle:index.of

"Apache/1.3.12 (Unix) mod_ssl/2.6.6 OpenSSL/0.9.5a" intitle:index.of

"Apache/1.3.12 Cobalt (Unix) Resin/2.0.5 StoreSense-Bridge/1.3 ApacheJServ/1.1.1 mod_ssl/2.6.4 OpenSSL/0.9.5a mod_auth_pam/1.0a FrontPage/4.0.4.3 mod_perl/1.24" intitle:index.of

"Apache/1.3.14 - PHP4.02 - Iprotect 1.6 CWIE (Unix) mod_fastcgi/2.2.12 PHP/4.0.3pl1" intitle:index.of

"Apache/1.3.14 Ben-SSL/1.41 (Unix) mod_throttle/2.11 mod_perl/1.24_01 PHP/4.0.3pl1 FrontPage/4.0.4.3 rus/PL30.0" intitle:index.of

"Apache/1.3.20 (Win32)" intitle:index.of

Continued

Table 3.3 continued Locating Specific and Esoteric Server Versions

Queries That Locate Specific and Esoteric Server Versions

"Apache/1.3.20 Sun Cobalt (Unix) PHP/4.0.3pl1 mod_auth_pam_external/0.1 FrontPage/4.0.4.3 mod_perl/1.25" intitle:index.of

"Apache/1.3.20 Sun Cobalt (Unix) PHP/4.0.4 mod_auth_pam_external/0.1 FrontPage/4.0.4.3 mod_ssl/2.8.4 OpenSSL/0.9.6b mod_perl/1.25" intitle:index.of

"Apache/1.3.20 Sun Cobalt (Unix) PHP/4.0.6 mod_ssl/2.8.4 OpenSSL/0.9.6 FrontPage/5.0.2.2510 mod_perl/1.26" intitle:index.of

"Apache/1.3.20 Sun Cobalt (Unix) mod_ssl/2.8.4 OpenSSL/0.9.6b PHP/4.0.3pl1 mod_auth_pam_external/0.1 FrontPage/4.0.4.3 mod_perl/1.25" intitle:index.of

"Apache/1.3.20 Sun Cobalt (Unix) mod_ssl/2.8.4 OpenSSL/0.9.6b PHP/4.0.3pl1 mod_fastcgi/2.2.8 mod_auth_pam_external/0.1 mod_perl/1.25" intitle:index.of

"Apache/1.3.20 Sun Cobalt (Unix) mod_ssl/2.8.4 OpenSSL/0.9.6b PHP/4.0.4 mod_auth_pam_external/0.1 mod_perl/1.25" intitle:index.of

"Apache/1.3.20 Sun Cobalt (Unix) mod_ssl/2.8.4 OpenSSL/0.9.6b PHP/4.0.6 mod_auth_pam_external/0.1 FrontPage/4.0.4.3 mod_perl/1.25" intitle:index.of

"Apache/1.3.20 Sun Cobalt (Unix) mod_ssl/2.8.4 OpenSSL/0.9.6b mod_auth_pam_external/0.1 mod_perl/1.25" intitle:index.of

"Apache/1.3.26 (Unix) Debian GNU/Linux PHP/4.1.2 mod_dtcl" intitle:index.of

"Apache/1.3.26 (Unix) PHP/4.2.2" intitle:index.of

"Apache/1.3.26 (Unix) mod_ssl/2.8.9 OpenSSL/0.9.6b" intitle:index.of

"Apache/1.3.26 (Unix) mod_ssl/2.8.9 OpenSSL/0.9.7" intitle:index.of

"Apache/1.3.26+PH" intitle:index.of

"Apache/1.3.27 (Darwin)" intitle:index.of

"Apache/1.3.27 (Unix) mod_log_bytes/1.2 mod_bwlimited/1.0 PHP/4.3.1 FrontPage/5.0.2.2510 mod_ssl/2.8.12 OpenSSL/0.9.6b" intitle:index.of

"Apache/1.3.27 (Unix) mod_ssl/2.8.11 OpenSSL/0.9.6g FrontPage/5.0.2.2510 mod_gzip/1.3.26 PHP/4.1.2 mod_throttle/3.1.2" intitle:index.of

One convention used by these sprawling tags is the use of parenthesis to offset the operating system of the server. For example, *Apache/1.3.26 (Unix)* indicates a UNIX-based operating system. Other more specific tags are used as well, some of which are listed below.

- CentOS
- Debian
- Debian GNU/Linux
- Fedora

- FreeBSD
- Linux/SUSE
- Linux/SuSE
- NETWARE
- Red Hat
- Ubuntu
- UNIX
- Win32

An attacker can use the information in these operating system tags in conjunction with the Web server version tag to formulate a specific attack. If this information does not hint at a specific vulnerability, an attacker can still use this information in a data-mining or information-gathering campaign, as we will see in a later chapter.

Going Out on a Limb: Traversal Techniques

The next technique we'll examine is known as *traversal*. Traversal in this context simply means *to travel across*. Attackers use traversal techniques to expand a small "foothold" into a larger compromise.

Directory Traversal

To illustrate how traversal might be helpful, consider a directory listing that was found with *intitle:index.of inurl: "admin",* as shown in Figure 3.12.

Figure 3.12 Traversal Example Found with *index.of*

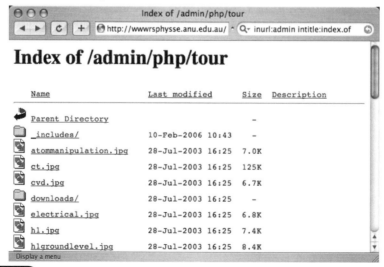

In this example, our query brings us to a relative URL of */admin/php/tour*. If you look closely at the URL, you'll notice an "admin" directory two directory levels above our current location. If we were to click the "parent directory" link, we would be taken up one directory, to the "php" directory. Clicking the "parent directory" link from the "envr" directory would take us to the "admin" directory, a potentially juicy directory. This is very basic directory traversal. We could explore each and every parent directory and each of the subdirectories, looking for juicy stuff. Alternatively, we could use a creative *site* search combined with an *inurl* search to locate a specific file or term inside a specific subdirectory, such as *site:anu.edu inurl:admin ws_ftp.log,* for example. We could also explore this directory structure by modifying the URL in the address bar.

Regardless of how we were to "walk" the directory tree, we would be traversing outside the Google search, wandering around on the target Web server. This is basic traversal, specifically *directory traversal*. Another simple example would be replacing the word *admin* with the word *student* or *public*. Another more serious traversal technique could allow an attacker to take advantage of software flaws to traverse to directories outside the Web server directory tree. For example, if a Web server is installed in the */var/www* directory, and public Web documents are placed in */var/www/htdocs*, by default any user attaching to the Web server's top-level directory is really viewing files located in */var/www/htdocs*. Under normal circumstances, the Web server will not allow Web users to view files above the */var/www/htdocs* directory. Now, let's say a poorly coded third-party software product is installed on the server that accepts directory names as arguments. A normal URL used by this product might be *www.somesadsite.org/badcode.pl?page=/index.html*. This URL would instruct the *badcode.pl* program to "fetch" the file located at */var/www/htdocs/index.html* and display it to the user, perhaps with a nifty header and footer attached. An attacker might attempt to take advantage of this type of program by sending a URL such as *www.somesadsite.org/badcode.pl?page=../../../etc/passwd*. If the *badcode.pl* program is vulnerable to a directory traversal attack, it would break out of the */var/www/htdocs* directory, crawl up to the *real root* directory of the server, dive down into the */etc* directory, and "fetch" the system password file, displaying it to the user with a nifty header and footer attached!

Automated tools can do a much better job of locating these types of files and vulnerabilities, if you don't mind all the noise they create. If you're a programmer, you will be very interested in the Libwhisker Perl library, written and maintained by Rain Forest Puppy (RFP) and available from www.wiretrip.net/rfp. Security Focus wrote a great article on using Libwhisker. That article is available from www.securityfocus.com/infocus/1798. If you aren't a programmer, RFP's Whisker tool, also available from the Wiretrip site, is excellent, as are other tools based on Libwhisker, such as nikto, written by sullo@cirt.net, which is said to be updated even more than the Whisker program itself. Another tool that performs (amongst other things) file and directory mining is Wikto from SensePost that can be downloaded at www.sensepost.com/research/wikto. The advantage of Wikto is that it does not suffer from false positives on Web sites that responds with friendly 404 messages.

Incremental Substitution

Another technique similar to traversal is *incremental substitution*. This technique involves replacing numbers in a URL in an attempt to find directories or files that are hidden, or unlinked from other pages. Remember that Google generally only locates files that are linked from other pages, so if it's not linked, Google won't find it. (Okay, there's an exception to every rule. See the FAQ at the end of this chapter.) As a simple example, consider a document called *exhc-1.xls*, found with Google. You could easily modify the URL for that document, changing the 1 to a 2, making the filename *exhc-2.xls*. If the document is found, you have successfully used the incremental substitution technique! In some cases it might be simpler to use a Google query to find other similar files on the site, but remember, not all files on the Web are in Google's databases. Use this technique only when you're sure a simple query modification won't find the files first.

This technique does not apply only to filenames, but just about anything that contains a number in a URL, even parameters to scripts. Using this technique to toy with parameters to scripts is beyond the scope of this book, but if you're interested in trying your hand at some simple file or directory substitutions, scare up some test sites with queries such as *filetype:xls inurl:1.xls* or *intitle:index.of inurl:0001* or even an images search for *1.jpg*. Now use substitution to try to modify the numbers in the URL to locate other files or directories that exist on the site. Here are some examples:

- */docs/bulletin/**1.xls*** could be modified to */docs/bulletin/**2.xls***
- */DigLib_thumbnail/spmg/hel/**0001**/H/* could be changed to */DigLib_thumbnail/spmg/hel/**0002**/H/*
- */gallery/wel008-**1.jpg*** could be modified to */gallery/wel008-**2.jpg***

Extension Walking

We've already discussed file extensions and how the *filetype* operator can be used to locate files with specific file extensions. For example, we could easily search for HTM files with a query such as *filetype:HTM[1]*. Once you've located HTM files, you could apply the substitution technique to find files with the same file name and different extension. For example, if you found */docs/index.htm*, you could modify the URL to */docs/index.asp* to try to locate an *index.asp* file in the *docs* directory. If this seems somewhat pointless, rest assured, this is, in fact, rather pointless. We can, however, make more intelligent substitutions. Consider the directory listing shown in Figure 3.13. This listing shows evidence of a very common practice, the creation of backup copies of Web pages.

Figure 3.13 Backup Copies of Web Pages Are Very Common

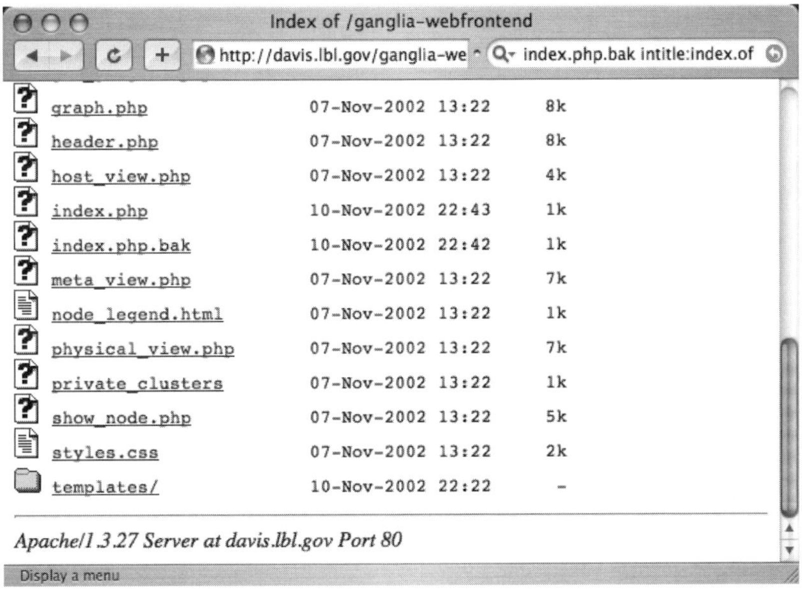

```
          Index of /ganglia-webfrontend
◄  ►  C  +   http://davis.lbl.gov/ganglia-we ▲    index.php.bak intitle:index.of

?  graph.php              07-Nov-2002 13:22      8k
?  header.php             07-Nov-2002 13:22      8k
?  host_view.php          07-Nov-2002 13:22      4k
?  index.php              10-Nov-2002 22:43      1k
?  index.php.bak          10-Nov-2002 22:42      1k
?  meta_view.php          07-Nov-2002 13:22      7k
   node_legend.html       07-Nov-2002 13:22      1k
?  physical_view.php      07-Nov-2002 13:22      7k
?  private_clusters       07-Nov-2002 13:22      1k
?  show_node.php          07-Nov-2002 13:22      5k
   styles.css             07-Nov-2002 13:22      2k
   templates/             10-Nov-2002 22:22      -

Apache/1.3.27 Server at davis.lbl.gov Port 80

Display a menu
```

Backup files can be a very interesting find from a security perspective. In some cases, backup files are older versions of an original file. This is evidenced in Figure 3.17. Backup files on the Web have an interesting side effect: they have a tendency to reveal source code. Source code of a Web page is quite a find for a security practitioner, because it can contain behind-the-scenes information about the author, the code creation and revision process, authentication information, and more.

To see this concept in action, consider the directory listing shown in Figure 3.13. Clicking the link for *index.php* will display that page in your browser with all the associated graphics and text, just as the author of the page intended. If this were an HTM or HTML file, viewing the source of the page would be as easy as right-clicking the page and selecting *view source*. PHP files, by contrast, are first *executed* on the server. The results of that executed program are then sent to your browser in the form of HTML code, which your browser then displays. Performing a *view source* on HTML code that was generated from a PHP script *will not* show you the PHP source code, only the HTML. It is not possible to view the actual PHP source code unless something somewhere is misconfigured. An example of such a misconfiguration would be *copying* the PHP code to a filename that ends in something other than PHP, like BAK. Most Web servers do not understand what a BAK file is. Those servers, then, will display a PHP.BAK file as text. When this happens, the actual PHP source code is displayed as text in your browser. As shown in Figure 3.14, PHP source code can be quite revealing, showing things like Structured Query Language (SQL) queries that list information about the structure of the SQL database that is used to store the Web server's data.

Figure 3.14 Backup Files Expose SQL Data

The easiest way to determine the names of backup files on a server is to locate a directory listing using *intitle:index.of* or to search for specific files with queries such as *intitle:index.of index.php.bak* or *inurl:index.php.bak*. Directory listings are fairly uncommon, especially among corporate-grade Web servers. However, remember that Google's cache captures a snapshot of a page in time. Just because a Web server isn't hosting a directory listing now doesn't mean the site never displayed a directory listing. The page shown in Figure 3.15 was found in Google's cache and was displayed as a directory listing because an *index.php* (or similar file) was missing. In this case, if you were to visit the server on the Web, it would look like a normal page because the index file has since been created. Clicking the cache link, however, shows this directory listing, leaving the list of files on the server exposed. This list of files can be used to intelligently locate files that still most likely exist on the server (via URL modification) without guessing at file extensions.

Figure 3.15 Cached Pages Can Expose Directory Listings

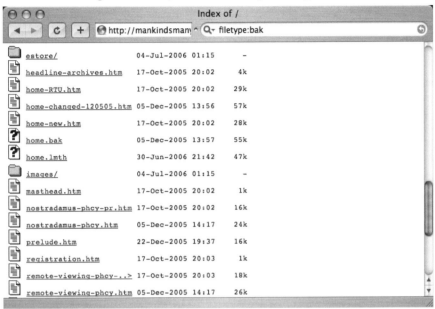

Directory listings also provide insight into the file extensions that are in use in other places on the site. If a system administrator or Web authoring program creates backup files with a *.BAK* extension in one directory, there's a good chance that BAK files will exist in other directories as well.

Summary

The Google cache is a powerful tool in the hands of the advanced user. It can be used to locate old versions of pages that may expose information that normally would be unavailable to the casual user. The cache can be used to highlight terms in the cached version of a page, even if the terms were not used as part of the query to find that page. The cache can also be used to view a Web page anonymously via the *&strip=1* URL parameter, and can be used as a basic transparent proxy server. An advanced Google user will always pay careful attention to the details contained in the cached page's header, since there can be important information about the date the page was crawled, the terms that were found in the search, whether the cached page contains external images, links to the original page, and the text of the URL used to access the cached version of the page. Directory listings provide unique behind-the-scenes views of Web servers, and directory traversal techniques allow an attacker to poke around through files that may not be intended for public view.

Solutions Fast Track

Anonymity with Caches

☑ Clicking the cache link will not only load the page from Google's database, it will also connect to the real server to access graphics and other non-HTML content.

☑ Adding *&strip=1* to the end of a cached URL will only show the HTML of a cached page. Accessing a cached page in this way will not connect to the real server on the Web, and could protect your anonymity if you use the cut and paste method shown in this chapter.

Locating Directory Listings

☑ Directory listings contain a great deal of invaluable information.

☑ The best way to home in on pages that contain directory listings is with a query such as *intitle:index.of "parent directory"* or *intitle:index.of name size*.

Locating Specific Directories in a Listing

☑ You can easily locate specific directories in a directory listing by adding a directory name to an *index.of* search. For example, *intitle:index.of inurl:backup* could be used to find directory listings that have the word *backup* in the URL. If the word *backup* is in the URL, there's a good chance it's a directory name.

Locating Specific Files in a Directory Listing

☑ You can find specific files in a directory listing by simply adding the filename to an *index.of* query, such as *intitle:index.of ws_ftp.log*.

Server Versioning with Directory Listings

☑ Some servers, specifically Apache and Apache derivatives, add a server tag to the bottom of a directory listing. These server tags can be located by extending an *index.of* search, focusing on the phrase *server at*—for example, *intitle:index.of server.at*.

☑ You can find specific versions of a Web server by extending this search with more information from a correctly formatted server tag. For example, the query *intitle:index.of server.at "Apache Tomcat/"* will locate servers running various versions of the Apache Tomcat server.

Directory Traversal

☑ Once you have located a specific directory on a target Web server, you can use this technique to locate other directories or subdirectories.

☑ An easy way to accomplish this task is via directory listings. Simply click the *parent directory* link, which will take you to the directory above the current directory. If this directory contains another directory listing, you can simply click links from that page to explore other directories. If the parent directory does not display a directory listing, you might have to resort to a more difficult method, guessing directory names and adding them to the end of the parent directory's URL. Alternatively, consider using *site* and *inurl* keywords in a Google search.

Incremental Substitution

☑ Incremental substitution is a fancy way of saying "take one number and replace it with the next higher or lower number."

☑ This technique can be used to explore a site that uses numbers in directory or filenames. Simply replace the number with the next higher or lower number, taking care to keep the rest of the file or directory name identical (watch those zeroes!). Alternatively, consider using *site* with either *inurl* or *filetype* keywords in a creative Google search.

Extension Walking

☑ This technique can help locate files (for example, backup files) that have the same filename with a different extension.

☑ The easiest way to perform extension walking is by replacing one extension with another in a URL—replacing *html* with *bak*, for example.

☑ Directory listings, especially cached directory listings, are easy ways to determine whether backup files exist and what kinds of file extensions might be used on the rest of the site.

Links to Sites

■ www.all-nettools.com/pr.htm A simple proxy checker that can help you test a proxy server you're using.

■ http://www.sensepost.com/research/wikto Sensepost's Wikto Tool, a great Web scanner that also incorporate Google query tests using the Google Hacking Database.

Frequently Asked Questions

Q: Searching for backup files seems cumbersome. Is there a better way?

A: Better, meaning faster, yes. Many automated Web tools (such as WebInspect from www.spidynamics.com) offer the capability to query a server for variations of existing filenames, turning an existing *index.html* file into queries for *index.html.bak* or *index.bak*, for example. These scans are generally very thorough but very noisy, and will almost certainly alert the site that you're scanning. WebInspect is better suited for this task than Google Hacking, but many times a low-profile Google scan can be used to get a feel for the security of a site without alerting the site's administrators or Intrusion Detection System (IDS). As an added benefit, any information gathered with Google can be reused later in an assessment.

Q: Backup files seem to create security problems, but these files help in the development of a site and provide peace of mind that changes can be rolled back. Isn't there some way to keep backup files around without the undue risk?

A: Yes. A major problem with backup files is that in most cases, the Web server displays them differently because they have a different file extension. So there are a few options. First, if you create backup files, keep the extensions the same. Don't copy *index.php* to *index.bak*, but rather to something like *index.bak.php*. This way the server still knows it's a

PHP file. Second, you could keep your backup files out of the Web directories. Keep them in a place you can access them, but where Web visitors can't get to them. The third (and best) option is to use a real configuration management system. Consider using a CVS-style system that allows you to register and check out source code. This way you can always roll back to an older version, and you don't have to worry about backup files sitting around.

[1] Remember that *filetype* searches *used to* require an search parameter. They don't any more. In the old days, all filetype searches required an addition of the extension. *Filetype:htm* would not work, but *filetype:htm htm* would!

Chapter 4

Document Grinding and Database Digging

Solutions in this chapter:

- **Configuration Files**
- **Log Files**
- **Office Documents**
- **Database Information**
- **Automated Grinding**
- **Google Desktop**
- **Links to Sites**

☑ **Summary**

☑ **Solutions Fast Track**

☑ **Frequently Asked Questions**

Introduction

There's no shortage of documents on the Internet. Good guys and bad guys alike can use information found in documents to achieve their distinct purposes. In this chapter we take a look at ways you can use Google to not only locate these documents but to search within these documents to locate information. There are so many different types of documents and we can't cover them all, but we'll look at the documents in distinct categories based on their function. Specifically, we'll take a look at configuration files, log files, and office documents. Once we've looked at distinct file types, we'll delve into the realm of database digging. We won't examine the details of the Structured Query Language (SQL) or database architecture and interaction; rather, we'll look at the many ways Google hackers can locate and abuse database systems armed with nothing more than a search engine.

One important thing to remember about document digging is that Google will only search the *rendered,* or visible, view of a document. For example, consider a Microsoft Word document. This type of document can contain *metadata,* as shown in Figure 4.1. These fields include such things as the subject, author, manager, company, and much more. Google will not search these fields. If you're interested in getting to the metadata within a file, you'll have to download the actual file and check the metadata yourself, as discussed in Chapter 5.

Figure 4.1 Microsoft Word Metadata

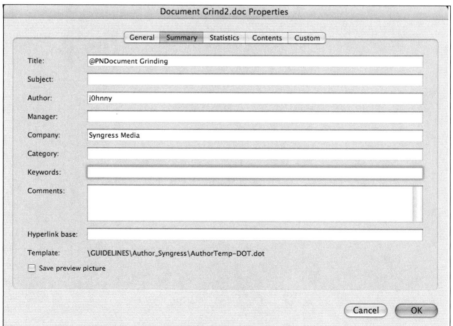

Configuration Files

Configuration files store program settings. An attacker (or "security specialist") can use these files to glean insight into the way a program is used and perhaps, by extension, into how the system or network it's on is used or configured. As we've seen in previous chapters, even the smallest tidbit of information can be of interest to a skilled attacker.

Consider the file shown in Figure 4.2. This file, found with a query such as *filetype:ini inurl:ws_ftp,* is a configuration file used by the WS_FTP client program. When the WS_FTP program is downloaded and installed, the configuration file contains nothing more than a list of popular, public Internet FTP servers. However, over time, this configuration file can be automatically updated to include the name, directory, username, and password of FTP servers the user connects to. Although the password is encoded when it is stored, some free programs can crack these passwords with relative ease.

Figure 4.2 The WS_FTP.INI File Contains Hosts, Usernames, and Passwords

Underground Googling

Locating Files

To locate files, it's best to try different types of queries. For example, *intitle:index.of ws_ftp.ini* will return results, but so will *filetype:ini inurl:ws_ftp.ini*. The *inurl* search, however, is often the better choice. First, the *filetype* search allows you to browse right to a cached version of the page. Second, the directory listings found by the *index.of* search might allow you to view a list of files but not allow you access to the actual file. Third, directory listings are not overly common. The *filetype* search will locate your file *no matter how* Google found it.

Regardless of the type of data in a configuration file, sometimes the mere existence of a configuration file is significant. If a configuration file is located on a server, there's a chance that the accompanying program is installed somewhere on that server or on neighboring machines on the network. Although this might not seem like a big deal in the case of FTP client software, consider a search like *filetype:conf inurl:firewall*, which can locate generic firewall configuration files. This example demonstrates one of the most generic naming conventions for a configuration file, the use of the *conf* file extension. Other generic naming conventions can be combined to locate other equally common naming conventions. One of the most common base searches for locating configuration files is simply *(inurl:conf OR inurl:config OR inurl:cfg)*, which incorporates the three most common configuration file prefixes. You may also opt to use the *filetype* operator.

If an attacker knows the name of a configuration file as it shipped from the software author or vendor, he can simply create a search targeting that filename using the *filetype* and *inurl* operators. However, most programs allow you to reference a configuration file of any name, making a Google search slightly more difficult. In these cases, it helps to get an idea of the *contents* of the configuration file, which could be used to extract unique strings for use in an effective base search. Sometimes, combining a generic base search with the name (or acronym) of a software product can have satisfactory results, as a search for *(inurl:conf OR inurl:config OR inurl:cfg) MRTG* shows in Figure 4.3.

Figure 4.3 Generic Configuration File Searching

Although this first search is not far off the mark, it's fairly common for even the best config file search to return page after page of sample or example files, like the sample MRTG configuration file shown in Figure 4.4.

Figure 4.4 Sample Config Files Need Filtering

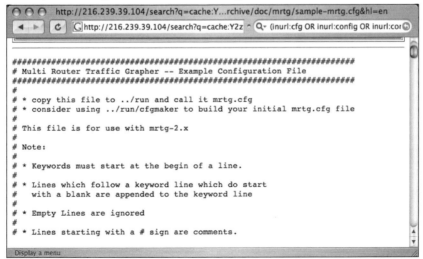

This brings us back, once again, to perhaps the most valuable weapon in a Google hacker's arsenal: effective search reduction. Here's a list of the most common points a Google hacker considers when trolling for configuration files:

- Create a strong base search using unique words or phrases from live files.

- Filter out the words *sample, example, test, howto,* and *tutorial* to narrow the obvious example files.

- Filter out CVS repositories, which often house default config files, with *–cvs.*

- Filter out *manpage* or *Manual* if you're searching for a UNIX program's configuration file.

- Locate the one most commonly changed field in a sample configuration file and perform a negative search on that field, reducing potentially "lame" or sample files.

To illustrate these points, consider the search *filetype:cfg mrtg "target[*]" -sample -cvs –example,* which locates potentially live MRTG files. As shown in Figure 4.5, this query uses a unique string *"target[*]"* (which is a bit ubiquitous to Google, but still a decent place to start) and removes potential example and CVS files, returning decent results.

Figure 4.5 A Common Search Reduction Technique

Some of the results shown in Figure 4.5 might not be real, live MRTG configuration files, but they all have potential, with the exception of the first hit, located in "/Squid-Book."

There's a good chance that this is a sample file, but because of the reduction techniques we've used, the other results are potentially live, production MRTG configuration files.

Table 4.1 lists a collection of searches that locate various configuration files. These entries were gathered by the many contributors to the GHDB. This list highlights the various methods that can be used to target configuration files. You'll see examples of CVS reduction, sample reduction, unique word and phrase isolation, and more. Most of these queries took imagination on the part of the creator and in many cases took several rounds of reduction by several searchers to get to the query you see here. Learn from these queries, and try them out for yourself. It might be helpful to remove some of the qualifiers, such as *–cvs* or *–sample,* where applicable, to get an idea of what the "messy" version of the search might look like.

Table 4.1 Configuration File Search Examples

Description	Query
PHP configuration file	intitle:index.of config.php
PHP configuration file	inurl:config.php dbuname dbpass
CGIIRC configuration file	intitle:index.of cgiirc.config
CGIIRG configuration file	inurl:cgiirc.config
IPSEC configuration file	inurl:ipsec.conf -intitle:manpage
ws_ftp configuration file	intitle:index.of ws_ftp.ini
eggdrop configuration file	eggdrop filetype:user user
samba configuration file filetype:conf	inurl:"smb.conf" intext:"workgroup"
firewall configuration file	filetype:conf inurl:firewall -intitle:cvs
vtunnelD configuration file	inurl:vtund.conf intext:pass -cvs
OpenLDAP configuration file	filetype:conf slapd.conf
PHP configuration file	inurl:php.ini filetype:ini
FTP configuration file	filetype:conf inurl:proftpd.conf -sample
WV Dial configuration file	inurl:"wvdial.conf" intext:"password"
OpenLDAP configuration file	inurl:"slapd.conf" intext:"credentials" -manpage -"Manual Page" -man: -sample
OpenLDAP configuration file	inurl:"slapd.conf" intext:"rootpw" -manpage -"Manual Page" -man: -sample
WS_FTP configuration file	filetype:ini ws_ftp pwd

Continued

Table 4.1 continued Configuration File Search Examples

Description	Query
MRTG configuration file	filetype:cfg mrtg "target[*]" -sample -cvs -example
WRQ Reflection configuration file	filetype:r2w r2w
Prestige router configuration file	"Welcome to the Prestige Web-Based Configurator"
GNU Zebra configuration file	inurl:zebra.conf intext:password -sample -test -tutorial -download
GNU Zebra configuration file	inurl:ospfd.conf intext:password -sample -test -tutorial -download
YAST configuration file	filetype:cfg ks intext:rootpw -sample -test -howto
Netscape server configuration file	allinurl:".nsconfig" -sample -howto -tutorial
UnrealIRCd configuration file	filetype:conf inurl:unrealircd.conf -cvs -gentoo
psyBNC configuration file	filetype:conf inurl:psybnc.conf "USER.PASS="
SSL configuration file	inurl:ssl.conf filetype:conf
LILO configuration file	inurl:lilo.conf filetype:conf password -tatercounter2000 -bootpwd -man
MySQL configuration file	filetype:cnf my.cnf -cvs -example
oracle client configuration file	filetype:ora ora
Mandrake configuration file	filetype:cfg auto_inst.cfg
Oekakibss configuration file	filetype:conf oekakibss
LeapFTP client configuration file	LeapFTP intitle:"index.of./" sites.ini modified
a .Net Web Application configuration file	filetype:config config intext:appSettings "User ID"
WS_FTP configuration file	"index of/" "ws_ftp.ini" "parent directory"
ODBC client configuration files	inurl:odbc.ini ext:ini -cvs
FlashFXP configuration file	filetype:ini inurl:flashFXP.ini
Generic configuration file	ext:ini intext:env.ini
Certificate Services configuration file	filetype:inf inurl:capolicy.inf
NoCatAuth configuration file	ext:conf NoCatAuth -cvs

Continued

Table 4.1 continued Configuration File Search Examples

Description	Query
Putty saved session data	inurl:"putty.reg"
Icecast configuration file	"liveice configuration file" ext:cfg -site:sourceforge.net
SoftCart configuration file	intitle:Configuration.File inurl:softcart.exe
Cisco configuration data	intext:"enable secret 5 $"
IIS Web.config file	filetype:config web.config -CVS
VMWare configuration files	ext:vmx vmx
Radiator Radius configuration file	ext:cfg radius.cfg
Rsync configuration file	ext:conf inurl:rsyncd.conf -cvs -man
Eudora configuration file	ext:ini eudora.ini
emule configuration file	inurl:preferences.ini "[emule]"
abyss webserver configuration file	intitle:index.of abyss.conf
Frontpage Extensions for Unix configuration file	filetype:cnf inurl:_vti_pvt access.cnf
Shoutcast configuration file	intitle:"Index of" sc_serv.conf sc_serv content
HP Ethernet switch configuration file	intitle:"DEFAULT_CONFIG - HP"
Oracle configuration files	filetype:ora tnsnames
Counterstrike configuration file	inurl:server.cfg rcon password
Steam configuration file	intext:"SteamUserPassphrase=" intext:"SteamAppUser=" -"username" -"user"
CGI Calendar configuration file	inurl:cgi-bin inurl:calendar.cfg
Cisco configuration file	intext:"enable password 7"
YABB Forum administration file	inurl:/yabb/Members/Admin.dat
FlashFXP site data file	inurl:"Sites.dat"+"PASS="
Ruby on Rails database connector file	ext:yml database inurl:config
Cisco configuration file	enable password | secret "current configuration" -intext:the
Generic configuration file	intitle:index.of.config

Log Files

Log files record information. Depending on the application, the information recorded in a log file can include anything from timestamps and IP addresses to usernames and passwords—even incredibly sensitive data such as credit card numbers!

Like configuration files, log files often have a default name that can be used as part of a base search. The most common file extension for a log file is simply *log*, making the simplest base search for log files simply *filetype:log inurl:log* or the even simpler *ext:log log*. Remember that the *ext (filetype)* operator requires at least one search argument. Log file searches seem to return fewer samples and example files than configuration file searches, but search reduction is still required in some cases. Refer to the rules for configuration file reduction listed previously.

Table 4.2 lists a collection of log file searches collected from the GHDB. These searches show the various techniques that are employed by Google hackers and serve as an excellent learning tool for constructing your own searches during a penetration test.

Table 4.2 Log File Search Examples

Query	Description
"ZoneAlarm Logging Client"	ZoneAlarm log files
"admin account info" filetype:log	Admin logs
"apricot - admin" 00h	Apricot logs
"by Reimar Hoven. All Rights Reserved. Disclaimer" | inurl: "log/logdb.dta"	PHP Web Statistik logs
"generated by wwwstat"	www statistics
"Index of" / "chat/logs"	Chat logs
"MacHTTP" filetype:log inurl:machttp.log	MacHTTP
"Most Submitted Forms and Scripts" "this section"	www statistics
"sets mode: +k"	IRC logs, channel key set
"sets mode: +p"	IRC chat logs
"sets mode: +s"	IRC logs, secret channel set
"The statistics were last updated" "Daily"-microsoft.com	Network activity logs
"This report was generated by WebLog"	weblog-generated statistics
"your password is" filetype:log	Password logs

Continued

Table 4.2 Log File Search Examples

Query	Description
QueryProgram "ZoneAlarm Logging Client"	ZoneAlarm log files
+htpasswd WS_FTP.LOG filetype:log	WS_FTP client log files
+intext:"webalizer" +intext: "Total Usernames" +intext:"Usage Statistics for"	Webalizer statistics
ext:log "Software: Microsoft Internet Information Services *.*"	IIS server log files
ext:log password END_FILE	Java password files
filetype:cfg login "LoginServer="	Ultima Online log files
filetype:log "PHP Parse error" | "PHP Warning" | "	PHP error logs
filetype:log "See `ipsec —copyright"	BARF log files
filetype:log access.log –CVS	HTTPD server access logs
filetype:log cron.log	UNIX cron logs
filetype:log hijackthis "scan saved"	Hijackthis scan log
filetype:log inurl:"password.log"	Password logs
filetype:log inurl:access.log TCP_HIT	Squid access log
filetype:log inurl:cache.log	Squid cache log
filetype:log inurl:store.log RELEASE	Squid disk store log
filetype:log inurl:useragent.log	Squid useragent log
filetype:log iserror.log	MS Install Shield logs
filetype:log iserror.log	MS Install Shield logs
filetype:log iserror.log	MS Install Shield logs
filetype:log username putty	Putty SSH client logs
filetype:log username putty	Putty SSH client logs
intext:"Session Start * * * *:*:* *" filetype:log	IRC/AIM log files
intitle:"HostMonitor log" | intitle: "HostMonitor report"	HostMonitor
intitle:"Index Of" -inurl:maillog maillog size	Mail log files
intitle:"LOGREP - Log file reporting system" -site:itefix.no	Logrep

Continued

www.syngress.com

Table 4.2 Log File Search Examples

Query	Description
intitle:index.of .bash_history	UNIX bash shell history file
intitle:index.of .sh_history	UNIX shell history file
intitle:index.of cleanup.log	Outlook Express cleanup logs
inurl:access.log filetype:log –cvs	Apache access log (Windows)
inurl:error.log filetype:log -cvs	Apache error log
inurl:log.nsf -gov	Lotus Domino
log inurl:linklint filetype:txt -"checking"	Linklint logs
Squid cache server reports	squid server cache reports

Log files reveal various types of information, as shown in the search for *filetype:log username putty* in Figure 4.6. This log file lists machine names and associated usernames that could be reused in an attack against the machine.

Figure 4.6 Putty Log Files Reveal Sensitive Data

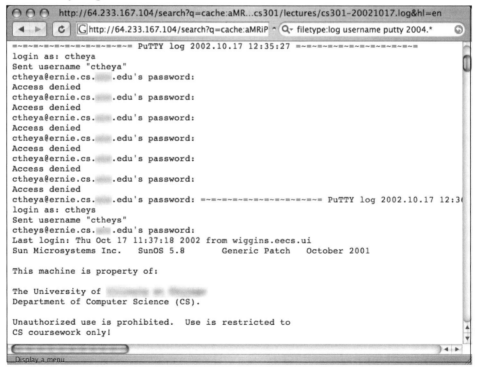

Office Documents

The term *office document* generally refers to documents created by word processing software, spreadsheet software, and lightweight database programs. Common word processing software includes Microsoft Word, Corel WordPerfect, MacWrite, and Adobe Acrobat. Common spreadsheet programs include Microsoft Excel, Lotus 1-2-3, and Linux's Gnumeric. Other documents that are generally lumped together under the office document category include Microsoft PowerPoint, Microsoft Works, and Microsoft Access documents. Table 4.3 lists some of the more common office document file types, organized roughly by their Internet popularity (based on number of Google hits).

Table 4.3 Popular Office Document File Types

File Type	Extension
Adobe Portable Document Format	Pdf
Adobe PostScript	Ps
Lotus 1-2-3	wk1, wk2, wk3, wk4, wk5, wki, wks, wku
Lotus WordPro	Lwp
MacWrite	Mw
Microsoft Excel	Xls
Microsoft PowerPoint	Ppt
Microsoft Word	Doc
Microsoft Works	wks, wps, wdb
Microsoft Write	Wri
Rich Text Format	Rtf
Shockwave Flash	Swf
Text	ans, txt

In many cases, simply searching for these files with *filetype* is pointless without an additional specific search. Google hackers have successfully uncovered all sorts of interesting files by simply throwing search terms such as *private* or *password* or *admin* onto the tail end of a *filetype* search. However, simple base searches such as *(inurl:xls OR inurl:doc OR inurl:mdb)* can be used as a broad search across many file types.

Table 4.4 lists some searches from the GHDB that specifically target office documents. This list shows quite a few specific techniques that we can learn from. Some searches, such as *filetype:xls inurl:password.xls,* focus on a file with a specific name. The *password.xls* file does not necessarily belong to any specific software package, but it sounds interesting simply because of the name. Other searches, such as *filetype:xls username password email,* shift the focus from the file's name to its contents. The reasoning here is that if an Excel spreadsheet contains the words *username password* and *e-mail*, there's a good chance the spreadsheet contains sensitive data such as passwords. The heart and soul of a good Google search involves refining a generic search to uncover something extremely relevant. Google's ability to search inside different types of documents is an extremely powerful tool in the hands of an advanced Google user.

Table 4.4 Sample Queries That Locate Potentially Sensitive Office Documents

Query	Potential Exposure
filetype:xls username password email	Passwords
filetype:xls inurl:"password.xls"	Passwords
filetype:xls private	Private data (use as base search)
Inurl:admin filetype:xls	Administrative data
filetype:xls inurl:contact	Contact information, e-mail addresses
filetype:xls inurl:"email.xls"	E-mail addresses, names
allinurl: admin mdb	Administrative database
filetype:mdb inurl:users.mdb	User lists, e-mail addresses
Inurl:email filetype:mdb	User lists, e-mail addresses
Data filetype:mdb	Various data (use as base search)
Inurl:backup filetype:mdb	Backup databases
Inurl:profiles filetype:mdb	User profiles
Inurl:*db filetype:mdb	Various data (use as base search)

Database Digging

There has been intense focus recently on the security of Web-based database applications, specifically the front-end software that interfaces with a database. Within the security community, talk of SQL injection has all but replaced talk of the once-common CGI vulnerability, indicating that databases have arguably become a greater target than the underlying operating system or Web server software.

An attacker will not generally use Google to *break into* a database or muck with a database front-end application; rather, Google hackers troll the Internet looking for bits and pieces of database information leaked from potentially vulnerable servers. These bits and pieces of information can be used to first select a target and then to mount a more educated attack (as opposed to a ground-zero blind attack) against the target. Bearing this in mind, understand that here we do not discuss the actual mechanics of the attack itself, but rather the surprisingly invasive information-gathering phase an accomplished Google hacker will employ prior to attacking a target.

Login Portals

As we discussed in Chapter 8, a login portal is the "front door" of a Web-based application. Proudly displaying a username and password dialog, login portals generally bear the scrutiny of most Web attackers simply because they are the one part of an application that is most carefully secured. There are obvious exceptions to this rule, but as an analogy, if you're going to secure your home, aren't you going to first make sure your front door is secure?

A typical database login portal is shown in Figure 4.7. This login page announces not only the existence of an SQL Server but also the Microsoft Web Data Administrator software package.

Figure 4.7 A Typical Database Login Portal

Regardless of its relative strength, the mere existence of a login portal provides a glimpse into the type of software and hardware that might be employed at a target. Put simply, a login portal is terrific for footprinting. In extreme cases, an unsecured login portal serves as a welcome mat for an attacker. To this end, let's look at some queries that an attacker might use to locate database front ends on the Internet. Table 4.5 lists queries that locate database front ends or interfaces. Most entries are pulled from the GHDB.

Table 4.5 Queries That Locate Database Interfaces

Query	Database Utility
allinurl: admin mdb	Administrative database
Inurl:backup filetype:mdb	Backup databases
"ClearQuest Web Logon"	ClearQuest (CQWEB)
inurl:/admin/login.asp	Common login page
inurl:login.asp	Common login page
filetype:fp5 fp5 -"cvs log"	FileMaker Pro
filetype:fp3 fp3	FileMaker Pro
filetype:fp7 fp7	FileMaker Pro
"Select a database to view" intitle: "filemaker pro"	FileMaker Pro
"Welcome to YourCo Financial"	IBM Websphere
"(C) Copyright IBM" "Welcome to Websphere"	IBM Websphere
inurl:names.nsf?opendatabase	Lotus Domino
inurl:"/catalog.nsf" intitle:catalog	Lotus Domino
intitle:"messaging login" "© Copyright IBM"	Lotus Messaging
intitle:"Web Data Administrator - Login"	MS SQL login
intitle:"Gateway Configuration Menu"	Oracle
inurl:/pls/sample/admin_/help/	Oracle default manuals
inurl:1810 "Oracle Enterprise Manager"	Oracle Enterprise Manager
inurl:admin_/globalsettings.htm	Oracle HTTP Listener
*intitle:"oracle http server index" "Copyright * Oracle Corporation."*	Oracle HTTP Server
inurl:pls/admin_/gateway.htm	Oracle login portal
inurl:orasso.wwsso_app_admin.ls_login	Oracle Single Sign-On
"phpMyAdmin" "running on" inurl:"main.php"	phpMyAdmin
"Welcome to phpMyAdmin" " Create new database"	phpMyAdmin

Continued

Table 4.5 continued Queries That Locate Database Interfaces

Query	Database Utility
intitle:"index of /phpmyadmin" modified	phpMyAdmin
*intitle:phpMyAdmin "Welcome to phpMyAdmin ***" "running on * as root@*"*	phpMyAdmin
inurl:main.php phpMyAdmin	phpMyAdmin
intitle:"phpPgAdmin - Login" Language	phpPgAdmin (PostgreSQL) Admin tool
intext:SQLiteManager inurl:main.php	SQLite Manager
Data filetype:mdb	Various data (use as base search)

Underground Googling

Login Portals

One way to locate login portals is to focus on the word *login*. Another way is to focus on the copyright at the bottom of a page. Most big-name portals put a copyright notice at the bottom of the page. Combine this with the product name, and a *welcome* or two, and you're off to a good start. If you run out of ideas for new databases to try, go to http://labs.google.com/sets, enter **oracle** and **mysql,** and click **Large Set** for a list of databases.

Support Files

Another way an attacker can locate or gather information about a database is by querying for support files that are installed with, accompany, or are created by the database software. These can include configuration files, debugging scripts, and even sample database files. Table 4.6 lists some searches that locate specific support files that are included with or are created by popular database clients and servers.

Table 4.6 Queries That Locate Database Support Files

Query	Description
inurl:default_content.asp ClearQuest	ClearQuest Web help files
intitle:"index of" intext:globals.inc	MySQL globals.inc file, lists connection and credential information
filetype:inc intext:mysql_connect	PHP MySQL Connect file, lists connection and credential information
filetype:inc dbconn	Database connection file, lists connection and credential information
intitle:"index of" intext:connect.inc	MySQL connection file, lists connection and credential information
filetype:properties inurl:db intext:password	db.properties file, lists connection information
intitle:"index of" mysql.conf OR mysql_config	MySQL configuration file, lists port number, version number, and path information to MySQL server
inurl:php.ini filetype:ini	PHP.INI file, lists connection and credential information
filetype:ldb admin	Microsoft Access lock files, list database and username
inurl:config.php dbuname dbpass	The old config.php script, lists user and password information
intitle:index.of config.php	The config.php script, lists user and password information
"phpinfo.php" -manual	The output from phpinfo.php, lists a great deal of information
intitle:"index of" +myd size	The MySQL data directory
filetype:cnf my.cnf -cvs -example	The MySQL my.cnf file, can list information, ranging from paths and database names to passwords and usernames
filetype:ora ora	ORA configuration files, list Oracle database information
filetype:pass pass intext:userid	dbman files, list encoded passwords
filetype:pdb pdb backup (Pilot | Pluckerdb)	Palm database files, can list all sorts of personal information

As an example of a support file, PHP scripts using the *mysql_connect* function reveal machine names, usernames, and cleartext passwords, as shown in Figure 4.8. Strictly speaking, this file contains PHP code, but the INC extension makes it an *include file*. It's the content of this file that is of interest to a Google hacker.

Figure 4.8 PHP Files Can Reveal Machine Names, Usernames, and Passwords

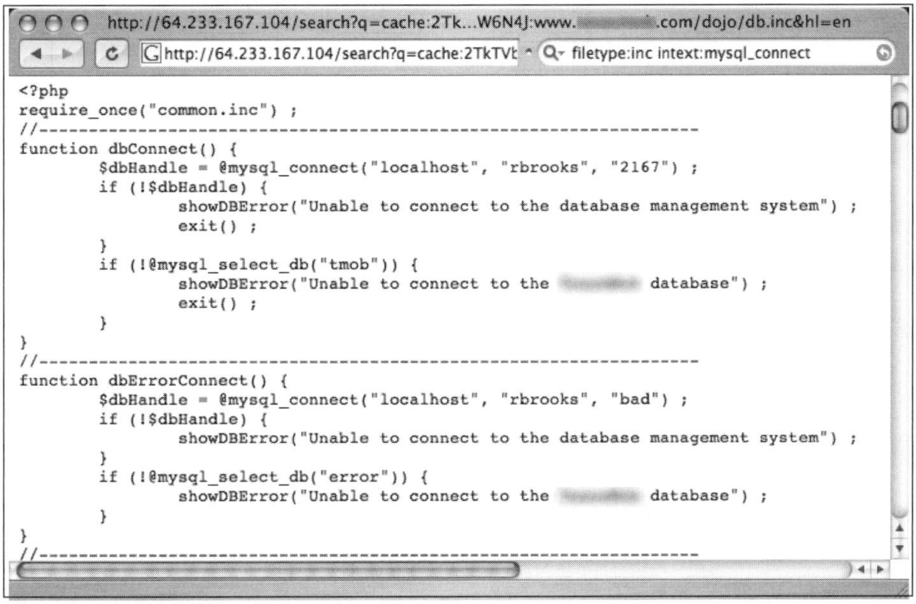

```
○ ○ ○         http://64.233.167.104/search?q=cache:2Tk...W6N4J:www._____.com/dojo/db.inc&hl=en
◄ ► C  G http://64.233.167.104/search?q=cache:2TkTVb ^  Q▼ filetype:inc intext:mysql_connect           ○

<?php
require_once("common.inc") ;
//------------------------------------------------------------------
function dbConnect() {
        $dbHandle = @mysql_connect("localhost", "rbrooks", "2167") ;
        if (!$dbHandle) {
                showDBError("Unable to connect to the database management system") ;
                exit() ;
        }
        if (!@mysql_select_db("tmob")) {
                showDBError("Unable to connect to the _____ database") ;
                exit() ;
        }
}
//------------------------------------------------------------------
function dbErrorConnect() {
        $dbHandle = @mysql_connect("localhost", "rbrooks", "bad") ;
        if (!$dbHandle) {
                showDBError("Unable to connect to the database management system") ;
        }
        if (!@mysql_select_db("error")) {
                showDBError("Unable to connect to the _____ database") ;
        }
}
//------------------------------------------------------------------
```

Error Messages

As we've discussed throughout this book, error messages can be used for all sorts of profiling and information-gathering purposes. Error messages also play a key role in the detection and profiling of database systems. As is the case with most error messages, database error messages can also be used to profile the operating system and Web server version. Conversely, operating system and Web server error messages can be used to profile and detect database servers. Table 4.7 shows queries that leverage database error messages.

Table 4.7 Queries That Locate Database Error Messages

Description	Query
.NET error message reveals data sources, and even authentication credentials	"ASP.NET_SessionId" "data source="
500 "Internal Server Error" reveals the server administrator's email address, and Apache server banners	"Internal Server Error" "server at"

Continued

Table 4.7 continued Queries That Locate Database Error Messages

Description	Query
500 "Internal Server Error" reveals the type of web server running on the site, and has the ability to show other information depending on how the message is internally formatted	intitle:"500 Internal Server Error" "server at"
ASP error message reveals compiler used, language used, line numbers, program names and partial source code	filetype:asp "Custom Error Message" Category Source
Access error message can reveal path names, function names, filenames and partial code	"Syntax error in query expression " -the
Apache Tomcat Error messages can reveal various kinds information depending on the type of error	intitle:"Apache Tomcat" "Error Report"
CGI error messages may reveal partial code listings, PERL version, detailed server information, usernames, setup file names, form and query information, port and path information, and more	intext:"Error Message : Error loading required libraries."
Chatologica MetaSearch error reveals Apache version, CGI environment vars, path names, stack dumps, process ID's, PERL version, and more	"Chatologica MetaSearch" "stack tracking:"
Cocoon XML reveals library functions, cocoon version number, and full and/or relative path names	"error found handling the request" cocoon filetype:xml
Cold fusion error messages trigger on SQL SELECT or INSERT statements which could help locate SQL injection points.	intitle:"Error Occurred While Processing Request" +WHERE (SELECT|INSERT) filetype:cfm
ColdFusion error message can reveal partial source code, full pathnames, SQL query info, database name, SQL state info and local time info	intitle:"Error Occurred" "The error occurred in" filetype:cfm

Continued

Table 4.7 continued Queries That Locate Database Error Messages

Description	Query
ColdFusion error message, can reveal SQL statements and server information	intitle:"Error Occurred While Processing Request"
ColdFusion error message, can reveal source code, full pathnames, SQL query info, database name, SQL state information, and local time information	intitle:"Error Occurred" "The error occurred in" filetype:cfm
Coldfusion Error Pages reveal many different types of information	"Error Diagnostic Information" intitle:"Error Occurred While"
DB2 error message can reveal path names, function names, filenames, partial code and program state	"detected an internal error [IBM][CLI Driver][DB2/6000]"
DB2 error message can reveal path names, function names, filenames, partial code and program state	An unexpected token "END-OF-STATE MENT" was found
DB2 error message, can reveal pathnames, function names, filenames, partial code, and program state	"detected an internal error [IBM] [CLI Driver][DB2/6000]"
DB2 error message, can reveal pathnames, function names, filenames, partial code, and program state	An unexpected token "END-OF-STATE MENT" was found
Discuz! Board error may reveal path information or partial SQL code listings	filetype:php inurl:"logging.php" "Discuz" error
Generic SQL message, can reveal pathnames and partial SQL code	"You have an error in your SQL syntax near"
Generic error can reveal path information	"Warning: Supplied argument is not a valid File-Handle resource in"
Generic error message can be used to determine operating system and web server version	intitle:"Under construction" "does not currently have"

Continued

Table 4.7 continued Queries That Locate Database Error Messages

Description	Query
Generic error message can reveal compiler used, language used, line numbers, program names and partial source code	"Fatal error: Call to undefined function" -reply -the -next
Generic error message reveals full path information	"Warning:" "SAFE MODE Restriction in effect." "The script whose uid is" "is not allowed to access owned by uid 0 in" "on line"
Generic error message, reveals various information	"Error Diagnostic Information" intitle:"Error Occurred While"
Generic error messages reveal path names, php file names, line numbers and include paths	intext:"Warning: Failed opening" "on line" "include_path"
Generic error reveals full path info	"Warning: Division by zero in" "on line" -forum
HyperNews error reveals the server software, server OS, server account user/group (unix), server administrator email address, and even stack traces	intitle:"Error using Hypernews" "Server Software"
IIS 4.0 error messages reveal the existence of an extremely old version of IIS	intitle:"the page cannot be found" inetmgr
IIS error message reveals somewhat unmodified (and perhaps unpatched) IIS servers	intitle:"the page cannot be found" "internet information services"
Informix error message can reveal path names, function names, filenames and partial code	"A syntax error has occurred" filetype:ihtml
Informix error message can reveal path names, function names, filenames and partial code	"An illegal character has been found in the statement" -"previous message"
MYSQL error message reveals path names	"supplied argument is not a valid MySQL result resource"
MySQL error message can reveal a variety of information.	"mySQL error with query"
MySQL error message can reveal database name, path names and partial SQL code	"Can't connect to local" intitle:warning

Continued

Table 4.7 continued Queries That Locate Database Error Messages

Description	Query
MySQL error message can reveal path names and partial SQL code	"You have an error in your SQL syntax near"
MySQL error message can reveal path names, function names, filenames and partial SQL code	"ORA-00921: unexpected end of SQL command"
MySQL error message can reveal path names, function names, filenames and partial SQL code	"Supplied argument is not a valid MySQL result resource"
MySQL error message can reveal path names, function names, filenames and partial code	"Incorrect syntax near"
MySQL error message can reveal path names, function names, filenames and partial code	"Incorrect syntax near" -the
MySQL error message can reveal path names, function names, filenames and partial code	"Unclosed quotation mark before the character string"
MySQL error message can reveal the username, database, path names and partial SQL code	"access denied for user" "using password"
MySQL error message, reveals real pathnames and listings of other PHP scripts on the server	"supplied argument is not a valid MySQL result resource"
MySQL error message, reveals various information	"MySQL error with query"
MySQL error reveals database schema and usernames.	"Warning: mysql_query()" "invalid query"
Netscape Application Server or iPlanet application servers error reveals the installation of extremely outdated software.	intitle:"404 SC_NOT_FOUND"
ODBC SQL error may reveal table or row queried, full database name and more	filetype:asp + "[ODBC SQL"
Oracle SQL error message, reveals full Web pathnames and/or php filenames	"ORA-00921: unexpected end of SQL command"

Continued

Table 4.7 continued Queries That Locate Database Error Messages

Description	Query
Oracle SQL error message, reveals pathnames, function names, filenames, and partial SQL code	"ORA-00933: SQL command not properly ended"
Oracle SQL error message, reveals pathnames, function names, filenames, and partial SQL code	"ORA-00936: missing expression"
Oracle error message can reveal path names, function names, filenames and partial SQL code	"ORA-00933: SQL command not properly ended"
Oracle error message can reveal path names, function names, filenames and partial database code	"ORA-00936: missing expression"
Oracle error message may reveal partial SQL code, path names, file names, and data sources	"ORA-12541: TNS:no listener" intitle: "error occurred"
Oracle error message, reveals SQL code, pathnames, filenames, and data sources	"ORA-12541: TNS:no listener" intitle: "error occurred"
PHP error logs can reveal various types of information	filetype:log "PHP Parse error" | "PHP Warning" | "PHP Error"
PHP error message can reveal path names, function names, filenames and partial code	"Warning: Cannot modify header information - headers already sent"
PHP error message can reveal the webserver's root directory and user ID	"The script whose uid is " "is not allowed to access"
PHP error messages reveal path names, PHP file names, line numbers and include paths.	PHP application warnings failing "include_path"
PHP error reveals web root path	"Parse error: parse error, unexpected T_VARIABLE" "on line" filetype:php
PostgreSQL error message can reveal path information and database names	"Warning: pg_connect(): Unable to connect to PostgreSQL server: FATAL"
PostgreSQL error message can reveal path names, function names, filenames and partial code	"PostgreSQL query failed: ERROR: parser: parse error"

Continued

Table 4.7 continued Queries That Locate Database Error Messages

Description	Query
PostgreSQL error message can reveal path names, function names, filenames and partial code	"Supplied argument is not a valid PostgreSQL result"
PostgreSQL error message, can reveal pathnames, function names, filenames, and partial code	"PostgreSQL query failed: ERROR: parser: parse error"
PostgreSQL error message, can reveal pathnames, function names, filenames, and partial code	"Supplied argument is not a valid PostgreSQL result"
Postgresql error message, reveals path information and database names	"Warning: pg_connect(): Unable to connect to PostgreSQL server: FATAL"
SQL error may reveal potential SQL injection points.	"[SQL Server Driver][SQL Server]Line 1: Incorrect syntax near" -forum -thread -showthread
SQL error message reveals full path info	"Invision Power Board Database Error"
SQL error message reveals full pathnames and/or PHP filenames.	"ORA-00921: unexpected end of SQL command"
SQL error message, can reveal pathnames, function names, filenames, and partial code (variation)	"Can't connect to local" intitle:warning
SQL error message, can reveal pathnames, function names, filenames, and partial code (variation)	"Incorrect syntax near" -the
SQL error message, can reveal pathnames, function names, filenames, and partial code (variation)	"access denied for user" "using password"
SQL error message, can reveal pathnames, function names, filenames, and partial code	"Incorrect syntax near"
SQL error message, can reveal pathnames, function names, filenames, and partial code	"Unclosed quotation mark before the character string"

Continued

Table 4.7 continued Queries That Locate Database Error Messages

Description	Query
Sablotron XML error can reveal partial source code, path and filename information and more	warning "error on line" php sablotron
Snitz Microsoft Access database error may reveal the location and name of the database, potentially making the forum vulnerable to unwanted download	databasetype. Code : 80004005. Error Description :
Softcart error message may reveal configuration file location and server file paths	intitle:Configuration.File inurl:softcart.exe
This dork reveals logins to databases that were denied for some reason.	"Warning: mysql_connect(): Access denied for user: '*@*'" "on line" -help -forum
Windows 2000 error messages reveal the existence of an extremely old version of Windows	intitle:"the page cannot be found" "2004 microsoft corporation"
cgiwrap error message reveals admin name and email, port numbers, path names, and may also include optional information like phone numbers for support personnel	intitle:"Execution of this script not permitted"
ht://Dig error can reveal administrative email, validation of a cgi-bin executable directory, directory structure, location of a search database file and possible naming conventions	intitle:"htsearch error" ht://Dig error
vbulletin error reveals SQL code snippets	"There seems to have been a problem with the" " Please try again by clicking the Refresh button in your web browser."

In addition to revealing information about the database server, error messages can also reveal much more dangerous information about potential vulnerabilities that exist in the server. For example, consider an error such as *"SQL command not properly ended"*, displayed in Figure 4.9. This error message indicates that a terminating character was not found at the end of an SQL statement. If a command accepts user input, an attacker could leverage the information in this error message to execute an SQL injection attack.

Figure 4.9 The Discovery of a Dangerous Error Message

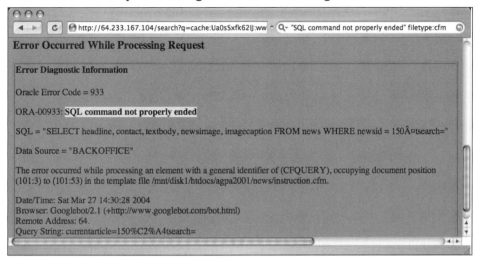

Database Dumps

The output of a database into any format can be constituted as a database dump. For the purposes of Google hacking, however, we'll us the term *database dump* to describe the text–based conversion of a database. As we'll see next in this chapter, it's entirely possible for an attacker to locate just about any type of binary database file, but standardized formats (such as the text-based SQL dump shown in Figure 4.10) are very commonplace on the Internet.

Figure 4.10 A Typical SQL Dump

```
--
-- Table structure for table 'artists'
--

CREATE TABLE artists (
  aID int(9) unsigned NOT NULL default '0',
  last char(30) NOT NULL default '',
  first char(30) NOT NULL default '',
  url char(80) NOT NULL default '',
  PRIMARY KEY  (aID)
) TYPE=MyISAM;

--
-- Dumping data for table 'artists'
--


--
-- Table structure for table 'blobs'
--

CREATE TABLE blobs (
  id int(9) unsigned NOT NULL default '0',
  type tinyint(2) unsigned NOT NULL default '0',
  body text NOT NULL,
  PRIMARY KEY  (id,type),
  FULLTEXT KEY body (body)
) TYPE=MyISAM;

--
```

Using a full database dump, a database administrator can completely rebuild a database. This means that a full dump details not only the structure of the database's tables but also every record in each and every table. Depending on the sensitivity of the data contained in the database, a database dump can be very revealing and obviously makes a terrific tool for an attacker. There are several ways an attacker can locate database dumps. One of the most obvious ways is by focusing on the headers of the dump, resulting in a query such as *"#Dumping data for table",* as shown in Figure 4.10. This technique can be expanded to work on just about any type of database dump headers by simply focusing on headers that exist in every dump and that are unique phrases that are unlikely to produce false positives.

Specifying additional specific interesting words or phrases such as *username, password,* or *user* can help narrow this search. For example, if the word *password* exists in a database dump, there's a good chance that a password of some sort is listed inside the database dump. With proper use of the *OR* symbol (|), an attacker can craft an extremely effective search, such as *"# Dumping data for table" (user | username | pass | password).* In addition, an attacker could focus on file extensions that some tools add to the end of a database dump by querying for *filetype:sql sql* and further narrowing to specific words, phrases, or sites. The SQL file extension is also used as a generic description of batched SQL commands. Table 4.8 lists queries that locate SQL database dumps.

Table 4.8 Queries That Locate SQL Database Dumps

Query	Description
inurl:nuke filetype:sql	php-nuke or postnuke CMS dumps
filetype:sql password	SQL database dumps or batched SQL com-
filetype:sql "IDENTIFIED BY" –cvs	SQL database dumps or batched SQL com-mands, focus on *"IDENTIFIED BY",* which can locate passwords
"# Dumping data for table (username|user|users|password)"	SQL database dumps or batched SQL commands, focus on interesting terms
"#mysql dump" filetype:sql	SQL database dumps
"# Dumping data for table"	SQL database dumps
"# phpMyAdmin MySQL-Dump" filetype:txt	SQL database dumps created by phpMyAdmin
"# phpMyAdmin MySQL-Dump" "INSERT INTO" -"the"	SQL database dumps created by phpMyAdmin (variation)

Actual Database Files

Another way an attacker can locate databases is by searching directly for the database itself. This technique does not apply to all database systems, only those systems in which the database is represented by a file with a specific name or extension. Be advised that Google will most likely not understand how to process or translate these files, and the summary (or "snippet") on the search result page will be blank and Google will list the file as an "unknown type," as shown in Figure 4.11.

Figure 4.11 Database Files Themselves Are Often Unknown to Google

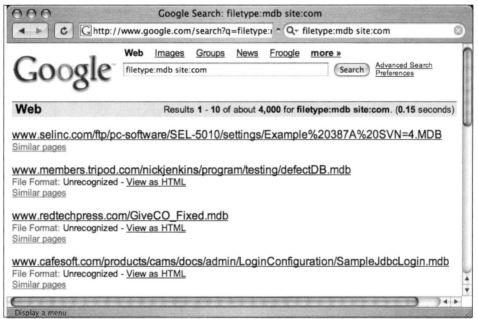

If Google does not understand the format of a binary file, as with many of those located with the *filetype* operator, you will be unable to search for strings *within* that file. This considerably limits the options for effective searching, forcing you to rely on *inurl* or *site* operators instead. Table 4.9 lists some queries that can locate database files.

Table 4.9 Queries That Locate Database Files

Query	Description
filetype:cfm "cfapplication name" password	ColdFusion source code
filetype:mdb inurl:users.mdb	Microsoft Access user database
inurl:email filetype:mdb	Microsoft Access e-mail database
inurl:backup filetype:mdb	Microsoft Access backup databases
inurl:forum filetype:mdb	Microsoft Access forum databases
inurl:/db/main.mdb	ASP-Nuke databases
inurl:profiles filetype:mdb	Microsoft Access user profile databases
*filetype:asp DBQ=" * Server. MapPath("*.mdb")*	Microsoft Access database connection string search
allinurl: admin mdb	Microsoft Access administration databases

Automated Grinding

Searching for files is fairly straightforward—especially if you know the type of file you're looking for. We've already seen how easy it is to locate files that contain sensitive data, but in some cases it might be necessary to search files offline. For example, assume that we want to troll for yahoo.com e-mail addresses. A query such as *"@yahoo.com" email* is not at all effective as a Web search, and even as a Group search it is problematic, as shown in Figure 4.12.

Figure 4.12 A Generic E-Mail Search Leaves Much to Be Desired

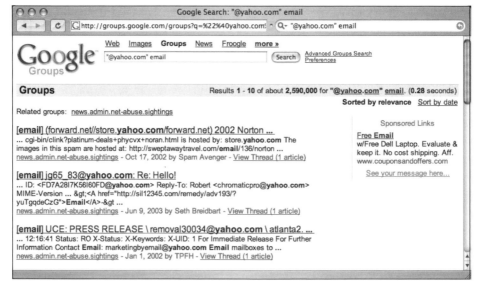

This search located one e-mail address, *jg65_83@yahoo.com*, but also keyed on *store.yahoo.com,* which is not a valid e-mail address. In cases like this, the best option for locating specific strings lies in the use of *regular expressions*. This involves downloading the documents you want to search (which you most likely found with a Google search) and parsing those files for the information you're looking for. You could opt to automate the process of downloading these files, as we'll show in Chapter 12, but once you have downloaded the files, you'll need an easy way to search the files for interesting information. Consider the following Perl script:

```perl
#!/usr/bin/perl
#
# Usage: ./ssearch.pl  FILE_TO_SEARCH  WORDLIST
#
# Locate words in a file, coded by James Foster
#
use strict;
open(SEARCHFILE,$ARGV[0]) || die("Can not open searchfile because $!");

open(WORDFILE,$ARGV[1]) || die("Can not open wordfile because $!");
my @WORDS=<WORDFILE>;
close(WORDFILE);

my $LineCount = 0;

while(<SEARCHFILE>) {
    foreach my $word (@WORDS) {
        chomp($word);
        ++$LineCount;
        if(m/$word/) {
            print "$&\n";
            last;
        }
    }
}
close(SEARCHFILE);
```

This script accepts two arguments: a file to search and a list of words to search for. As it stands, this program is rather simplistic, acting as nothing more than a glorified *grep* script. However, the script becomes much more powerful when instead of words, the word list contains regular expressions. For example, consider the following regular expression, written by Don Ranta:

```
[a-zA-Z0-9._-]+@(([a-zA-Z0-9_-]{2,99}\.)+[a-zA-Z]{2,4})|((25[0-5]|2[0-
4]\d|1\d\d|[1-9]\d|[1-9])\.(25[0-5]|2[0-4]\d|1\d\d|[1-9]\d|[1-9])\.(25[0-5]|2[0-
4]\d|1\d\d|[1-9]\d|[1-9])\.(25[0-5]|2[0-4]\d|1\d\d|[1-9]\d|[1-9]))
```

Unless you're somewhat skilled with regular expressions, this might look like a bunch of garbage text. This regular expression is very powerful, however, and will locate various forms of e-mail address.

Let's take a look at this regular expression in action. For this example, we'll save the results of a Google Groups search for *"@yahoo.com" email* to a file called results.html, and we'll enter the preceding regular expression all on one line of a file called wordlfile.txt. As shown in Figure 4.13, we can grab the search results from the command line with a program like Lynx, a common text-based Web browser. Other programs could be used instead of Lynx—Curl, Netcat, Telnet, or even "save as" from a standard Web browser. Remember that Google's terms of service frown on any form of automation. In essence, Google prefers that you simply execute your search from the browser, saving the results manually. However, as we've discussed previously, if you honor the *spirit* of the terms of service, taking care not to abuse Google's free search service with excessive automation, the folks at Google will most likely not turn their wrath upon you. Regardless, most people will ultimately decide for themselves how strictly to follow the terms of service.

Back to our Google search: Notice that the URL indicates we're grabbing the first hundred results, as demonstrated by the use of the *num=100* parameter. This will potentially locate more e-mail addresses. Once the results are saved to the *results.html* file, we'll run our ssearch.pl script against the results.html file, searching for the e-mail expression we've placed in the wordfile.txt file. To help narrow our results, we'll pipe that output into *"grep yahoo | head −15 | sort −u"* to return at most 15 unique addresses that contain the word *yahoo*. The final (obfuscated) results are shown in Figure 4.13.

Figure 4.13 ssearch.pl Hunting for E-Mail Addresses

As you can see, this combination of commands works fairly well at unearthing e-mail addresses. If you're familiar with UNIX commands, you might have already noticed that there is little need for *two* separate commands. This entire process could have been easily combined into one command by modifying the Perl script to read standard input and piping the output from the Lynx command directly into the ssearch.pl script, effectively bypassing the results.html file. Presenting the commands this way, however, opens the door for *irresponsible* automation techniques, which isn't overtly encouraged.

Other regular expressions can come in handy as well. This expression, also by Don Ranta, locates URLs:

```
[a-zA-Z]{3,4}[sS]?://((([\w\d\-]+\.)+[ a-zA-Z]{2,4})|((25[0-5]|2[0-4]\d|1\d\d|[1-
9]\d|[1-9])\.(25[0-5]|2[0-4]\d|1\d\d|[1-9]\d|[1-9])\.(25[0-5]|2[0-4]\d|1\d\d|[1-
9]\d|[1-9])\.(25[0-5]|2[0-4]\d|1\d\d|[1-9]\d|[1-9])))((\?|/)[\w/=+#_~&:;%\-\?\.]*)*
```

This expression, which will locate URLs and parameters, including addresses that consist of either IP addresses or domain names, is great at processing a Google results page, returning all the links on the page. This doesn't work as well as the API-based methods, but it is simpler to use than the API method. This expression locates IP addresses:

```
(25[0-5]|2[0-4]\d|1\d\d|[1-9]\d|[1-9])\.(25[0-5]|2[0-4]\d|1\d\d|[1-9]\d|[1-
9])\.(25[0-5]|2[0-4]\d|1\d\d|[1-9]\d|[1-9])\.(25[0-5]|2[0-4]\d|1\d\d|[1-9]\d|[1-9])
```

We can use an expression like this to help map a target network. These techniques could be used to parse not only HTML pages but also practically any type of document. However, keep in mind that many files are binary, meaning that they should be converted into text before they're searched. The UNIX *strings* command (usually implemented with *strings −8* for this purpose) works very well for this task, but don't forget that Google has the built-in capability to translate many different types of documents for you. If you're searching for visible text, you should opt to use Google's translation, but if you're searching for nonprinted text such as metadata, you'll need to first download the original file and search it offline. Regardless of how you implement these techniques, it should be clear to you by now that Google can be used as an extremely powerful information-gathering tool when it's combined with even a little automation.

Google Desktop Search

The Google Desktop, available from http://desktop.google.com, is an application that allows you to search files on your local machine. Available for Windows Mac and Linux, Google Desktop Search allows you to search many types of files, depending on the operating system you are running. The following fil types can be searched from the Mac OS X operating system:

- Gmail messages
- Text files (.txt)
- PDF files
- HTML files
- Apple Mail and Microsoft Entourage emails
- iChat transcripts
- Microsoft Word, Excel, and PowerPoint documents
- Music and Video files
- Address Book contacts
- System Preference panes
- File and folder names

Google Desktop Search will also search file types on a Windows operating system:

- Gmail
- Outlook Express
- Word
- Excel
- PowerPoint
- Internet Explorer
- AOL Instant Messenger
- MSN Messenger
- Google Talk
- Netscape Mail/Thunderbird
- Netscape / Firefox / Mozilla
- PDF
- Music
- Video
- Images
- Zip Files

The Google Desktop search offers many features, but since it's a beta product, you should check the desktop Web page for a current list of features. For a document-grinding tool, you can simply download content from the target server and use Desktop Search to search through those files. Desktop Search also captures Web pages that are viewed in Internet Explorer 5 and newer. This means you can always view an older version of a page you've visited online, even when the original page has changed. In addition, once Desktop Search is installed, any online Google Search you perform in Internet Explorer will also return results found on your local machine.

Summary

The subject of document grinding is topic worthy of an entire book. In a single chapter, we can only hope to skim the surface of this topic. An attacker (black or white hat) who is skilled in the art of document grinding can glean loads of information about a target. In this chapter we've discussed the value of configuration files, log files, and office documents, but obviously there are many other types of documents we could focus on as well. The key to document grinding is first discovering the types of documents that exist on a target and then, depending on the number of results, to narrow the search to the more interesting or relevant documents. Depending on the target, the line of business they're in, the document type, and many other factors, various keywords can be mixed with *filetype* searches to locate key documents.

Database hacking is also a topic for an entire book. However, there is obvious benefit to the information Google can provide prior to a full-blown database audit. Login portals, support files, and database dumps can provide various information that can be recycled into an audit. Of all the information that can be found from these sources, perhaps the most telling (and devastating) is source code. Lines of source code provide insight into the way a database is structured and can reveal flaws that might otherwise go unnoticed from an external assessment. In most cases, though, a thorough code review is required to determine application flaws. Error messages can also reveal a great deal of information to an attacker.

Automated grinding allows you to search many documents programmatically for bits of important information. When it's combined with Google's excellent document location features, you've got a very powerful information-gathering weapon at your disposal.

Solutions Fast Track

Configuration Files

- ☑ Configuration files can reveal sensitive information to an attacker.
- ☑ Although the naming varies, configuration files can often be found with file extensions like INI, CONF, CONFIG, or CFG.

Log Files

- ☑ Log files can also reveal sensitive information that is often more current than the information found in configuration files.
- ☑ Naming convention varies, but log files can often be found with file extensions like LOG.

Office Documents

☑ In many cases, office documents are intended for public release. Documents that are inadvertently posted to public areas can contain sensitive information.

☑ Common office file extensions include PDF, DOC, TXT, or XLS.

☑ Document content varies, but strings like private, password, backup, or admin can indicate a sensitive document.

Database Digging

☑ Login portals, especially default portals supplied by the software vendor, are easily searched for and act as magnets for attackers seeking specific versions or types of software. The words *login, welcome,* and *copyright statements* are excellent ways of locating login portals.

☑ Support files exist for both server and client software. These files can reveal information about the configuration or usage of an application.

☑ Error messages have varied content that can be used to profile a target.

☑ Database dumps are arguably the most revealing of all database finds because they include full or partial contents of a database. These dumps can be located by searching for strings in the headers, like *"# Dumping data for table"*.

Links to Sites

■ **www.filext.com** A great resource for getting information about file extensions.

■ **http://desktop.google.com** The Google Desktop Search application.

■ **http://johnny.ihackstuff.com** The home of the Google Hacking Database, where you can find more searches like those listed in this chapter.

Frequently Asked Questions

The following Frequently Asked Questions, answered by the authors of this book, are designed to both measure your understanding of the concepts presented in this chapter and to assist you with real-life implementation of these concepts. To have your questions about this chapter answered by the author, browse to **www.syngress.com/solutions** and click on the **"Ask the Author"** form.

Q: What can I do to help prevent this form of information leakage?

A: To fix this problem on a site you are responsible for, first review all documents available from a Google search. Ensure that the returned documents are, in fact, supposed to be in the public view. Although you might opt to scan your site for database information leaks with an automated tool (see the Protection chapter), the best way to prevent this is at the source. Your database remote administration tools should be locked down from outside users, default login portals should be reviewed for safety and checked to ensure that software versioning information has been removed, and support files should be removed from your public servers. Error messages should be tailored to ensure that excessive information is not revealed, and a full application review should be performed on all applications in use. In addition, it doesn't hurt to configure your Web server to only allow certain file types to be downloaded. It's much easier to list the file types you will allow than to list the file types you *don't* allow.

Q: I'm concerned about excessive metadata in office documents. Can I do anything to clean up my documents?

A: Microsoft provides a Web page dedicated to the topic: http://support.microsoft.com/default.aspx?scid=kb;EN-US;Q223396. In addition, several utilities are available to automate the cleaning process. One such product, ezClean, is available from www.kklsoftware.com.

Q: Many types of software rely on *include files* to pull in external content. As I understand it, include files, like the INC files discussed in this chapter, are a problem because they often reveal sensitive information meant for programs, not Web visitors. Is there any way to resolve the dangers of include files?

A: Include files are in fact a problem because of their file extensions. If an extension such as .INC is used, most Web servers will display them as text, revealing sensitive data. Consider blocking .INC files (or whatever extension you use for includes) from being downloaded. This server modification will keep the file from presenting in a browser but will still allow back-end processes to access the data within the file.

Q: Our software uses .INC files to store database connection settings. Is there another way?

A: Rename the extension to .PHP so that the contents are not displayed.

Q: How can I avoid our application database from being downloaded by a Google hacker?

A: Read the documentation. Some badly written software has hardcoded paths but most allow you to place the file outside the Web server's *docroot*.

## Chapter 5

Google's Part in an Information Collection Framework

Solutions in this chapter:

- The Principles of Automating Searches
- Applications of Data Mining
- Collecting Search Terms

Introduction

There are various reasons for hacking. When most of us hear hacker we think about computer and network security, but lawyers, salesmen, and policemen are also hackers at heart. It's really a state of mind and a way of thinking rather than a physical attribute. Why do people hack? There are a couple of motivators, but one specific reason is to be able to know things that the ordinary man on the street doesn't. From this flow many of the other motivators. Knowledge is power—there's a rush to seeing what others are doing without them knowing it. Understanding that the thirst for knowledge is central to hacking, consider Google, a massively distributed super computer, with access to all known information and with a deceivingly simple user interface, just waiting to answer any query within seconds. It is almost as if Google was made for hackers.

The first edition of this book brought to light many techniques that a hacker (or penetration tester) might use to obtain information that would help him or her in conventional security assessments (e.g., finding networks, domains, e-mail addresses, and so on). During such a conventional security test (or pen test) the aim is almost always to breach security measures and get access to information that is restricted. However, this information can be reached simply by assembling related pieces of information together to form a bigger picture. This, of course, is not true for all information. The chances that I will find your super secret double encrypted document on Google is extremely slim, but you can bet that the way to get to it will eventually involve a lot of information gathering from public sources like Google.

If you are reading this book you are probably already interested in information mining, getting the most from search engines by using them in interesting ways. In this chapter I hope to show interesting and clever ways to do just that.

The Principles of Automating Searches

Computers help automate tedious tasks. Clever automation can accomplish what a thousand disparate people working simultaneously cannot. But it's impossible to automate something that cannot be done manually. If you want to write a program to perform something, you need to have done the entire process by hand, and have that process work every time. It makes little sense to automate a flawed process. Once the manual process is ironed out, an algorithm is used to translate that process into a computer program.

Let's look at an example. A user is interested in finding out which Web sites contain the e-mail address *andrew@syngress.com*. As a start, the user opens Google and types the e-mail address in the input box. The results are shown in Figure 5.1.

Figure 5.1 A Simple Search for an E-mail Address

The user sees that there are three different sites with that e-mail address listed: *g.bookpool*.com, *www.networksecurityarchive.org*, and *book.google.com*. In the back of his or her mind is the feeling that these are not the only sites where the e-mail address appears, and remembers that he or she has seen places where e-mail addresses are listed as *andrew at syngress dot com*. When the user puts this search into Google, he or she gets different results, as shown in Figure 5.2.

Clearly the lack of quotes around the query gave incorrect results. The user adds the quotes and gets the results shown in Figure 5.3.

Figure 5.2 Expanding the search

Figure 5.3 Expansion with Quotes

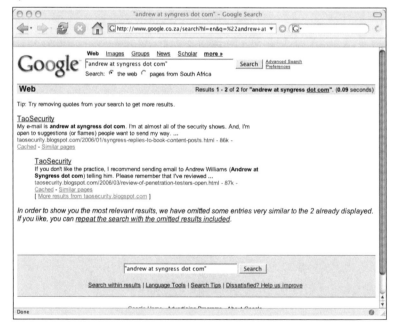

By formulating the query differently, the user now has a new result: *taosecurity.blogspot.com.* The manipulation of the search query worked, and the user has found another site reference.

If we break this process down into logical parts, we see that there are actually many different steps that were followed. Almost all searches follow these steps:

- Define an original search term
- Expand the search term
- Get data from the data source
- Parse the data
- Post-process the data into information

Let's look at these in more detail.

The Original Search Term

The goal of the previous example was to find Web pages that reference a specific e-mail address. This seems rather straightforward, but clearly defining a goal is probably the most difficult part of any search. Brilliant searching won't help attain an unclear goal. When automating a search, the same principles apply as when doing a manual search: garbage in, garbage out.

Tools & Traps…

Garbage in, garbage out

Computers are bad at "thinking" and good at "number crunching." Don't try to make a computer think for you, because you will be bitterly disappointed with the results. The principle of garbage in, garbage out simply states that if you enter bad information into a computer from the start, you will only get garbage (or bad information) out. Inexperienced search engine users often wrestle with this basic principle.

In some cases, goals may need to be broken down. This is especially true of broad goals, like trying to find e-mail addresses of people that work in cheese factories in the Netherlands. In this case, at least one sub-goal exists—you'll need to define the cheese factories first. Be sure your goals are clearly defined, then work your way to a set of core search terms. In some cases, you'll need to play around with the results of a single query in order to work your way towards a decent starting search term. I have often seen results of a query and thought, "Wow, I never thought that my query would return these results. If I shape the query a little differently each time with automation, I can get loads of interesting information."

In the end the only real limit to what you can get from search engines is your own imagination, and experimentation is the best way to discover what types of queries work well.

Expanding Search Terms

In our example, the user quickly figured out that they could get more results by changing the original query into a set of slightly different queries. Expanding search terms is fairly natural for humans, and the real power of search automation lies in thinking about that human process and translating it into some form of algorithm. By programmatically changing the standard form of a search into many different searches, we save ourselves from manual repetition, and more importantly, from having to remember all of the expansion tricks. Let's take a look at a few of these expansion techniques.

E-mail Addresses

Many sites try obscure e-mail addresses in order to fool data mining programs. This is done for a good reason: the majority of the data mining programs troll sites to collect e-mail addresses for spammers. If you want a sure fire way to receive a lot of spam, post to a mailing list that does not obscure your e-mail address. While it's a good thing that sites automatically obscure the e-mail address, it also makes our lives as Web searchers difficult. Luckily, there are ways to beat this; however, these techniques are also not unknown to spammers.

When searching for an e-mail address we can use the following expansions. The e-mail address *andrew@syngress.com* could be expanded as follows:

- *andrew at syngress.com*
- *andrew at syngress dot com*
- *andrew@syngress dot com*
- *andrew_at_syngress.com*
- *andrew_at_syngress dot com*
- *andrew_at_syngress_dot_com*
- *andrew@syngress.remove.com*
- *andrew@_removethis_syngress.com*

Note that the "@" sign can be written in many forms (e.g., − (at), _at_ or -at-). The same goes for the dot ("."). You can also see that many people add "remove" or "removethis" in an e-mail address. At the end it becomes an 80/20 thing—you will find 80 percent of addresses when implementing the top 20 percent of these expansions.

At this stage you might feel that you'll never find every instance of the address (and you may be right). But there is a tiny light at the end of the tunnel. Google ignores certain characters in a search. A search for *andrew@syngress.com* and *"andrew syngress com"* returns the same results. The @ sign and the dot are simply ignored. So when expanding search terms, don't include both, because you are simply wasting a search.

Tools & Traps…

Verifying an e-mail address

Here's a quick hack to verify if an e-mail address exists. While this might not work on all mail servers, it works on the majority of them – including Gmail. Have a look:

- Step 1 – Find the mail server:

```
$ host -t mx gmail.com
gmail.com mail is handled by 5 gmail-smtp-in.l.google.com.
gmail.com mail is handled by 10 alt1.gmail-smtp-in.l.google.com.
gmail.com mail is handled by 10 alt2.gmail-smtp-in.l.google.com.
gmail.com mail is handled by 50 gsmtp163.google.com.
gmail.com mail is handled by 50 gsmtp183.google.com.
```

- Step 2 – Pick one and Telnet to port 25

```
$ telnet gmail-smtp-in.l.google.com 25
Trying 64.233.183.27...
Connected to gmail-smtp-in.l.google.com.
Escape character is '^]'.
220 mx.google.com ESMTP d26si15626330nfh
```

- Step 3: Mimic the Simple Mail Transfer Protocol (SMTP):

```
HELO test
250 mx.google.com at your service
MAIL FROM: <test@test.com>
250 2.1.0 OK
```

- Step 4a: Positive test:

```
RCPT TO: <roelof.temmingh@gmail.com>
250 2.1.5 OK
```

Continued

■ **Step 4b: Negative test:**

```
RCPT TO: <kosie.kramer@gmail.com>
550 5.1.1 No such user d26si15626330nfh
```

■ **Step 5: Say goodbye:**

```
quit
221 2.0.0 mx.google.com closing connection d26si15626330nfh
```

By inspecting the responses from the mail server we have now verified that *roelof.temmingh@gmail.com* exists, while *kosie.kramer@gmail.com* does not. In the same way, we can verify the existence of other e-mail addresses.

NOTE

On Windows platforms you will need to use the *nslookup* command to find the e-mail servers for a domain. You can do this as follows:
nslookup -qtype=mx gmail.com

Telephone Numbers

While e-mail addresses have a set format, telephone numbers are a different kettle of fish. It appears that there is no standard way of writing down a phone number. Let's assume you have a number that is in South Africa and the number itself is 012 555 1234. The number can appear on the Internet in many different forms:

- 012 555 1234 (local)
- 012 5551234 (local)
- 012555124 (local)
- +27 12 555 1234 (with the country code)
- +27 12 5551234 (with the country code)
- +27 (0)12 555 1234 (with the country code)
- 0027 (0)12 555 1234 (with the country code)

One way of catching all of the results would be to look for the most significant part of the number, "555 1234" and "5551234." However, this has a drawback as you might find that the same number exists in a totally different country, giving you a false positive.

An interesting way to look for results that contain telephone numbers within a certain range is by using Google's *numrange* operator. A shortcut for this is to specify the start number, then ".." followed by the end number. Let's see how this works in real life. Imagine I want to see what results I can find on the area code +1 252 793. You can use the *numrange* operator to specify the query as shown in Figure 5.4.

Figure 5.4 Searching for Telephone Number Ranges

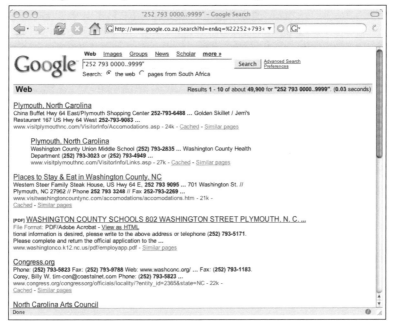

We can clearly see that the results all contain numbers located in the specified range in North Carolina. We will see how this ability to restrict results to a certain area is very useful later in this chapter.

People

One of the best ways to find information about someone is to Google them. If you haven't Googled for yourself, you are the odd one out. There are many ways to search for a person and most of them are straightforward. If you don't get results straight away don't worry, there are numerous options. Assuming you are looking for Andrew Williams you might search for:

- "Andrew Williams"
- "Williams Andrew"
- "A Williams"
- "Andrew W"
- Andrew Williams
- Williams Andrew

Note that the last two searches do not have quotes around them. This is to find phrases like "Andrew is part of the Williams family".

With a name like Andrew Williams you can be sure to get a lot of false positives as there are probably many people named Andrew Williams on the Internet. As such, you need to add as many additional search terms to your search as possible. For example, you may try something like *"Andrew Williams" Syngress publishing security*. Another tip to reduce false positives is to restrict the site to a particular country. If Andrew stayed in England, adding the *site:uk* operator would help limit the results. But keep in mind that your searches are then limited to sites in the UK. If Andrew is indeed from the UK but posts on sites that end in any other top level domains (TLD), this search won't return hits from those sites.

Getting Lots of Results

In some cases you'd be interested in getting a lot of results, not just specific results. For instance, you want to find all Web sites or e-mail addresses within a certain TLD. Here you want to combine your searches with keywords that do two things: get past the 1,000 result restriction and increase your yield per search. As an example, consider finding Web sites in the ****.*gov* domain, as shown in Figure 5.5.

Figure 5.5 Searching for a Domain

You will get a maximum of 1,000 sites from the query, because it is most likely that you will get more than one result from a single site. In other words, if 500 pages are located on one server and 500 pages are located on another server you will only get two site results.

Also, you will be getting results from sites that are not within the ****.*gov* domain. How do we get more results and limit our search to the ****.*gov* domain? By combining the query with keywords and other operators. Consider the query *site:****.gov -www.****.gov*. The query means find any result within sites that are located in the ****.*gov* domain, but that are not on their main Web site. While this query works beautifully, it will again only get a maximum of 1,000 results. There are some general additional keywords we can add to each query. The idea here is that we use words that will raise sites that were below the 1,000 mark surface to within the first 1,000 results. Although there is no guarantee that it will lift the other sites out, you could consider adding terms like *about*, *official*, *page*, *site*, and so on. While Google says that words like *the, a, or*, and so on are ignored during searches, we do see that results differ when combining these words with the *site:* operator. Looking at these results in Figure 5.6 shows that Google is indeed honoring the "ignored" words in our query.

Figure 5.6 Searching for a Domain Using the *site* Operator

More Combinations

When the idea is to find lots of results, you might want to combine your search with terms that will yield better results. For example, when looking for e-mail addresses, you can add keywords like *contact, mail, e-mail, send,* and so on. When looking for telephone numbers you might use additional keywords like *phone, telephone, contact, number, mobile,* and so on.

Using "Special" Operators

Depending on what it is that we want to get from Google, we might have to use some of the other operators. Imagine we want to see what Microsoft Office documents are located on a Web site. We know we can use the *filetype:* operator to specify a certain file type, but we can only specify one type per query. As a result, we will need to automate the process of asking for each Office file type at a time. Consider asking Google these questions:

- *filetype:ppt site:www.* * * * *.gov*
- *filetype:doc site:www.* * * * *.gov*
- *filetype:xls site:www.* * * * *.gov*
- *filetype:pdf site:www.* * * * *.gov*

Keep in mind that in certain cases, these expansions can now be combined again using boolean logic. In the case of our Office document search, the search *filetype:ppt* or *filetype:doc site www.* * * * *.gov* could work just as well.

Keep in mind that we can change the *site:* operator to be *site:* * * * *.gov*, which will fetch results from any Web site within the * * * *.gov* domain. We can use the *site:* operator in other ways as well. Imagine a program that will see how many time the word *iPhone* appears on sites located in different countries. If we monitor the Netherlands, France, Germany, Belgium, and Switzerland our query would be expanded as such:

- *iphone site:nl*
- *iphone site:fr*
- *iphone site:de*
- *iphone site:be*
- *iphone site:ch*

At this stage we only need to parse the returned page from Google to get the amount of results, and monitor how the iPhone campaign is/was spreading through Western Europe over time. Doing this right now (at the time of writing this book) would probably not give you meaningful results (as the hype has already peaked), but having this monitoring system in place before the release of the actual phone could have been useful. (For a list of all country codes see http://ftp.ics.uci.edu/pub/websoft/wwwstat/country-codes.txt, or just Google for internet country codes.)

Getting the Data From the Source

At the lowest level we need to make a Transmission Control Protocol (TCP) connection to our data source (which is the Google Web site) and ask for the results. Because Google is a Web application, we will connect to port 80. Ordinarily, we would use a Web browser, but if we are interested in automating the process we will need to be able to speak programmatically to Google.

Scraping it Yourself— Requesting and Receiving Responses

This is the most flexible way to get results. You are in total control of the process and can do things like set the number of results (which was never possible with the Application Programming Interface [API]). But it is also the most labor intensive. However, once you get it going, your worries are over and you can start to tweak the parameters.

> **WARNING**
>
> Scraping is not allowed by most Web applications. Google disallows scraping in their Terms of Use (TOU) unless you've cleared it with them. From www.google.com/accounts/TOS:
>
> *"5.3 You agree not to access (or attempt to access) any of the Services by any means other than through the interface that is provided by Google, unless you have been specifically allowed to do so in a separate agreement with Google. You specifically agree not to access (or attempt to access) any of the Services through any automated means (including use of scripts or Web crawlers) and shall ensure that you comply with the instructions set out in any robots.txt file present on the Services."*

To start we need to find out how to ask a question/query to the Web site. If you normally Google for something (in this case the word *test)*, the returned Uniform Resource Locator (URL) looks like this:

http://www.google.co.za/search?hl=en&q=test&btnG=Search&meta=

The interesting bit sits after the first slash (/)—*search?hl=en&q=test&btnG= Search&meta=*). This is a GET request and parameters and their values are separated with an "&" sign. In this request we have passed four parameters:

- *hl*

- *q*

- *btnG*

- *meta*

The values for these parameters are separated from the parameters with the equal sign (=). The "*hl*" parameter means "home language," which is set to English. The "*q*" parameter means "question" or "query," which is set to our query "test." The other two parameters are not of importance (at least not now). Our search will return ten results. If we set our preferences to return 100 results we get the following GET request:

http://www.google.co.za/search?num=100&hl=en&q=test&btnG=Search&meta=

Note the additional parameter that is passed; "*num*" is set to 100. If we request the second page of results (e.g., results 101–200), the request looks as follows:

http://www.google.co.za/search?q=test&num=100&hl=en&start=100&sa=N

There are a couple of things to notice here. The order in which the parameters are passed is ignored and yet the "*start*" parameter is added. The *start* parameter tells Google on which page we want to start getting results and the "*num*" parameter tell them how many results we want. Thus, following this logic, in order to get results 301–400 our request should look like this:

http://www.google.co.za/search?q=test&num=100&hl=en&start=300&sa=N

Let's try that and see what we get (see Figure 5.7).

Figure 5.7 Searching with a 100 Results from Page three

It seems to be working. Let's see what happens when we search for something a little more complex. The search *"testing testing 123" site:uk* results in the following query:

http://www.google.co.za/search?num=100&hl=en&q=%22testing+testing+123%22+site%3A uk&btnG=Search&meta=

What happened there? Let's analyze it a bit. The *num* parameter is set to 100. The *btnG* and *meta* parameters can be ignored. The *site:* operator does not result in an extra parameter, but rather is located within the question or query. The question says *%22testing+testing+123%22+site%3Auk*. Actually, although the question seems a bit intimidating at first, there is really no magic there. The *%22* is simply the hexadecimal encoded form of a quote ("). The *%3A* is the encoded form of a colon (:). Once we have replaced the encoded characters with their unencoded form, we have our original query back: *"testing testing 123" site:uk.*

So, how do you decide when to encode a character and when to use the unencoded form? This is a topic on it's own, but as a rule of thumb you cannot go wrong to encode everything that's not in the range A–Z, a–z, and 0–9. The encoding can be done programmatically, but if you are curious you can see all the encoded characters by typing man ascii in a UNIX terminal, by Googling for ascii hex encoding, or by visiting http://en.wikipedia.org/wiki/ASCII.

Now that we know how to formulate our request, we are ready to send it to Google and get a reply back. Note that the server will reply in Hypertext Markup Language (HTML). In it's simplest form, we can Telnet directly to Google's Web server and send the request by hand. Figure 5.8 shows how it is done:

Figure 5.8 A Raw HTTP Request and Response from Google for Simple Search

```
login

Mips:~ roeloftemmingh$ telnet www.google.com 80
Trying 64.233.183.103...
Connected to www.l.google.com.
Escape character is '^]'.
GET /search?hl=en&q=test&btnG=Search&meta= HTTP/1.0
Host: www.google.com

HTTP/1.0 200 OK
Date: Mon, 02 Jul 2007 11:55:47 GMT
Content-Type: text/html; charset=ISO-8859-1
Cache-Control: private
Set-Cookie: PREF=ID=65d2ba4ed6bd9544:TM=1183377347:LM=1183377347:S=T2xjyi3xSSKmD
cdR; expires=Sun, 17-Jan-2038 19:14:07 GMT; path=/; domain=.google.com
Server: GWS/2.1
Via: 1.1 netcachejhb-2 (NetCache NetApp/5.5R6)

<html><head><meta http-equiv="content-type" content="text/html; charset=ISO-8859
-1"><title>test - Google Search</title><style><!--
div,td{color:#000}
.f{color:#666}
.flc,.fl:link,.ft a:link,.ft a:hover,.ft a:active{color:#77c}
a:link,.w,a.w:link,.w a:link,.q:visited,.q:link,.q:active,.q{color:#00c}
a:visited,.fl:visited{color:#551a8b}
a:active,.fl:active{color:red}
```

The resultant HTML is truncated for brevity. In the screen shot above, the commands that were typed out are highlighted. There are a couple of things to notice. The first is that we need to connect (Telnet) to the Web site on port 80 and wait for a connection before issuing our Hypertext Transfer Protocol (HTTP) request. The second is that our request is a GET that is followed by "*HTTP/1.0*" stating that we are speaking HTTP version 1.0 (you could also decide to speak 1.1). The last thing to notice is that we added the Host header, and ended our request with two carriage return line feeds (by pressing **Enter** two times). The server replied with a HTTP header (the part up to the two carriage return line feeds) and a body that contains the actual HTML (the bit that starts with *<html>*).

This seems like a lot of work, but now that we know what the request looks like, we can start building automation around it. Let's try this with Netcat.

Notes from the Underground…

Netcat

Netcat has been described as the Swiss Army Knife of TCP/Internet Protocol (IP). It is a tool that is used for good and evil; from catching the reverse shell from an exploit (evil) to helping network administrators dissect a protocol (good). In this case we will use it to send a request to Google's Web servers and show the resulting HTML on the screen. You can get Netcat for UNIX as well as Microsoft Windows by Googling "netcat download."

To describe the various switches and uses of Netcat is well beyond the scope of this chapter; therefore, we will just use Netcat to send the request to Google and catch the response. Before bringing Netcat into the equation, consider the following commands and their output:

```
$ echo "GET / HTTP/1.0";echo "Host: www.google.com"; echo
GET / HTTP/1.0
Host: www.google.com
```

Note that the last echo command (the blank one) adds the necessary carriage return line feed (CRLF) at the end of the HTTP request. To hook this up to Netcat and make it connect to Google's site we do the following:

```
$ (echo "GET / HTTP/1.0";echo "Host: www.google.com"; echo) | nc www.google.com 80
```

The output of the command is as follows:

```
HTTP/1.0 302 Found
Date: Mon, 02 Jul 2007 12:56:55 GMT
```

```
Content-Length: 221
Content-Type: text/html
```

The rest of the output is truncated for brevity. Note that we have parenthesis () around the echo commands, and the pipe character (|) that hooks it up to Netcat. Netcat makes the connection to www.google.com on port 80 and sends the output of the command to the left of the pipe character to the server. This particular way of hooking Netcat and echo together works on UNIX, but needs some tweaking to get it working under Windows.

There are other (easier) ways to get the same results. Consider the "*wget*" command (a Windows version of wget is available at http://xoomer.alice.it/hherold/). *Wget* in itself is a great tool, and using it only for sending requests to a Web server is a bit like contracting a rocket scientist to fix your microwave oven. To see all the other things *wget* can do, simply type *wget -h*. If we want to use *wget* to get the results of a query we can use it as follows:

   wget http://www.google.co.za/search?hl=en&q=test -O output

The output looks like this:

```
--15:41:43--  http://www.google.com/search?hl=en&q=test
           => `output'
Resolving www.google.com... 64.233.183.103, 64.233.183.104, 64.233.183.147, ...
Connecting to www.google.com|64.233.183.103|:80... connected.
HTTP request sent, awaiting response... 403 Forbidden
15:41:44 ERROR 403: Forbidden.
```

The output of this command is the first indication that Google is not too keen on automated processes. What went wrong here? HTTP requests have a field called "*User-Agent*" in the header. This field is populated by applications that request Web pages (typically browsers, but also "grabbers" like *wget*), and is used to identify the browser or program. The HTTP header that *wget* generates looks like this:

```
GET /search?hl=en&q=test HTTP/1.0
User-Agent: Wget/1.10.1
Accept: */*
Host: www.google.com
Connection: Keep-Alive
```

You can see that the *User-Agent* is populated with *Wget/1.10.1*. And that's the problem. Google inspects this field in the header and decides that you are using a tool that can be used for automation. Google does not like automating search queries and returns HTTP error code 403, Forbidden. Luckily this is not the end of the world. Because *wget* is a flexible program, you can set how it should report itself in the *User Agent* field. So, all we need to do is tell *wget* to report itself as something different than *wget*. This is done easily with an additional switch. Let's see what the header looks like when we tell *wget* to report itself as "*my_diesel_driven_browser*." We issue the command as follows:

```
$ wget -U my_diesel_drive_browser "http://www.google.com/search?hl=en&q=test" -O
output
```

The resultant HTTP request header looks like this:

```
GET /search?hl=en&q=test HTTP/1.0
User-Agent: my_diesel_drive_browser
Accept: */*
Host: www.google.com
Connection: Keep-Alive
```

Note the changed *User-Agent*. Now the output of the command looks like this:

```
--15:48:55--  http://www.google.com/search?hl=en&q=test
          => `output'
Resolving www.google.com... 64.233.183.147, 64.233.183.99, 64.233.183.103, ...
Connecting to www.google.com|64.233.183.147|:80... connected.
HTTP request sent, awaiting response... 200 OK
Length: unspecified [text/html]

    [   <=>                                ] 17,913        37.65K/s

15:48:56 (37.63 KB/s) - `output' saved [17913]
```

The HTML for the query is located in the file called *'output'*. This example illustrates a very important concept—changing the *User-Agent*. Google has a large list of User-Agents that are not allowed.

Another popular program for automating Web requests is called "*curl*," which is available for Windows at http://fileforum.betanews.com/detail/cURL_for_Windows/966899018/1. For Secure Sockets Layer (SSL) use, you may need to obtain the file *libssl32.dll* from somewhere else. Google for *libssl32.dll download*. Keep the EXE and the DLL in the same directory. As with *wget*, you will need to set the *User-Agent* to be able to use it. The default behavior of *curl* is to return the HTML from the query straight to standard output. The following is an example of using *curl* with an alternative *User-Agent* to return the HTML from a simple query. The command is as follows:

```
$ curl -A zoemzoemspecial "http://www.google.com/search?hl=en&q=test"
```

The output of the command is the raw HTML response. Note the changed *User-Agent*.

Google also uses the user agent of the Lynx text-based browser, which tries to render the HTML, leaving you without having to struggle through the HTML. This is useful for quick hacks like getting the amount of results for a query. Consider the following command:

```
$ lynx -dump "http://www.google.com/search?q=google" | grep Results | awk -F "of
about" '{print $2}' | awk '{print $1}'
1,020,000,000
```

Clearly, using UNIX commands like *sed*, *grep*, *awk*, and so on makes using Lynx with the dump parameter a logical choice in tight spots.

There are many other command line tools that can be used to make requests to Web servers. It is beyond the scope of this chapter to list all of the different tools. In most cases, you will need to change the *User-Agent* to be able to speak to Google. You can also use your favorite programming language to build the request yourself and connect to Google using sockets.

Scraping it Yourself – The Butcher Shop

In the previous section, we learned how to Google a question and how to get HTML back from the server. While this is mildly interesting, it's not really that useful if we only end up with a heap of HTML. In order to make sense of the HTML, we need to be able to get individual results. In any scraping effort, this is the messy part of the mission. The first step of parsing results is to see if there is a structure to the results coming back. If there is a structure, we can unpack the data from the structure into individual results.

The FireBug extension from FireFox (https://addons.mozilla.org/en-US/firefox/addon/1843) can be used to easily map HTML code to visual structures. Viewing a Google results page in FireFox and inspecting a part of the results in FireBug looks like Figure 5.9:

Figure 5.9 Inspecting a Google Search Results with FireBug

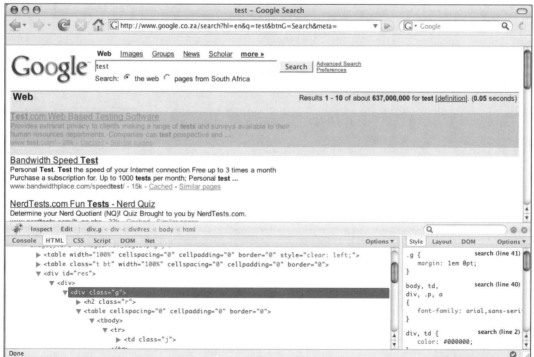

With FireBug, every result snippet starts with the HTML code *<div class="g">*. With this in mind, we can start with a very simple PERL script that will only extract the first of the snippets. Consider the following code:

```perl
1 #!/bin/perl
2 use strict;
3 my $result=`curl -A moo "http://www.google.co.za/search?q=test&hl=en"`;
4 my $start=index($result,"<div class=g>");
5 my $end=index($result,"<div class=g",$start+1);
6 my $snippet=substr($result,$start,$end-$start);
7 print "\n\n".$snippet."\n\n";
```

In the third line of the script, we externally call *curl* to get the result of a simple request into the *$result* variable (the question/query is *test* and we get the first 10 results). In line 4, we create a scalar (*$start*) that contains the position of the first occurrence of the "*<div class=g>*" token. In Line 5, we look at the next occurrence of the token, the end of the snippet (which is also the beginning of the second snippet), and we assign the position to *$end*. In line 6, we literally cut the first snippet from the entire HTML block, and in line 7 we display it. Let's see if this works:

```
$ perl easy.pl
  % Total    % Received % Xferd  Average Speed   Time    Time     Time  Current
                                 Dload  Upload   Total   Spent    Left  Speed
100 14367    0 14367    0     0  13141      0 --:--:--  0:00:01 --:--:-- 54754
```

```
<div class=g><a href="http://www.test.com/" class=l><b>Test</b>.com Web Based
Testing Software</a><table border=0 cellpadding=0 cellspacing=0><tr><td
class="j"><font size=-1>Provides extranet privacy to clients making a range of
<b>tests</b> and surveys available to their human resources departments. Companies
can <b>test</b> prospective and <b>...</b><br><span class=a>www.<b>test</b>.com/ -
28k - </span><nobr><a class=fl
href="http://64.233.183.104/search?q=cache:S9XHtkEncW8J:www.test.com/+test&hl=en&ct
=clnk&cd=1&gl=za&ie=UTF-8">Cached</a> - <a class=fl href="/search?hl=en&ie=UTF-
8&q=related:www.test.com/">Similar pages</a></nobr></font></td></tr></table></div>
```

It looks right when we compare it to what the browser says. The script now needs to somehow work through the entire HTML and extract all of the snippets. Consider the following PERL script:

```perl
1 #!/bin/perl
2 use strict;
3 my $result=`curl -A moo "http://www.google.com/search?q=test&hl=en"`;
4
5 my $start;
```

```
6 my $end;
7 my $token="<div class=g>";
8
9  while (1){
10  $start=index($result,$token,$start);
11  $end=index($result,$token,$start+1);
12  if ($start == -1 || $end == -1 || $start == $end){
13    last;
14  }
15
16  my $snippet=substr($result,$start,$end-$start);
17  print "\n-----\n".$snippet."\n----\n";
18  $start=$end;
19 }
```

While this script is a little more complex, it's still really simple. In this script we've put the "*<div class=g>*" string into a token, because we are going to use it more than once. This also makes it easy to change when Google decides to call it something else. In lines 9 through 19, a loop is constructed that will continue to look for the existence of the token until it is not found anymore. If it does not find a token (line 12), then the loop simply exists. In line 18, we move the position from where we are starting our search (for the token) to the position where we ended up in our previous search.

Running this script results in the different HTML snippets being sent to standard output. But this is only so useful. What we really want is to extract the URL, the title, and the summary from the snippet. For this we need a function that will accept four parameters: a string that contains a starting token, a string that contains the ending token, a scalar that will say where to search from, and a string that contains the HTML that we want to search within. We want this function to return the section that was extracted, as well as the new position where we are within the passed string. Such a function looks like this:

```
1 sub cutter{
2    my ($starttok,$endtok,$where,$str)=@_;
3    my $startcut=index($str,$starttok,$where)+length($starttok);
4    my $endcut=index($str,$endtok,$startcut+1);
5    my $returner=substr($str,$startcut,$endcut-$startcut);
6    my @res;
7    push @res,$endcut;
8   push @res,$returner;
9   return @res;
10 }
```

Now that we have this function, we can inspect the HTML and decide how to extract the URL, the summary, and the title from each snippet. The code to do this needs to be located within the main loop and looks as follows:

```
1   my ($pos,$url) = cutter("<a href=\"","\"",0,$snippet);
2   my ($pos,$heading) = cutter(">","</a>",$pos,$snippet);
3   my ($pos,$summary) = cutter("<font size=-1>","<br>",$pos,$snippet);
```

Notice how the URL is the first thing we encounter in the snippet. The URL itself is a hyper link and always start with "*<a href=* and ends with a quote. Next up is the heading, which is within the hyper link and as such starts with a ">" and ends with "*</a>*". Finally, it appears that the summary is always in a "*<font size=-1>*" and ends in a "*
*". Putting it all together we get the following PERL script:

```perl
#!/bin/perl
use strict;
my $result=`curl -A moo "http://www.google.com/search?q=test&hl=en"`;

my $start;
my $end;
my $token="<div class=g>";

while (1){
  $start=index($result,$token,$start);
  $end=index($result,$token,$start+1);
  if ($start == -1 || $end == -1 || $start == $end){
    last;
  }

  my $snippet=substr($result,$start,$end-$start);
  my ($pos,$url) = cutter("<a href=\"","\"",0,$snippet);
  my ($pos,$heading) = cutter(">","</a>",$pos,$snippet);
  my ($pos,$summary) = cutter("<font size=-1>","<br>",$pos,$snippet);

  # remove <b> and </b>
  $heading=cleanB($heading);
  $url=cleanB($url);
  $summary=cleanB($summary);

  print "--->\nURL: $url\nHeading: $heading\nSummary:$summary\n<---\n\n";
  $start=$end;
}
```

```perl
sub cutter{
  my ($starttok,$endtok,$where,$str)=@_;
  my $startcut=index($str,$starttok,$where)+length($starttok);
  my $endcut=index($str,$endtok,$startcut+1);
  my $returner=substr($str,$startcut,$endcut-$startcut);
  my @res;
  push @res,$endcut;
  push @res,$returner;
  return @res;
}

sub cleanB{
  my ($str)=@_;
  $str=~s/<b>//g;
  $str=~s/<\/b>//g;
  return $str;
}
```

Note that Google highlights the search term in the results. We therefore take the ** and ** tags out of the results, which is done in the "*cleanB*" subroutine. Let's see how this script works (see Figure 5.10).

Figure 5.10 The PERL Scraper in Action

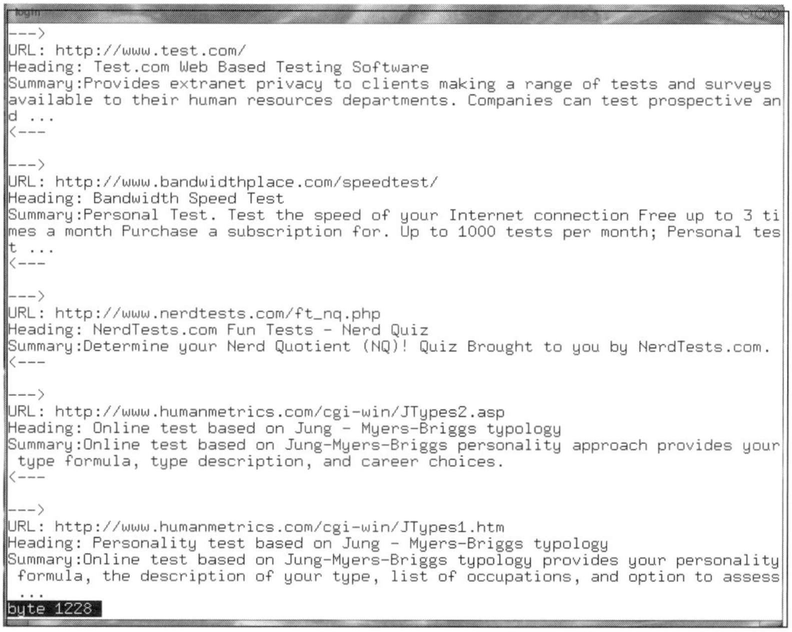

```
--->
URL: http://www.test.com/
Heading: Test.com Web Based Testing Software
Summary:Provides extranet privacy to clients making a range of tests and surveys
available to their human resources departments. Companies can test prospective an
d ...
<---

--->
URL: http://www.bandwidthplace.com/speedtest/
Heading: Bandwidth Speed Test
Summary:Personal Test. Test the speed of your Internet connection Free up to 3 ti
mes a month Purchase a subscription for. Up to 1000 tests per month; Personal tes
t ...
<---

--->
URL: http://www.nerdtests.com/ft_nq.php
Heading: NerdTests.com Fun Tests - Nerd Quiz
Summary:Determine your Nerd Quotient (NQ)! Quiz Brought to you by NerdTests.com.
<---

--->
URL: http://www.humanmetrics.com/cgi-win/JTypes2.asp
Heading: Online test based on Jung - Myers-Briggs typology
Summary:Online test based on Jung-Myers-Briggs personality approach provides your
 type formula, type description, and career choices.
<---

--->
URL: http://www.humanmetrics.com/cgi-win/JTypes1.htm
Heading: Personality test based on Jung - Myers-Briggs typology
Summary:Online test based on Jung-Myers-Briggs typology provides your personality
 formula, the description of your type, list of occupations, and option to assess
...
byte 1228
```

It seems to be working. There could well be better ways of doing this with tweaking and optimization, but for a first pass it's not bad.

Dapper

While manual scraping is the most flexible way of getting results, it also seems like a lot of hard, messy work. Surely there must be an easier way. The Dapper site (www.dapper.net) allows users to create what they call *Dapps*. These Dapps are small "programs" that will scrape information from any site and transform the scraped data into almost any format (e.g., XML, CSV, RSS, and so on). What's nice about Dapper is that programming the Dapp is facilitated via a visual interface. While Dapper works fine for scraping a myriad of sites, it does not work the way we expected for Google searches. Dapps created by other people also appear to return inconsistent results. Dapper shows lots of promise and should be investigated. (See Figure 5.11.)

Figure 5.11 Struggling with Dapper

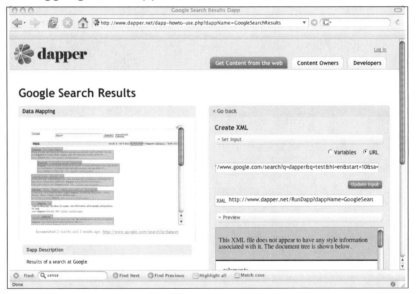

Aura/EvilAPI

Google used to provide an API that would allow you to programmatically speak to the Google engine. First, you would sign up to the service and receive a key. You could pass the key along with other parameters to a Web service, and the Web service would return the data nicely packed in eXtensible Markup Language (XML) structures. The standard key could be used for up to 1,000 searches a day. Many tools used this API, and some still do. This used to work really great, however, since December 5, 2006, Google no longer issues new API keys. The older keys still work, and the API is still there (who knows for how long) but new users will not be able to access it. Google now provides an AJAX interface which is really interesting, but does not allow for automation from scripts or applications (and it has some key features missing). But not all is lost.

The need for an API replacement is clear. An application that intercepts Google API calls and returns Simple Object Access Protocol (SOAP) XML would be great—applications that rely on the API could still be used, without needing to be changed in any way. As far as the application would be concerned, it would appear that nothing has changed on Google's end. Thankfully, there are two applications that do exactly this: Aura from SensePost and EvilAPI from Sitening.

EvilAPI (http://sitening.com/evilapi/h) installs as a PERL script on your Web server. The *GoogleSearch.wsdl* file that defines what functionality the Web service provides (and where to find it) must then be modified to point to your Web server.

After battling to get the PERL script working on the Web server (think two different versions of PERL), Sitening provides a test gateway where you can test your API scripts. After again modifying the WSDL file to point to their site and firing up the example script, Sitening still seems not to work. The word on the street is that their gateway is "mostly down" because "Google is constantly blacklisting them." The PERL-based scraping code is so similar to the PERL code listed earlier in this chapter, that it almost seems easier to scrape yourself than to bother getting all this running. Still, if you have a lot of Google API-reliant legacy code, you may want to investigate Sitening.

SensePost's Aura (www.sensepost.com/research/aura) is another proxy that performs the same functionality. At the moment it is running only on Windows (coded in .NET), but sources inside SensePost say that a Java version is going to be released soon. The proxy works by making a change in your host table so that *api.google.com* points to the local machine. Requests made to the Web service are then intercepted and the proxy does the scraping for you. Aura currently binds to localhost (in other words, it does not allow external connections), but it's believed that the Java version will allow external connections. Trying the example code via Aura did not work on Windows, and also did not work via a relayed connection from a UNIX machine. At this stage, the integrity of the example code was questioned. But when it was tested with an old API key, it worked just fine. As a last resort, the Googler section of Wikto was tested via Aura, and thankfully that combination worked like a charm.

The bottom line with the API clones is that they work really well when used as intended, but home brewed scripts will require some care and feeding. Be careful not to spend too much time getting the clone to work, when you could be scraping the site yourself with a lot less effort. Manual scraping is also extremely flexible.

Using Other Search Engines

Believe it or not, there are search engines other than Google! The MSN search engine still supports an API and is worth looking into. But this book is not called MSN Hacking for

Penetration Testers, so figuring out how to use the MSN API is left as an exercise for the reader.

Parsing the Data

Let's assume at this stage that everything is in place to connect to our data source (Google in this case), we are asking the right questions, and we have something that will give us results in neat plain text. For now, we are not going to worry how exactly that happens. It might be with a proxy API, scraping it yourself, or getting it from some provider. This section only deals with what you can do with the returned data.

To get into the right mindset, ask yourself what you as a human would do with the results. You may scan it for e-mail addresses, Web sites, domains, telephone numbers, places, names, and surnames. As a human you are also able to put some context into the results. The idea here is that we put some of that human logic into a program. Again, computers are good at doing things over and over, without getting tired or bored, or demanding a raise. And as soon as we have the logic sorted out, we can add other interesting things like counting how many of each result we get, determining how much confidence we have in the results from a question, and how close the returned data is to the original question. But this is discussed in detail later on. For now let's concentrate on getting the basics right.

Parsing E-mail Addresses

There are many ways of parsing e-mail addresses from plain text, and most of them rely on regular expressions. Regular expressions are like your quirky uncle that you'd rather not talk to, but the more you get to know him, the more interesting and cool he gets. If you are afraid of regular expressions you are not alone, but knowing a little bit about it can make your life a lot easier. If you are a regular expressions guru, you might be able to build a one-liner regex to effectively parse e-mail addresses from plain text, but since I only know enough to make myself dangerous, we'll take it easy and only use basic examples. Let's look at how we can use it in a PERL program.

```
use strict;
my $to_parse="This is a test for roelof\@home.paterva.com - yeah right blah";
my @words;
#convert to lower case
$to_parse =~ tr/A-Z/a-z/;

#cut at word boundaries
push @words,split(/ /,$to_parse);

foreach my $word (@words){
    if ($word =~ /[a-z0-9._%+-]+@[a-z0-9.-]+\.[a-z]{2,4}/) {
```

```
       print $word."\n";
  }
}
```

This seems to work, but in the real world there are some problems. The script cuts the text into words based on spaces between words. But what if the text was "*Is your address roelof@paterva.com?*" Now the script fails. If we convert the @ sign, underscores (_), and dashes (-) to letter tokens, and then remove all symbols and convert the letter tokens back to their original values, it could work. Let's see:

```
use strict;
my $to_parse="Hey !! Is this a test for roelof-temmingh\@home.paterva.com? Right
!";
my @words;

print "Before: $to_parse\n";
#convert to lower case
$to_parse =~ tr/A-Z/a-z/;

#convert 'special' chars to tokens
$to_parse=convert_xtoX($to_parse);
#blot all symbols
$to_parse=~s/\W/ /g;
#convert back
$to_parse=convert_Xtox($to_parse);
print "After: $to_parse\n";

#cut at word boundaries
push @words,split(/ /,$to_parse);

print "\nParsed email addresses follows:\n";
foreach my $word (@words){
  if ($word =~ /[a-z0-9._%+-]+@[a-z0-9.-]+\.[a-z]{2,4}/) {
    print $word."\n";
  }
}

sub convert_xtoX {
  my ($work)=@_;
  $work =~ s/\@/AT/g;    $work =~ s/\./DOT/g;
  $work =~ s/_/UNSC/g;   $work =~ s/-/DASH/g;
  return $work;
```

```
}

sub convert_Xtox{
   my ($work)=@_;
   $work =~ s/AT/\@/g;    $work =~ s/DOT/\./g;
   $work =~ s/UNSC/_/g;   $work =~ s/DASH/-/g;
   return $work;
}
```

```
Right - let's see how this works.
```

```
$ perl parse-email-2.pl
Before: Hey !! Is this a test for roelof-temmingh@home.paterva.com? Right !
After: hey    is this a test for roelof-temmingh@home.paterva.com   right
```

```
Parsed email addresses follows:
roelof-temmingh@home.paterva.com
```

It seems to work, but still there are situations where this is going to fail. What if the line reads "*My e-mail address is roelof@paterva.com.*"? Notice the period after the e-mail address? The parsed address is going to retain that period. Luckily that can be fixed with a simple replacement rule; changing a dot space sequence to two spaces. In PERL:

```
$to_parse =~ s/\. /  /g;
```

With this in place, we now have something that will effectively parse 99 percent of valid e-mail addresses (and about 5 percent of invalid addresses). Admittedly the script is not the most elegant, optimized, and pleasing, but it works!

Remember the expansions we did on e-mail addresses in the previous section? We now need to do the exact opposite. In other words, if we find the text "*andrew at syngress.com*" we need to know that it's actually an e-mail address. This has the disadvantage that we will create false positives. Think about a piece of text that says "*you can contact us at paterva.com.*" If we convert *at* back to @, we'll parse an e-mail that reads *us@paterva.com*. But perhaps the pros outweigh the cons, and as a general rule you'll catch more real e-mail addresses than false ones. (This depends on the domain as well. If the domain belongs to a company that normally adds a *.com* to their name, for example *amazon.com*, chances are you'll get false positives before you get something meaningful). We furthermore want to catch addresses that include the *_remove_* or *removethis* tokens.

To do this in PERL is a breeze. We only need to add these translations in front of the parsing routines. Let's look at how this would be done:

```
sub expand_ats{
   my ($work)=@_;
```

```
$work=~s/remove//g;
$work=~s/removethis//g;
$work=~s/_remove_//g;
$work=~s/\(remove\)//g;
$work=~s/_removethis_//g;
$work=~s/\s*(\@)\s*/\@/g;
$work=~s/\s+at\s+/\@/g;
$work=~s/\s*\(at\)\s*/\@/g;
$work=~s/\s*\[at\]\s*/\@/g;
$work=~s/\s*\.at\.\s*/\@/g;
$work=~s/\s*_at_\s*/\@/g;
$work=~s/\s*\@\s*/\@/g;
$work=~s/\s*dot\s*/\./g;
$work=~s/\s*\[dot\]\s*/\./g;
$work=~s/\s*\(dot\)\s*/\./g;
$work=~s/\s*_dot_\s*/\./g;
$work=~s/\s*\.\s*/\./g;
return $work;
}
```

These replacements are bound to catch lots of e-mail addresses, but could also be prone to false positives. Let's give it a run and see how it works with some test data:

```
$ perl parse-email-3.pl
Before: Testing test1 at paterva.com
This is normal text. For a dot matrix printer.
This is normal text...no really it is!
At work we all need to work hard
 test2@paterva dot com
 test3 _at_ paterva dot com
 test4(remove) (at) paterva [dot] com
 roelof  @  paterva  .  com
 I want to stay at home. Really I do.
```

After: testing *test1@paterva.com* this is normal text.for a.matrix printer.this is normal text...no really it is @work we all need to work hard test2@paterva.com test3 @paterva.com test4 @paterva . com roelof@paterva.com i want to stay@home.really i do.

```
Parsed email addresses follows:
test1@paterva.com
test2@paterva.com
test3@paterva.com
```

```
roelof@paterva.com
stay@home.really
```

For the test run, you can see that it caught four of the five test e-mail addresses and included one false positive. Depending on the application, this rate of false positives might be acceptable because they are quickly spotted using visual inspection. Again, the 80/20 principle applies here; with 20 percent effort you will catch 80 percent of e-mail addresses. If you are willing to do some post processing, you might want to check if the e-mail addresses you've mined ends in any of the known TLDs (see next section). But, as a rule, if you want to catch all e-mail addresses (in all of the obscured formats), you can be sure to either spend a lot of effort or deal with plenty of false positives.

Domains and Sub-domains

Luckily, domains and sub-domains are easier to parse if you are willing to make some assumptions. What is the difference between a host name and a domain name? How do you tell the two apart? Seems like a silly question. Clearly *www.paterva.com* is a host name and *paterva.com* is a domain, because *www.paterva.com* has an IP address and *paterva.com* does not. But the domain *google.com* (and many others) resolve to an IP address as well. Then again, you know that *google.com* is a domain. What if we get a Google hit from *fpd.gsfc.* ∗∗∗∗ *.gov*? Is it a hostname or a domain? Or a CNAME for something else? Instinctively you would add *www.* to the name and see if it resolves to an IP address. If it does then it's a domain. But what if there is no *www* entry in the zone? Then what's the answer?

A domain needs a name server entry in its zone. A host name does not have to have a name server entry, in fact it very seldom does. If we make this assumption, we can make the distinction between a domain and a host. The rest seems easy. We simply cut our Google URL field into pieces at the dots and put it back together. Let's take the site *fpd.gsfc.* ∗∗∗∗ *.gov* as an example. The first thing we do is figure out if it's a domain or a site by checking for a name server. It does not have a name server, so we can safely ignore the *fpd* part, and end up with *gsfc.* ∗∗∗∗ *.gov*. From there we get the domains:

- *gsfc.* ∗∗∗∗ *.gov* ∗∗∗∗ *.gov*
- *gov*

There is one more thing we'd like to do. Typically we are not interested in TLDs or even sub-TLDs. If you want to you can easily filter these out (a list of TLDs and sub-TLDs are at www.neuhaus.com/domaincheck/domain_list.htm). There is another interesting thing we can do when looking for domains. We can recursively call our script with any new information that we've found. The input for our domain hunting script is typically going to be a domain, right? If we feed the domain ∗∗∗∗ *.gov* to our script, we are limited to 1,000 results. If our script digs up the domain *gsfc.* ∗∗∗∗ *.gov*, we can now feed it back into the same script, allowing for 1,000 fresh results on this sub-domain (which might give us deeper sub-domains). Finally, we can have our script terminate when no new sub-domains are found.

Another sure fire way of obtaining domains without having to perform the host/domain check is to post process-mined e-mail addresses. As almost all e-mail addresses are already at a domain (and not a host), the e-mail address can simply be cut after the @ sign and used in a similar fashion.

Telephone Numbers

Telephone numbers are very hard to parse with an acceptable rate of false positives (unless you limit it to a specific country). This is because there is no standard way of writing down a telephone number. Some people add the country code, but on regional sites (or mailing lists) it's seldom done. And even if the country code is added, it could be added by using a plus sign (e.g. +44) or using the local international dialing method (e.g., 0044). It gets worse. In most cases, if the city code starts with a zero, it is omitted if the internal dialing code is added (e.g., +27 12 555 1234 versus 012 555 1234). And then some people put the zero in parentheses to show it's not needed when dialing from abroad (e.g., +27 (0)12 555 1234). To make matters worse, a lot of European nations like to split the last four digits in groups of two (e.g., 012 12 555 12 34). Of course, there are those people that remember numbers in certain patterns, thereby breaking all formats and making it almost impossible to determine which part is the country code (if at all), the city, and the area within the city (e.g., +271 25 551 234).

Then as an added bonus, dates can look a lot like telephone numbers. Consider the text "*From 1823-1825 1520 people couldn't parse telephone numbers.*" Better still are time frames such as "*Andrew Williams: 1971-04-01 – 2007-07-07.*" And, while it's not that difficult for a human to spot a false positive when dealing with e-mail addresses, you need to be a local to tell the telephone number of a plumber in Burundi from the ISBN number of "Stealing the network." So, is all lost? Not quite. There are two solutions: the hard but cheap solution and the easy but costly solution. In the hard but cheap solution, we will apply all of the logic we can think of to telephone numbers and live with the false positives. In the easy (OK, it's not even that easy) solution, we'll buy a list of country, city, and regional codes from a provider. Let's look at the hard solution first.

One of the most powerful principles of automation is that if you can figure out how to do something as a human being, you can code it. It is when you cannot write down what you are doing when automation fails. If we can code all the things we know about telephone numbers into an algorithm, we have a shot at getting it right. The following are some of the important rules that I have used to determine if something is a real telephone number.

- Convert *00* to +, but only if the number starts with it.
- Remove instances of *(0)*.

- Length must be between 9 and 13 numbers.

- Has to contain at least one space (optional for low tolerance).

- Cannot contain two (or more) single digits (e.g., 2383 5 3 231 will be thrown out).

- Should not look like a date (various formats).

- Cannot have a plus sign if it's not at the beginning of the number.

- Less than four numbers before the first space (unless it starts with a + or a *0*).

- Should not have the string "ISBN" in near proximity.

- Rework the number from the last number to the first number and put it in *+XX-XXX-XXX-XXXX* format.

To find numbers that need to comply to these rules is not easy. I ended up not using regular expressions but rather a nested loop, which counts the number of digits and accepted symbols (pluses, dashes, and spaces) in a sequence. Once it's reached a certain number of acceptable characters followed by a number of unacceptable symbols, the result is sent to the verifier (that use the rules listed above). If verified, it is repackaged to try to get in the right format.

Of course this method does not always work. In fact, approximately one in five numbers are false positives. But the technique seldom fails to spot a real telephone number, and more importantly, it does not cost anything.

There are better ways to do this. If we have a list of all country and city codes we should be able to figure out the format as well as verify if a sequence of numbers is indeed a telephone number. Such a list exists but is not in the public domain. Figure 5.12 is a screen shot of the sample database (in CSV):

Figure 5.12 Telephone City and Area Code Sample

Not only did we get the number, we also got the country, provider, if it is a mobile or geographical number, and the city name. The numbers in Figure 5.12 are from Spain and go six digits deep. We now need to see which number in the list is the closest match for the number that we parsed. Because I don't have the complete database, I don't have code for this, but suspect that you will need to write a program that will measure the distance between the first couple of numbers from the parsed number to those in the list. You will surely end up in a situation where there is more than one possibility. This will happen because the same number might exist in multiple countries and if they are specified on the Web page without a country code it's impossible to determine in which country they are located.

The database can be bought at www.numberingplans.com, but they are rather strict about selling the database to just anyone. They also provide a nifty lookup interface (limited to just a couple of lookups a day), which is not just for phone numbers. But that's a story for another day.

Post Processing

Even when we get good data back from our data source there might be the need to do some form of post processing on it. Perhaps you want to count how many of each result you mined in order to sort it by frequency. In the next section we look at some things that you should consider doing.

Sorting Results by Relevance

If we parse an e-mail address when we search for "Andrew Williams," that e-mail address would almost certainly be more interesting than the e-mail addresses we would get when searching for "A Williams." Indeed, some of the expansions we've done in the previous section borders on desperation. Thus, what we need is a method of implementing a "confidence" to a search. This is actually not that difficult. Simply assign this confidence index to every result you parse.

There are other ways of getting the most relevant result to bubble to the top of a result list. Another way is simply to look at the frequency of a result. If you parse the e-mail address *andrew@syngress.com* ten times more than any other e-mail address, the chances are that that e-mail address is more relevant than an e-mail address that only appears twice.

Yet another way is to look at how the result correlates back to the original search term. The result *andrew@syngress.com* looks a lot like the e-mail address for Andrew Williams. It is not difficult to write an algorithm for this type of correlation. An example of such a correlation routine looks like this:

```
sub correlate{
  my ($org,$test)=@_;
  print " [$org] to [$test] : ";
  my $tester;  my $beingtest;
  my $multi=1;
```

```
#determine which is the longer string
if (length($org) > length($test)){
  $tester=$org;    $beingtest=$test;
} else {
  $tester=$test;    $beingtest=$org;
}
#loop for every 3 letters
for (my $index=0; $index<=length($tester)-3; $index++){
  my $threeletters=substr($tester,$index,3);
  if ($beingtest =~ /$threeletters/i){
    $multi=$multi*2;
  }
}
print "$multi\n";
return $multi;
}
```

This routine breaks the longer of the two strings into sections of three letters and compares these sections to the other (shorter) string. For every section that matches, the resultant return value is doubled. This is by no means a "standard" correlation function, but will do the trick, because basically all we need is something that will recognize parts of an e-mail address as looking similar to the first name or the last name. Let's give it a quick spin and see how it works. Here we will "weigh" the results of the following e-mail addresses to an original search of "Roelof Temmingh":

```
[Roelof Temmingh] to [roelof.temmingh@abc.co.za] : 8192
[Roelof Temmingh] to [rtemmingh@abc.co.za] : 64
[Roelof Temmingh] to [roeloft@abc.co.za] : 16
[Roelof Temmingh] to [TemmiRoe882@abc.co.za] : 16
[Roelof Temmingh] to [kosie@temmingh.org] : 64
[Roelof Temmingh] to [kosie.kramer@yahoo.com] : 1
[Roelof Temmingh] to [Tempest@yahoo.com] : 2
```

This seems to work, scoring the first address as the best, and the two addresses containing the entire last name as a distant second. What's interesting is to see that the algorithm does not know what is the user name and what is a domain. This is something that you might want to change by simply cutting the e-mail address at the @ sign and only comparing the first part. On the other hand, it might be interesting to see domains that look like the first name or last name.

There are two more ways of weighing a result. The first is by looking at the distance between the original search term and the parsed result on the resultant page. In other words, if the e-mail address appears right next to the term that you searched for, the chances are more likely that it's more relevant than when the e-mail address is 20 paragraphs away from the search term. The second is by looking at the importance (or popularity) of the site that gives the result. This means that results coming from a site that is more popular is more relevant than results coming from sites that only appear on page five of the Google results. Luckily by just looking at Google results, we can easily implement both of these requirements. A Google snippet only contains the text surrounding the term that we searched for, so we are guaranteed some proximity (unless the parsed result is separated from the parsed results by "..."). The importance or popularity of the site can be obtained by the Pagerank of the site. By assigning a value to the site based on the position in the results (e.g., if the site appears first in the results or only much later) we can get a fairly good approximation of the importance of the site.

A note of caution here. These different factors need to be carefully balanced. Things can go wrong really quickly. Imagine that Andrew's e-mail address is whipmaster@midgets.com, and that he always uses the alias "*WhipMaster*" when posting from this e-mail address. As a start, our correlation to the original term (assuming we searched for *Andrew Williams*) is not going to result in a null value. And if the e-mail address does not appear many times in different places, it will also throw the algorithm off the trail. As such, we may choose to only increase the index by 10 percent for every three-letter word that matches, as the code stands a 100 percent increase if used. But that's the nature of automation, and the reason why these types of tools ultimately assist but do not replace humans.

Beyond Snippets

There is another type of post processing we can do, but it involves lots of bandwidth and loads of processing power. If we expand our mining efforts to the actual page that is returned (i.e., not just the snippet) we might get many more results and be able to do some other interesting things. The idea here is to get the URL from the Google result, download the entire page, convert it to plain text (as best as we can), and perform our mining algorithms on the text. In some cases, this expansion would be worth the effort (imagine looking for e-mail addresses and finding a page that contains a list of employees and their e-mail addresses. What a gold mine!). It also allows for parsing words and phrases, something that has a lot less value when only looking at snippets.

Parsing and sorting words or phrases from entire pages is best left to the experts (think the PhDs at Google), but nobody says that we can't try our hand at some very elementary processing. As a start we will look at the frequency of words across all pages. We'll end up with common words right at the top (e.g., *the*, *and*, and *friends*). We can filter these words using one of the many lists that provides the top ten words in a specific language. The resultant text will give us a general idea of what words are common across all the pages; in other words, an idea of "what this is about." We can extend the words to phrases by simply concatenating words together. A next step would be looking at words or phrases that are not used in high frequency in a single page, but that has a high frequency when looking across many pages. In other words, what we are looking for are words that are only used once or twice in a document (or Web page), but that are used on all the different pages. The idea here is that these words or phrases will give specific information about the subject.

Presenting Results

As many of the searches will use expansion and thus result in multiple searches, with the scraping of many Google pages we'll need to finally consolidate all of the sub-results into a single result. Typically this will be a list of results and we will need to sort the results by their relevance.

Applications of Data Mining

Mildly Amusing

Let's look at some basic mining that can be done to find e-mail addresses. Before we move to more interesting examples, let us first see if all the different scraping/parsing/weighing techniques actually work. The Web interface for Evolution at www.paterva.com basically implements all of the aforementioned techniques (and some other magic trade secrets). Let's see how Evolution actually works.

   As a start we have to decide what type of entity ("thing") we are going to look for. Assuming we are looking for Andrew Williams' e-mail address, we'll need to set the type to "*Person*" and set the function (or transform) to "*toEmailGoogle*" as we want Evolution to search for e-mail addresses for Andrew on Google. Before hitting the submit button it looks like Figure 5.13:

Figure 5.13 Evolution Ready to Go

By clicking **submit** we get the results shown in Figure 5.14.

Figure 5.14 Evolution Results page

There are a few things to notice here. The first is that Evolution is giving us the top 30 words found on resultant pages for this query. The second is that the results are sorted by their relevance index, and that moving your mouse over them gives the related snippets where it was found as well as populating the search box accordingly. And lastly, you should notice that there is no trace of Andrew's Syngress address, which only tells you that there is more than one Andrew Williams mentioned on the Internet. In order to refine the search to look for the Andrew Williams that works at Syngress, we can add an additional search term. This is done by adding another comma (,) and specifying the additional term. Thus it becomes "*Andrew, Williams, syngress*." The results look a lot more promising, as shown in Figure 5.15.

It is interesting to note that there are three different encodings of Andrew's e-mail address that were found by Evolution, all pointing to the same address (i.e., andrew@syngress.com, Andrew at Syngress dot com, and Andrew (at) Syngress.com). His alternative e-mail address at Elsevier is also found.

Figure 5.15 Getting Better Results When Adding an Additional Search Term Evolution

Let's assume we want to find lots of addresses at a certain domain such as ****.*gov*. We set the type to "*Domain*," enter the domain ****.*gov*, set the results to 100, and select the "*ToEmailAtDomain*." The resultant e-mail addresses all live at the ****.*gov* domain, as shown in Figure 5.16:

Figure 5.16 Mining E-mail Addresses with Evolution

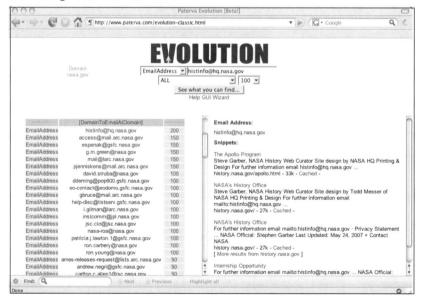

As the mouse moves over the results, the interface automatically readies itself for the next search (e.g., updating the type and value). Figure 5.16 shows the interface "pre-loaded" with the results of the previous search).

In a similar way we can use Evolution to get telephone numbers; either lots of numbers or a specific number. It all depends on how it's used.

Most Interesting

Up to now the examples used have been pretty boring. Let's spice it up somewhat by looking at one of those three letter agencies. You wouldn't think that the cloak and dagger types working at xxx.gov (our cover name for the agency) would list their e-mail addresses. Let's see what we can dig up with our tools. We will start by searching on the domain *xxx.gov* and see what telephone numbers we can parse from there. Using Evolution we supply the domain *xxx.gov* and set the transform to "*ToPhoneGoogle.*" The results do not look terribly exciting, but by looking at the area code and the city code we see a couple of numbers starting with 703 444. This is a fake extension we've used to cover up the real name of the agency, but these numbers correlate with the contact number on the real agency's Web site. This is an excellent starting point. By no means are we sure that the entire exchange belongs to them, but let's give it a shot. As such we want to search for telephone numbers starting with 703 444 and then parse e-mail addresses, telephone numbers, and site names that are connected to those numbers. The hope is that one of the cloak-and-dagger types has listed his private e-mail address with his office number. The way to go about doing this is by setting the Entity type to "*Telephone,*" entering "*+1 703 444*" (omitting the latter four digits of the phone number), setting the results to 100, and using the combo "*ToEmailPhoneSiteGoogle.*" The results look like Figure 5.17:

Figure 5.17 Transforming Telephone Numbers to E-mail Addresses Using Evolution

This is not to say that Jean Roberts is working for the xxx agency, but the telephone number listed at the Tennis Club is in close proximity to that agency.

Staying on the same theme, let's see what else we can find. We know that we can find documents at a particular domain by setting the *filetype* and *site* operators. Consider the following query, *filetype:doc site:xxx.gov* in Figure 5.18.

Figure 5.18 Searching for Documents on a Domain

While the documents listed in the results are not that exciting, the meta information within the document might be useful. The very handy *ServerSniff.net* site provides a useful page where documents can be analyzed for interesting meta data (www.serversniff.net/file-info.php). Running the *32CFR.doc* through Tom's script we get:

Figure 5.19 Getting Meta Information on a Document From ServerSniff.netWe can get a lot of information from this. The username of the original author is "Macuser" and he or she worked at Clator Butler Web Consulting, and the user "*clator*" clearly had a mapped drive that had a copy of the agency Web site on it. Had, because this was back in March 2003.

It gets really interesting once you take it one step further. After a couple of clicks on Evolution it found that Clator Butler Web Consulting is at www.clator.com, and that Mr. Clator Butler is the manager for David Wilcox's (the artist) forum. When searching for "Clator Butler" on Evolution, and setting the transform to "*ToAffLinkedIn*" we find a LinkedIn profile on Clator Butler as shown in Figure 5.20:

Figure 5.20 The LinkedIn Profile of the Author of a Government Document

Can this process of grabbing documents and analyzing them be automated? Of course! As a start we can build a scraper that will find the URLs of Office documents (*.doc*, *.ppt*, *.xls*, *.pps*). We then need to download the document and push it through the meta information parser. Finally, we can extract the interesting bits and do some post processing on it. We already have a scraper (see the previous section) and thus we just need something that will extract the meta information from the file. Thomas Springer at ServerSniff.net was kind enough to provide me with the source of his document information script. After some slight changes it looks like this:

```perl
#!/usr/bin/perl

# File-analyzer 0.1, 07/08/2007, thomas springer
# stripped-down version
# slightly modified by roelof temmingh @ paterva.com
# this code is public domain - use at own risk
# this code is using phil harveys ExifTool - THANK YOU, PHIL!!!!
# http://www.ebv4linux.de/images/articles/Phil1.jpg
```

```perl
use strict;
use Image::ExifTool;

#passed parameter is a URL
my ($url)=@ARGV;

# get file and make a nice filename
my $file=get_page($url);
my $time=time;
my $frand=rand(10000);
my $fname="/tmp/".$time.$frand;

# write stuff to a file
 open(FL, ">$fname");
 print FL $file;
 close(FL);

# Get EXIF-INFO
 my $exifTool=new Image::ExifTool;
 $exifTool->Options(FastScan => '1');
 $exifTool->Options(Binary => '1');
 $exifTool->Options(Unknown => '2');
 $exifTool->Options(IgnoreMinorErrors => '1');
 my $info = $exifTool->ImageInfo($fname); # feed standard info into a hash

# delete tempfile
unlink ("$fname");

my @names;
print "Author:".$$info{"Author"}."\n";
print "LastSaved:".$$info{"LastSavedBy"}."\n";
print "Creator:".$$info{"creator"}."\n";
print "Company:".$$info{"Company"}."\n";
print "Email:".$$info{"AuthorEmail"}."\n";

exit; #comment to see more fields

foreach (keys %$info){
    print "$_ = $$info{$_}\n";
}
```

```
sub get_page{
  my ($url)=@_;
  #use curl to get it - you might want change this
  # 25 second timeout - also modify as you see fit
  my $res=`curl -s -m 25 $url`;
  return $res;
}
```

Save this script as *docinfo.pl*. You will notice that you'll need some PERL libraries to use this, specifically the *Image::ExifTool* library, which is used to get the meta data from the files. The script uses curl to download the pages from the server, so you'll need that as well. Curl is set to a 25-second timeout. On a slow link you might want to increase that. Let's see how this script works:

```
$ perl docinfo.pl http://www.elsevier.com/framework_support/permreq.doc
Author:Catherine Nielsen
LastSaved:Administrator
Creator:
Company:Elsevier Science
Email:
```

The scripts looks for five fields in a document: *Author, LastedSavedBy, Creator, Company*, and *AuthorEmail*. There are many other fields that might be of interest (like the software used to create the document). On it's own this script is only mildly interesting, but it really starts to become powerful when combining it with a scraper and doing some post processing on the results. Let's modify the existing scraper a bit to look like this:

```
#!/usr/bin/perl
use strict;

my ($domain,$num)=@ARGV;
my @types=("doc","xls","ppt","pps");
my $result;
foreach my $type (@types){
  $result=`curl -s -A moo
"http://www.google.com/search?q=filetype:$type+site:$domain&hl=en&
num=$num&filter=0"`;
  parse($result);
}

sub parse {
  ($result)=@_;
```

```perl
my $start;
my $end;
my $token="<div class=g>";

my $count=1;
while (1){
  $start=index($result,$token,$start);
  $end=index($result,$token,$start+1);
  if ($start == -1 || $end == -1 || $start == $end){
    last;
  }

  my $snippet=substr($result,$start,$end-$start);
  my ($pos,$url) = cutter("<a href=\"","\"",0,$snippet);
  my ($pos,$heading) = cutter(">","</a>",$pos,$snippet);
  my ($pos,$summary) = cutter("<font size=-1>","<br>",$pos,$snippet);

  # remove <b> and </b>
  $heading=cleanB($heading);
  $url=cleanB($url);
  $summary=cleanB($summary);

  print $url."\n";
  $start=$end;
  $count++;
  }
}

sub cutter{
  my ($starttok,$endtok,$where,$str)=@_;
  my $startcut=index($str,$starttok,$where)+length($starttok);
  my $endcut=index($str,$endtok,$startcut+1);
  my $returner=substr($str,$startcut,$endcut-$startcut);
  my @res;
  push @res,$endcut;
  push @res,$returner;
  return @res;
}

sub cleanB{
```

```
  my ($str)=@_;
  $str=~s/<b>//g;
  $str=~s/<\/b>//g;
  return $str;
}
```

Save this script as *scraper.pl*. The scraper takes a domain and number as parameters. The number is the number of results to return, but multiple page support is not included in the code. However, it's child's play to modify the script to scrape multiple pages from Google. Note that the scraper has been modified to look for some common Microsoft Office formats and will loop through them with a *site:domain_parameter filetype:XX* search term. Now all that is needed is something that will put everything together and do some post processing on the results. The code could look like this:

```perl
#!/bin/perl
use strict;
my ($domain,$num)=@ARGV;

my %ALLEMAIL=(); my %ALLNAMES=();
my %ALLUNAME=(); my %ALLCOMP=();

my $scraper="scrape.pl";
my $docinfo="docinfo.pl";
print "Scraping...please wait...\n";
my @all_urls=`perl $scraper $domain $num`;
if ($#all_urls == -1 ){
  print "Sorry - no results!\n";
  exit;
}
my $count=0;
foreach my $url (@all_urls){
  print "$count / $#all_urls : Fetching $url";
  my @meta=`perl $docinfo $url`;
  foreach my $item (@meta){
    process($item);
  }
  $count++;
}


#show results
```

```perl
print "\nEmails:\n-------------\n";
foreach my $item (keys %ALLEMAIL){
  print "$ALLEMAIL{$item}:\t$item";
}
print "\nNames (Person):\n------------\n";
foreach my $item (keys %ALLNAMES){
  print "$ALLNAMES{$item}:\t$item";
}
print "\nUsernames:\n------------\n";
foreach my $item (keys %ALLUNAME){
  print "$ALLUNAME{$item}:\t$item";
}
print "\nCompanies:\n------------\n";
foreach my $item (keys %ALLCOMP){
  print "$ALLCOMP{$item}:\t$item";
}


sub process {
  my ($passed)=@_;
  my ($type,$value)=split(/:/,$passed);
  $value=~tr/A-Z/a-z/;
  if (length($value)<=1) {return;}
  if ($value =~ /[a-zA-Z0-9]/){
    if ($type eq "Company"){$ALLCOMP{$value}++;}
    else {
      if (index($value,"\@")>2){$ALLEMAIL{$value}++; }
      elsif (index($value," ")>0){$ALLNAMES{$value}++; }
      else{$ALLUNAME{$value}++; }
    }
  }
}
```

This script first kicks off *scraper.pl* with domain and the number of results that was passed to it as parameters. It captures the output (a list of URLs) of the process in an array, and then runs the *docinfo.pl* script against every URL. The output of this script is then sent for further processing where some basic checking is done to see if it is the company name, an e-mail address, a user name, or a person's name. These are stored in separate hash tables for later use. When everything is done, the script displays each collected piece of information and the number of times it occurred across all pages. Does it actually work? Have a look:

```
# perl combined.pl xxx.gov 10
Scraping...please wait...
0 / 35 : Fetching http://www.xxx.gov/8878main_C_PDP03.DOC
1 / 35 : Fetching http://***.xxx.gov/1329NEW.doc
2 / 35 : Fetching http://***.xxx.gov/LP_Evaluation.doc
3 / 35 : Fetching http://*******.xxx.gov/305.doc
... <cut>

Emails:
-------------
1:      ***zgpt@***.ksc.xxx.gov
1:      ***ikrb@kscems.ksc.xxx.gov
1:      ***ald.l.***mack@xxx.gov
1:      ****ie.king@****.xxx.gov

Names (Person):
-------------
1:      audrey sch***
1:      corina mo****
1:      frank ma****
2:      eileen wa****
2:      saic-odin-**** hq
1:      chris wil****
1:      nand lal****
1:      susan ho****
2:      john jaa****
1:      dr. paul a. cu****
1:      *** project/code 470
1:      bill mah****
1:      goddard, pwdo - bernadette fo****
1:      joanne wo****
2:      tom naro****
1:      lucero ja****
1:      jenny rumb****
1:      blade ru****
1:      lmit odi****
2:      **** odin/osf seat
1:      scott w. mci****
2:      philip t. me****
1:      annie ki****
```

```
Usernames:
-------------
1:        cgro****
1:        ****
1:        gidel****
1:        rdcho****
1:        fbuchan****
2:        sst****
1:        rbene****
1:        rpan****
2:        l.j.klau****
1:        gane****h
1:        amh****
1:        caroles****
2:        mic****e
1:        baltn****r
3:        pcu****
1:        md****
1:        ****wxpadmin
1:        mabis****
1:        ebo****
2:        grid****
1:        bkst****
1:        ***(at&l)


Companies:
-------------


1:        shadow conservatory
[SNIP]
```

The list of companies has been chopped way down to protect the identity of the government agency in question, but the script seems to work well. The script can easily be modified to scrape many more results (across many pages), extract more fields, and get other file types. By the way, what the heck is the one unedited company known as the "Shadow Conservatory?"

Figure 5.21 Zero Results for "Shadow Conservatory"

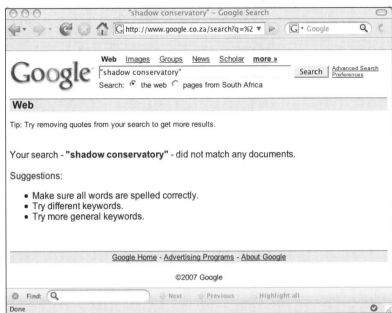

The tool also works well for finding out what (and if) a user name format is used. Consider the list of user names mined from ... somewhere:

Usernames:

```
1:      79241234
1:      78610276
1:      98229941
1:      86232477
2:      82733791
2:      02000537
1:      79704862
1:      73641355
2:      85700136
```

From the list it is clear that an eight-digit number is used as the user name. This information might be very useful in later stages of an attack.

Taking It One Step Further

Sometimes you end up in a situation where you want to hook the output of one search as the input for another process. This process might be another search, or it might be something like looking up an e-mail address on a social network, converting a DNS name to a domain, resolving a DNS name, or verifying the existence of an e-mail account. How do I link two e-mail addresses together? Consider Johnny's e-mail address *johnny@ihackstuff.com* and my previous e-mail address at SensePost *roelof@sensepost.com*. To link these two addresses together we can start by searching for one of the e-mail addresses and extracting sites, e-mail addresses, and phone numbers. Once we have these results we can do the same for the other e-mail address and then compare them to see if there are any common results (or nodes). In this case there are common nodes (see Figure 5.22).

Figure 5.22 Relating Two E-mail Addresses from Common Data Sources

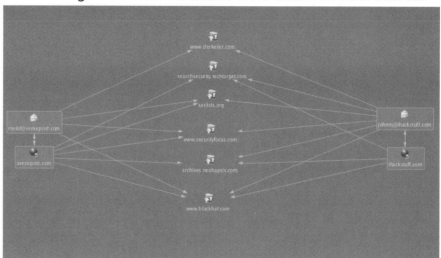

If there are no matches, we can loop through all of the results of the first e-mail address, again extracting e-mail addresses, sites, and telephone numbers, and then repeat it for the second address in the hope that there are common nodes.

What about more complex sequences that involve more than searching? Can you get locations of the Pentagon data centers by simply looking at public information? Consider Figure 5.23.

What's happening here? While it looks seriously complex, it really isn't. The procedure to get to the locations shown in this figure is as follows:

Figure 5.23 Getting Data Center Geographical Locations Using Public Information

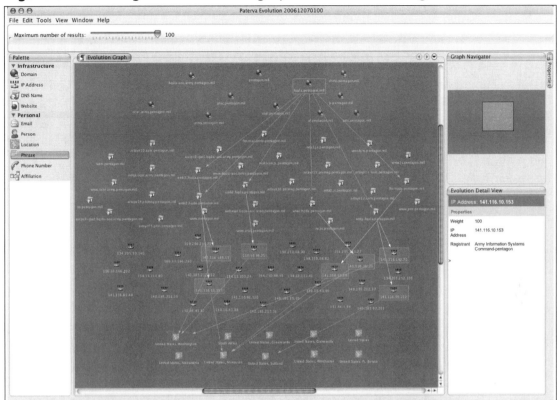

- Mine e-mail addresses at pentagon.mil (not shown on the screen shot)

- From the e-mail addresses, extract the domains (mentioned earlier in the domain and sub-domain mining section). The results are the nodes at the top of the screen shot.

- From the sub-domains, perform brute-force DNS look ups, basically looking for common DNS names. This is the second layer of nodes in the screen shot.

- Add the DNS names of the MX records for each domain.

- Once that's done resolve all of the DNS names to IP addresses. That is the third layer of nodes in the screen shot.

- From the IP addresses, get the geographical locations, which are the last layer of nodes.

There are a couple of interesting things you can see from the screen shot. The first is the location, *South Africa*, which is linked to www.pentagon.mil. This is because of the use of Akamai. The lookup goes like this:

```
$ host www.pentagon.mil
www.pentagon.mil is an alias for www.defenselink.mil.edgesuite.net.
www.defenselink.mil.edgesuite.net is an alias for a217.g.akamai.net.
a217.g.akamai.net has address 196.33.166.230
a217.g.akamai.net has address 196.33.166.232
```

As such, the application sees the location of the IP as being in South Africa, which it is. The application that shows these relations graphically (as in the screen shot above) is the Evolution Graphical User Interface (GUI) client that is also available at the Paterva Web site.

The number of applications that can be built when linking data together with searching and other means are literally endless. Want to know who in your neighborhood is on Myspace? Easy. Search for your telephone number, omit the last 4 digits (covered earlier), and extract e-mail addresses. Then feed these e-mail addresses into MySpace as a person search, and voila, you are done! You are only limited by your own imagination.

Collecting Search Terms

Google's ability to collect search terms is very powerful. If you doubt this, visit the Google ZeitGeist page. Google has the ability to know what's on the mind of just about everyone that's connected to the Internet. They can literally read the minds of the (online) human race.

If you know what people are looking for, you can provide them (i.e., sell to them) that information. In fact, you can create a crude economic model. The number of searches for a phrase is the "demand "while the number of pages containing the phrase is the "supply." The price of a piece of information is related to the demand divided by the supply. And while Google will probably (let's hope) never implement such billing, it would be interesting to see them adding this as some form of index on the results page.

Let's see what we can do to get some of that power. This section looks at ways of obtaining the search terms of other users.

On the Web

In August 2006, AOL released about 20 million search records to researchers on a Web site. Not only did the data contain the search term, but also the time of the search, the link that the user clicked on, and a number that related to the user's name. That meant that while you couldn't see the user's name or e-mail address, you could still find out exactly when and for what the user searched. The collection was done on about 658,000 users (only 1.5 percent of all searches) over a three-month period. The data quickly made the rounds on the Internet. The original source was removed within a day, but by then it was too late.

Manually searching through the data was no fun. Soon after the leak sites popped up where you could search the search terms of other people, and once you found something interesting, you could see all of the other searches that the person performed. This keyhole view on someone's private life proved very popular, and later sites were built that allowed users to list interesting searches and profile people according to their searches. This profiling led to the positive identification of at least one user. Here is an extract from an article posted on securityfocus.com:

The New York Times combed through some of the search results to discover user 4417749, whose search terms included, "homes sold in shadow lake subdivision gwinnett county georgia" along with several people with the last name of Arnold. This was enough to reveal the identity of user 4417749 as Thelma Arnold, a 62-year-old woman living in Georgia. Of the 20 million search histories posted, it is believed there are many more such cases where individuals can be identified.

…Contrary to AOL's statements about no personally-identifiable information, the real data reveals some shocking search queries. Some researchers combing through the data have claimed to have discovered over 100 social security numbers, dozens or hundreds of credit card numbers, and the full names, addresses and dates of birth of various users who entered these terms as search queries.

The site http://data.aolsearchlog.com provides an interface to all of the search terms, and also shows some of the profiles that have been collected (see Figure 5.24):

Figure 5.24 Site That Allows You to Search AOL Search Terms

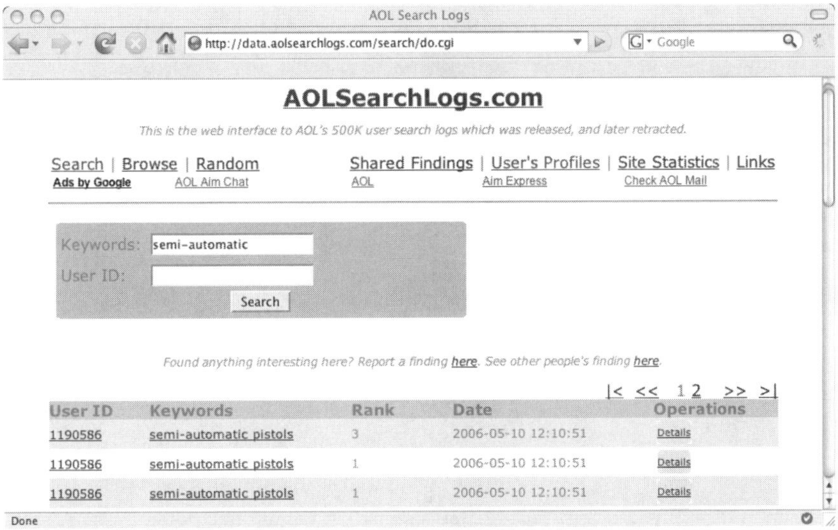

While this site could keep you busy for a couple of minutes, it contains search terms of people you don't know and the data is old and static. Is there a way to look at searches in a more real time, live way?

Spying on Your Own

Search Terms

When you search for something, the query goes to Google's computers. Every time you do a search at Google, they check to see if you are passing along a cookie. If you are not, they instruct your browser to set a cookie. The browser will be instructed to pass along that cookie for every subsequent request to any Google system (e.g., *.google.com), and to keep doing it until 2038. Thus, two searches that were done from the same laptop in two different countries, two years apart, will both still send the same cookie (given that the cookie store was never cleared), and Google will know it's coming from the same user. The query has to travel over the network, so if I can get it as it travels to them, I can read it. This technique is called "sniffing." In the previous sections, we've seen how to make a request to Google. Let's see what a cookie-less request looks like, and how Google sets the cookie:

```
$ telnet www.google.co.za 80
Trying 64.233.183.99...
Connected to www.google.com.
Escape character is '^]'.
GET / HTTP/1.0
Host: www.google.co.za

HTTP/1.0 200 OK
Date: Thu, 12 Jul 2007 08:20:24 GMT
Content-Type: text/html; charset=ISO-8859-1
Cache-Control: private
Set-Cookie:
PREF=ID=329773239358a7d2:TM=1184228424:LM=1184228424:S=MQ6vKrgT4f9up_gj;
expires=Sun, 17-Jan-2038 19:14:07 GMT; path=/; domain=.google.co.za
Server: GWS/2.1
Via: 1.1 netcachejhb-2 (NetCache NetApp/5.5R6)

<html><head>....snip...
```

Notice the *Set-Cookie* part. The ID part is the interesting part. The other cookies (*TM* and *LM*) contain the birth date of the cookie (in seconds from 1970), and when the preferences were last changed. The ID stays constant until you clear your cookie store in the browser. This means every subsequent request coming from your browser will contain the cookie.

If we have a way of reading the traffic to Google we can use the cookie to identify subsequent searches from the same browser. There are two ways to be able to see the requests going to Google. The first involves setting up a sniffer somewhere along the traffic, which will monitor requests going to Google. The second is a lot easier and involves infrastructure that is almost certainly already in place; using proxies. There are two ways that traffic can be proxied. The user can manually set a proxy in his or her browser, or it can be done transparently somewhere upstream. With a transparent proxy, the user is mostly unaware that the traffic is sent to a proxy, and it almost always happens without the user's consent or knowledge. Also, the user has no way to switch the proxy on or off. By default, all traffic going to port 80 is intercepted and sent to the proxy. In many of these installations other ports are also intercepted, typically standard proxy ports like 3128, 1080, and 8080. Thus, even if you set a proxy in your browser, the traffic is intercepted before it can reach the manually configured proxy and is sent to the transparent proxy. These transparent proxies are typically used at boundaries in a network, say at your ISP's Internet gateway or close to your company's Internet connection.

On the one hand, we have Google that is providing a nice mechanism to keep track of your search terms, and on the other hand we have these wonderful transparent devices that collect and log all of your traffic. Seems like a perfect combination for data mining.

Let's see how can we put something together that will do all of this for us. As a start we need to configure a proxy to log the entire request header and the GET parameters as well as accepting connections from a transparent network redirect. To do this you can use the popular Squid proxy with a mere three modifications to the stock standard configuration file. These three lines that you need are:

The first tells Squid to accept connections from the transparent redirect on port 3128:

```
http_port 3128 transparent
```

The second tells Squid to log the entire HTTP request header:

```
log_mime_hdrs on
```

The last line tells Squid to log the GET parameters, not just the host and path:

```
strip_query_terms off
```

With this set and the Squid proxy running, the only thing left to do is to send traffic to it. This can be done in a variety of ways and it is typically done at the firewall. Assuming you are running FreeBSD with all the kernel options set to support it (and the Squid proxy is on the same box), the following one liner will direct all outgoing traffic to port 80 into the Squid box:

```
ipfw add 10 fwd 127.0.0.1,3128 tcp from any to any 80
```

Similar configurations can be found for other operating systems and/or firewalls. Google for "transparent proxy network configuration" and choose the appropriate one. With this set we are ready to intercept all Web traffic that originates behind the firewall. While there is a lot of interesting information that can be captured from these types of Squid logs, we will focus on Google-related requests.

Once your transparent proxy is in place, you should see requests coming in. The following is a line from the proxy log after doing a simple search on the phrase "test phrase":

```
1184253638.293    752 196.xx.xx.xx TCP_MISS/200 4949 GET
http://www.google.co.za/search?hl=en&q=test+phrase&btnG=Google+Search&meta= -
DIRECT/72.14.253.147 text/html [Host: www.google.co.za\r\nUser-Agent: Mozilla/5.0
(Macintosh; U; Intel Mac OS X; en-US; rv:1.8.1.4) Gecko/20070515
Firefox/2.0.0.4\r\nAccept:
text/xml,application/xml,application/xhtml+xml,text/html;q=0.9,text/plain;q=0.8,ima
ge/png,*/*;q=0.5\r\nAccept-Language: en-us,en;q=0.5\r\nAccept-Encoding:
gzip,deflate\r\nAccept-Charset: ISO-8859-1,utf-8;q=0.7,*;q=0.7\r\nKeep-Alive:
300\r\nProxy-Connection: keep-alive\r\nReferer: http://www.google.co.za/\r\nCookie:
PREF=ID=35d1cc1c7089ceba:TM=1184106010:LM=1184106010:S=gBAPGByiXrA7ZPQN\r\n]
[HTTP/1.0 200 OK\r\nCache-Control: private\r\nContent-Type: text/html; charset=UTF-
8\r\nServer: GWS/2.1\r\nContent-Encoding: gzip\r\nDate: Thu, 12 Jul 2007 09:22:01
GMT\r\nConnection: Close\r\n\r]
```

Notice the search term appearing as the value of the "*q*" parameter "*test+phrase.*" Also notice the ID cookie which is set to "*35d1cc1c7089ceba.*" This value of the cookie will remain the same regardless of subsequent search terms. In the text above, the IP number that made the request is also listed (but mostly X-ed out). From here on it is just a question of implementation to build a system that will extract the search term, the IP address, and the cookie and shove it into a database for further analysis. A system like this will silently collect search terms day in and day out.

While at SensePost, I wrote a very simple (and unoptimized) application that will do exactly that, and called it PollyMe (www.sensepost.com/research/PollyMe.zip). The application works the same as the Web interface for the AOL searches, the difference being that you are searching logs that you've collected yourself. Just like the AOL interface, you can search the search terms, find out the cookie value of the searcher, and see all of the other searches associated with that value. As a bonus, you can also view what other sites the user visited during a time period. The application even allows you to search for terms in the visited URL.

Tools & Tips...

How to Spot a Transparent Proxy

In some cases it is useful to know if you are sitting behind a transparent proxy. There is a quick way of finding out. Telnet to port 80 on a couple of random IP addresses that are outside of your network. If you get a connection every time, you are behind a transparent proxy. (Note: try not to use private IP address ranges when conducting this test.)

Another way is looking up the address of a Web site, then Telnetting to the IP number, issuing a GET/HTTP/1.0 (without the Host: header), and looking at the response. Some proxies use the Host: header to determine where you want to connect, and without it should give you an error.

```
$ host www.paterva.com

www.paterva.com has address 64.71.152.104


$ telnet 64.71.152.104 80

Trying 64.71.152.104...

Connected to linode.

Escape character is '^]'.

GET / HTTP/1.0


HTTP/1.0 400 Bad Request

Server: squid/2.6.STABLE12
```

Not only do we know we are being transparently proxied, but we can also see the type and server of the proxy that's used. Note that the second method does not work with all proxies, especially the bigger proxies in use at many ISPs.

Gmail

Collecting search terms and profiling people based on it is interesting but can only take you so far. More interesting is what is happening inside their mail box. While this is slightly out of the scope of this book, let's look at what we can do with our proxy setup and Gmail. Before we delve into the nitty gritty, you need to understand a little bit about how (most) Web applications work. After successfully logging into Gmail, a cookie is passed to your Web browser (in the same way it is done with a normal search), which is used to identify you. If it was not for the cookie, you would have had to provide your user name and password for every page you'd navigate to, as HTTP is a stateless protocol. Thus, when you are logged into Gmail, the only thing that Google uses to identify you is your cookie. While your credentials are passed to Google over SSL, the rest of the conversation happens in the clear (unless you've forced it to SSL, which is not default behavior), meaning that your cookie travels all the way in the clear. The cookie that is used to identify me is in the clear and my entire request (including the HTTP header that contains the cookie) can be logged at a transparent proxy somewhere that I don't know about.

At this stage you may be wondering what the point of all this is. It is well known that unencrypted e-mail travels in the clear and that people upstream can read it. But there is a subtle difference. Sniffing e-mail gives you access to the e-mail itself. The Gmail cookie gives you access to the user's Gmail *application*, and the application gives you access to address books, the ability to search old incoming and outgoing mail, the ability to send e-mail as that user, access to the user's calendar, search history (if enabled), the ability to chat online to contact via built-in Gmail chat, and so on. So, yes, there is a big difference. Also, mention the word "sniffer" at an ISP and all the alarm bells go off. But asking to tweak the proxy is a different story.

Let's see how this can be done. After some experimentation it was found that the only cookie that is really needed to impersonate someone on Gmail is the "GX" cookie. So, a typical thing to do would be to transparently proxy users on the network to a proxy, wait for some Gmail traffic (a browser logged into Gmail makes frequent requests to the application and all of the requests carry the GX cookie), butcher the GX cookie, and craft the correct request to rip the user's contact list and then search his or her e-mail box for some interesting phrases.

The request for getting the address book is as follows:

```
GET /mail?view=cl&search=contacts&pnl=a HTTP/1.0
Host: mail.google.com
Cookie: GX=xxxxxxxxxx
```

The request for searching the mailbox looks like this:

```
GET /mail?view=tl&search=query&q=__stuff_to_search_for__ HTTP/1.0
Host: mail.google.com
Cookie: GX=xxxxxxxxxx
```

The GX cookie needs to be the GX that you've mined from the Squid logs. You will need to do the necessary parsing upon receiving the data, but the good stuff is all there. Automating this type of on-the-fly rip and search is trivial. In fact, a nefarious system administrator can go one step further. He or she could mine the user's address book and send e-mail to everyone in the list, then wait for them to read their e-mail, mine their GXes, and start the process again. Google will have an interesting time figuring out how an innocent looking e-mail became viral (of course it won't really be viral, but will have the same characteristics of a worm given a large enough network behind the firewall).

A Reminder...

It's Not a Google-only Thing

At this stage you might think that this is something Google needs to address. But when you think about it for a while you'll see that this is the case with all Web applications. The only real solution that they can apply is to ensure that the entire conversation is happening over SSL, which in terms of computational power is a huge overhead. Other Web mail providers suffer from exactly the same problem. The only difference is that their application does not have the same number of features as Gmail (and probably a smaller user base), making them less of a target.

A word of reassurance. Although it is possible for network administrators of ISPs to do these things, they are most likely bound by serious privacy laws. In most countries, you have do something really spectacular for law enforcement to get a lawful intercept (e.g., sniffing all your traffic and reading your e-mail). As a user, you should be aware that when you want to keep something really private, you need to properly encrypt it.

Honey Words

Imagine you are running a super secret project code name "Sookha." Nobody can ever know about this project name. If someone searches Google for the word Sookha you'd want to know without alerting the searcher of the fact that you do know. What you can do is register an Adword with the word Sookha as the keyword. The key to this is that Adwords not only tell you when someone clicks on your ad, but also tells you how many impressions were shown (translated), and how many times someone searched for that word.

So as to not alert your potential searcher, you should choose your ad in such a way as to not draw attention to it. The following screen shot (Figure 5.25) shows the set up of such an ad:

Figure 5.25 Adwords Set Up for Honey words

Once someone searches for your keyword, the ad will appear and most likely not draw any attention. But, on the management console you will be able to see that an impression was created, and with confidence you can say "I found a leak in our organization."

Figure 5.26 Adwords Control Panel Showing A Single Impression

Referrals

Another way of finding out what people are searching for is to look at the *Referer:* header of requests coming to your Web site. Of course there are limitations. The idea here being that someone searches for something on Google, your site shows up on the list of results, and they click on the link that points to your site. While this might not be super exciting for those with none or low traffic sites, it works great for people with access to very popular sites. How does it actually work? Every site that you visit knows about the previous site that you visited. This is sent in the HTTP header as a referrer. When someone visits Google, their search terms appear as part of the URL (as it's a GET request) and is passed to your site once the user arrives there. This gives you the ability to see what they searched for before they got to your site, which is very useful for marketing people.

Typically an entry in an Apache log that came from a Google search looks like this:

```
68.144.162.191 - - [10/Jul/2007:11:45:25 -0400] "GET /evolution-gui.html HTTP/1.1"
304 - "http://www.google.com/search?hl=en&q=evolution+beta+gui&btnG=Search"
"Mozilla/5.0 (Windows; U; Windows NT 5.1; en-GB; rv:1.8.1.4) Gecko/20070515
Firefox/2.0.0.4"
```

From this entry we can see that the user was searching for "*evolution beta gui*" on Google before arriving at our page, and that he or she then ended up at the "*/evolution-gui.html*" page. A lot of applications that deal with analyzing Web logs have the ability to automatically extract these terms for your logs, and present you with a nice list of terms and their frequency.

Is there a way to use this to mine search terms at will? Not likely. The best option (and it's really not that practical) is to build a popular site with various types of content and see if you can attract visitors with the only reason to mine their search terms. Again, you'll surely have better uses for these visitors than just their search terms.

Summary

In this chapter we looked at various ways that you can use Google to dig up useful information. The power of searching really comes to life when you have the ability to automate certain processes. This chapter showed how this automation can be achieved using simple scripts. Also, the fun really starts when you have the means of connecting bits of information together to form a complete picture (e.g., not just searching, but also performing additional functions with the mined information). The tools and tricks shown in the chapter is really only the top of a massive iceberg called *data collection* (or *mining*). Hopefully it will open your mind as to what can be achieved. The idea was never to completely exhaust every possible avenue in detail, but rather to get your mind going in the right direction and to stimulate creative thoughts. If the chapter has inspired you to hack together your own script to perform something amazing, it has served it's purpose (and I would love to hear from you).

## Chapter 6

Locating Exploits and Finding Targets

Solutions in this chapter:

- Locating Exploit Code
- Locating Vulnerable Targets
- Links to Sites

☑ Summary

☑ Solutions Fast Track

☑ Frequently Asked Questions

Introduction

Exploits, are tools of the hacker trade. Designed to penetrate a target, most hackers have many different exploits at their disposal. Some exploits, termed *zero day* or *0day*, remain underground for some period of time, eventually becoming public, posted to newsgroups or Web sites for the world to share. With so many Web sites dedicated to the distribution of exploit code, it's fairly simple to harness the power of Google to locate these tools. It can be a slightly more difficult exercise to locate potential targets, even though many modern Web application security advisories include a Google search designed to locate potential targets.

In this chapter we'll explore methods of locating exploit code and potentially vulnerable targets. These are not strictly "dark side" exercises, since security professionals often use public exploit code during a vulnerability assessment. However, only black hats use those tools against systems without prior consent.

Locating Exploit Code

Untold hundreds and thousands of Web sites are dedicated to providing exploits to the general public. Black hats generally provide exploits to aid fellow black hats in the hacking community. White hats provide exploits as a way of eliminating false positives from automated tools during an assessment. Simple searches such as *remote exploit* and *vulnerable exploit* locate exploit sites by focusing on common lingo used by the security community. Other searches, such as *inurl:0day,* don't work nearly as well as they used to, but old standbys like *inurl:sploits* still work fairly well. The problem is that most security folks don't just troll the Internet looking for exploit caches; most frequent a handful of sites for the more mainstream tools, venturing to a search engine only when their bookmarked sites fail them. When it comes time to troll the Web for a specific security tool, Google's a great place to turn first.

Locating Public Exploit Sites

One way to locate exploit code is to focus on the file extension of the source code and then search for specific content within that code. Since source code is the text-based representation of the difficult-to-read machine code, Google is well suited for this task. For example, a large number of exploits are written in C, which generally uses source code ending in a .c extension. Of course, a search for *filetype:c c* returns nearly 500,000 results, meaning that we need to narrow our search. A query for *filetype:c exploit* returns around 5,000 results, most of which are exactly the types of programs we're looking for. Bearing in mind that these are the most popular sites hosting C source code containing the word *exploit*, the returned list is a good start for a list of bookmarks. Using page-scraping techniques, we can isolate these sites by running a UNIX command such as:

```
grep Cached exploit_file  | awk -F" -" '{print $1}' | sort -u
```

against the dumped Google results page. Using good, old–fashioned cut and paste or a command such as *lynx —dump* works well for capturing the page this way. The slightly polished results of scraping 20 results from Google in this way are shown in the list below.

download2.rapid7.com/r7-0025

securityvulns.com/files

www.outpost9.com/exploits/unsorted

downloads.securityfocus.com/vulnerabilities/exploits

packetstorm.linuxsecurity.com/0101-exploits

packetstorm.linuxsecurity.com/0501-exploits

packetstormsecurity.nl/0304-exploits

www.packetstormsecurity.nl/0009-exploits

www.0xdeadbeef.info

archives.neohapsis.com/archives/

packetstormsecurity.org/0311-exploits

packetstormsecurity.org/0010-exploits

www.critical.lt

synnergy.net/downloads/exploits

www.digitalmunition.com

www.safemode.org/files/zillion/exploits

vdb.dragonsoft.com.tw

unsecure.altervista.org

www.darkircop.org/security

www.w00w00.org/files/exploits/

Underground Googling...

Google Forensics

Google also makes a great tool for performing digital forensics. If a suspicious tool is discovered on a compromised machine, it's pretty much standard practice to run the tool through a UNIX command such as *strings –8* to get a feel for the readable text in the program. This usually reveals information such as the usage text for the tool, parts of which can be tweaked into Google queries to locate similar tools. Although obfuscation programs are becoming more and more commonplace, the combination of *strings* and Google is very powerful, when used properly—capable of taking some of the mystery out of the vast number of suspicious tools on a compromised machine.

Locating Exploits Via Common Code Strings

Since Web pages display source code in various ways, a source code listing could have practically any file extension. A PHP page might generate a text view of a C file, for example, making the file extension from Google's perspective .PHP instead of .C.

Another way to locate exploit code is to focus on common strings within the source code itself. One way to do this is to focus on common inclusions or header file references. For example, many C programs include the standard input/output library functions, which are referenced by an *include* statement such as *#include <stdio.h>* within the source code. A query such as *"#include <stdio.h>" exploit* would locate C source code that contained the word *exploit,* regardless of the file's extension. This would catch code (and code fragments) that are displayed in HTML documents. Extending the search to include programs that include a friendly usage statement with a query such as *"#include <stdio.h>" usage exploit* returns the results shown in Figure 6.1.

Figure 6.1 Searching for Exploit Code with Nonstandard Extensions

This search returns quite a few hits, nearly all of which contain exploit code. Using traversal techniques (or simply hitting up the main page of the site) can reveal other exploits or tools. Notice that most of these hits are HTML documents, which our previous *filetype:c*

query would have excluded. There are lots of ways to locate source code using common code strings, but not all source code can be fit into a nice, neat little box. Some code can be nailed down fairly neatly using this technique; other code might require a bit more query tweaking. Table 6.1 shows some suggestions for locating source code with common strings.

Table 6.1 Locating Source Code with Common Strings

Language	Extension (Optional)	Sample String
asp.net (C#)	Aspx	*"<%@ Page Language="C#"" inherits*
asp.net (VB)	Aspx	*"<%@ Page Language="vb"" inherits*
asp.net (VB)	Aspx	*<%@ Page LANGUAGE="JScript"*
C	C	*"#include <stdio.h>"*
C#	Cs	*"using System;" class*
c++	Cpp	*"#include "stdafx.h""*
Java	J, JAV	*class public static*
JavaScript	JS	*"<script language="JavaScript">"*
Perl	PERL, PL, PM	*"#!/usr/bin/perl"*
Python	Py	*"#!/usr/bin/env"*
VBScript	.vbs	*"<%@ language="vbscript" %>"*
Visual Basic	Vb	*"Private Sub"*

In using this table, a *filetype* search is optional. In most cases, you might find it's easier to focus on the sample strings so that you don't miss code with funky extensions.

Locating Code with Google Code Search

Google Code Search (www.google.com/codesearch) can be used to search for public source code. In addition to allowing queries that include powerful regular expressions, code search introduces unique operators, some of which are listed in Table 6.2.

Table 6.2 Google Code Search Operators

Operator	Description	Example
file	Search for specific types of files. Parameters can include file names, extensions, or full path names.	file:js
package	Search within a specific package, often listed as a URL or CVS server name	package:linux.*.tar.gz buggy

Continued

Table 6.2 Google Code Search Operators

Operator	Description	Example
lang	Search for code written in specific languages	lang:"c++"
license	Search for code written under specific licenses	license:gpl

Code search is a natural alternative to the techniques we covered in the previous section. For example, in Table 6.1 we used the web search term "*#include <stdio.h>*" to locate programs written in the *C* programming language. This search is effective, and locates *C* code, regardless of the file extension. This same query could be reformatted as a code search query by simply removing the quotes as shown in Figure 6.2.

Figure 6.2 Code Search used to locate Header Strings

If we're trying to locate *C* code, it makes more sense to query code search for *lang:c* or *lang:c++*. Although this may feel an awful lot like searching by file extension, this is a bit more advanced than a file extension search. Google's Code Search does a decent job of analyzing the code (regardless of extension) to determine the programming language the code was written in. Check out the second hit in Figure 6.2. As the snippet clearly shows, this is *C* code, but is embedded in an HTML file, as revealed by the file name, *perlos390.html*.

As many researchers and bloggers have reported, Google Code Search can also be used to locate software that contains potential vulnerabilities, as shown in Table Table 6.3.

Table 6.3 Google Code Searches for Vulnerable Code

Google Code Search Query	Description	Author
lang:php (echo|print).*\$_(GET|POST|COOKIE|REQUEST)	Code which displays untrusted variables passed GET/POST or cookies. Classic XSS (Cross-Site scripting) vulnerability.	Ilia Alshanetsky
<%=.*getParameter*	Code that allows XSS in Java due to HTML-encoded user input.	Nitesh Dhanjani
lang:php echo.*\$_SERVER\ ['PHP_SELF']	XSS vulnerability due to echo of PHP_SELF.	
echo.*\$_(GET|POST).*	Generic version of above query.	Chris Shiflett
lang:php query\(.*\$_(GET|POST|COOKIE|REQUEST).*\)	SQL queries built from user-supplied GET/POST requests. This could be an SQL injection point.	Ilia Alshanetsky
.*mysql_query\(.*\$_(GET|POST).*	SQL queries built from user-supplied GET/POST requests. This could be an SQL injection point. MySQL-specific.	Nitesh Dhanjani
lang:php "WHERE username='$_"	SQL injection due to raw input to WHERE clause.	Chris Shiflett
.*executeQuery.*getParameter.*	SQL injection in Java code due to execution of an SQL query executed with untrusted user input.	Stephen de Vries

Continued

Table 6.3 continued Google Code Searches for Vulnerable Code

Google Code Search Query	Description	Author
lang:php header\s*\("Location:.*\$_ (GET|POST|COOKIE|REQUEST).*\)	Code import built from user-supplied GET/POST requests and cookies. This may allow execution of malicious code.	Ilia Alshanetsky
lang:php (system|popen|shell_exec| exec)\s*\(\$_(GET|POST|COOKIE| REQUEST).*\)	Code that passes untrusted GET/ POST/COOKIE data to the system for execution. This allows remote code execution.	Ilia Alshanetsky

Locating Malware and Executables

Since the first edition of this book was published, researchers discovered that Google not only crawls, but analyzes *binary,* or *executable* files. The query *"Time Date Stamp: 4053c6c2"* (shown in Figure 6.3) returns one hit for a program named *Message.pif.* A PIF (or Program Information File) is a type of Windows executable.

Since executable files are machine (and not human) readable, it might seem odd to see text in the snippet of the search result. However, the snippet text is the result of Google's *analysis* of the binary file. Clicking the *View as HTML* link for this result displays the full analysis of the file, as shown in Figure 6.4. If the listed information seems like hardcore geek stuff, it's because the listed information is hardcore geek stuff.

Figure 6.3 Google Digs into Executable Files

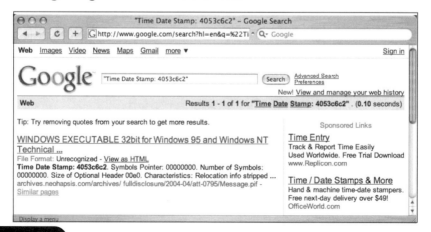

Figure 6.4 Google Analyzes Binary Files

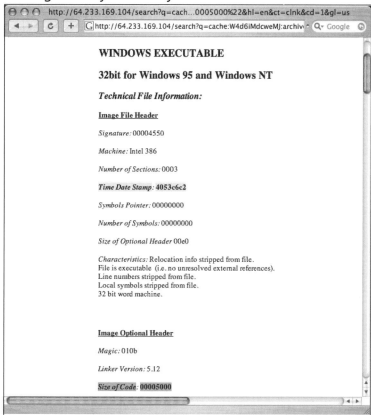

Clicking the file link (instead of the HTML link) will most likely freak out your browser, as shown in Figure 6.5.

Figure 6.5 Binary Browser Garbage

Binary files were just not meant to be displayed in a browser. However, if we right-click the file link and choose *Save As…* to save it to our local machine, we can run our own basic analysis on the file to determine exactly what it is. For example, running the *file* command on a Linux or Mac OS X machine reveals that Message.pif is indeed a Windows Executable file:

```
$ file Message.pif.txt
Message.pif.txt: MS Windows PE 32-bit Intel 80386 GUI executable not relocatable
```

So Google snatches and analyzes binary files it finds on the web. So what? Well, first, it's interesting to see that Google has moved into this space. It's an indication that they're expanding their capabilities. For example, Google now has the ability to recognize malware. Consider the search for *Backup4all* backup software shown in Figure 6.6.

Figure 6.6 Google Warning about Malware

Notice the warning below the site description: This site may harm your computer. Clicking on the file link will not take you to the systemutils.net URL, but will instead present a warning page as show in Figure 6.7.

Figure 6.7 Google's Malware Wrapping Page

So this is certainly a handy feature, but since this book is about Google Hacking, not about Google's plans to save the world's Internet surfers from themselves, it's only right that we get to the dark heart of the matter: Google can be used to *search* for live malware. As Websense announced in 2006, this feature can be leveraged to search for very specific executables by focusing on specific details of individual files, such as the *Time Stamp, Size* and *Entry Point* fields. H.D. Moore took this one step further and created a sort of malware search engine, which can be found at http://metasploit.com/research/misc/mwsearch, as shown in Figure 6.8.

Figure 6.8 H.D. Moore's Malware Search Engine based on Google Binary Search

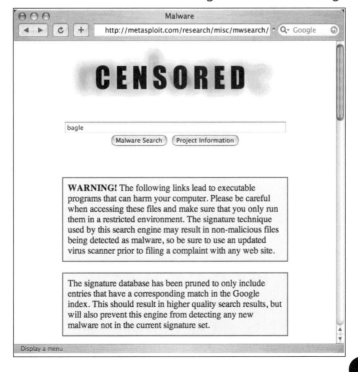

A search for *bagle*, for example, reveals several hits, as shown in Figure 6.9.

Figure 6.9 A Malware Search for Bagles (With No Cream Cheese)

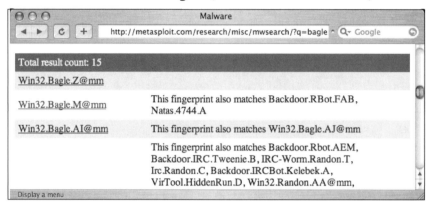

Clicking the second link in this search result will forward you to a Google web search results page for *"Time Date Stamp: 4053c6c2" "Size of Image: 00010000" "Entry Point: 0000e5b0" "Size of Code: 00005000"*—a very long query that uniquely describes the binary signature for the Win32.Bagle.M worm. The Google results page for this query is shown in Figure 6.3. Remember this file? It's the one we successfully downloaded and plopped right onto our desktop!

So even though Google's binary analysis capability has the potential for good, skillful attackers can use it for malicious purposes as well.

Locating Vulnerable Targets

Attackers are increasingly using Google to locate Web-based targets vulnerable to specific exploits. In fact, it's not uncommon for public vulnerability announcements to contain Google links to potentially vulnerable targets, as shown in Figure 6.10.

Figure 6.10 Google Link to Vulnerable Targets in Advisory

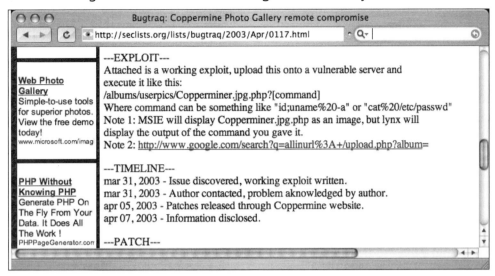

Locating Targets Via Demonstration Pages

The process of locating vulnerable targets can be fairly straightforward, as we'll see in this section. Other times, the process can be a bit more involved, as we'll see in the next section. Let's take a look at a Web application security advisory posted to Secunia (www.secunia.com) on October 10, 2004, as shown in Figure 6.11.

Figure 6.11 Typical Web Application Security Advisory

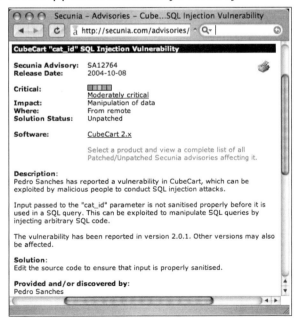

This particular advisory displays a link to the affected software vendor's Web site. Not all advisories list such a link, but a quick Google query should help you locate the vendor's page. Since our goal is to develop a query string to locate vulnerable targets on the Web, the vendor's Web site is a good place to discover what exactly the product's Web pages look like. Like many software vendors' Web sites, the CubeCart site shows links for product demonstrations and live sites that are running the product, as shown in Figure 6.12.

Figure 6.12 Vendor Web Pages Often Provide Product Demonstrations

At the time of this writing, this site's demonstration pages were offline, but the list of live sites was active. Live sites are often better for this purpose because we can account for potential variations in how a Web site is ultimately displayed. For example, some administrators might modify the format of a vendor-supplied Web page to fit the theme of the site. These types of modifications can impact the effectiveness of a Google search that targets a vendor-supplied page format.

Perusing the list of available live sites in Figure 6.4, we find that most sites look very similar and that nearly every site has a "powered by" message at the bottom of the main page, as shown in the (highly edited) example in Figure 6.13.

Figure 6.13 "Powered by" Tags Are Common Query Fodder for Finding Web Apps

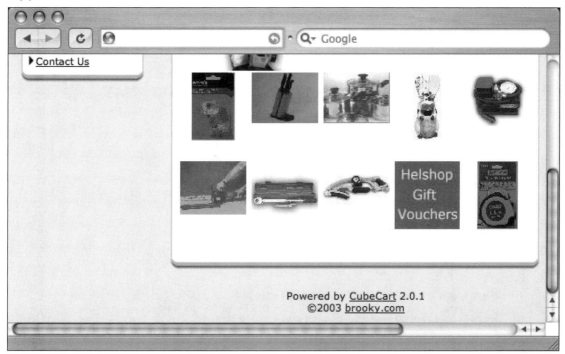

In this case, the live page displays "Powered by CubeCart 2.0.1" as a footer on the main page. Since CubeCart 2.0.1 is the version listed as vulnerable in the security advisory, we need do little else to create a query that locates vulnerable targets on the Web. The final query, *"Powered by CubeCart 2.0.1"*, returns results of over 27,000 potentially vulnerable targets, as shown in Figure 6.14.

Combining this list of sites with the exploit tool released in the Secunia security advisory, an attacker has access to a virtual smorgasbord of online retailers that could likely be compromised, potentially revealing sensitive customer information such as address, products purchased, and payment details.

Figure 6.14 A Query That Locates Vulnerable CubeCart Sites

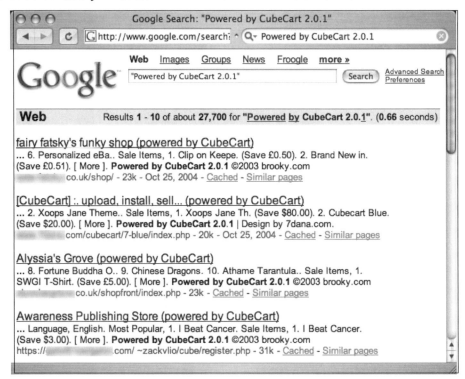

Locating Targets Via Source Code

In some cases, a good query is not as easy to come by, although as we'll see, the resultant query is nearly identical in construction. Although this method is more drawn out (and could be short-circuited by creative thinking), it shows a typical process for detecting an exact working query for locating vulnerable targets. Here we take a look at how a hacker might use the source code of a program to discover ways to search for that software with Google. For example, an advisory was released for the CuteNews program, as shown in Figure 6.15.

As explained in the security advisory, an attacker could use a specially crafted URL to gain information from a vulnerable target. To find the best search string to locate potentially vulnerable targets, we can visit the Web page of the software vendor to find the source code of the offending software. In cases where source code is not available, an attacker might opt to simply download the offending software and run it on a machine he controls to get ideas for potential searches. In this case, version 1.3.1 of the CuteNews software was readily available for download from the author's Web page.

Figure 6.15 The CuteNews Advisory

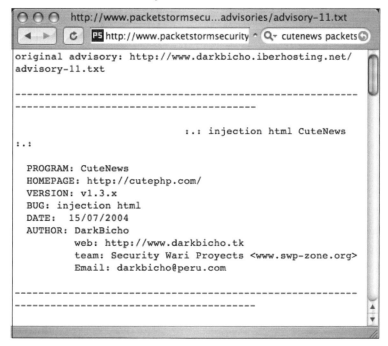

Once the software is downloaded and optionally unzipped, the first thing to look for is the main Web page that would be displayed to visitors. In the case of this particular software, PHP files are used to generate Web pages. Figure 6.16 shows the contents of the top-level CuteNews directory.

Figure 6.16 Files Included with CuteNews 1.3.1

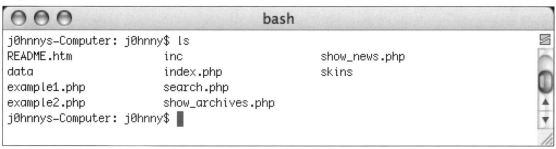

Of all the files listed in the main directory of this package, index.php is the most likely candidate to be a top-level page. Parsing through the index.php file, line 156 would most likely catch our eye.

```
156 // If User is Not Logged In, Display The Login Page
```

Line 156 shows a typical informative comment. This comment reveals the portion of the code that would display a login page. Scrolling down farther in the login page code, we come to lines 173–178:

```
173        <td width=80>Username: </td>
174        <td><input tabindex=1 type=text
           name=username value='$lastusername' style=\"width:134\"></td>
175        </tr>
176        <tr>
177        <td>Password: </td>
178        <td><input type=password name=password style=\"width:134\"></td>
```

These lines show typical HTML code and reveal username and password prompts that are displayed to the user. Based on this code, a query such as *"username:" "password:"* would seem reasonable, except for the fact that this query returns millions of results that are not even close to the types of pages we are looking for. This is because the colons in the query are effectively ignored and the words *username* and *password* are far too common to use for even a base search. Our search continues to line 191 of index.php, shown here:

```
191 echofooter();
```

This line prints a footer at the bottom of the Web page. This line is a function, an indicator that it is used many times through the program. A common footer that displays on several CuteNews pages could make for a very nice base query. We'll need to uncover what exactly this footer looks like by locating the code for the *echofooter* function. Running a command such as *grep −r echofooter* * will search every file in each directory for the word *echofooter*. This returns too many results, as shown in this abbreviated output:

```
j0hnnys-Computer: j0hnny$ grep -r echofooter *
inc/about.mdu:   echofooter();
inc/addnews.mdu:     echofooter();
inc/categories.mdu:echofooter();
inc/editnews.mdu:     echofooter();
inc/editnews.mdu:     echofooter();
inc/editusers.mdu:    echofooter();
inc/functions.inc.php:  echofooter();
inc/functions.inc.php:// Function:      echofooter
inc/functions.inc.php:function echofooter(){
inc/help.mdu:    echofooter();
```

Most of the lines returned by this command are *calls* to the *echofooter* function, not the definition of the function itself. One line, however, precedes the word *echofooter* with the word *function*, indicating the definition of the function. Based on this output, we know that the file inc/functions.inc.php contains the code to print the Web page footer. Although there is a great deal of information in this function, as shown in Figure 6.17, certain things will catch the eye of any decent Google hacker. For example, line 168 shows that copyrights are printed and that the term "Powered by" is printed in the footer.

Figure 6.17 The *echofooter* Function Reveals Potential Query Strings

```
                                 vim
159
160        global $PHP_SELF, $is_loged_in, $config_skin, $skin_footer, $lan
       g_content_type, $skin_menu, $skin_prefix, $config_version_name;
161
162      if($is_loged_in == TRUE){ $skin_footer = preg_replace("/{menu}/", "$
       skin_menu", "$skin_footer"); }
163      else { $skin_footer = preg_replace("/{menu}/", "   $config_vers
       ion_name", "$skin_footer"); }
164
165      $skin_footer = preg_replace("/{image-name}/", "${skin_prefix}${image
       }", $skin_footer);
166      $skin_footer = preg_replace("/{header-text}/", $header_text, $skin_f
       ooter);
167      $skin_footer = preg_replace("/{content-type}/", $lang_content_type,
       $skin_footer);
168      $skin_footer = preg_replace("/{copyrights}/", "<div style='font-size
       : 9px'>Powered by <a style='font-size: 9px' href=\"http://cutephp.com/cu
       tenews/\" target=_blank>$config_version_name</a> ? 2003  <a style='font-
       size: 9px' href=\"http://cutephp.com/\" target=_blank>CutePHP</a>.</div>
       ", $skin_footer);
169
170      echo $skin_footer;
171
172 }
173
```

A phrase like "Powered by" can be very useful in locating specific targets due to their high degree of uniqueness. Following the "Powered by" phrase is a link to http://cutephp.com/cutenews/ and the string *$config_version_name*, which will list the version name of the CuteNews program. To have a very specific "Powered by" search to feed Google, the attacker must either guess the exact version number that would be displayed (remembering that version 1.3.1 of CuteNews was downloaded) or the actual version number displayed must be located in the source code. Again, *grep* can quickly locate this string for us. We can either search for the string directly or put an equal sign (=) after the string to find where it is defined in the code. A *grep* command such as *grep −r "\$config_version_name ="* * will do the trick:

```
johnny-longs-g4 root$ grep -r "\$config_version_name =" *
inc/install.mdu:\$config_version_name = "CuteNews v1.3.1";
inc/options.mdu:    fwrite($handler, "<?PHP \n\n//System
Configurations\n\n\$config_version_name =
\"$config_version_name\";\n\n\$config_version_id = $config_version_id;\n\n");
johnny-longs-g4 root$
```

As shown here, the version name is listed as *CuteNews v1.3.1*. Putting the two pieces of the footer together creates a very specific string: *"Powered by CuteNews v1.3.1"*. This in turn creates a very nice Google query, as shown in Figure 6.18. This very specific query returns nearly perfect results, displaying nearly 500 sites running the potentially vulnerable version 1.3.1 of the CuteNews software.

Figure 6.18 A Completed Vulnerability Search

Too many examples of this technique are in action to even begin to list them all, but in the tradition of the rest of this book, Table 6.4 lists examples of some queries designed to locate targets running potentially vulnerable Web applications. These examples were all pulled from the Google Hacking Database.

Table 6.4 Vulnerable Web Application Examples from the GHDB

Google Query	Vulnerability Description
inurl:custva.asp	EarlyImpact Productcart contains multiple vulnerabilities in versions YaBB Gold - Sp 1.3.1 and others.
"Powered by mnoGoSearch— free web search engine software"	Certain versions of mnGoSearch contain a buffer overflow vulnerability
intitle:guestbook "advanced guestbook 2.2 powered"	Advanced Guestbook v2.2 has an SQL injection vulnerability

Continued

Table 6.4 continued Vulnerable Web Application Examples from the GHDB

Google Query	Vulnerability Description
filetype:asp inurl: "shopdisplayproducts.asp"	Versions of VP-ASP (Virtual Programming— ASP) contains multiple cross-site scripting attacks vulnerabilities
"Powered by: vBulletin * 3.0.1" inurl:newreply.php	vBulletin 3.01 does not correctly sanitize the input, allowing malicious code injection.
"Powered by Invision Power Board(U) v1.3 Final"	Invision Power Board v.13 Final has an SQL injection vulnerability in its 'ssi.php' script.
"powered by sphider" -exploit -ihackstuff -www.cs.ioc.ee	Versions of the sphider search engine script allow arbitrary remote code inclusion.
inurl:gotoURL.asp?url=	Asp Nuke version 1.2, 1.3, and 1.4 does not sanitize the input vars, creating an SQL injection problem.
inurl:comersus_message.asp	Certain versions of Comersus Open Technologies Comersus Cart have Multiple Vulnerabilities, including XSS.
ext:pl inurl:cgi intitle:"FormMail *" -"*Referrer" -"* Denied" -sourceforge -error -cvs -input	Certain versions of FormMail contain configuration problems and invalid referrer checks.
inurl:"dispatch.php?atknodetype" | inurl:class.at	Certain versions of Achievo allow remote code execution.
"Powered by Gallery v1.4.4"	Gallery v1.44 contains a vulnerability that may allow a remote attacker to execute malicious scripts
"Powered by Ikonboard 3.1.1"	IkonBoard 3.1.1 contains poor user input validation, allowing an attacker to evaluate arbitrary Perl and run arbitrary commands.
inurl:/cgi-bin/index.cgi inurl:topics inurl:viewca	Certain versions of WebAPP contain a serious reverse directory traversal vulnerability.
inurl:"/becommunity/community/ index.php?pageurl="	Certain versions of E-market allow arbitrary code injection.
"Powered *: newtelligence" ("dasBlog 1.6"| "dasBlog 1.5"| "dasBlog 1.4"|"dasBlog 1.3")	DasBlog 1.3-1.6 is reportedly susceptible to an HTML injection.
"Powered by DCP-Portal v5.5"	DCP-Portal 5.5 is vulnerable to sql injection.
"FC Bigfeet" -inurl:mail	Certain versions of TYPO3 allow demo logins.

Continued

Table 6.4 continued Vulnerable Web Application Examples from the GHDB

Google Query	Vulnerability Description
filetype:cgi inurl:tseekdir.cgi	Certain versions of Turbo Seek allow for file enumeration.
filetype:php inurl:index.php inurl: "module=subjects" inurl:"func=*" (listpages| viewpage | listcat)	Certain versions of the PostNuke Modules Factory Subjects module contain an SQL injection vulnerability.
filetype:cgi inurl:pdesk.cgi	Certain versions of PerlDesk contain multiple vulnerabilities.
"Powered by IceWarp Software" inurl:mail	IceWarp Web Mail prior to v 5.2.8 contains multiple input validation vulnerabilities.
intitle:"MRTG/RRD" 1.1* (inurl:mrtg.cgi | inurl:14all.cgi |traffic.cgi)	MRTG v1.1.* allow partial file enumeration.
inurl:com_remository	Certain versions of the ReMOSitory module for Mambo are prone to an SQL injection vulnerability.
intitle:"WordPress > * > Login form" inurl:"wp-login.php"	Certain versions of WordPress contain XSS vulnerabilities.
inurl:"comment.php?serendipity"	Certain versions of Serendipity are vulnerable to SQL injection.
"Powered by AJ-Fork v.167"	AJ-Fork v.167 is vulnerable to a full path disclosure.
"Powered by Megabook *" inurl :guestbook.cgi	Certain versions of MegaBook are prone to multiple HTML injection vulnerabilities.
"Powered by yappa-ng"	Certain versions of yappa-ng contain an authentication vulnerability.
"Active Webcam Page" inurl:8080	Certain versions of Active WebCam contain directory traversal and XSS vulnerabilities.
"Powered by A-CART"	Certain versions of A-CART allow for the downloading of customer databases.
"Online Store - Powered by ProductCart"	Certain versions of ProductCart contain multiple SQL injection vulnerabilities.
"Powered by FUDforum"	Certain versions of FUDforum contain SQL injection problems and file manipulation problems.
"BosDates Calendar System " "powered by BosDates v3.2 by BosDev"	BosDates 3.2 has an SQL injection vulnerability.

Continued

Table 6.4 continued Vulnerable Web Application Examples from the GHDB

Google Query	Vulnerability Description
intitle:"EMUMAIL - Login" "Powered by EMU Webmail"	EMU Webmail version 5.0 and 5.1.0 contain XSS vulnerabilities.
intitle:"WebJeff - FileManager" intext:"login" intext:Pass|PAsse	WebJeff-Filemanager 1.x has a directory traversal vulnerability.
inurl:"messageboard/Forum.asp?"	Certain versions of GoSmart Message Board suffer from SQL injection and XSS problems.
"1999-2004 FuseTalk Inc" -site:fusetalk.com	Fusetalk forums v4 are susceptible to XSS attacks.
"2003 DUware All Rights Reserved"	Certain versions of multiple DUware products suffer from SQL injection and HTML injection.
"This page has been automatically generated by Plesk Server Administrator"	Certain versions of Plesk Server Administrator (PSA) contain input validation errors.
inurl:ttt-webmaster.php	Turbo traffic trader Nitro v1.0 suffers from multiple vulnerabilities.
"Copyright Ã,Â© 2002 Agustin Dondo Scripts"	Certain versions of CoolPHP suffer from multiple vulnerabilities.
"Powered by CubeCart"	CubeCart 2.0.1 has a full path disclosure and SQL injection problem.
"Ideal BB Version: 0.1" -idealbb.com	Ideal BB 0.1 is reported prone to multiple unspecified input validation vulnerabilities.
"Powered by YaPig V0.92b"	YaPiG v0.92b is reported to contain an HTML injection vulnerability.
inurl:"/site/articles.asp?idcategory="	Certain versions of Dwc_Articles suffer from possible sql injections.
filetype:cgi inurl:nbmember.cgi	Certain versions of Netbilling nbmember.cgicontains an information disclosure vulnerability.
"Powered by Coppermine Photo Gallery"	Coppermine Photo Gallery Coppermine Photo Gallery 1.0, 1.1, 1.2, 1.2.1, 1.3, 1.3.1 and 1.3.2 contains a design error that may allow users to cast multiple votes for a picture.
"Powered by WowBB" -site:wowbb.com	Certain versions of WowBB are reportedly affected by multiple input validation vulnerabilities.

Continued

Table 6.4 continued Vulnerable Web Application Examples from the GHDB

Google Query	Vulnerability Description
"Powered by ocPortal" -demo -ocportal.com	Certain versions of ocPortal is affected by a remote file include vulnerability.
inurl:"slxweb.dll"	Certain versions of SalesLogix contain authentication vulnerability.
"Powered by DMXReady Site Chassis Manager" -site:dmxready.com	Certain versions of the DMXReady Site Chassis Manager are susceptible to two remotely exploitable input validation vulnerabilities.
"Powered by My Blog" intext: "FuzzyMonkey.org"	FuzzyMonkey My Blog versions 1.15-1.20 are vulnerable to multiple input validation vulnerabilities.
inurl:wiki/MediaWiki	MediaWiki versions 1.3.1-6 are reported prone to a cross-site scripting vulnerability. This issue arises due to insufficient sanitization of user-supplied data.
"inurl:/site/articles.asp?idcategory="	Dwc_Articles version prior to v1.6 suffers from SQL injection vulnerabilities.
"Enter ip" inurl:"php-ping.php"	Certain versions of php-ping may be prone to a remote command execution vulnerabilities.
intitle:welcome.to.horde	Certain versions of Horde Mail suffer from several vulnerabilities.
"BlackBoard 1.5.1-f | Ã,Â© 2003-4 by Yves Goergen"	BlackBoard Internet Newsboard System v1.5.1is reported prone to a remote file include vulnerability.
inurl:"forumdisplay.php" +"Powered by: vBulletin Version 3.0.0..4"	vBulletin 3.0.0.4 is reported vulnerable to a remote SQL injection vulnerability.
inurl:technote inurl:main.cgi *filename=*	Certain versions of Technote suffer from a remote command execution vulnerability.
"running: Nucleus v3.1" -.nucleuscms.org -demo	Multiple unspecified vulnerabilities reportedly affect Nucleus CMS v3.1.
"driven by: ASP Message Board"	Infuseum ASP Message Board 2.2.1c suffers from multiple unspecified vulnerabilities.
"Obtenez votre forum Aztek" -site:forum-aztek.com	Certain versions of Atztek Forum are prone to multiple input validation vulnerabilities.

Continued

Table 6.4 continued Vulnerable Web Application Examples from the GHDB

Google Query	Vulnerability Description
intext:("UBB.threadsÃ¢â?žÂ¢ 6.2" |"UBB.threadsÃ¢â?žÂ¢ 6.3") intext: "You * not logged *" -site:ubbcentral.com	UBB.Threads 6.2.*-6.3.* contains a one character brute force vulnerability.
inurl:/SiteChassisManager/	Certain versions of DMXReady Site Chassis Manager suffer from SQL and XSS vulnerabilities.
inurl:directorypro.cgi	Certain versions of DirectoryPro suffer from directory traversal vulnerabilities.
inurl:cal_make.pl	Certain versions of PerlCal allows remote attackers to access files that reside outside the normally bounding HTML root directory.
"Powered by PowerPortal v1.3"	PowerPortal 1.3 is reported vulnerable to remote SQL injection.
"powered by minibb" -site:www.minibb.net -intext:1.7f	miniBB versions prior to 1.7f are reported vulnerable to remote SQL injection.
inurl:"/cgi-bin/loadpage.cgi?user_id="	Certain versions of EZshopper allow Directory traversal.
intitle:"View Img" inurl:viewimg.php	Certain versions of the 'viewing.php' script does not properly validate user-supplied input in the 'path' variable.
+"Powered by Invision Power Board v2.0.0.2"	Inivision Power Board v2.0.0-2.0.2 suffers from an SQL injection vulnerability.
+"Powered by phpBB 2.0.6..10" -phpbb.com -phpbb.pl	phpbb 2.0.6-20.10 is vulnerable to SQL Injection.
ext:php intext:"Powered by phpNewMan Version"	Certain versions of PHP News Manager are vulnerable to a directory traversal problem.
"Powered by WordPress" -html filetype:php -demo -wordpress.org -bugtraq	Certain versions of WordPress are vulnerable to a few SQL injection queries.
intext:Generated.by.phpix.1.0? inurl:$mode=album	PHPix v1.0 suffers from a directory traversal vulnerability.
inurl:citrix/metaframexp/default/ login.asp? ClientDetection=On	Certain versions of Citrix contain an XSS vulnerability in a widely used version of their Web Interface.

Continued

Table 6.4 continued Vulnerable Web Application Examples from the GHDB

Google Query	Vulnerability Description
"SquirrelMail version 1.4.4" inurl:src ext:php	SquirrelMail v1.4.4 contains an inclusion vulnerability.
"IceWarp Web Mail 5.3.0" "Powered by IceWarp"	IceWarp Web Mail 5.3.0 contains multiple cross-site scripting and HTML injection vulnerabilities.
"Powered by MercuryBoard [v1"	MercuryBoard v1 contains an unspecified vulnerability.
"delete entries" inurl: admin/delete.asp	Certain versions of AspJar contain a flaw that may allow a malicious user to delete arbitrary messages.
allintitle:aspjar.com guestbook	Certain versions of the ASPJar guestbook contain an input validation vulnerability.
"powered by CubeCart 2.0"	Brooky CubeCart v2.0 is prone to multiple vulnerabilities due to insufficient sanitization of user-supplied data.
Powered.by:.vBulletin.Version ...3.0.6	vBulletin 3.0.6 is reported prone to an arbitrary PHP script code execution vulnerability.
filetype:php intitle:"paNews v2.0b4"	PaNews v2.0b4 is reported prone to a remote PHP script code execution vulnerability.
"Powered by Coppermine Photo Gallery" ("v1.2.2 b" | "v1.2.1" | "v1.2" | "v1.1" | "v1.0")	Coppermine Photo Gallery versions 1.0, 1.1, 1.2, 1.2.1 and 1.2.2b are prone to multiple input validation vulnerabilities, some of which may lead to arbitrary command execution.
powered.by.instaBoard.version.1.3	InstaBoard v1.3 is vulnerable to SQL Injection.
intext:"Powered by phpBB 2.0.13" inurl:"cal_view_month.php"|inurl: "downloads.php"	phpBB 2.0.13 with installed Calendar Pro MOD are vulnerable to SQL injection attacks.
intitle:"myBloggie 2.1.1..2— by myWebland"	myBloggie v2.1.1-2.1.2 is affected by multiple vulnerabilities.
intitle:"osTicket :: Support Ticket System"	Certain versions of osTicket contains several vulnerabilities.
inurl:sphpblog intext:"Powered by Simple PHP Blog 0.4.0"	Simple PHP Blog v0.4.0 is vulnerable to multiple attacks including full path disclosure, XSS and other disclosures.

Continued

Table 6.4 continued Vulnerable Web Application Examples from the GHDB

Google Query	Vulnerability Description
intitle:"PowerDownload" ("PowerDownload v3.0.2 Ã‚Â©" | "PowerDownload v3.0.3 Ã‚Â©") -site:powerscripts.org	PowerDownload version 3.0.2 and 3.0.3 contains a remote execution vulnerability.
"portailphp v1.3" inurl:"index.php ?affiche" inurl:"PortailPHP" -site:safari-msi.com	PortailPHP v1.3 suffers from an SQL injection vulnerability.
+intext:"powered by MyBulletinBoard"	MyBB <= 1.00 RC4 contains an SQL injection vulnerability.
intext:"Powered by flatnuke-2.5.3" +"Get RSS News" -demo	FlatNuke 2.5.3 contains multiple vulnerabilities.
intext:"Powered By: Snitz Forums 2000 Version 3.4.00..03"	Snitz Forum 2000 v 3.4.03 and older are vulnerable to many things including XSS.
inurl:"/login.asp?folder=" "Powered by: i-Gallery 3.3"	i-Gallery 3.3 (and possibly older) are vulnerable to many things, including directory traversals.
intext:"Calendar Program Ã‚Â© Copyright 1999 Matt Kruse" "Add an event"	Certain versions of CalendarScript is vulnerable to HTML injection.
"powered by PhpBB 2.0.15" -site:phpbb.com	phpBB 2.0.15 Viewtopic.PHP contains a remote code execution vulnerability.
inurl:index.php fees shop link.codes merchantAccount	EPay Pro version 2.0 is vulnerable to a directory traversal issue.
intitle:"blog torrent upload"	Certain versions of Blog Torrent contain a password revelation issue.
"Powered by Zorum 3.5"	Zorum 3.5 contains a remote code execution vulnerability.
"Powered by FUDForum 2.6" -site:fudforum.org -johnny.ihackstuff	FUDforum 2.6 is prone to a remote arbitrary PHP file upload vulnerability.
intitle:"Looking Glass v20040427" "When verifying	Looking Glass v20040427 allows arbitrary commands execution and cross site scripting.
phpLDAPadmin intitle: phpLDAPadmin filetype:php inurl: tree.php | inurl:login.php | inurl: donate.php (0.9.6 | 0.9.7)	phpLDAPadmin 0.9.6 - 0.9.7/alpha5 (and possibly prior versions) contains system disclosure, remote code execution, and XSS vulnerabilities.

Continued

Table 6.4 continued Vulnerable Web Application Examples from the GHDB

Google Query	Vulnerability Description
"powered by ITWorking"	SaveWebPortal 3.4 contains a remote code execution, admin check bypass and remote file inclusion vulnerability.
intitle:guestbook inurl:guestbook "powered by Adva	Certain versions of Advanced Guestbook are prone to HTML injection vulnerabilities.
"Powered by FUDForum 2.7" -site:fudforum.org -johnny.ihackstuff	FUDforum 2.7 is prone to a remote arbitrary PHP file upload vulnerability.
inurl:chitchat.php "choose graphic"	Cyber-Cats ChitCHat 2.0 contains multiple vulnerabilities.
"Calendar programming by AppIdeas.com" filetype:php bypass and XSS.	phpCommunityCalendar 4.0.3 (and possibly prior versions) allows SQL injection, login
"Powered by MD-Pro"	"made with MD-Pro"	MAXdev MD-Pro 1.0.73 (and possibly prior versions) allow remote code execution, XSS and path disclosure.
"Software PBLang" 4.65 filetype:php	PBLang 4.65 (and possibly prior versions) allow remote code execution, administrative credentials disclosure, system information disclosure, XSS and path disclosure.
"Powered by and copyright class-1" 0.24.4	Class-1 Forum Software v 0.24.4 allows remote code execution.
"Powered by AzDg" (2.1.3 | 2.1.2 | 2.1.1)	AzDGDatingLite V 2.1.3 (and possibly prior versions) allows remote code execution.
"Powered by: Land Down Under 800"	"Powered by: Land Down Under 801" - www.neocrome.net	Land Down Under 800 and 900 are prone to an HTML injection vulnerability.
"powered by Gallery v" "[slideshow]" |"images" inurl:gallery	Certain versions of Gallery suffer from a script injection vulnerability.
intitle:guestbook inurl:guestbook "powered by Advanced guestbook 2.*" "Sign the Guestbook"	Advanced Guestbook v2.* is prone to an HTML injection vulnerability.
"Copyright 2004 Ã‚Â© Digital Scribe v.1.4"	Digital Scribe v1.4 alows login bypass, SQL injection and remote code execution.
"Powered by PHP Advanced Transfer Manager v1.30"	PHP Advanced Transfer Manager v1.30 allows underlying system disclosure, remote command execution and cross site scripting.

Continued

Table 6.4 continued Vulnerable Web Application Examples from the GHDB

Google Query	Vulnerability Description
"Powered by CuteNews"	CuteNews 1.4.0 (and possibly prior versions) allows remote code execution.
"Powered by GTChat 0.95"+ "User Login"+"Remember my login information"	GTChat v0.95 contains a remote denial of service vulnerability.
intitle:"WEB//NEWS Personal Newsmanagement" intext:"Ã,Â © 2002-2004 by Christian Scheb— Stylemotion.de"+"Version 1.4 "+ "Login"	WEB//NEWS 1.4 is prone to multiple SQL injection vulnerabilities.
"Mimicboard2 086"+"2000 Nobutaka Makino"+"password"+ "message" inurl:page=1	Mimicboard2 v086 is prone to multiple HTML injection vulnerabilities.
"Maintained with Subscribe Me 2.044.09p"+"Professional" inurl:"s.pl"	Subscribe Me Pro 2.0.44.09p is prone to a directory traversal vulnerability.
"Powered by autolinks pro 2.1" inurl:register.php	AutoLinksPro v2.1 contains a remote PHP File include vulnerability.
"CosmoShop by Zaunz Publishing" inurl:"cgi-bin/cosmoshop/lshop.cgi" -johnny.ihackstuff.com -V8.10.106 - V8.10.100 -V.8.10.85 - V8.10.108 -V8.11*	Cosmoshop versions 8.10.85, 8.10.100, 8.10.106, 8.10.108 and 8.11* are vulnerable to SQL injection, and cleartext password enumeration.
"Powered by Woltlab Burning Board" -"2.3.3" -"v2.3.3" -"v2.3.2" -"2.3.2"	Woltlab Burning Board versions 2.3.32 and 2.3.3 are vulnerable to SQL injection.
intitle:"PHP TopSites FREE Remote Admin"	Certain versions of PHP TopSites discloses configuration data to remote users.
Powered by PHP-Fusion v6.00.109 Ã,Â© 2003-2005. -php-fusion.co.uk	PHP-Fusion v6.00.109 is prone to SQL Injection and administrative credentials disclosure.
"Powered By: lucidCMS 1.0.11"	Lucid CMS 1.0.11 has SQL injection and login bypass vulnerabilities.
"News generated by Utopia News Pro"	"Powered By: Utopia News Pro"	Utopia News Pro 1.1.3 (and prior versions) contain SQL Injection and XSS vulnerabilities.
intitle:Mantis "Welcome to the bugtracker" "0.15	0.16	0.17	0.18"	Mantis versions 0.19.2 or less contain XSS and SQL injection vulnerabilities.

Continued

Table 6.4 continued Vulnerable Web Application Examples from the GHDB

Google Query	Vulnerability Description
"Cyphor (Release:" -www.cynox.ch	Cyphor 0.19 (and possibly prior versions) allow SQL injection, board takeover and XSS.
"Welcome to the versatileBulletinBoard" | "Powered by versatileBulletinBoard"	VersatileBulletinBoard V1.0.0 RC2 (and possibly prior versions) contains multiple vulnerabilities.
inurl:course/category.php | inurl:course/info.php | inurl:iplookup/ipatlas/plot.php	Moodle <=1.6 allows blind SQL injection.
"Powered by XOOPS 2.2.3 Final"	XOOPS 2.2.3 allows arbitrary local file inclusion.
inurl:"wfdownloads/viewcat.php?list="	XOOPS WF_Downloads (2.05) module allows SQL injection.
"This website was created with phpWebThings 1.4"	phpWebThings 1.4 contains several vulnerabilities.
"Copyright 2000 - 2005 Miro International Pty Ltd. All rights reserved" "Mambo is Free Software released"	Mambo 4.5.2x allows remote command execution.
("Skin Design by Amie of Intense")|("Fanfiction Categories" "Featured Stories")|("default2, 3column, Romance, eFiction")	eFiction <=2.0 contains multiple vulnerabilities.
"Powered by UPB" (b 1.0)|(1.0 final)|(Public Beta 1.0b)	UPB versions b1.0, 1.0 final and Public Beta 1.0b Contains several vulnerabilities.
"powered by GuppY v4"|"Site crÃƒÂ©ÃƒÂ© avec GuppY v4"	Guppy <= 4.5.9 allows remote code execution and arbitrary inclusion.
"Powered by Xaraya" "Copyright 2005"	Xaraya <=1.0.0 RC4 contains a denial of service.
"This website powered by PHPX" -demo	PhpX <= 3.5.9 allows SQL injection and login bypass.
"Based on DoceboLMS 2.0"	DoceboLMS 2.0 contains multiple vulnerabilities.
"2005 SugarCRM Inc. All Rights Reserved" "Powered By SugarCRM"	Sugar Suite 3.5.2a & 4.0beta allow remote code execution.

Continued

Table 6.4 continued Vulnerable Web Application Examples from the GHDB

Google Query	Vulnerability Description
"Powered By phpCOIN 1.2.2"	PhpCOIN 1.2.2 allows arbitrary remote\local inclusion, blind SQL injection and path disclosure.
intext:"Powered by SimpleBBS v1.1"*	SimpleBBS v1.1 contains a flaw that may allow an attacker to carry out an SQL injection attack.
"Site powered By Limbo CMS"	Limbo Cms <= 1.0.4.2 allows remote code execution.
intext:"Powered by CubeCart 3.0.6" intitle:"Powered by CubeCart"	CubeCart 3.0.6 allows remote command execution.
intext:"PhpGedView Version" intext:"final - index" -inurl:demo	PHPGedView <=3.3.7 allows remote code execution.
intext:"Powered by DEV web management system" -dev-wms.sourceforge.net -demo	DEV cms <=1.5 allows SQL injection.
intitle:"phpDocumentor web interface"	Php Documentor < = 1.3.0 rc4 allows remote code execution.
inurl:install.pl intitle:GTchat	Certain versions of Gtchat allow unauthorized configuration changes.
intitle:"4images - Image Gallery Management System" and intext:"Powered by 4images 1.7.1"	4Images v1.7.1 allows remote code execution.
(intitle:"metaframe XP Login")|(intitle:"metaframe Presentation server Login")	Certain versions of Metaframe Presentation Server may allow unauthorized admin access.
"Powered by Simplog"	Simplog v1.0.2 allows directory traversal and XSS.
"powered by sblog" +"version 0.7"	Sblog v0.7 allows HTML injection.
"Thank You for using WPCeasy"	Certain versions of WPC.easy, allow SQL injection.
"Powered by Loudblog"	LoudBlog <= 0.4 contains an arbitrary remote inclusion vulnerability.
"This website engine code is copyright" "2005 by Clever Copy" -inurl:demo	Clever Copy <= 3.0 allows SQL injection.
"index of" intext:fckeditor inurl:fckeditor	FCKEditor script 2.0 and 2.2 contain multiple vulnerabilities.

Continued

Table 6.4 continued Vulnerable Web Application Examples from the GHDB

Google Query	Vulnerability Description
"powered by runcms" -runcms.com -runcms.org	Runcms versions <=1.2 are vulnerable to an arbitrary remote inclusion.
(intitle:"Flyspray setup"|"powered by flyspray 0.9.7") -flyspray.rocks.cc	Flyspray v0.9.7contains multiple vulnerabilities.
intext:"LinPHA Version" intext: "Have fun"	Linpha <=1.0 allows arbitrary local inclusion.
("powered by nocc" intitle:"NOCC Webmail") -site:sourceforge.net -Zoekinalles.nl -analysis	Certain versions of NOCC Webmail allow arbitrary local inclusion, XSS and possible remote code execution.
intitle:"igenus webmail login"	Igenus webmail allows local file enumeration.
"powered by 4images"	4images <= 1.7.1 allows remote code execution.
intext:"Powered By Geeklog" -geeklog.net	Certain versions of Geeklog contains multiple vulnerabilities.
intitle:admbook intitle:version filetype:php	Admbook version: 1.2.2 allows remote execution.
WEBalbum 2004-2006 duda -ihackstuff -exploit	WEBalbum 2004-2006 contains multiple vulnerabilities.
intext:"powered by gcards" -ihackstuff -exploit	Gcards <=1.45 contains multiple vulnerabilities.
"powered by php icalendar" -ihackstuff -exploit	php iCalendar <= 2.21 allows remote command execution.
"Powered by XHP CMS" -ihackstuff -exploit -xhp.targetit.ro	XHP CMS 0.5 allows remote command execution.
inurl:*.exe ext:exe inurl:/*cgi*/	Many CGI-bin executables allow XSS and html injection.
"powered by claroline" -demo	Claroline e-learning platform <= 1.7.4 contains multiple vulnerabilities.
"PhpCollab . Log In" | "NetOffice . Log In" | (intitle:"index.of." intitle: phpcollab|netoffice inurl:phpcollab |netoffice -gentoo)	PhpCollab 2.x / NetOffice 2.x allows SQL injection.
intext:"2000-2001 The phpHeaven Team" -sourceforge	PHPMyChat <= 0.14.5 contains an SQL injection vulnerability.
"2004-2005 ReloadCMS Team."	ReloadCMS <= 1.2.5stable allows XSS and remote command execution.

Continued

Table 6.4 continued Vulnerable Web Application Examples from the GHDB

Google Query	Vulnerability Description
intext:"2000-2001 The phpHeaven Team" -sourceforge	Certain versions of phpHeaven allow remote command execution.
inurl:server.php ext:php intext:"No SQL" -Released	Certain versions of PHPOpenChat contain multiple vulnerabilities.
intitle:PHPOpenChat inurl: "index.php?language="	Certain versions of PHPOpenchat allow SQL injection and information disclosure.
"powered by phplist" | inurl:" lists/?p=subscribe" | inurl:"lists/index. php?p=subscribe" -ubbi -bugs +phplist -tincan.co.uk	PHPList 2.10.2 allows arbitrary local file inclusion.
inurl:"extras/update.php" intext: mysql.php -display	Certain versions of osCommerce allow local file enumeration.
inurl:sysinfo.cgi ext:cgi	Sysinfo 1.2.1allows remote command execution.
inurl:perldiver.cgi ext:cgi	Certain versions of perldiver.cgi allow XSS.
inurl:tmssql.php ext:php mssql pear adodb -cvs -akbk	Certain versions of tmssql.php allow remote code execution.
"powered by php photo album" | inurl:"main.php?cmd=album" -demo2 -pitanje	Certain versions of PHP photo album allow local file enumeration and remote exploitation.
inurl:resetcore.php ext:php	Certain versions of e107 contain multiple vulnerabilities.
"This script was created by Php-ZeroNet" "Script. Php-ZeroNet"	Php-ZeroNet v 1.2.1 contains multiple vulnerabilities.
"You have not provided a survey identification num	PHP Surveyor 0995 allows SQL injection.
intitle:"HelpDesk" "If you need additional help, please email helpdesk at"	PHP Helpdesk 0.6.16 allows remote execution of arbitrary data.
inurl:database.php | inurl:info_ db.php ext:php "Database V2.*" "Burning Board *"	Woltlab Burning Board 2.x contains multiple vulnerabilities.
intext:"This site is using phpGraphy" | intitle:"my phpgraphy site"	phpGraphy 0911 allows XSS and denial of service.
intext:"Powered by PCPIN.com" -site:pcpin.com -ihackstuff -"works with" -findlaw	Certain versions of PCPIN Chat allow SQL injection, login bypass and arbitrary local inclusion.

Continued

Table 6.4 continued Vulnerable Web Application Examples from the GHDB

Google Query	Vulnerability Description
intitle:"X7 Chat Help Center" | "Powered By X7 Chat" -milw0rm -exploit	X7 Chat <=2.0 allows remote command execution.
allinurl:tseekdir.cgi	Certain versions of tseekdir.cgi allows local file enumeration.
Copyright. Nucleus CMS v3.22 . Valid XHTML 1.0 Strict. Valid CSS. Back to top -demo -"deadly eyes"	Nucleus 3.22 CMS allows arbitrary remote file inclusion.
"powered by pppblog v 0.3.(.)"	pppblog 0.3.x allows system information disclosure.
"Powered by PHP-Fusion v6.00.110" | "Powered by PHP-Fusion v6.00.2." | "Powered by PHP-Fusion v6.00.3." -v6.00.400 -johnny.ihackstuff	PHP-Fusion 6.00.3 and 6.00.4 contains multiple vulnerabilities.
intitle:"XOOPS Site" intitle:"Just Use it!" | "powered by xoops (2.0)| (2.0.....)"	XOOPS 2.x allows file overwrite.
inurl:wp-login.php +Register Username Password "remember me" -echo -trac -footwear	Wordpress 2.x allows remote command execution.
"powered by ubbthreads"	Certain versions of ubbthreads are vulnerable to file inclusion.
"Powered by sendcard - an advanced PHP e-card program" -site:sendcard.org	Certain versions of Sendcard allow remote command execution.
"powered by xmb"	XMB <=1.9.6 Final allows remote command execution and SQL injection.
"powered by minibb forum software"	Certain versions of minibb forum software allow arbitrary remote file inclusion.
inurl:eStore/index.cgi?	Certain versions of eStore allow directory traversal.[1]

This table and associated GHDB entries provided by many members of the community, listed here by the number of contributions: rgod (85), Joshua Brashars (18), klouw (18), Fr0zen (10), MacUK (8), renegade334 (7), webby_guy (7), CP (6), cybercide (5), jeffball55 (5), JimmyNeutron (5), murfie (4), FiZiX (4), sfd (3), ThePsyko (2), wolveso (2), Deeper (2), HaVoC88 (2), l0om (2), Mac (2), rar (2), GIGO (2), urban (1), demonio (1), ThrowedOff (1), plaztic (1), Vipsta (1), golfo (1), xlockex (1), hevnsnt (1), none90810 (1), hermes (1), blue_matrix (1), Kai (1), good-virus (1), Ronald MacDonald (1), ujen (1), Demonic_Angel (1), zawa (1), Stealth05 (1), maveric (1), MERLiiN (1), norocosul_alex R00t (1), abinidi (1), Brasileiro (1), ZyMoTiCo (1), TechStep (1), sylex (1), QuadsteR (1), ghooli (1)

Locating Targets Via CGI Scanning

One of the oldest and most familiar techniques for locating vulnerable Web servers is through the use of a *CGI scanner*. These programs parse a list of known "bad" or vulnerable Web files and attempt to locate those files on a Web server. Based on various response codes, the scanner could detect the presence of these potentially vulnerable files. A CGI scanner can list vulnerable files and directories in a data file, such as the snippet shown here:

```
/cgi-bin/userreg.cgi
/cgi-bin/cgiemail/uargg.txt
/random_banner/index.cgi
/random_banner/index.cgi
/cgi-bin/mailview.cgi
/cgi-bin/maillist.cgi
/iissamples/ISSamples/SQLQHit.asp
/iissamples/ISSamples/SQLQHit.asp
/SiteServer/admin/findvserver.asp
/scripts/cphost.dll
/cgi-bin/finger.cgi
```

Instead of connecting directly to a target server, an attacker could use Google to locate servers that might be hosting these potentially vulnerable files and directories by converting each line into a Google query. For example, the first line searches for a filename userreg.cgi located in a directory called cgi-bin. Converting this to a Google query is fairly simple in this case, as a search for *inurl:/cgi-bin/userreg.cgi* shows in Figure 6.19.

This search locates many hosts that are running the supposedly vulnerable program. There is certainly no guarantee that the program Google detected is the vulnerable program. This highlights one of the biggest problems with CGI scanner programs. The mere existence of a file or directory does not necessarily indicate that a vulnerability is present. Still, there is no shortage of these types of scanner programs on the Web, each of which provides the potential for many different Google queries.

Figure 6.19 A Single CGI Scan-Style Query

There are other ways to go after CGI-type files. For example, the *filetype* operator can be used to find the actual CGI program, even outside the context of the parent cgi-bin directory, with a query such as *filetype:cgi inurl:userreg.cgi*. This locates more results, but unfortunately, this search is even more sketchy, since the cgi-bin directory is an indicator that the program is in fact a CGI program. Depending on the configuration of the server, the userreg.cgi program might be a text file, not an executable, making exploitation of the program interesting, if not altogether impossible!

Another even sketchier way of finding this file is via a directory listing with a query such as *intitle:index.of userreg.cgi*. This query returns no hits at the time of this writing, and for good reason. Directory listings are not nearly as common as URLs on the Web, and a directory listing containing a file this specific is a rare occurrence indeed.

Underground Googling...

Automated CGI Scanning Via Google

Obviously, automation is required to effectively search Google in this way, but two tools, Wikto (from www.sensepost.com) and Gooscan (from http://Johnny. ihackstuff.com) both perform automated Google and CGI scanning. The Wikto tool uses the Google API; Gooscan does not. See the Protection chapter for more details about these tools.

Summary

There are so many ways to locate exploit code that it's nearly impossible to categorize them all. Google can be used to search the Web for sites that host public exploits, and in some cases you might stumble on "private" sites that host tools as well. Bear in mind that many exploits are not posted to the Web. New (or 0day) exploits are guarded very closely in many circles, and an open public Web page is the *last* place a competent attacker is going to stash his or her tools. If a toolkit is online, it is most likely encrypted or at least password protected to prevent dissemination, which would alert the community, resulting in the eventual lockdown of potential targets. This isn't to say that new, unpublished exploits are *not* online, but frankly it's often easier to build relationships with those in the know. Still, there's nothing wrong with having a nice hit list of public exploit sites, and Google is great at collecting those with simple queries that include the words *exploit, vulnerability,* or *vulnerable.* Google can also be used to locate source code by focusing on certain strings that appear in that type of code.

Locating potential targets with Google is a fairly straightforward process, requiring nothing more than a unique string presented by a vulnerable Web application. In some cases these strings can be culled from demonstration applications that a vendor provides. In other cases, an attacker might need to download the product or source code to locate a string to use in a Google query. Either way, a public Web application exploit announcement, combined with the power of Google, leaves little time for a defender to secure a vulnerable application or server.

Solutions Fast Track

Locating Exploit Code

- ☑ Public exploit sites can be located by focusing on common strings like *exploit* or *vulnerability.* To narrow the results, the *filetype* operator can be added to the query to locate exploits written in a particular programming language.

- ☑ Exploit code can be located by focusing either on the file extension with *filetype* or on strings commonly found in that type of source code, such as *"include <stdio.h>"* for C programs.

Google Code Search

- ☑ Google's Code Search (www.google.com/codesearch) can be used to search inside of program code, but it can also be used to find programming flaws that lead to vulnerabilities.

Locating Malware

☑ Google's binary search feature can be used to profile executables, but it can also be used to locate live malware on the web. See H.D. Moore's search engine at http://metasploit.com/research/misc/mwsearch.

Locating Vulnerable Targets

☑ Attackers can locate potential targets by focusing on strings presented in a vulnerable application's demonstration installation provided by the software vendor.

☑ Attackers can also download and optionally install a vulnerable product to locate specific strings the application displays.

☑ Regardless of how a string is obtained, it can easily be converted into a Google query, drastically narrowing the time a defender has to secure a site after a public vulnerability announcement.

Links to Sites

☑ www.sensepost.com/research/wikto/ Wikto, an excellent Google and Web scanner.

☑ www.cirt.net/code/nikto.shtml Nikto, an excellent Web scanner.

☑ http://packetstormsecurity.com/ An excellent site for tools and exploits.

☑ Ilia Alshanetsky http://ilia.ws/archives/133-Google-Code-Search-Hackers-best-friend.html

☑ Nitesh Dhanjani http://dhanjani.com/archives/2006/10/using_google_code_search_to_fi.html

☑ Chris Shiflett http://shiflett.org/blog/2006/oct/google-code-search-for-security-vulnerabilities

☑ Stephen de Vries http://www.securityfocus.com/archive/107/447729/30/0

Michael Sutton's Blog:

☑ http://portal.spidynamics.com/blogs/msutton/archive/2006/09/26/How-Prevalent-Are-SQL-Injection-Vulnerabilities_3F00_.aspx

☑ http://portal.spidynamics.com/blogs/msutton/archive/2007/01/31/How-Prevalent-Are-XSS-Vulnerabilities_3F00_.aspx

☑ Jose Nazario's page on Google Code Search insecurity stats: http://monkey.org/~jose/blog/viewpage.php?page=google_code_search_stats

☑ Static Code Analysis with Google by Aaron Campbell: http://asert.arbornetworks.com/2006/10/static-code-analysis-using-google-code-search/

☑ HD Moore's Malware Search http://metasploit.com/research/misc/mwsearch

Frequently Asked Questions

The following Frequently Asked Questions, answered by the authors of this book, are designed to both measure your understanding of the concepts presented in this chapter and to assist you with real-life implementation of these concepts. To have your questions about this chapter answered by the author, browse to **www.syngress.com/solutions** and click on the **"Ask the Author"** form.

Q: CGI scanning tools have been around for years and have large scan databases with contributions from many hackers. What's the advantage of using Google, which depends on a site having been crawled by Googlebot? Doesn't that give fewer results?

A: Although this is true, Google provides some level of anonymity because it can show the cached pages using the *strip=1* parameter, so the attacker's IP (black or white) is not logged at the server. Check out the Nikto code in Chapter 12, which combines the power of Google with the Nikto database!

Q: Are there any generic techniques for locating known vulnerable Web applications?

A: Try combining *INURL:["parameter="]* with *FILETYPE:[ext]* and *INURL:[scriptname]* using information from the security advisory. In some cases, version information might not always appear on the target's page. If you're searching for version information, remember that each digit counts as a word, so 1.4.2 is three words according to Google. You could hit the search word limit fast.

Also remember that for Google to show a result, the site must have been crawled earlier. If that's not the case, try using a more generic search such as *"powered by XYZ"* to locate pages that could be running a particular family of software.

## Chapter 7

Ten Simple Security Searches That Work

Solutions in this chapter:

- *site*
- *intitle:index.of*
- *error | warning*
- *login | logon*
- *username | userid | employee.ID | "your username is"*
- *password | passcode | "your password is"*
- *admin | administrator*
- *–ext:html –ext:htm –ext:shtml –ext:asp –ext:php*
- *inurl:temp | inurl:tmp | inurl:backup | inurl:bak*
- *intranet | help.desk*
- List of Sites

Introduction

Although we see literally hundreds of Google searches throughout this book, sometimes it's nice to know there's a few searches that give good results just about every time. In the context of security work, we'll take a look at 10 searches that work fairly well during a security assessment, especially when combined with the *site* operator, which secures the first position in our list. As you become more and more comfortable with Google, you'll certainly add to this list, modifying a few searches and quite possibly deleting a few, but the searches here should serve as a very nice baseline for your own top 10 list. Without further ado, let's dig into some queries.

site

The *site* operator is absolutely invaluable during the information-gathering phase of an assessment. Combined with a host or domain name, this query presents results that can be overwhelming, to say the least. However, the *site* operator is meant to be used as a base search, not necessarily as a standalone search. Sure, it's possible (and not entirely discouraged) to scan through *every single* page of results from this query, but in most cases it's just downright impractical.

Important information can be gained from a straight-up site search, however. First, remember that Google lists results in page-ranked order. In other words, the most popular pages float to the top. This means you can get a quick idea about what the rest of the Internet thinks is most worthwhile about a site. The implications of this information are varied, but at a basic level you can at least get an idea of the public image or consensus about an online presence by looking at what floats to the top. Outside the specific site search itself, it can be helpful to read into the context of links originating from other sites. If a link's text says something to the effect of "CompanyXYZ sucks!" there's a good chance that someone is discontent about CompanyXYZ.

As we saw in Chapter 5, the site search can also be used to gather information about the servers and hosts that a target maintains. Using simple reduction techniques, we can quickly get an idea about a target's online presence. Consider the simple example of *site:nytimes.com –site:www.nytimes.com* shown in Figure 7.1.

Figure 7.1 Site Reduction Reveals Domain Names

This query effectively locates hosts on the nytimes.com domain other than www. nytimes.com. Just from a first pass, Figure 7.1 shows three hosts: theater.nytimes.com, www2.nytimes.com, salary.nytimes.com and realestate.nytimes.com. These may be hosts, or they may be subdomains. Further investigation would be required to determine this. Also remember to validate your Google results before unleashing your mega-scanner of choice.

intitle:index.of

intitle:index.of is the universal search for directory listings. Directory listings are chock-full of juicy details, as we saw in Chapter 3. Firing an *intitle:index.of* query against a target is fast and easy and could produce a killer payoff.

error | warning

As we've seen throughout this book, error messages can reveal a great deal of information about a target. Often overlooked, error messages can provide insight into the application or operating system software a target is running, the architecture of the network the target is on, information about users on the system, and much more. Not only are error messages informative, they are prolific. This query will take some playing with, and is best when combined with a *site* query. For example, a query of *("for more information" | "not found") (error | warning)* returns interesting results, as shown in Figure 7.2.

Figure 7.2 The Word *Error* Is Very Common in a Document Title

Unfortunately, some error messages don't actually display the word *error*, as shown in the SQL located with a query of *"access denied for user" "using password"* shown in Figure 7.3.

Figure 7.3 Where Errors Hide, Warnings Lurk

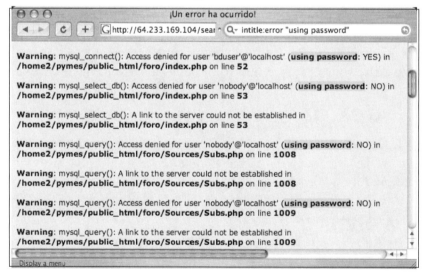

This error page reveals usernames, filenames, path information, IP addresses, and line numbers, yet the word *error* does not occur anywhere on the page. Nearly as prolific as error messages, warning messages can be generated from application programs. In some cases, however, the word *warning* is specifically written into the text of a page to alert the Web user that something important has happened or is about to happen. Regardless of how they are generated, pages containing these words may be of interest during an assessment, as long as you don't mind teasing out the results a bit.

login | logon

As we'll see in Chapter 8, a login portal is a "front door" to a Web site. Login portals can reveal the software and operating system of a target, and in many cases "self-help" documentation is linked from the main page of a login portal. These documents are designed to assist users who run into problems during the login process. Whether the user has forgotten a password or even a username, this documents can provide clues that might help an attacker, or in our case a security tester, gain access to the site.

Many times, documentation linked from login portals lists e-mail addresses, phone numbers, or URLs of human assistants who can help a troubled user regain lost access. These assistants, or help desk operators, are perfect targets for a social engineering attack. Even the smallest security testing team should not be without a social engineering whiz who could talk an Eskimo out of his thermal underwear. The vast majority of all security systems has one common weakest link: a human behind a keyboard. The words *login* and *logon* are widely used on the Internet, occurring on millions of pages, as shown in Figure 7.4.

Figure 7.4 *login* and *logon* Locate Login Portals

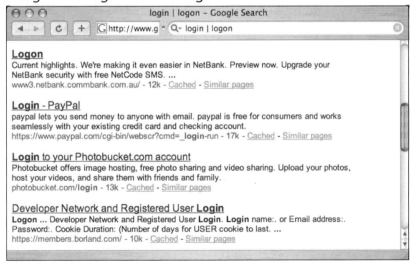

Also common is the phrase *login trouble* in the text of the page. A phrase like this is designed to steer wayward users who have forgotten their login credentials. This info is of course very valuable to attackers and pen testers alike.

username | userid | employee.ID | "your username is"

As we'll see in Chapter 9, there are many different ways to obtain a username from a target system. Even though a username is the less important half of most authentication mechanisms, it should at least be marginally protected from outsiders. Figure 7.5 shows that even sites that reveal very little information in the face of a barrage of probing Google queries return many potentially interesting results to this query. To avoid implying anything negative about the target used in this example, some details of the figure have been edited.

Figure 7.5 Even "Tight-Lipped" Sites Provide Login Portals

The mere existence of the word *username* in a result is not indicative of a vulnerability, but results from this query provide a starting point for an attacker. Since there's no good reason to remove derivations of the word *username* from a site you protect, why not rely on this common set of words to at least get a foothold during an assessment?

password | passcode | "your password is"

The word *password* is so common on the Internet, there are over a billion results for this one-word query. Launching a query for derivations of this word makes little sense unless you actually combine that search with the *site* operator.

During an assessment, it's very likely that results for this query combined with a *site* operator will include pages that provide help to users who have forgotten their passwords. In some cases, this query will locate pages that provide policy information about the *creation* of a password. This type of information can be used in an intelligent-guessing or even a brute-force campaign against a password field.

Despite how this query looks, it's quite uncommon for this type of query to return *actual* passwords. Passwords do exist on the Web, but this query isn't well suited for locating them. (We'll look at queries to locate passwords in Chapter 9.) Like the login portal and username queries, this query can provide an informational foothold into a system. Most often, this query should be used alongside a *site* operator, but with a little tweaking, the query can be used without *site* to illustrate the point, as shown in Figure 7.6. "Forgotten password" pages like these can be very informative.

Figure 7.6 Even Without *site*, This Query Can Locate User Login Help Pages

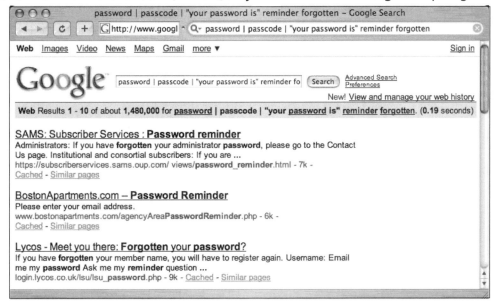

admin | administrator

The word *administrator* is often used to describe the person in control of a network or system. There are so many references to the word on the Web that a query for *admin | administrator* weighs in at a half a billion results. This suggests that these words will likely be referenced on a site you're charged with assessing. However, the value of these and other words in a query does not lie in the number of results but in the contextual relevance of the words. Tweaking this query, with the addition of "change your" can return interesting results, even without the addition of a *site* operator, as shown in Figure 7.7.

Figure 7.7 Admin Query Tweaked and Focused

The phrase *Contact your system administrator* is a fairly common phrase on the Web, as are several basic derivations. A query such as *"please contact your ★ administrator"* will return results that reference local, company, site, department, server, system, network, database, e-mail, and even tennis administrators. If a Web user is told to contact an administrator, odds are that there's data of at least moderate importance to a security tester.

The word *administrator* can also be used to locate administrative login pages, or login portals. (We'll take a closer look at login portal detection in Chapter 8.) A query for *"administrative login"* returns millions of results, many of which are administrative login pages. A security tester can profile Web servers using seemingly insignificant clues found on these types of login pages. Most login portals provide clues to an attacker about what software is in use on the server and act as a magnet, drawing attackers who are armed with an exploit for that particular type of software. As shown in Figure 7.8, many of the results for the combined admin query reveal administrative login pages.

Figure 7.8 *admin login* Reveals Administrative Login Pages

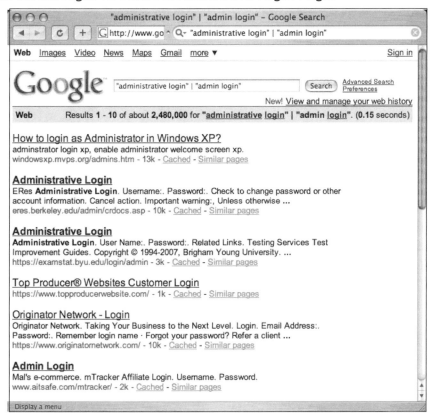

Another interesting use of the *administrator* derivations is to search for them in the URL of a page using an *inurl* search. If the word *admin* is found in the hostname, a directory name, or a filename within a URL, there's a decent chance that the URL has some administrative function, making it interesting from a security standpoint.

–ext:html –ext:htm
–ext:shtml –ext:asp –ext:php

The *–ext:html –ext:htm –ext:shtml –ext:asp –ext:php* query uses *ext*, a synonym for the *filetype* operator, and is a negative query. It returns no results when used alone and should be combined with a *site* operator to work properly. The idea behind this query is to exclude some of the most common Internet file types in an attempt to find files that might be more interesting for our purposes.

As you'll see through this book, there are certainly lots of HTML, PHP, and ASP pages that reveal interesting information, but this chapter is about cutting to the chase, and that's what this query attempts to do. The documents returned by this search often have great potential for document grinding, which we'll explore in more detail in Chapter 10. The file extensions used in this search were selected very carefully. First, www.filext.com (one of the Internet's best resources for all known file extensions) was consulted to obtain a list of every known file extension. Each entry in the list of over 8000 file extensions was converted into a Google query using the *filetype* operator. For example, if we wanted to search for the PDF extension, we might use a query like *filetype:PDF* to get the number of known results on the Internet. This type of Google query was performed for each and every known file extension from filext.com, which can take quite some time, especially when done in accordance with Google Terms of Use agreement. (★cough★) Once the results were gathered, they were sorted in descending order by the number of hits. The top thirty results of this query are shown in Table 7.1.

Table 7.1 Top 30 File Extensions on the Internet

Extension	Approximate Number of Hits
HTML	4,960,000,000
HTM	1,730,000,000
PHP	1,050,000,000
ASP	831,000,000
CFM	481,000,000
ASPX	442,000,000
SHTML	310,000,000
PDF	260,000,000
JSP	240,000,000
CGI	83,000,000
DO	63,400,000
PL	54,500,000
XML	53,100,000
DOC	42,000,000
SWF	40,000,000
PHTML	38,800,000
PHP3	38,100,000
FCGI	30,300,000
TXT	30,100,000
STM	29,900,000
FILE	18,400,000

Continued

Table 7.1 continued Top 30 File Extensions on the Internet

Extension	Approximate Number of Hits
EXE	17,000,000
JHTML	16,300,000
XLS	16,100,000
PPT	13,000,000
DLL	12,900,000
PS	10,400,000
GZ	10,400,000
STORY	9,850,000
X	8,640,000

This table reveals the most common file types on the Internet, according to Google. So a site search combined with a *negative* search for the top ten most common file types can lead you right to some potentially interesting documents. In some cases, this query will need to be refined, especially if the site uses a less common server-generated file extension. For example, consider this query combined with a *site* operator, as shown in Figure 7.9. (To protect the identity of the target, certain portions of the figure have been edited.)

Figure 7.9 A Base Search Combined with the *site* Operator

As revealed in the search results, this site uses the ASPX extension for some Web content. By adding *–ext:aspx* to the query and resubmitting it, that type of content is removed

from the search results. This modified search reveals some interesting information, as shown in Figure 7.10.

Figure 7.10 New and Improved, Juicier and Tastier

By adding a common file extension used on this site, after a few pages of mediocre results we discover a page full of interesting information. Result line 1 reveals that the site supports the HTTPS protocol, a secured version of HTTP used to protect sensitive information. The mere existence of the HTTPS protocol often indicates that this server houses something worth protecting. Result line 1 also reveals several nested subdirectories (/research/files/summaries) that could be explored or traversed to locate other information. This same line also reveals the existence of a PDF document dated the first quarter of 2003.

Result line 2 reveals the existence of what is most likely a development server named DEV. This server also contains subdirectories (/events/archives/strategiesNAM2003) that could be traversed to uncover more information. One of the subdirectory names, strategiesNAM2003, contains a the string 2003, most likely a reference to the year 2003. Using the incremental substitution technique discussed in Chapter 3, it's possible to modify the year in this directory name to uncover similarly named directories. Result line 2 also reveals the existence of an attendee list that could be used to discover usernames, e-mail addresses, and so on.

Result line 3 reveals another machine name, JOBS, which contains a ColdFusion application that accepts parameters. Depending on the nature and security of this application, an attack based on user input might be possible. Result line 4 reveals new directory names, /help/emp, which could be traversed or fed into other third-party assessment applications.

The results continue, but the point is that once common, purposefully placed files are removed from a search, interesting information tends to float to the top. This type of reduction can save an attacker or a security technician a good deal of time in assessing a target.

inurl:temp | inurl:tmp | inurl:backup | inurl:bak

The *inurl:temp | inurl:tmp | inurl:backup | inurl:bak* query, combined with the *site* operator, searches for temporary or backup files or directories on a server. Although there are many possible naming conventions for temporary or backup files, this search focuses on the most common terms. Since this search uses the *inurl* operator, it will also locate files that contain these terms as file extensions, such as index.html.bak, for example. Modifying this search to focus on file extensions is one option, but these terms are more interesting if found in a URL.

intranet | help.desk

The term *intranet*, despite more specific technical meanings, has become a generic term that describes a network confined to a small group. In most cases the term *intranet* describes a closed or private network, unavailable to the general public. However, many sites have configured portals that allow access to an intranet from the Internet, bringing this typically closed network one step closer to potential attackers.

In rare cases, private intranets have been discovered on the public Internet due to a network device misconfiguration. In these cases, network administrators were completely unaware that their private networks were accessible to anyone via the Internet. Most often, an Internet-connected intranet is only partially accessible from the outside. In these cases, filters are employed that only allow access to certain pages from specific addresses, presumably inside a facility or campus. There are two major problems with this type of configuration. First, it's an administrative nightmare to keep track of the access rights of specific pages. Second, this is not true access control. This type of restriction can be bypassed very easily if an attacker gains access to a local proxy server, bounces a request off a local misconfigured Web server, or simply compromises a machine on the same network as trusted intranet users. Unfortunately, it's nearly impossible to provide a responsible example of this technique in action. Each example we considered for this section was too easy for an attacker to reconstruct with a few simple Google queries.

Help desks have a bad reputation of being, well, too helpful. Since the inception of help desks, hackers have been donning alternate personalities in an attempt to gain sensitive information from unsuspecting technicians. Recently, help desk procedures have started to address the hacker threat by insisting that technicians validate callers before attempting to assist them. Most help desk workers will (or should) ask for identifying information such as usernames, Social Security numbers, employee numbers, and even PIN numbers to properly validate callers' identities. Some procedures are better than others, but for the most part, today's help desk technicians are at least *aware* of the potential threat that is posed by an imposter.

In Chapter 4, we discussed ways Google can be used to harvest the identification information a help desk may require, but the *intranet | help.desk* query is not designed to bypass help desk procedures but rather to locate pages describing help desk procedures. When this query is combined with a *site* search, the results could indicate the location of a help desk (Web page, telephone number, or the like), the information that might be requested by help desk technicians (which an attacker could gather before calling), and in many cases links that describe troubleshooting procedures. Self-help documentation is often rather verbose, and a crafty attacker can use the information in these documents to profile a target network or server. There are exceptions to every rule, but odds are that this query, combined with the *site* operator, will dig up information about a target that can feed a future attack.

Summary

This list may not be perfect, but these 10 searches should serve you well as you seek to compile your own list of killer searches. It's important to realize that a search that works against one target might not work well against other targets. Keep track of the searches that work for you, and try to reach some common ground about what works and what doesn't. Automated tools, discussed in Chapters 11 and 12, can be used to feed longer lists of Google queries such as those found in the Google Hacking Database, but in some cases, simpler might be better. If you're having trouble finding common ground in some queries that work for you, don't hesitate to keep them in a list for use in one of the automated tools we'll discuss later.

Solutions Fast Track

site

☑ The *site* operator is great for trolling through all the content Google has gathered for a target.

☑ This operator is used in conjunction with many of the other queries presented here to narrow the focus of the search to one target.

intitle:index.of

☑ The universal search for Apache-style directory listings.

☑ Directory listings provide a wealth of information for an attacker.

error | warning

☑ Error messages are also very revealing in just about every context.

☑ In some cases, warning text can provide important insight into the behind-the-scenes code used by a target.

login | logon

☑ This query locates login portals fairly effectively.

☑ It can also be used to harvest usernames and troubleshooting procedures.

username | userid | employee.ID | "your username is"

- ☑ This is one of the most generic searches for username harvesting.

- ☑ In cases where this query does not reveal usernames, the context around these words can reveal procedural information an attacker can use in later offensive action.

password | passcode | "your password is"

- ☑ This query reflects common uses of the word *password*.

- ☑ This query can reveal documents describing login procedures, password change procedures, and clues about password policies in use on the target. *Passcode* is specifically interesting for locating information about conference calls, especially when used in a Google calendar search.

admin | administrator

- ☑ Using the two most common terms for the owner or maintainer of a site, this query can also be used to reveal procedural information ("contact your administrator") and even admin login portals.

−ext:html −ext:htm −ext:shtml −ext:asp −ext:php

- ☑ This query, when combined with the *site* operator, gets the most common files out of the way to reveal more interesting documents.

- ☑ This query should be modified to reduce other common file types on a target-by-target basis.

inurl:temp | inurl:tmp | inurl:backup | inurl:bak

- ☑ This query locates backup or temporary files and directories.

intranet | help.desk

- ☑ This query locates intranet sites (which are often supposed to be protected from the general public) and help desk contact information and procedures.

Frequently Asked Questions

The following Frequently Asked Questions, answered by the authors of this book, are designed to both measure your understanding of the concepts presented in this chapter and to assist you with real-life implementation of these concepts. To have your questions about this chapter answered by the author, browse to **www. syngress.com/solutions** and click on the **"Ask the Author"** form.

Q: If automation is an option, what's so great about 10 measly searches?

A: Automation tools, such as those discussed in Chapters 11 and 12, have their place. However, the vast majority of the searches covered in large query lists are very specific searches that target a very small minority of Internet sites. Although the effects of these specific queries are often devastating, it's often nice to have a short list of powerful searches to get the creative juices flowing during an assessment, especially if you've reached a dead end using more conventional means.

Q: Doesn't it make more sense to base a list like this off a more popular list like the SANS Top 20 list at www.sans.org/top20?

A: There's nothing wrong with the SANS Top 20 list, except for the fact that the vast majority of the items on the list describe vulnerabilities that are not Web-based. This means that in most cases the vulnerabilities described there cannot be detected or exploited via Web-based services such as Google.

## Chapter 8

Tracking Down Web Servers, Login Portals, and Network Hardware

Solutions in this chapter:

- **Locating and Profiling Web Servers**
- **Locating Login Portals**
- **Locating Other Network Hardware**
- **Using and Locating Various Web Utilities**
- **Targeting Web-Enabled Network Devices**

☑ Summary

☑ Solutions Fast Track

☑ Frequently Asked Questions

Introduction

Penetration (pen) testers are sometimes thought of as professional hackers since they essentially break into their customers' networks in an attempt to locate, document, and ultimately help resolve security flaws in a system or network. However, pen testers and hackers differ quite a bit in several ways.

For example, most penetration testers are provided with specific instructions about which networks and systems they will be testing. Their targets are specified for many reasons, but in all cases, their targets are clearly defined or bounded in some fashion. Hackers, on the other hand, have the luxury of selecting from a wider target base. Depending on his or her motivations and skill level, the attacker might opt to select a target based on known exploits at his disposal. This reverses the model used by pen testers, and as such it affects the structure we will use to explore the topic of Google hacking. The techniques we'll explore in the next few chapters are most often employed by hackers—the "bad guys."

Penetration testers have access to the techniques we'll explore in these chapters, but in many cases these techniques are too cumbersome for use during a vulnerability assessment, when time is of the essence. Security professionals often use specialized tools that perform these tasks in a much more streamlined fashion, but these tools make lots of noise and often overlook the simplest form of information leakage that Google is so capable of revealing—and revealing in a way that's nearly impossible to catch on the "radar." The techniques we'll examine here are used on a daily basis to locate and explore the systems and networks attached to the Internet, so it's important that we explore how these techniques are used to better understand the level of exposure and how that exposure can be properly mitigated.

The techniques we explore in this chapter are used to locate and analyze the front-end systems on an Internet-connected network. We look at ways an attacker can profile Web servers using seemingly insignificant clues found with Google queries. Next, we'll look at methods used to locate login portals, the literal front door of most Web sites. As we will see, some login portals provide administrators of a system an access point for performing various administrative functions. Most login portals provide clues to an attacker about what software is in use on the server, and act as a magnet, drawing attackers that are armed with an exploit for that particular type of software. We round out the chapter by showing techniques that can be used to locate all sorts of network devices—firewalls, routers, network printers, and even Web cameras.

Locating and Profiling Web Servers

If an attacker hasn't already decided on a target, he might begin with a Google search for specific targets that match an exploit at his disposal. He might focus specifically on the operating system, the version and brand of Web server software, default configurations, vulnerable scripts, or any combination of factors.

There are many different ways to locate a server. The most common way is with a simple portscan. Using a tool such as Nmap, a simple scan of port 80 across a class C network will expose potential Web servers. Integrated tools such as Nessus, H.E.A.T., or Retina will run some type of portscan, followed by a series of security tests. These functions can be replicated with Google queries, although in most cases the results are nowhere near as effective as the results from a well thought out vulnerability scanner or Web assessment tool. Remember, though, that Google queries are less obvious and provide a degree of separation between an attacker and a target. Also remember that hackers can use Google hacking techniques to find systems you may be charged with protecting. The bottom line is that it's important to understand the capabilities of the Google hacker and realize the role Google can play in an attacker's methodology.

Directory Listings

We discussed directory listings in Chapter 3, but the importance of directory listings with regard to profiling methods is important. The *server* tag at the bottom of a directory listing can provide explicit detail about the type of Web server software that's running. If an attacker has an exploit for Apache 2.0.52 running on a UNIX server, a query such as *server.at* *"Apache/2.0.52"* will locate servers that host a directory listing with an Apache 2.0.52 *server* tag, as shown in Figure 8.1.

Figure 8.1 Standard *Server* Tags Can Be Used for Locating Servers

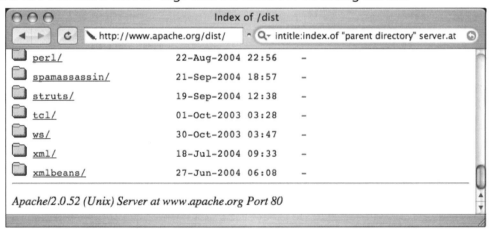

TIP

Remember to always check the real page (as opposed to the cached page), because server version numbers could change between crawls.

Not all Web servers place this tag at the bottom of directory listings, but most Apache derivatives turn on this feature by default. Other platforms, such as Microsoft's Internet Information Server (IIS), display server tags as well, as a query for *"Microsoft-IIS/5.0 server at"* shows in Figure 8.2.

Figure 8.2 Finding IIS 5.0 Servers

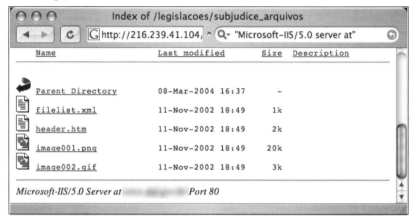

When searching for these directory tags, keep in mind that your syntax is very important. There are many irrelevant results from a query for *"Microsoft-IIS/6.0" "server at"*, whereas a query like *"Microsoft-IIS/6.0 server at"* provides very relevant results. Since we've already covered directory listings, we won't dwell on it here. Refer back to Chapter 3 if you need a refresher on directory listings.

Web Server Software Error Messages

Error messages contain a lot of useful information, but in the context of locating specific servers, we can use portions of various error messages to locate servers running specific software versions. We'll begin our discussion by looking at error messages that are generated by the Web server software itself.

Microsoft IIS

The absolute best way to find error messages is to figure out what messages the server is capable of generating. You could gather these messages by examining the server source code or configuration files or by actually generating the errors on the server yourself. The best way to get this information from IIS is by examining the source code of the error pages themselves.

IIS 5.0 and 6.0, by default, display static Hypertext Transfer Protocol (HTTP)/1.1 error messages when the server encounters some sort of problem. These error pages are stored by default in the *%SYSTEMROOT%\help\iisHelp\common* directory. These files are essentially

Hypertext Markup language (HTML) files named by the type of error they produce, such as 400.htm, 401-1.htm, 501.htm, and so on. By analyzing these files, we can come up with trends and commonalities between the pages that are essential for effective Google searching. For example, the file that produces 400 error pages, 400.htm, contains a line (line 12) that looks like this:

```
<title>The page cannot be found</title>
```

This is a dead giveaway for an effective *intitle* query such as *intitle:" "The page cannot be found"*. Unfortunately, this search yields (as you might guess) far too many results. We'll need to dig deeper into the 400.htm file to get more clues about what to look for. Lines 65–88 of 400.htm are shown here:

```
65.    <p>Please try the following:</p>
66.    <ul>
67.    <li>If you typed the page address in the Address bar, make sure that it is
spelled correctly.</li>
68.
69.    <li>Open the
70.
71.    <script language="JavaScript">
72.    <!--
73.    if (!((window.navigator.userAgent.indexOf("MSIE") > 0) &&
(window.navigator.appVersion.charAt(0) == "2")))
74.    {
75.    Homepage();
76.    }
77.    -->
78.    </script>
79.
80.    home page, and then look for links to the information you want.</li>
81.
82.    <li>Click the
83.    <a href="javascript:history.back(1)">
84.    Back</a> button to try another link.</li>
85.    </ul>
86.
87.    <h2 style="COLOR:000000; FONT: 8pt/11pt verdana">HTTP 400 - Bad Request<br>
88.    Internet Information Services</h2>
```

The phrase "*Please try the following*" in line 65 exists in *every single* error file in this directory, making it a perfect candidate for part of a good base search. This line could effectively be reduced to *"please * * following."* Line 88 shows another phrase that appears in every error document; *"Internet Information Services,"* These are "golden terms" to use to search for IIS HTTP/1.1 error pages that Google has crawled. A query such as *intitle:"The page cannot be found" "please ＊ ＊ following" "Internet ＊ Services"* can be used to search for IIS servers that present a 400 error page, as shown in Figure 8.3.

Figure 8.3 Smart Search for Locating IIS Servers

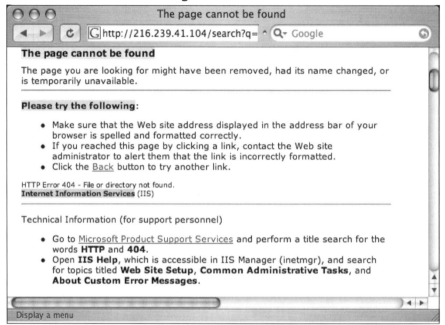

Looking at this cached page carefully, you'll notice that the actual error code itself is printed on the page, about halfway down. This error line is also printed on each of IIS's error pages, making for another good limiter for our searching. The line on the page begins with *"HTTP Error 404,"* which might seem out of place, considering we were searching for a 400 error code, not a 404 error code. This occurs because several IIS error pages produce similar pages. Although commonalities are often good for Google searching, they could lead to some confusion and produce ineffective results if we are searching for a specific, less benign error page. It's obvious that we'll need to sort out exactly what's what in these error page files. Table 8.1 lists all the unique HTML error page titles and error codes from a default IIS 5 installation.

Table 8.1 IIS HTTP/1.1 Error Page Titles

Error Code	Page Title
400	The page cannot be found
401.1, 401.2, 401.3, 401.4, 401.5	You are not authorized to view this page
403.1, 403.2	The page cannot be displayed
403.3	The page cannot be saved
403.4	The page must be viewed over a secure channel
403.5 Web browser	The page must be viewed with a high-security
403.6	You are not authorized to view this page
403.7	The page requires a client certificate
403.8	You are not authorized to view this page
403.9	The page cannot be displayed
403.10, 403.11	You are not authorized to view this page
403.12, 403.13	The page requires a valid client certificate
403.15	The page cannot be displayed
403.16, 403.17	The page requires a valid client certificate
404.1, 404b	The Web site cannot be found
405	The page cannot be displayed
406	The resource cannot be displayed
407	Proxy authentication required
410	The page does not exist
412	The page cannot be displayed
414	The page cannot be displayed
500, 500.11, 500.12, 500.13, 500.14, 500.15	The page cannot be displayed
502	The page cannot be displayed

These page titles, used in an *intitle* search, combined with the other golden IIS error searches, make for very effective searches, locating all sorts of IIS servers that generate all sorts of telling error pages. To troll for IIS servers with the esoteric 404.1 error page, try a query such *as intitle:"The Web site cannot be found" "please ★ ★ following"*. A more common error can be found with a query such as *intitle:"The page cannot be displayed" "Internet Information Services" "please ★ ★ following"*, which is very effective because this error page is shown for many different error codes.

In addition to displaying the default static HTTP/1.1 error pages, IIS can be configured to display custom error messages, configured via the Management Console. An example of this type of custom error page is shown in Figure 8.4. This type of functionality makes the job of the Google hacker a bit more difficult since there is no apparent way to home in on a customized error page. However, some error messages, including 400, 403.9, 411, 414, 500, 500.11, 500.14, 500.15, 501, 503, and 505 pages, cannot be customized. In terms of Google hacking, this means that there is no easy way an IIS 6.0 server can prevent displaying the static HTTP/1.1 error pages we so effectively found previously. This opens the door for locating these servers through Google, even if the server has been configured to display custom error pages.

Besides trolling through the IIS error pages looking for exact phrases, we can also perform more generic queries, such as *intitle:"the page cannot be found" inetmgr"*, which focuses on the fairly unique term used to describe the IIS Management console, *inetmgr,* as shown near the bottom of Figure 8.3. Other ways to perform this same search might be *intitle:"the page cannot be found" "internet information services",* or *intitle:"Under construction" "Internet Information Services".*

Other, more specific searches can reveal the exact version of the IIS server, such as a query for *intext:" "404 Object Not Found" Microsoft-IIS/5.0,* as shown in Figure 8.4.

Figure 8.4 *"Object Not Found"* **Error Message Used to Find IIS 5.0**

Apache Web Server

Apache Web servers can also be located by focusing on server-generated error messages. Some generic searches such as *"Apache/1.3.27 Server at" "-intitle:index.of intitle:inf"* or *"Apache/1.3.27 Server at" -intitle:index.of intitle:error* (shown in Figure 8.5) can be used to locate servers that might be advertising their server version via an info or error message.

Figure 8.5 A Generic Error Search Locates Apache Servers

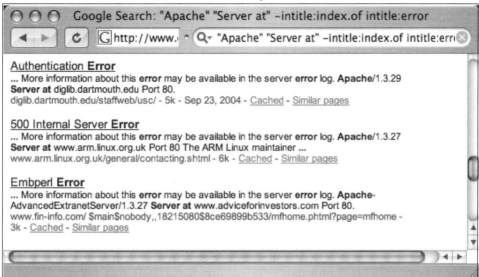

A query such as *"Apache/2.0.40" intitle:"Object not found!"* will locate Apache 2.0.40 Web servers that presented this error message. Figure 8.6 shows an error page from an Apache 2.0.40 server shipped with Red Hat 9.0.

Figure 8.6 A Common Error Message from Apache 2.0.40

Although there might be nothing wrong with throwing queries around looking for commonalities and good base searches, we've already seen in the IIS section that it's more effective to consult the server software itself for search clues. Most Apache installations rely on a configuration file called *httpd.conf*. Searching through Apache 2.0.40's *httpd.conf* file reveals the location of the HTML templates for error messages. The referenced files (which follow) are located in the Web root directory, such as */error/http_BAD_REQUEST.html.var*, which refers to the */var/www/error* directory on the file system:

```
ErrorDocument 400 /error/HTTP_BAD_REQUEST.html.var
ErrorDocument 401 /error/HTTP_UNAUTHORIZED.html.var
ErrorDocument 403 /error/HTTP_FORBIDDEN.html.var
ErrorDocument 404 /error/HTTP_NOT_FOUND.html.var
ErrorDocument 405 /error/HTTP_METHOD_NOT_ALLOWED.html.var
ErrorDocument 408 /error/HTTP_REQUEST_TIME_OUT.html.var
ErrorDocument 410 /error/HTTP_GONE.html.var
ErrorDocument 411 /error/HTTP_LENGTH_REQUIRED.html.var
ErrorDocument 412 /error/HTTP_PRECONDITION_FAILED.html.var
ErrorDocument 413 /error/HTTP_REQUEST_ENTITY_TOO_LARGE.html.var
ErrorDocument 414 /error/HTTP_REQUEST_URI_TOO_LARGE.html.var
ErrorDocument 415 /error/HTTP_SERVICE_UNAVAILABLE.html.var
ErrorDocument 500 /error/HTTP_INTERNAL_SERVER_ERROR.html.var
ErrorDocument 501 /error/HTTP_NOT_IMPLEMENTED.html.var
ErrorDocument 502 /error/HTTP_BAD_GATEWAY.html.var
ErrorDocument 503 /error/HTTP_SERVICE_UNAVAILABLE.html.var
ErrorDocument 506 /error/HTTP_VARIANT_ALSO_VARIES.html.var
```

Taking a look at one of these template files, we can see recognizable HTML code and variable listings that show the construction of an error page. The file itself is divided into sections by language. The English portion of the *HTTP_NOT_FOUND.html.var* file is shown here:

```
Content-language: en
Content-type: text/html
Body:----------en--
<!-#set var="TITLE" value="Object not found!" ->
<!-#include virtual="include/top.html" ->

    The requested URL was not found on this server.

  <!--#if expr="$HTTP_REFERER" -->

    The link on the
```

```
<a href="<!--#echo encoding="url" var="HTTP_REFERER"-->">referring
page</a> seems to be wrong or outdated. Please inform the author of
<a href="<!--#echo encoding="url" var="HTTP_REFERER"-->">that page</a>
about the error.

<!--#else -->

If you entered the URL manually please check your
spelling and try again.

<!--#endif -->

<!--#include virtual="include/bottom.html" ->
----------en--
```

Notice that the sections of the error page are clearly labeled, making it easy to translate into Google queries. The *TITLE* variable, shown near the top of the listing, indicates that the text "*Object not found!*" will be displayed in the browser's title bar. When this file is processed and displayed in a Web browser, it will look like Figure 8.2. However, Google hacking is not always this easy. A search for *intitle:"Object not found!"* is too generic, returning the results shown in Figure 8.7.

Figure 8.7 Error Message Text Is Not Enough for Profiling

These results are not what we're looking for. To narrow our results, we need a better base search. Constructing our base search from the template files included with the Apache 2.0 source code not only enables us to locate all the potential error messages the server is capable of producing, it also shows us how those messages are translated into other languages, resulting in very solid multilingual base searches.

The *HTTP_NOT_FOUND.html.var* file listed previously references two *virtual include* lines, one near the top (*include/top.html*) and one near the bottom (*include/bottom.html*). These lines instruct Apache to read and insert the contents of these two files (located in our case in the */var/www/error/include* directory) into the current file. The following code lists the contents of the *bottom.html* file and show some subtleties that will help construct that perfect base search:

```
</dd></dl><dl><dd>
<!--#include virtual="../contact.html.var" -->
</dd></dl>
<h2>Error <!--#echo encoding="none" var="REDIRECT_STATUS" --></h2>
<dl>
<dd>
<address>
<a href="/"><!--#echo encoding="url" var="SERVER_NAME" --></a>
<br />
<!--#config timefmt="%c" -->
<small><!--#echo encoding="none" var="DATE_LOCAL" --></small>
<br />
<small><!--#echo encoding="none" var="SERVER_SOFTWARE" --></small>
</address>
</dd>
</dl>
</body>
</html>
```

First, notice line 4, which will display the word "*Error*" on the page. Although this might seem very generic, it's an important subtlety that would keep results like the ones in Figure 8.7 from displaying. Line 2 shows that another file (*/var/www/error/contact.html.var*) is read and included into this file. The contents of this file, listed as follows, contain more details that we can include into our base search:

```
1.    Content-language: en
2.    Content-type: text/html
3.    Body:----------en--
4.    If you think this is a server error, please contact
```

```
5.      the <a href="mailto:<!--#echo encoding="none" var="SERVER_ADMIN" --
>">webmaster</a>
6.      ----------en--
```

This file, like the file that started this whole "include chain," is broken up into sections by language. The portion of this file listed here shows yet another unique string we can use. We'll select a fairly unique piece of this line, *"think this is a server error,"* as a portion of our base search instead of just the word *error*, which we used initially to remove some false positives. The other part of our base search, *intitle:"Object not found!"*, was originally found in the */error/http_BAD_REQUEST.html.var* file. The final base search for this file then becomes *intitle:"Object Not Found!" "think this is a server error"*, which returns more accurate results, as shown in Figure 8.8.

Figure 8.8 A Good Base Search Evolved

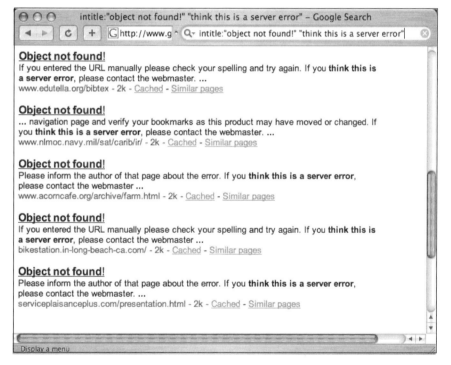

Now that we've found a good base search for one error page, we can automate the query-hunting process to determine good base searches for the other error pages referenced in the *httpd.conf* file, helping us create solid base searches for each and every default Apache (2.0) error page. The *contact.html.var* file that we saw previously is included in each and every Apache 2.0 error page via the *bottom.html* file. This means that *"think this is a server error"* will work for all the different error pages that Apache 2.0 will produce. The other critical element to our search was the *intitle* search, which we could *grep* for in each of the error files.

While we're at it, we should also try to grab a snippet of the text that is printed in each of the error pages, remembering that in some cases a more specific search might be needed. Using some basic shell commands, we can isolate both the title of an error page and the text that might appear on the error page:

```
grep -h -r "Content-language: en" * -A 10 | grep -A5 "TITLE" | grep -v virtual
```

This Linux bash shell command, when run against the Apache 2.0 source code tree, will produce output similar to that shown in Table 8.2. This table lists the title of each English Apache (2.0 and newer) error page as well as a portion of the text that will be located on the page. Instead of searching for English messages only, we could search for errors in other Apache-supported languages by simply replacing the *Content-language* string in the previous *grep* command from *en* to either *de, es, fr,* or *sv*, for German, Spanish, French, or Swedish, respectively.

Table 8.2 The Title and Partial Text of English Apache 2.0 Error Pages

Error Page Title	Error Page Partial Text
Bad gateway!	The proxy server received an invalid response from an upstream server.
Bad request!	Your browser (or proxy) sent a request that this server could not understand.
Access forbidden!	You don't have permission to access the requested directory. Either there is no index document or the directory is read-protected.
Resource is no longer available!	The requested URL is no longer available on this server and there is no forwarding address.
Server error!	The server encountered an internal error and was unable to complete your request.
Method not allowed!	A request with the method is not allowed for the requested URL.
No acceptable object found!	An appropriate representation of the requested resource could not be found on this server.
Object not found!	The requested Uniform Resource Locator (URL) was not found on this server.
Cannot process request!	The server does not support the action requested by the browser.
Precondition failed!	The precondition on the request for the URL failed positive evaluation.

Continued

Table 8.2 continued The Title and Partial Text of English Apache 2.0 Error Pages

Error Page Title	Error Page Partial Text
Request entity too large!	The method does not allow the data transmitted, or the data volume exceeds the capacity limit.
Request time-out!	The server closed the network connection because the browser didn't finish the request within the specified time.
Submitted URI too large!	The length of the requested URL exceeds the capacity limit for this server. The request cannot be processed.
Service unavailable!	The server is temporarily unable to service your request due to maintenance downtime or capacity problems. Please try again later.
Authentication required!	This server could not verify that you are authorized to access the URL. You either supplied the wrong credentials (such as a bad password), or your browser doesn't understand how to supply the credentials required.
Unsupported media type!	The server does not support the media type transmitted in the request.
Variant also varies!	A variant for the requested entity is itself a negotiable resource. Access not possible.

To use this table, simply supply the text in the Error Page Title column as an *intitle* search and a portion of the text column as an additional phrase in the search query. Since some of the text is lengthy, you might need to select a unique portion of the text or replace common words with an asterisk, which will reduce your search query to the 10-word limit imposed on Google queries. For example, a good query for the first line of the table might be *"response from * upstream server." intitle:"Bad Gateway!"*. Alternately, you could also rely on the *"think this is a server error"* phrase combined with a title search, such as *"think this is a server error" intitle:"Bad Gateway!"*. Different versions of Apache will display slightly different error messages, but the process of locating and creating solid base searches from software source code is something you should get comfortable with to stay ahead of the ever-changing software market.

This technique can be expanded to find Apache servers in other languages by reviewing the rest of the *contact.html.var* file. The important strings from that file are listed in Table 8.3. Because these sentences and phrases are included in every Apache 2.0 error message, they should appear *in the text* of *every error page* that the Apache server produces, making them ideal for base searches. It is possible (and fairly easy) to modify these error pages to provide a more polished appearance when a user encounters an error, but remember, hackers have different motivations. Some are simply interested in locating particular versions of a server, perhaps to exploit. Using this criteria, there is no shortage of servers on the Internet that are using these default error phrases, and by extension may have a default, less-secured configuration.

Table 8.3 Phrases Located on All Default Apache (2.0.28–2.0.52) Error Pages

Language	Phrases
German	Sofern Sie dies für eine Fehlfunktion des Servers halten, informieren Sie bitte den hierüber.
English	If you think this is a server error, please contact.
Spanish	En caso de que usted crea que existe un error en el servidor.
French	Si vous pensez qu'il s'agit d'une erreur du serveur, veuillez contacter.
Swedish	Om du tror att detta beror på ett serverfel, vänligen kontakta.

Besides Apache and IIS, other servers (and other versions of these servers) can be located by searching for server-produced error messages, but we're trying to keep this book just a bit thinner than your local yellow pages, so we'll draw the line at just these two servers.

Application Software Error Messages

The error messages we've looked at so far have all been generated by the Web server itself. In many cases, applications running on the Web server can generate errors that reveal information about the server as well. There are untold thousands of Web applications on the Internet, each of which can generate any number of error messages. Dedicated Web assessment tools such as SPI Dynamic's WebInspect excel at performing detailed Web application assessments, making it seem a bit pointless to troll Google for application error messages. However, we search for error message output throughout this book simply because the data contained in error messages should not be overlooked.

We've looked at various error messages in previous chapters, and we'll see more error messages in later chapters, but let's take a quick look at how error messages can help profile a Web server and its applications. Admittedly, we will hardly scratch the surface of this topic, but we'll make an effort to stimulate your thinking about Google's ability to locate these sometimes very telling error messages.

One query, *"Fatal error: Call to undefined function" -reply -the –next*, will locate Active Server Page (ASP) error messages. These messages often reveal information about the database software in use on the server as well as information about the application that caused the error (see Figure 8.9).

Figure 8.9 ASP Custom Error Messages

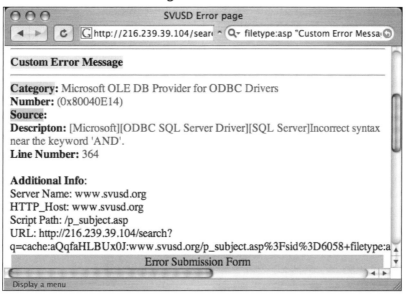

Although this ASP message is fairly benign, some ASP error messages are much more revealing. Consider the query *"ASP.NET_SessionId" "data source="*, which locates unique strings found in ASP.NET application state dumps, as shown in Figure 8.10. These dumps reveal all sorts of information about the running application and the Web server that hosts that application. An advanced attacker could use encrypted password data and variable information in these stack traces to subvert the security of the application and perhaps the Web server itself.

Figure 8.10 ASP Dumps Provide Dangerous Details

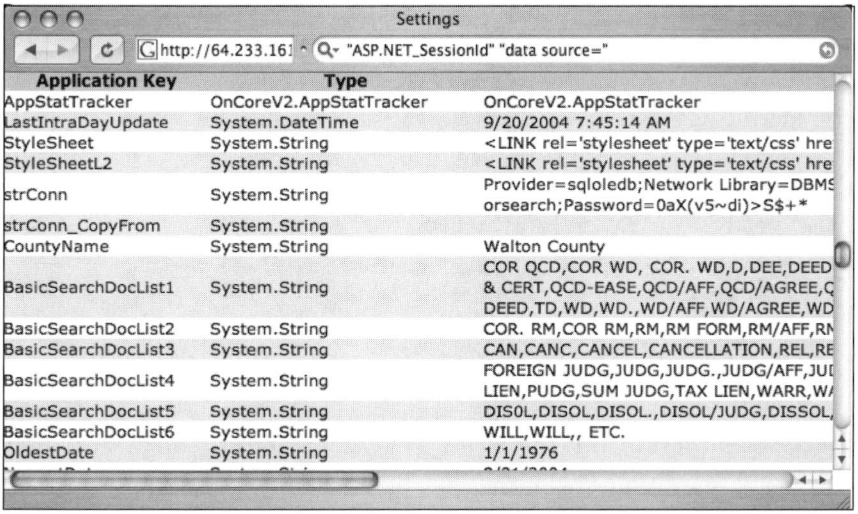

Hypertext Preprocessor (PHP) application errors are fairly commonplace. They can reveal all sorts of information that an attacker can use to profile a server. One very common error can be found with a query such as *intext:"Warning: Failed opening" include_path,* as shown in Figure 8.11.

Figure 8.11 Many Errors Reveal Pathnames and Filenames

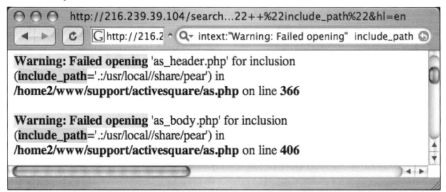

CGI programs often reveal information about the Web server and its applications in the form of environment variable dumps. A typical environmental variable output page is shown in Figure 8.12.

Figure 8.12 CGI Environment Listings Reveal Lots of Information

```
  http://64.233.161.104/search?q=cac...bot.com+%22Server_Software".&hl=en
  http://64.233.1  "HTTP_FROM=googlebot" googlebot.com "Server_Softwa
HTTP_ACCEPT : text/html,text/plain
HTTP_USER_AGENT : Googlebot/2.1 (+http://www.google.com/bot.html)
GATEWAY_INTERFACE : CGI/1.1
HTTP_HOST : www.uib.no
SERVER_SOFTWARE : Apache/1.3.26 (Unix) PHP/4.2.1
SERVER_ADMIN : webmaster@uib.no
REMOTE_ADDR : 66.249.64.183
HTTP_IF_MODIFIED_SINCE : Tue, 31 Aug 2004 01:10:34 GMT
SCRIPT_NAME : /cgi-bin/env
SERVER_NAME : www.uib.no
DOCUMENT_ROOT : /www
REQUEST_URI : /cgi-bin/env
SCRIPT_FILENAME : /local/apache/cgi-bin/env
REQUEST_METHOD : GET
PATH : /usr/sbin:/usr/bin
HTTP_FROM : googlebot(at)google.com
SERVER_PORT : 80
```

This screen shows information about the Web server and the client that connected to the page when the data was produced. Since Google's bot crawls pages for us, one way to find these CGI environment pages is to focus on the trail left by the bot, reflected in these pages as the *"HTTP_FROM=googlebot"* line. We can search for pages like this with a query such as *"HTTP_FROM=googlebot" googlebot.com "Server_Software"*. These pages are dynamically generated, which means that you must look at Google's cache to see the document as it was crawled.

To locate good base searches for a particular application, it's best to look at the source code of that application. Using the techniques we've explored so far, it's simple to create these searches.

Default Pages

Another way to locate specific types of servers or Web software is to search for default Web pages. Most Web software, including the Web server software itself, ships with one or more default or test pages. These pages can make it easy for a site administrator to test the installation of a Web server or application. By providing a simple page to test, the administrator can simply connect to his own Web server with a browser to validate that the Web software was installed correctly. Some operating systems even come with Web server software already installed. In this case, the owner of the machine might not even realize that a Web server is running on his machine. This type of casual behavior on the part of the owner will lead an attacker to rightly assume that the Web software is not well maintained and is, by extension, insecure. By further extension, the attacker can also assume that the entire operating system of the server might be vulnerable by virtue of poor maintenance.

In some cases, Google crawls a Web server while it is in its earliest stages of installation, still displaying a set of default pages. In these cases there's generally a short window of time between the moment when Google crawls the site and when the intended content is actually placed on the server. This means that there could be a disparity between what the live page is displaying and what Google's cache displays. This makes little difference from a Google hacker's perspective, since even the past existence of a default page is enough for profiling purposes. Remember, we're essentially searching Google's cached version of a page when we submit a query. Regardless of the reason a server has default pages installed, there's an attacker somewhere who will eventually show interest in a machine displaying default pages found with a Google search.

A classic example of a default page is the Apache Web server default page, shown in Figure 8.13.

Figure 8.13 A Typical Apache Default Web Page

Notice that the administrator's e-mail is generic as well, indicating that not a lot of attention was paid to detail during the installation of this server. These default pages do not list the version number of the server, which is a required piece of information for a successful attack. It is possible, however, that an attacker could search for specific variations in these default pages to find specific ranges of server versions. As shown in Figure 8.14, an Apache server running versions 1.3.11 through 1.3.26 shows a slightly different page than the Apache server version 1.3.11 through 1.3.26, as shown in Figure 8.13.

Figure 8.14 Subtle Differences in Apache Default Pages

Using these subtle differences to our advantage, we can use specific Google queries to locate servers with these default pages, indicating that they are most likely running a specific version of Apache. Table 8.4 shows queries that can be used to locate specific families of Apache running default pages.

Table 8.4 Queries That Locate Default Apache Installations

Apache Server Version	Query
Apache 1.2.6	intitle:"Test Page for Apache Installation" "You are free"
Apache 1.3.0–1.3.9	intitle:"Test Page for Apache" "It worked!" "this Web site!"
Apache 1.3.11–1.3.31	intitle:Test.Page.for.Apache seeing.this.instead
Apache 2.0	intitle:Simple.page.for.Apache Apache.Hook.Functions
Apache SSL/TLS	intitle:test.page "Hey, it worked !" "SSL/TLS-aware"
Apache on Red Hat	"Test Page for the Apache Web Server on Red Hat Linux"
Apache on Fedora	intitle:"test page for the apache http server on fedora core"
Apache on Debian	intitle:"Welcome to Your New Home Page!" debian
Apache on other Linux	intitle:"Test Page * * Apache Web Server on " -red.hat -fedora

IIS also displays a default Web page when first installed. A query such as *intitle: "Welcome to IIS 4.0"* can locate very specific versions of IIS, as shown in Figure 8.15.

Table 8.5 Queries That Locate Specific IIS Server Versions

IIS Server Version	Query
Many	intitle:"welcome to" intitle:internet IIS
Unknown	intitle:"Under construction" "does not currently have"
IIS 4.0	intitle:"welcome to IIS 4.0"
IIS 4.0	allintitle:Welcome to Windows NT 4.0 Option Pack
IIS 4.0	allintitle:Welcome to Internet Information Server
IIS 5.0	allintitle:Welcome to Windows 2000 Internet Services
IIS 6.0	allintitle:Welcome to Windows XP Server Internet Services

Figure 8.15 Locating Default Installations of IIS 4.0 on Windows NT 4.0/OP

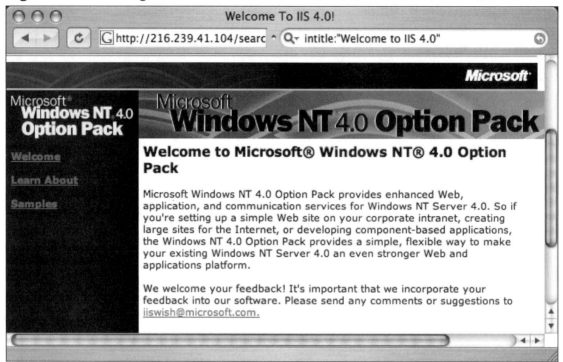

Although each version of IIS displays distinct default Web pages, in some cases service packs or hotfixes could alter the content of a default page. In these cases, the subtle page changes can be incorporated into the search to find not only the operating system version and Web server version, but also the service pack level and security patch level. This information is invaluable to an attacker bent on hacking not only the Web server, but hacking beyond the Web server and into the operating system itself. In most cases, an attacker with control of the operating system can wreak more havoc on a machine than a hacker who controls only the Web server.

Netscape servers can also be located with simple queries such as *allintitle:Netscape Enterprise Server Home Page,* as shown in Figure 8.16.

Figure 8.16 Locating Netscape Web Servers

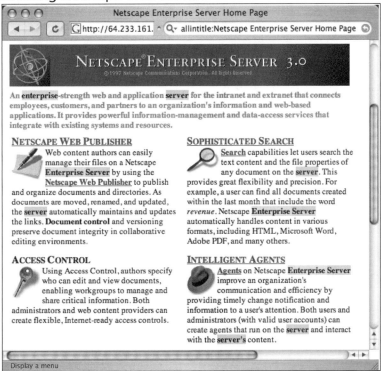

Other Netscape servers can be found with simple *allintitle* searches, as shown in Table 8.6.

Table 8.6 Queries That Locate Netscape Servers

Netscape Server Type	Query
Enterprise Server	*allintitle:Netscape Enterprise Server Home Page*
FastTrack Server	*allintitle:Netscape FastTrack Server Home Page*

Many different types of Web server can be located by querying for default pages as well. Table 8.7 lists a sample of more esoteric Web servers that can be profiled with this technique.

Table 8.7 Queries That Locate More Esoteric Servers

Server/Version	Query
Cisco Micro Webserver 200	*"micro webserver home page"*
Generic Appliance	*"default web page" congratulations "hosting appliance"*
HP appliance sa1*	*intitle:"default domain page" "congratulations" "hp web"*
iPlanet/Many	*intitle:"web server, enterprise edition"*
Intel Netstructure	*"congratulations on choosing" intel netstructure*
JWS/1.0.3–2.0	*allintitle:default home page java web server*
J2EE/Many	*intitle:"default j2ee home page"*
Jigsaw/2.2.3	*intitle:"jigsaw overview" "this is your"*
Jigsaw/Many	*intitle:"jigsaw overview"*
KFSensor honeypot	*"KF Web Server Home Page"*
Kwiki	*"Congratulations! You've created a new Kwiki website."*
Matrix Appliance	*"Welcome to your domain web page" matrix*
NetWare 6	*intitle:"welcome to netware 6"*
Resin/Many	*allintitle:Resin Default Home Page*
Resin/Enterprise	*allintitle:Resin-Enterprise Default Home Page*
Sambar Server	*intitle:"sambar server" "1997..2004 Sambar"*
Sun AnswerBook Server	*inurl:"Answerbook2options"*
TivoConnect Server	*inurl:/TiVoConnect*

Default Documentation

Web server software often ships with manuals and documentation that ends up in the Web directories. An attacker could use this documentation to either profile or locate Web software. For example, Apache Web servers ship with documentation in HTML format, as shown in Figure 8.17.

Figure 8.17 Apache Documentation Used for Profiling

In most cases, default documentation does not as accurately portray the server version as well as error messages or default pages, but this information can certainly be used to locate targets and to gain an understanding of the potential security posture of the server. If the server administrator has forgotten to delete the default documentation, an attacker has every reason to believe that other details such as security have been overlooked as well. Other Web servers, such as IIS, ship with default documentation as well, as shown in Figure 8.18.

In most cases, specialized programs such as CGI scanners or Web application assessment tools are better suited for finding these default pages and programs, but if Google has crawled the pages (from a link on a default main page for example), you'll be able to locate these pages with Google queries. Some queries that can be used to locate default documentation are listed in Table 8.8.

Figure 8.18 IIS Server Profiled Via Default Manuals

Table 8.8 Queries That Locate Default Documentation

	Query
Apache 1.3	intitle:"Apache 1.3 documentation"
Apache 2.0	intitle: "Apache 2.0 documentation"
Apache Various	intitle:"Apache HTTP Server" intitle:" documentation" \
ColdFusion	inurl:cfdocs
EAServer	intitle:"Easerver" "Easerver Version * Documents"
iPlanet Server 4.1/Enterprise Server 4.0	inurl:"/manual/servlets/" intitle:"programmer"
IIS/Various	inurl:iishelp core
Lotus Domino 6	intext:/help/help6_client.nsf
Novell Groupwise 6	inurl:/com/novell/gwmonitor
Novell Groupwise WebAccess	inurl:"/com/novell/webaccess"
Novell Groupwise WebPublisher	inurl:"/com/novell/webpublisher"

Sample Programs

In addition to documentation and manuals that ship with Web software, it is fairly common for default applications to be included with a software package. These default applications, like default Web pages, help demonstrate the functionality of the software and serve as a starting point for developers, providing sample routines and code that could be used as learning tools. Unfortunately, these sample programs can be used to not only profile a Web server; often these sample programs contain flaws or functionality an attacker could use to compromise the server. The Microsoft Index Server simple content query page, shown in Figure 8.19, allows Web visitors to search through the content of a Web site. In some cases, this query page could locate pages that are not linked from any other page or that contain sensitive information.

Figure 8.19 Microsoft Index Server Simple Content Query Page

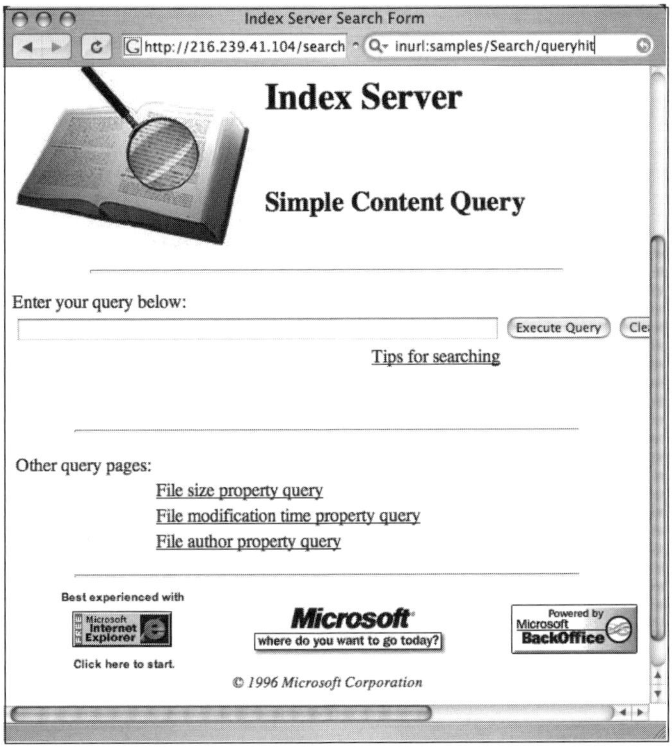

As with default pages, specialized programs designed to crawl a Web site in search of these default programs are much better suited for finding these pages. However, if a default page provided with a Web server contains links to demonstration pages and programs, Google will find them. In some cases, the cache of these pages will remain even after the main page has been updated and the links removed. And remember, you can use the cache page, along with the *&strip=1* option to view the page anonymously. This keeps the information gathering exercise away from the watchful eye of the server's admin. Table 8.9 shows some queries that can be used to locate default-installed programs.

Table 8.9 Queries That Locate Default Programs

Software	Query
Apache Cocoon	*inurl:cocoon/samples/welcome*
Generic	*inurl:demo | inurl:demos*
Generic	*inurl:sample | inurl:samples*
IBM Websphere	*inurl:WebSphereSamples*
Lotus Domino 4.6	*inurl: /sample/framew46*
Lotus Domino 4.6	*inurl:/sample/faqw46*
Lotus Domino 4.6	*inurl:/sample/pagesw46*
Lotus Domino 4.6	*inurl:/sample/siregw46*
Lotus Domino 4.6	*inurl:/sample/faqw46*
Lotus Domino 4.6	*inurl:/sample/faqw46*
Lotus Domino 4.6	*inurl:/sample/faqw46*
Lotus Domino 4.6	*inurl:/sample/faqw46*
Microsoft Index Server	*inurl:samples/Search/queryhit*
Microsoft Site Server	*inurl:siteserver/docs*
Novell NetWare 5	*inurl:/lcgi/sewse.nlm*
Novell GroupWise WebPublisher	*inurl:/servlet/webpub groupwise*
Netware WebSphere	*inurl:/servlet/SessionServlet*
OpenVMS!	*inurl:sys$common*
Oracle Demos	*inurl:/demo/sql/index.jsp*
Oracle JSP Demos	*inurl:demo/basic/info*
Oracle JSP Scripts	*inurl:ojspdemos*
Oracle 9i	*inurl:/pls/simpledad/admin_*
IIS/Various	*inurl:iissamples*
IIS/Various	*inurl:/scripts/samples/search*
Sambar Server	*intitle:"Sambar Server Samples"*

Locating Login Portals

Login portal is a term I use to describe a Web page that serves as a "front door" to a Web site. Login portals are designed to allow access to specific features or functions after a user logs in. Google hackers search for login portals as a way to profile the software that's in use on a target, and to locate links and documentation that might provide useful information for an attack. In addition, if an attacker has an exploit for a particular piece of software, and that software provides a login portal, the attacker can use Google queries to locate potential targets.

Some login portals, like the one shown in Figure 8.20, captured with *"microsoft outlook" "web access" version,* are obviously default pages provided by the software manufacturer—in this case, Microsoft. Just as an attacker can get an idea of the potential security of a target by simply looking for default pages, a default login portal can indicate that the technical skill of the server's administrators is generally low, revealing that the security of the site will most likely be poor as well. To make matters worse, default login portals like the one shown in Figure 8.20, indicate the software revision of the program—in this case, version 5.5 SP4. An attacker can use this information to search for known vulnerabilities in that software version.

Figure 8.20 Outlook Web Access Default Portal

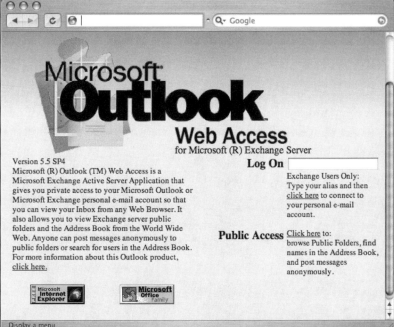

By following links from the login portal, an attacker can often gain access to other information about the target. The Outlook Web Access portal is particularly renowned for this type of information leak, because it provides an anonymous public access area that can be viewed without logging in to the mail system. This public access area sometimes provides access to a public directory or to broadcast e-mails that can be used to gather usernames or information, as shown in Figure 8.21.

Figure 8.21 Public Access Areas Can Be Found from Login Portals

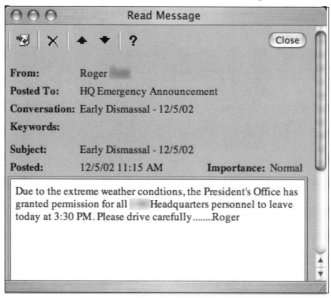

Some login portals provide more details than others. As shown in Figure 8.22, the Novell Management Portal provides a great deal of information about the server, including server software version and revision, application software version and revision, software upgrade date, and server uptime. This type of information is very handy for an attacker staging an attack against the server.

Figure 8.22 Novell Management Portal Reveals a Great Deal of Information

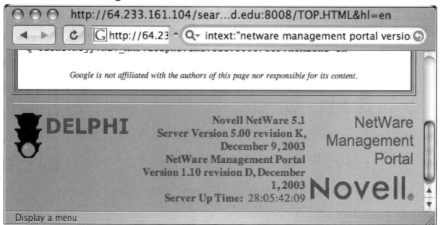

Table 8.9 shows some queries that can be used to locate various login portals. Refer to Chapter 4 for more information about login portals and the information they reveal.

Table 8.9 Queries That Locate Login Portals

Login Portal	Query
.NET login pages	ASP.login_aspx "ASP.NET_SessionId"
4images Gallery	"4images Administration Control Panel"
Aanval Intrusion Detection Console	intitle:"remote assessment" OpenAanval Console
ActiveX Login	inurl:"Activex/default.htm" "Demo"
Affiliate Tracking Software	intitle:"iDevAffiliate - admin" -demo
Aimoo	intitle:"Login to the forums - @www.aimoo.com" inurl:login.cfm?id=
AlternC Desktop	intitle:"AlternC Desktop"
Ampache	intitle:Ampache intitle:"love of music" password | login | "Remember Me." -welcome
Anyboard Login Portals	intitle:"Login Forum Powered By AnyBoard" intitle:"If you are a new user:" intext:"Forum Powered By AnyBoard" inurl:gochat -edu
aspWebCalendar	inurl:"calendar.asp?action=login"
Asterisk Recording Interface	intitle:ARI "Phone System Administrator"
Athens Access Management system	intitle:"Athens Authentication Point"
b2evolution	intitle:"b2evo > Login form" "Login form. You must log in! You will have to accept cookies in order to log in" -demo -site:b2evolution.net
Bariatric Advantage	inurl:"/?pagename=AdministratorLogin"
BEA WebLogic Server 8.1	intitle:"WebLogic Server" intitle:"Console Login" inurl:console
betaparticle	"bp blog admin" intitle:login | intitle:admin -site:johnny.ihackstuff.com
bitboard2	intext:""BiTBOARD v2.0" BiTSHiFTERS Bulletin Board"
Blogware Login Portal	intitle:"Admin Login" "admin login" "blogware"
Cacti	intitle:"Login to Cacti"
Cash Crusader	"site info for" "Enter Admin Password"

Continued

Table 8.9 continued Queries That Locate Login Portals

Login Portal	Query
CGIIRC	filetype:cgi inurl:"irc.cgi" | intitle:"CGI:IRC Login"
CGIIRC	inurl:irc filetype:cgi cgi:irc
Cisco CallManager CallManager	intitle:"Cisco CallManager User Options Log On" "Please enter your User ID and Password in the spaces provided below and click the Log On button to co
Cisco VPN 3000 concentrators	intitle:"inc. vpn 3000 concentrator"
Cisco WebVPN Services Module	inurl:webvpn.html "login" "Please enter your"
Citrix Metaframe	inurl:metaframexp/default/login.asp | intitle:"Metaframe XP Login"
Citrix Metaframe	inurl:/Citrix/Nfuse17/
CMS/Blogger	inurl:textpattern/index.php
ColdFusion	intitle:"ColdFusion Administrator Login"
ColdFusion	inurl:login.cfm
Communigate Pro	intitle:communigate pro entrance
Confixx	inurl:confixx inurl:login|anmeldung
Coranto	inurl:coranto.cgi intitle:Login (Authorized Users Only)
CPanel	inurl::2082/frontend -demo
Create Pro.	inurl:csCreatePro.cgi
CUPS	inurl:"631/admin" (inurl:"op=*") | (intitle:CUPS)
CuteNews	"powered by CuteNews" "2003..2005 CutePHP"
Cyclades TS1000 and TS2000 Web Management Service	allintitle:"Welcome to the Cyclades"
Dell OpenManage	inurl:"usysinfo?login=true"
Dell Remote Access Controller	intitle:"Dell Remote Access Controller"
Docutek Eres	intitle:"Docutek ERes - Admin Login" -edu
DWMail	"Powered by DWMail" password intitle:dwmail
Easy File Sharing Web Server	intitle:"Login - powered by Easy File Sharing Web
EasyAccess Web	inurl:ids5web

Continued

Table 8.9 continued Queries That Locate Login Portals

Login Portal	Query
EasySite	"You have requested access to a restricted area of our website. Please authenticate yourself to continue."
Ecommerce	inurl:"vsadmin/login" | inurl:"vsadmin/admin" inurl:.php|.asp -"Response.Buffer = True" -javascript
eHealth	inurl:bin.welcome.sh | inurl:bin.welcome.bat | intitle:eHealth.5.0
Emergisoft	"Emergisoft web applications are a part of our"
eMule	intitle:"eMule *" intitle:"- Web Control Panel" intext:"Web Control Panel" "Enter your password here."
Ensim WEBppliance Pro.	intitle:"Welcome Site/User Administrator" "Please select the language" -demos
Enterprise Manager 10g Grid Control	inurl:1810 "Oracle Enterprise Manager"
ePowerSwitch D4 Guard	intitle:"ePowerSwitch Login"
eRecruiter	intitle:"OnLine Recruitment Program - Login" -johnny.ihackstuff
eXist	intitle:"eXist Database Administration" -demo
Extranet login pages	intitle:"EXTRANET login" -.edu -.mil -.gov -johnny.ihackstuff
eZ publish	Admin intitle:"eZ publish administration"
EZPartner	intitle:"EZPartner" -netpond
Fiber Logic Management	"Web-Based Management" "Please input password to login" -inurl:johnny.ihackstuff.com
Flash Operator Panel	intitle:"Flash Operator Panel" -ext:php -wiki -cms -inurl:asternic -inurl:sip -intitle:ANNOUNCE -inurl:lists
FlashChat	FlashChat v4.5.7
Free Perl Guestbook (FPG)	ext:cgi intitle:"control panel" "enter your owner password to continue!"
Generic	inurl:login.asp
Generic	inurl:/admin/login.asp
Generic	"please log in"

Continued

Table 8.9 continued Queries That Locate Login Portals

Login Portal	Query
Generic	"This section is for Administrators only. If you are an administrator then please"
Generic	intitle:"Member Login" "NOTE: Your browser must have cookies enabled in order to log into the site." ext:php OR ext:cgi
Generic (with password)	intitle:"please login" "your password is *"
GNU GNATS	inurl:gnatsweb.pl
GradeSpeed	inurl:"gs/adminlogin.aspx"
GreyMatter	"login prompt" inurl:GM.cgi
Group-Office	intitle:Group-Office "Enter your username and password to login"
HostingAccelerator ControlPanel	"HostingAccelerator" intitle:"login" +"Username" -"news" -demo
HP WBEM Clients	intitle:"*- HP WBEM Login" | "You are being prompted to provide login account information for *" | "Please provide the information requested and press
H-SPHERE	intext:"Welcome to" inurl:"cp" intitle:"H-SPHERE" inurl:"begin.html" -Fee
IBM TotalStorage Open Software	intext:"Storage Management Server for" intitle:"Server Administration"
IBM WebSphere	allinurl:wps/portal/ login
Icecast	intext:"Icecast Administration Admin Page" intitle:"Icecast Administration Admin Page"
iCMS	intitle:"Content Management System" "user name"|"password"|"admin" "Microsoft IE 5.5" -mambo -johnny.ihackstuff
iCMS	intitle:"Content Management System" "user name"|"password"|"admin" "Microsoft IE 5.5" -mambo -johnny.ihackstuff
iCONECTnxt	"iCONECT 4.1 :: Login"
IlohaMail	intitle:ilohamail intext:"Version 0.8.10" "Powered by IlohaMail"
IlohaMail	intitle:ilohamail "Powered by IlohaMail"
IMail Server	"IMail Server Web Messaging" intitle:login

Continued

Table 8.9 continued Queries That Locate Login Portals

Login Portal	Query
INDEXU	+"Powered by INDEXU" inurl:(browse|top_rated|power
Inspanel	"inspanel" intitle:"login" -"cannot" "Login ID" -site:inspediumsoft.com
Intranet login pages	intitle:"Employee Intranet Login"
iPlanet Messenger Express	"This is a restricted Access Server" "Javascript Not Enabled!"|"Messenger Express" -edu -ac
I-Secure	intitle:"i-secure v1.1" -edu
ISPMan	intitle:"ISPMan : Unauthorized Access prohib-ited"
Jetbox	Login ("Powered by Jetbox One CMS" | "Powered by Jetstream *")
Kerio Mail server	inurl:"default/login.php" intitle:"kerio"
Kurant StoreSense admin logon	intitle:"Kurant Corporation StoreSense" file-type:bok
Lights Out	"Establishing a secure Integrated Lights Out session with" OR intitle:"Data Frame - Browser not HTTP 1.1 compatible" OR intitle:"HP Integrated Lights-
Linux Openexchange Server	filetype:pl "Download: SuSE Linux Openexchange Server CA"
Listmail	intitle:"ListMail Login" admin -demo
Lotus Domino	inurl:names.nsf?opendatabase
Lotus Domino Web Administration.	inurl:"webadmin" filetype:nsf
MailEnable Standard Edition	inurl:mewebmail
MailMan	intitle:"MailMan Login"
Mailtraq WebMail	intitle:"Welcome to Mailtraq WebMail"
Mambo	inurl:administrator "welcome to mambo"
MDaemon	intitle:"WorldClient" intext:"(2003|2004) Alt-N Technologies."
Merak Email Server	"Powered by Merak Mail Server Software" -.gov -.mil -.edu -site:merakmailserver.com -johnny.ihackstuff
Merak Email Server	intitle:"Merak Mail Server Web Administration" -ihackstuff.com

Continued

Table 8.9 continued Queries That Locate Login Portals

Login Portal	Query
MetaFrame Presentation Server	inurl:Citrix/MetaFrame/default/default.aspx
Microsoft Certificate Services Authority (CA)	intitle:"microsoft certificate services" inurl:certsrv
Microsoft CRM Login portal.	"Microsoft CRM : Unsupported Browser Version"
Microsoft Outlook or Microsoft Exchange	allinurl:"exchange/logon.asp"
Microsoft Outlook or Microsoft Exchange	inurl:"exchange/logon.asp" OR intitle:"Microsoft Outlook Web Access - Logon"
Microsoft Software Update Services	inurl:/SUSAdmin intitle:"Microsoft Software Update Services"
Microsoft's Remote Desktop Web Connection	intitle:Remote.Desktop.Web.Connection inurl:tsweb
Midmart Messageboard	"Powered by Midmart Messageboard" "Administrator Login"
Mikro Tik Router	intitle:"MikroTik RouterOS Managing Webpage"
Mitel 3300 Integrated Communications Platform (ICP)	"intitle:3300 Integrated Communications Platform" inurl:main.htm
Miva Merchant	inurl:/Merchant2/admin.mv | inurl:/Merchant2/admin.mvc | intitle:"Miva Merchant Administration Login" -inurl:cheap-malboro.net
Monster Top List	"Powered by Monster Top List" MTL numrange:200-
MX Logic	intitle:"MX Control Console" "If you can't remember"
Neoteris Instant Virtual Extranet (IVE)	inurl:/dana-na/auth/welcome.html
Netware servers (v5 and up)	Novell NetWare intext:"netware management portal version"
Novell Groupwise	intitle:Novell intitle:WebAccess "Copyright *-* Novell, Inc"
Novell GroupWise	intitle:"Novell Web Services" intext:"Select a service and a language."

Continued

Table 8.9 continued Queries That Locate Login Portals

Login Portal	Query
Novell GroupWise	intitle:"Novell Web Services" "GroupWise" -inurl:"doc/11924" -.mil -.edu -.gov -filetype:pdf
Novell login portals	intitle:"welcome to netware *" -site:novell.com
oMail-webmail	intitle:"oMail-admin Administration - Login" -inurl:omnis.ch
Open groupware	intitle:opengroupware.org "resistance is obsolete" "Report Bugs" "Username" "password"
Openexchange Server	intitle:"SuSE Linux Openexchange Server" "Please activate JavaScript!"
Openexchange Server	inurl:"suse/login.pl"
OpenSRS Domain Management System	"OPENSRS Domain Management" inurl:manage.cgi
Open-Xchange 5	intitle:open-xchange inurl:login.pl
Oracle Single Sign-On solution	inurl:orasso.wwsso_app_admin.ls_login
Oscommerce Admin	inurl:"/admin/configuration. php?" Mystore
Outlook Web Access Login Portal	inurl:exchweb/bin/auth/owalogon.asp
Ovislink	intitle:Ovislink inurl:private/login
pcANYWHERE EXPRESS Java Client	"pcANYWHERE EXPRESS Java Client"
Philex	intitle:"Philex 0.2*" -script -site:freelists.org
Photo Gallery Managment Systems	"Please authenticate yourself to get access to the management interface"
PhotoPost	-Login inurl:photopost/uploadphoto.php
PHP Advacaned TRansfer	intitle:"PHP Advanced Transfer" inurl:"login.php"
PHP iCalendar	intitle:"php icalendar administration" -site:sourceforge.net
PHP iCalendar	intitle:"php icalendar administration" -site:sourceforge.net
PHP Poll Wizard 2	Please enter a valid password! inurl:polladmin
PHP121	inurl:"php121login.php"
PHPhotoalbum	intitle:"PHPhotoalbum - Upload"	inurl:"PHPhotoalbum/upload"
PHPhotoalbum	inurl:PHPhotoalbum/statistics intitle:"PHPhotoalbum - Statistics"

Continued

Table 8.9 continued Queries That Locate Login Portals

Login Portal	Query
phpMySearch	inurl:search/admin.php
PhpNews	intitle:phpnews.login
phpPgAdmin	intitle:"phpPgAdmin - Login" Language
PHProjekt	intitle:"PHProjekt - login" login password
PHPsFTPd	"Please login with admin pass" -"leak" -sourceforge
PhpWebMail	filetype:php login (intitle:phpWebMail|WebMail)
Plesk	intitle:plesk inurl:login.php3
Plesk	inurl:+:8443/login.php3
Polycom WebCommander	inurl:default.asp intitle:"WebCommander"
Postfix	intext:"Mail admins login here to administrate your domain."
Postfix Admin login pages	inurl:postfixadmin intitle:"postfix admin" ext:php
Qmail	intext:"Master Account" "Domain Name" "Password" inurl:/cgi-bin/qmailadmin
Qmail	intext:"Master Account" "Domain Name" "Password" inurl:/cgi-bin/qmailadmin
Quicktime streaming server	inurl:"1220/parse_xml.cgi?"
Real Estate	intitle:"site administration: please log in" "site designed by emarketsouth"
RemotelyAnywhere	inurl:2000 intitle:RemotelyAnywhere -site:realvnc.comg
Request System	(inurl:"ars/cgi-bin/arweb?O=0" | inurl:arweb.jsp)
RT	intitle:Login intext:"RT is * Copyright"
rymo	(intitle:"rymo Login")|(intext:"Welcome to rymo") -family
Sak Mail	intitle:endymion.sak.mail.login.page | inurl:sake.servlet
SalesLogix	inurl:"/slxweb.dll/external?name= (custportal|webticketcust)"
SAP Internet Transaction Server	intitle:"ITS System Information" "Please log on to the SAP System"

Continued

Table 8.9 continued Queries That Locate Login Portals

Login Portal	Query
ServiceDesk	intitle:"AdventNet ManageEngine ServiceDesk Plus" intext:"Remember Me"
SFXAdmin	intitle:"SFXAdmin - sfx_global" | intitle:"SFXAdmin - sfx_local" | intitle:"SFXAdmin - sfx_test"
Shockwave (Flash) login	inurl:login filetype:swf swf
SHOUTcast	intitle:"SHOUTcast Administrator" inurl:admin.cgi
Sift Group	intitle:"Admin login" "Web Site Administration" "Copyright"
SilkRoad Eprise	inurl:/eprise/
SilkyMail	(intitle:"SilkyMail by Cyrusoft International, Inc
SquirrelMail	inurl:login.php "SquirrelMail version"
SquirrelMail	"SquirrelMail version" "By the SquirrelMail Development Team"
SQWebmail.	inurl:/cgi-bin/sqwebmail?noframes=1
Sun Cobalt RaQ	"Login - Sun Cobalt RaQ"
Supero Doctor III Remote Management	intitle:"Supero Doctor III" -inurl:supermicro
Surgemail	"SurgeMAIL" inurl:/cgi/user.cgi ext:cgi
Synchronet Bulletin Board System	intitle:Node.List Win32.Version.3.11
SysCP	"SysCP - login"
Tarantella	"ttawlogin.cgi/?action="
TeamSpeak	intitle:"teamspeak server-administration
Terracotta web manager	"You have requested to access the management functions" -.edu
This finds login portals for Apache Tomcat, an open source Java servlet container which can run as a standalone server or with an Apache web server.	intitle:"Tomcat Server Administration"
Topdesk	intitle:"TOPdesk ApplicationServer"
TrackerCamÃ	intitle:("TrackerCam Live Video")|("TrackerCam Application Login")|("Trackercam Remote") -trackercam.com
TUTOS	intitle:"TUTOS Login"

Continued

Table 8.9 continued Queries That Locate Login Portals

Login Portal	Query
TWIG	intitle:"TWIG Login"
TYPO3	inurl:"typo3/index.php?u=" -demo
UBB.classic	inurl:cgi-bin/ultimatebb.cgi?ubb=login
UBB.threads	(intitle:"Please login - Forums powered by UBB.threads")|(inurl:login.php "ubb")
UebiMiau	"Powered by UebiMiau" -site:sourceforge.net
Ultima Online game.	filetype:cfg login "LoginServer="
UltiPro Workforce Management	inurl:"utilities/TreeView.asp"
Usermin	"Login to Usermin" inurl:20000
vBulletin	inurl:/modcp/ intext:Moderator+vBulletin
vBulletin Admin Control Panel	intext:"vbulletin" inurl:admincp
VHCS	"VHCS Pro ver" -demo
vHost	intitle:"vhost" intext:"vHost . 2000-2004"
VISAS	intitle:"Virtual Server Administration System"
VisNetic WebMail	intitle:"VisNetic WebMail" inurl:"/mail/"
VitalQIP Web Client	intitle:"VitalQIP IP Management System"
VMware GSX Server	intitle:"VMware Management Interface:" inurl:"vmware/en/"
VNC	"VNC Desktop" inurl:5800
VNC	intitle:"VNC viewer for Java"
VOXBOX	intitle:asterisk.management.portal web-access
webadmin.	filetype:php inurl:"webeditor.php"
WebConnect	inurl:WCP_USER
Web-cyradm	intitle:"web-cyradm"|"by Luc de Louw" "This is only for authorized users" -tar.gz -site:web-cyradm.org -johnny.ihackstuff
WebEdit	inurl:/webedit.* intext:WebEdit Professional -html
WebExplorer Server	"WebExplorer Server - Login" "Welcome to WebExplorer Server"
Webmail	intitle:Login * Webmailer
Webmail	inurl:webmail./index.pl "Interface"
Webmail	intitle:"Login to @Mail" (ext:pl | inurl:"index") -dwaffleman

Continued

Table 8.9 continued Queries That Locate Login Portals

Login Portal	Query
Webmail	intitle:IMP inurl:imp/index.php3
Webmail	intitle:"Login to @Mail" (ext:pl | inurl:"index") -dwaffleman
Webmin	inurl:":10000" intext:webmin
WebMyStyle	(intitle:"WmSC e-Cart Administration")|(intitle:"WebMyStyle e-Cart Administration")
WEBppliance	inurl:ocw_login_username
WebSTAR	"WebSTAR Mail - Please Log In"
W-Nailer	uploadpics.php?did= -forum
WorkZone Extranet Solution	intitle:"EXTRANET * - Identification"
WRQ Reflection	filetype:r2w r2w
WWWthreads	(intitle:"Please login - Forums powered by WWWThreads")|(inurl:"wwwthreads/login.php")|(inurl:"wwwthreads/login.pl?Cat=")
xams	intitle:"xams 0.0.0..15 - Login"
XcAuction	intitle:"XcAuctionLite" | "DRIVEN BY XCENT" Lite inurl:admin
XMail	intitle:"XMail Web Administration Interface" intext:Login intext:password
Zope Help System	intitle:"Zope Help System" inurl:HelpSys
ZyXEL Prestige Router	intitle:"ZyXEL Prestige Router" "Enter password"

Login portals provide great information for use during a vulnerability assessment. Chapter 4 provides more details on getting the most from these pages.

Using and Locating Various Web Utilities

Google is amazing and very flexible, but it certainly can't do *everything*. Some things are much easier when you don't use Google. Tasks like WHOIS lookups, "pings," traceroutes, and port scans are much easier when performed *outside* of Google. There is a wealth of tools available that can perform these functions, but with a bit of creative Googling, it's possible to perform all of these arduous functions and more, preserving the level of anonymity Google hackers have come to expect. Consider a tool called the Network Query Tool (NQT), shown in Figure 8.23.

Figure 8.23 The NQT NQT, the Network Query Tool Offers Interesting Options

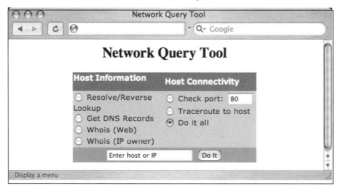

Default installations of NQT allow any Web user to perform Internet Protocol (IP) host name and address lookups, Domain Name Server (DNS) queries, WHOIS queries, port testing, and traceroutes. This is a Web-based application, meaning that any user who can view the page can generally perform these functions against just about any target. This is a very handy tool for any security person, and for good reason. NQT functions appear to originate from the site hosting the NQT application. The Web server masks the real address of the user. The use of an anonymous proxy server would further mask the user's identity.

We can use Google to locate servers hosting the NQT program with a very simple query. The NQT program is usually called nqt.php, and in its default configuration displays the title "Network Query Tool." A simple query like *inurl:nqt.php intitle:"Network Query Tool"* returns many results, as shown in Figure 5.11.

Figure 8.24 Using Google to Locate NQT Installations

After submitting this query, it's a simple task to simply click on the results pages to locate a working NQT program. However, the NQT program accepts remote POSTS, which means it's possible to send an NQT "command" from your Web server to the *foo.com* server, which would execute the NQT "command" on your behalf. If this seems pointless, consider the fact that this would allow for simple extension of NQT's layout and capabilities. We could, for example, easily craft an NQT "rotator" that would execute NQT commands against a target, first bouncing it off an Internet NQT server. Let's take a look at how that might work.

First, we'll scrape the results page shown in Figure 8.24, creating a list of sites that host NQT. Consider the following Linux/Mac OS X command:

```
lynx -dump "
http://www.google.com/search?q=inurl:nqt.php+%22Network+\
Query+Tool%22&num=100" | grep "nqt.php$" | grep -v google |
awk '{print $2}' | sort -u
```

This command grabs 100 results of the Google query *inurl:nqt.php intitle:"Network Query Tool"*, locates the word *nqt.php* at the end of a line, removes any line that contains the word *google*, prints the second field in the list (which is the URL of the NQT site), and uniquely sorts that list. This command will not catch NQT URLs that contain parameters (since *nqt.php* will not be the last word in the link), but it produces clean output that might look something like this:

```
http://bevmo.dynsample.org/uptime/nqt.php
http://biohazard.sifsample7.com/nqt.php
http://cahasample.com/nqt.php
http://samplehost.net/resources/nqt.php
http://linux.sample.nu/phpwebsite_v1/nqt.php
http://noc.bogor.indo.samplenet.id/nqt.php
http://noc.cbn.samplenet.id/nqt.php
http://noc.neksample.org/nqt.php
http://portal.trgsample.de/network/nqt.php
```

We could dump this output into a file by appending *>> nqtfile.txt* to the end of the previous *sort* command. Now that we have a working list of NQT servers, we'll need a copy of the NQT code that produces the interface displayed in Figure 8.23. This interface, with its buttons and "*enter host or IP*" field, will serve as the interface for our "rotator" program. Getting a copy of this interface is as easy as viewing the source of an existing *nqt.php* Web page (say, from the list of sites in the *nqtfile.txt* file), and saving the HTML content to a file we'll call *rotator.php* on our own Web server. At this point, we have two files in the same directory of our Web server—an *nqtfile.txt* file containing a list of NQT servers, and a *rotator.php* file that contains the HTML source of NQT. We'll be replacing a single line in the *rotator.php* file to create our "rotator" program. This line, which is the beginning of the NQT input form, reads:

```
<form method="post" action="/nqt.php">
```

This line indicates that once the "Do it" button is pressed, data will be sent to a script called nqt.php. If we were to modify this form field to *<form method="post" action="http://foo.com/nqt.php">*, our rotator program would send the NQT command to the NQT program located at *foo.com,* which would execute it on our behalf. We're going to take this one step further, inserting PHP code that will read a random site from the *nqtfile.txt* program, inserting it into the form line for us. This code might look something like this (lines numbered for clarity):

```
1.      <?php
2.      $array = file("./nqtsites.txt");
3.      $site=substr($array[rand(0,count($array)-1)],0,-1);
4.      print "<form method=\"post\" action=$site><br>";
5.      print "Using NQT Site: $site for this session.<br>";
6.      print "Reload this page for a new NQT site.<br><br>";
7.      ?>
```

This PHP code segment is meant to replace the *<form method="post" action="/nqt.php">* line in the original NQT HTML code. Line 1 indicates that a PHP code segment is about to begin. Since the rest of the *rotator.php* file is HTML, this line, as well as line 7 that terminates the PHP code segment, is required. Line 2 reads our *nqtsites.txt* file, assigning each line in the file (a URL to an NQT site) to an array element. Line 3, included as a separate line for readability, assigns one random line from the *nqtsites.txt* program to the variable *$site*. Line 4 outputs the modified version of the original *form* line, modifying the action target to point to a random remote NQT site. Lines 5 and 6 simply output informative messages about the NQT site that was selected, and instructions for loading a new NQT site. The next line in the *rotator.php* script would be the *table* line that draws the main NQT table. When *rotator.php* is saved and viewed in a browser, it should look similar to Figure 8.25.

Figure 8.25 The NQT Rotator in Action

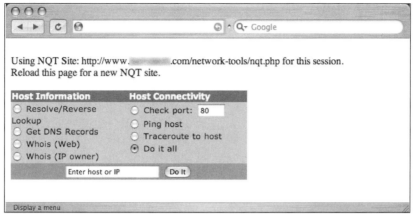

Our rotator program looks very similar to the standard NQT program interface, with the addition of the two initial lines of text. However, when the "check port" box is checked, www.microsoft.com is entered into the host field, and the Do It button is clicked, we are whisked away to the results page on a remote NQT server that displays the results—port 80 is, in fact, open and accepting connections, as shown in Figure 8.26.

Figure 8.26 NQT "Rotator" Output

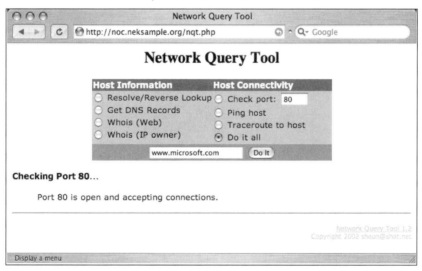

This example is designed to suggest that Google can be used to supplement the use of many Web-based applications. All that's required is a bit of Google know-how and a healthy dose of creativity.

Targeting Web-Enabled Network Devices

Google can also be used to detect the presence of many Web-enabled network devices. Many network devices come preinstalled with a Web interface to allow an administrator to query the status of the device or to change device settings with a Web browser. While this is convenient, and can even be primitively secured through the use of an Secure Sockets Layer (SSL)-enabled connection, if the Web interface of a device is crawled with Google, even the mere existence of that device can add to a silently created network map. For example, a query like *intitle:"BorderManager information alert"* can reveal the existence of a Novell BorderManager Proxy/Firewall server, as shown in Figure 8.27.

Figure 8.27 Google Reveals Novell BorderManager Proxy/Firewall

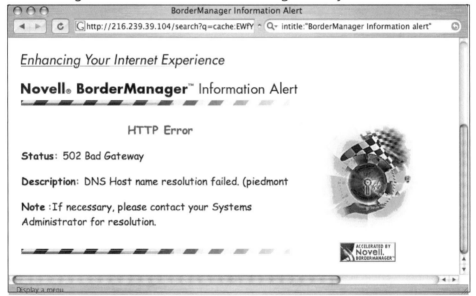

A crafty attacker could use the mere existence of this device to craft his attack against the target network. For example, if this device is acting as a proxy server, the attacker might attempt to use it to gain access to machines inside a trusted network by bouncing connections off this server. Additionally, an attacker might search for any public vulnerabilities for this product in an attempt to exploit this device directly. Although many different devices can be located in this way, it's generally easier to harvest IP and network data using the output from network statistical programs as we'll see in the next section. To get an idea of the types of devices that can be located with this technique, consider queries like *"Version Info" "Boot Version" "Internet Settings"*, which locate Belkin Cable/DSL routers; *intitle:"wbem" compaq login*, which locates HP Insight Management Agents; *intitle:"lantronix web-manager"*, which locates Lantronix Web managers; *inurl:tech-support inurl:show Cisco* or *intitle:"switch*

home page" "cisco systems" "Telnet - to", which locates various Cisco products; or *intitle:"axis storpoint CD" intitle:"ip address"*, which can locate Axis StorPoint servers. Each of these queries reveals pages that report various bits of information about the networks on which they're installed.

Locating Various Network Reports

In addition to targeting network devices directly, various network documents and status reports can be located with Google that give an outsider access to everything from IP addresses on the network to complete, ready-to-use network diagrams. For example, the query *"Looking Glass" (inurl:"lg/" | inurl:lookingglass)* will locate looking glass servers that show router statistical information, as shown in Figure 8.28.

Figure 8.28 Looking Glass Router Information

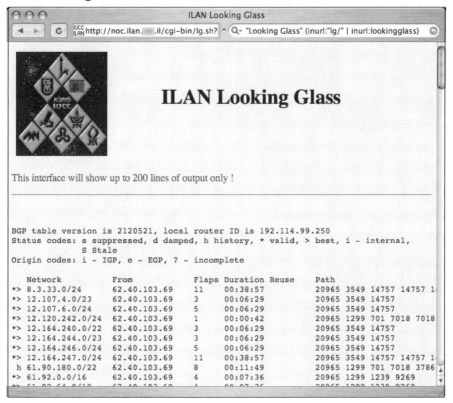

The ntop program shows network traffic statistics that can be used to determine the network architecture of a target. The query *intitle:"Welcome to ntop!"* will locate servers that have publicized their ntop programs, which produces the output shown in Figure 8.29.

Figure 8.29 NTOP Output Reveals Network Statistics

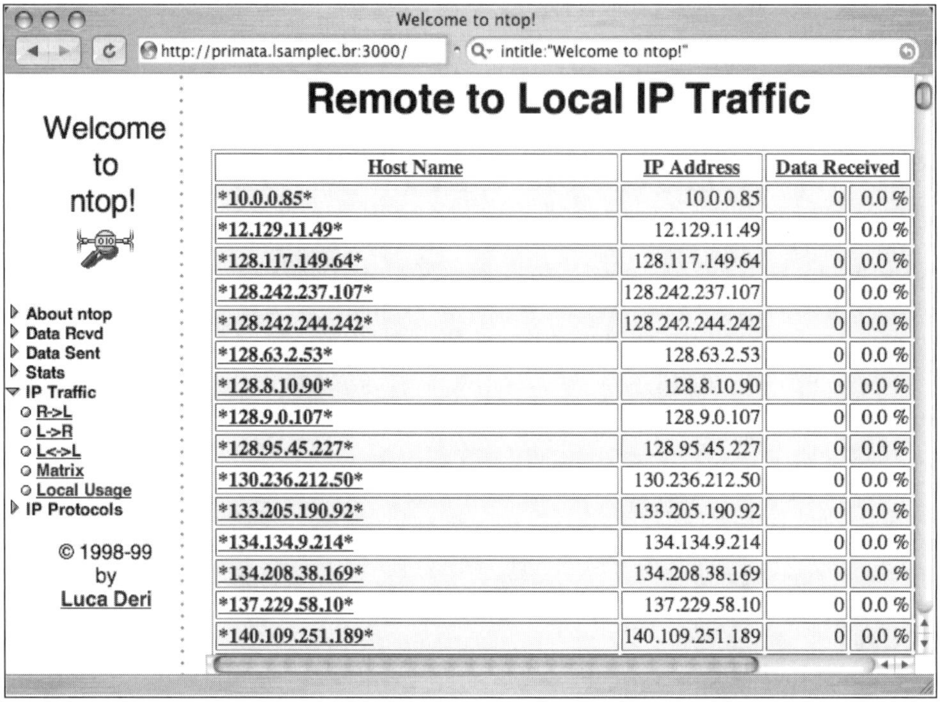

Practically any Web-based network statistics package can be located with Google. Table 8.10 reveals several examples from the Google Hacking Database (GHDB) that show searches for various network documentation.

Table 8.10 Examples of Network Documentation from the GHDB

Query	Device/Report
intitle:"statistics of" "advanced web statistics"	awstats shows statistics for Web servers.
intitle:"Big Sister" +"OK Attention Trouble"	Big Sister program reveals network information.
inurl:"cacti" +inurl:"graph_view.php" +"Settings Tree View" -cvs -RPM	cacti reveals internal network information including architecture, hosts, and services.
inurl:fcgi-bin/echo	fastcgi echo program reveals detailed server information.
"These statistics were produced by getstats"	Getstats program reveals server statistical information.

Continued

Table 8.10 continued Examples of Network Documentation from the GHDB

Query	Device/Report
inurl:"/cricket/grapher.cgi"	grapher.cgi reveals networks information like configuration, services, and bandwidth.
intitle:"Object not found" netware "apache 1.."	HP Switch Web Interface.
((inurl:ifgraph "Page generated at") OR ("This page was built using ifgraph"))	ifGraph SNMP data collector.
"Looking Glass" (inurl:"lg/" | inurl:lookingglass)	Looking Glass network stats output.
filetype:reg "Terminal Server Client"	Microsoft Terminal Services connection settings Registry files reveal credentials and configuration data.
intext:"Tobias Oetiker" "traffic analysis"	MRTG analysis pages reveals various network statistical information.
intitle:"Welcome to ntop!"	ntop program shows current network usage.
inurl:"smb.conf" intext:"workgroup" filetype:conf	Samba config file reveals server and network data.
intitle:"Ganglia" "Cluster Report for"	Server Cluster Reports
intitle:"System Statistics" "System and Network Information Center"	SNIC reveals internal network information including network configuration, ping times, services, and host information.
intitle:"ADSL Configuration page"	SolWise ADSL Modem Network Stats.
"cacheserverreport for" "This analysis was produced by calamaris"	Squid Cache Server Reports.
inurl:vbstats.php "page generated"	vbstats report reveals server statistical information.
filetype:vsd vsd network -samples -examples	Visio network drawings.

This type of information is a huge asset during a security audit, which can save a lot of time, but realize that any information found in this manner should be validated before using it in any type of finished report.

Locating Network Hardware

It's not uncommon for a network-connected device to have a Web page of some sort. If that device is connected to the Internet and a link to that device's Web page ever existed, there's a good chance that that page is in Google's database, waiting to be located with a crafty query. As we discussed in Chapter 5, these pages can reveal information about the target network, as shown in Figure 8.30. This type of information can play a very important role in mapping a target network.

Figure 8.30 Network Device Web Pages Reveal Network Data

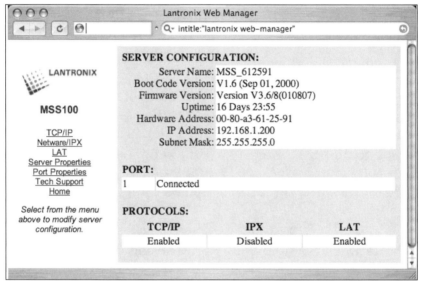

All types of devices can be connected to a network. These devices, ranging from switches and routers to printers and even firewalls, are considered great finds for any attacker interested in network reconnaissance, but some devices such as Webcams are interesting finds for an attacker as well.

In most cases, a network-connected Webcam is not considered a security threat but more a source of entertainment for any Web surfer. Keep a few things in mind, however. First, some companies consider it trendy and cool to provide customers a look around their workplace. Netscape was known for this back in its heyday. The Webcams located on these companies' premises were obviously authorized by upper management. A look inside a facility can be a huge benefit if your job boils down to a physical assessment. Second, it's not all that uncommon for a Webcam to be placed outside a facility, as shown in Figure 8.31. This type of cam is a boon for a physical assessment. Also, don't forget that what an employee does at work doesn't necessarily reflect what he does on his own time. If you locate an employee's personal Web space, there's a fair chance that these types of devices will exist.

Figure 8.31 Webcams Placed Outside a Facility

Most network printers manufactured these days have some sort of Web-based interface installed. If these devices (or even the documentation or drivers supplied with these devices) are linked from a Web page, various Google queries can be used to locate them.

Once located, network printers can provide an attacker with a wealth of information. As shown in Figure 8.32, it is very common for a network printer to list details about the surrounding network, naming conventions, and more. Many devices located through a Google search are still running a default, insecure configuration with no username or password needed to control the device. In a worst-case scenario, attackers can view print jobs and even coerce these printers to store files or even send network commands.

Figure 8.32 Networked Printers Provide Lots of Details

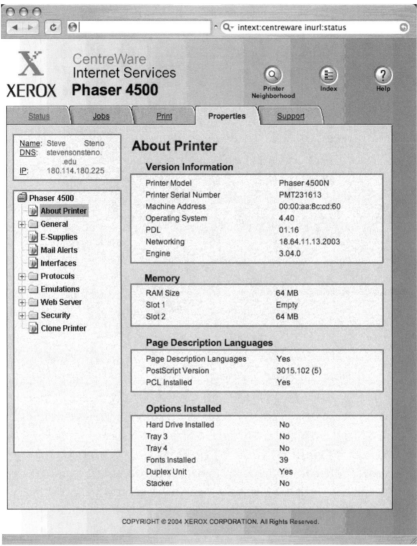

Table 8.11 shows queries that can be used to locate various network devices.

Table 8.11 Queries That Locate Various Network Devices

Network Device	Query
AXIS 2400	inurl:indexFrame.shtml Axis
PhaserLink Printers	intitle:"View and Configure PhaserLink"
Panasonic Network Cameras	inurl:"ViewerFrame?Mode="

Continued

Table 8.11 Queries That Locate Various Network Devices

Network Device	Query
Sony NC RZ30 Camers	SNC-RZ30 HOME
Sony NC RZ20 Cameras	intitle:snc-z20 inurl:home/
Mobotix netcams	(intext:"MOBOTIX M1" | intext:"MOBOTIX M10") intext:"Open Menu" Shift-Reload
Panasonic WJ-NT104	intitle:"WJ-NT104 Main Page"
XP PRO Webcams	"powered by webcamXP" "Pro|Broadcast"
AXIS Cameras	intitle:"Live View / - AXIS"
Phaser 6250N Printer	"Phaser 6250" "Printer Neighborhood" "XEROX CORPORATION"
Xerox Phaser Printer	"Phaser740 Color Printer" "printer named: "
Phaser 8200 Printer	"Phaser 8200" "Xerox" "refresh" " Email Alerts"
Xerox Phaser 840 Color Printer	"Phaser 840 Color Printer" "Current Status" "printer named:"
Canon "WebView LiveScope"	intitle:liveapplet inurl:LvAppl
Xerox Phaser 4500/6250/ 8200/8400	intext:centreware inurl:status
Linux Dreamboxes	intitle:"dreambox web"
Axis Netcams	intitle:"Live View / - AXIS" | inurl:view/view.sht
Axis 200	intitle:"The AXIS 200 Home Page"
Fiery WebTools	("Fiery WebTools" inurl:index2.html) | "WebTools enable * * observe, *, * * * flow * print jobs"
Konica Network Printer	intitle:"network administration" inurl:"nic"
Ricoh Aficio 1022	inurl:sts_index.cgi
Ricoh Afficio Printer	intitle:RICOH intitle:"Network Administration"
Canon ImageReady 3300, 5000 & 60000.	intitle:"remote ui:top page"
HP Printers.	inurl:hp/device/this.LCDispatcher
Webeye webcams.	intitle:webeye inurl:login.ml
AXIS StorPoint CD+.	intitle:"axis storpoint CD" intitle:"ip address"
Cisco Switches	intitle:"switch home page" "cisco systems" "Telnet - to"
HP switches	intitle:"DEFAULT_CONFIG - HP"
Linksys webcam	camera linksys inurl:main.cgi
My webcamXP server	intitle:"my webcamXP server!" inurl:":8080"

Continued

Table 8.11 continued Queries That Locate Various Network Devices

Network Device	Query
Ricoh Aficio 2035 (fax/scanner)	(inurl:webArch/mainFrame.cgi) | (intitle:"web image monitor" -htm -solutions)
Axis Network Camera	inurl:netw_tcp.shtml
Tivo Devices	inurl:TiVoConnect?Command=QueryServer
Embedded DVR	intitle:"DVR Web client"
Panasonic Network Camera	site:.viewnetcam.com -www.viewnetcam.com
Toshiba netcams	intitle:"toshiba network camera - User Login"
CCTV webcams	"please visit" intitle:"i-Catcher Console" Copyright "iCode Systems"
AMX Netlink	WebControl intitle:"AMX NetLinx"
XeroxDocuPrint printer.	intitle:"Home" "Xerox Corporation" "Refresh Status"
Xerox 860 and 8200 Printers.	intext:"Ready with 10/100T Ethernet"
Lexmark printers	intext:"UAA (MSB)" Lexmark -ext:pdf
Axis Netcams	inurl:axis-cgi
SiteZap webcam	"Starting SiteZAP 6.0"
EvoCam	intitle:"EvoCam" inurl:"webcam.html"
Tandberg video conferencing appliances	intext:"Videoconference Management System" ext:htm
Novell Iprint	inurl:"ipp/pdisplay.htm"
Phaser printers	"Copyright (c) Tektronix, Inc." "printer status"
Xerox DocuPrint printer	intext:"MaiLinX Alert (Notify)" -site:net-workprinters.com
Brother HL Printers	inurl:"printer/main.html" intext:"settings"
Axis Storpoint	axis storpoint "file view" inurl:/volumes/
Netsnap Online Cameras	intitle:"Live NetSnap Cam-Server feed"
V-Gear Bee Web Cameras	intitle:"V-Gear BEE"
Audio ReQuest home CD/MP3 player	intitle:"AudioReQuest.web.server"
CUPS Printers	inurl:":631/printers" -php -demo
iVista Camera	intitle:"iVISTA.Main.Page"
Axis Video Cameras	
Linksys Wireless-G web cams.	inurl:"next_file=main_fs.htm" inurl:img inurl:image.cgi

Continued

Table 8.11 continued Queries That Locate Various Network Devices

Network Device	Query
SnapStream Digital Video Recorder	filetype:cgi transcoder.cgi
Axis Network Print Server	intitle:"Network Print Server" filetype:shtm (inurl:u_printjobs | inurl:u_server | inurl:a_server | inurl:u_generalhelp | u_printjobs)
Axis Network Print Server	intitle:"Network Print Server" intext:"http://www.axis.com" filetype:shtm
ActiveX webcam	intitle:"Browser Launch Page"
Sweex, Orite Web Cameras	allinurl:index.htm?cus?audio
EDSR video cameras	intitle:"EverFocus.EDSR.applet"
Epson Web Assist	intitle:"EpsonNet WebAssist Rev"
Brother printers	intitle:"Brother" intext:"View Configuration" intext:"Brother Industries, Ltd."
Linksys webcams	intitle:Linksys site:ourlinksys.com
SupervisionCam	intitle:"supervisioncam protocol"
Vivotec webcams	inurl:camctrl.cgi
mmEye webcam	allintitle:Brains, Corp. camera
Dell ESW Printers	intitle:"Dell Laser Printer" ews
HomeSeer home automation server	intitle:HomeSeer.Web.Control | Home.Status.Events.Log
Samsung webthru cameras	"Webthru User Login"
Lexmark printers (4 models)	intitle:"Lexmark *" inurl:port_0
Aficio printers	inurl:/en/help.cgi "ID=*"
HP Officejet help page.	intitle:jdewshlp "Welcome to the Embedded Web Server!"
Xerox Phaser printers.	"display printer status" intitle:"Home"
GeoHttpServer	inurl:JPGLogin.htm
Winamp Servers	"About Winamp Web Interface" intitle:"Winamp Web Interface"
NeroNet Servers	intitle:"NeroNET - burning online"
Xerox (*Centre) Printers	ext:dhtml intitle:"document centre|(home)" OR intitle:"xerox"
Lexmark and Dell Printers	inurl:"port_255" -htm
Adobe's PrintGear	intext:"Powered by: Adobe PrintGear" inurl:admin

Continued

www.syngress.com

Table 8.11 continued Queries That Locate Various Network Devices

Network Device	Query
AVTech Video Web Server	intitle:"—- VIDEO WEB SERVER —-" intext:"Video Web Server" "Any time & Any where" username password
VPON (Video Picture On Net) video surveillance system	inurl:start.htm?scrw=
Dell Printers	intitle:"Dell *" inurl:port_0
Kpix Java Based Traffic Cameras	(cam1java)|(cam2java)|(cam3java)| (cam4java)|(cam5java)|(cam6java) -navy.mil -backflip -power.ne.jp
Mobile Cameras	inurl:"S=320x240"	inurl:"S=160x120" inurl:"Q=Mob
Panasonic IP cameras	inurl:"CgiStart?page="
Dell and Lexmark Printers	intitle:"configuration" inurl:port_0
Dell Laser Printer M5200	intitle:"Dell Laser Printer M5200" port_0
AXIS 240 Camera Servers	intitle:"AXIS 240 Camera Server" intext:"server push" -help
Veo Observer Web Client	intitle:"Veo Observer Web Client"
Standalone Network Camera	intitle:"Java Applet Page" inurl:ml
DVR Systems	intitle:"WEBDVR" -inurl:product -inurl:demo
sensorProbe Environmental Monitoring Device	"Summary View of Sensors"	"sensorProbe8 v *"	"
iDVR Camera	intitle:iDVR -intitle:"com	net	shop" -inurl:"asp	htm	pdf	html	php	shtml	com	at	cgi	tv"
INTELLINET IP camera	intitle:"INTELLINET" intitle:"IP Camera Homepage"
StarDot netcam	intitle:"NetCam Live Image" -.edu -.gov - johnny.ihackstuff.com
Netbotz devices	intitle:"netbotz appliance" -inurl:.php -inurl:.asp - inurl:.pdf -inurl:securitypipeline -announces
Phaser Network Printers	Phaser numrange:100-100000 Name DNS IP "More Printers" index help filetype:html	filetype:shtml
Orite 301 Netcams	intitle:"Orite IC301"	intitle:"ORITE Audio IP-Camera IC-301" -the -a
Brimsoft webcam	intitle:"Biromsoft WebCam" -4.0 -serial -ask -crack - software -a -the -build -download -v4 -3.01 -num-range:1-10000

Continued

Table 8.11 continued Queries That Locate Various Network Devices

Network Device	Query
VisionGS Webcam	(intitle:"VisionGS Webcam Software")|(intext:"Powered by VisionGS Webcam") -showthread.php -showpost.php -"Search Engine" -computersglobal.com -site:g
IQeye netcam	intitle:"IQeye302 | IQeye303 | IQeye601 | IQeye602 | IQeye603" intitle:"Live Images"
Samsung printers	"This page is for configuring Samsung Network Printer" | printerDetails.htm
Intel Netport Express Print Server.	intitle:"SNOIE Intel Web Netport Manager" OR intitle:"Intel Web Netport Manager Setup/Status"
Express6 live video controller	Display Cameras intitle:"Express6 Live Image"
Sony SNT-V304 Video Network Station	intitle:"Sony SNT-V304 Video Network Station" inurl:hsrindex.shtml
Windows 2003 Remote Printing	inurl:Printers/ipp_0001.asp
Linksys wireless G Camera	inurl:/img/vr.htm
Sony DCS-950 Web Camera	DCS inurl:"/web/login.asp"
Dell laser printers	intitle:"Dell Laser Printer *" port_0 -johnny.ihack-stuff
INTELLINET IP Camera	intitle:"::::: INTELLINET IP Camera Homepage :::::"
Celestix Taurus Server	intext:"Welcome to Taurus" "The Taurus Server Appliance" intitle:"The Taurus Server Appliance"
Sharp printers	intitle:"AR-*" "browser of frame dealing is necessary"
Watchdogs WxGoos Camera	intitle:"WxGoos-" ("Camera image"|"60 seconds")
Nuvico DVR	intitle:"DVR Client" -the -free -pdf -downloads -blog -download -dvrtop
Hunt Electronics web cams	"OK logout" inurl:vb.htm?logout=1
EverFocus DVR	intitle:"Edr1680 remote viewer"
IVC Security Cameras	intitle:"IVC Control Panel"
MOBOTIX Cameras	(intitle:MOBOTIX intitle:PDAS) | (intitle:MOBOTIX intitle:Seiten) | (inurl:/pda/index.html +camera)
Netbotz devices	intitle:"Device Status Summary Page" -demo
iGuard Fingerprint Security System	intitle:"iGuard Fingerprint Security System"

Continued

Table 8.11 continued Queries That Locate Various Network Devices

Network Device	Query
Veo Observer XT	intitle:"Veo Observer XT" -inurl:shtml|pl|php|htm|asp|aspx|pdf|cfm -intext:observer
EyeSpyFX or OptiCamFX Camera	(intitle:(EyeSpyFX|OptiCamFX) "go to camera"))|(inurl:servlet/DetectBrowser)
MOBOTIX cameras	inurl:cgi-bin/guestimage.html
Sony SNC-RZ30 IP camera	intitle:"SNC-RZ30" -demo
Everfocus EDSR400	allintitle: EverFocus | EDSR | EDSR400 Applet
Everfocus EDR1680	allintitle:Edr1680 remote viewer
Everfocus EDR1600	allintitle: EDR1600 login | Welcome
Everfocus EDR400	allintitle: EDR400 login | Welcome
Boshe/Divar Net Cameras	intitle:"Divar Web Client"
Axis Cameras	intitle:"Live View / - AXIS" | inurl:view/view.shtml OR inurl:view/indexFrame.shtml | intitle:"MJPG Live Demo" | "intext:Select preset position"
Axis Cameras 2XXX Series	allintitle: Axis 2.10 OR 2.12 OR 2.30 OR 2.31 OR 2.32 OR 2.33 OR 2.34 OR 2.40 OR 2.42 OR 2.43 "Network Camera "
BlueNet Video Viewer	intitle:"BlueNet Video Viewer"
Stingray File Transfer Server	intitle:"stingray fts login" | (login.jsp intitle:StingRay)
Softwell Technology "Wit-Eye" DVR	allintitle:"DVR login"
WR Control Lite Multi-Camera View	inurl:wrcontrollite
Device	Query
Axis Video Server (CAM)	*inurl:indexFrame.shtml Axis*
AXIS Video Live Camera	*intitle:"Live View / - AXIS"*
AXIS Video Live View	*intitle:"Live View / - AXIS" | inurl:view/view.sht*
AXIS 200 Network Camera	*intitle:"The AXIS 200 Home Page"*
Canon Network Camera	*intitle:liveapplet inurl:LvAppl*
Mobotix Network Camera	*intext:"MOBOTIX M1" intext:"Open Menu"*
Panasonic Network Camera	*intitle:"WJ-NT104 Main Page"*
Panasonic Network Camera	*inurl:"ViewerFrame?Mode="*
Sony Network Camera	*SNC-RZ30 HOME*

Continued

Table 8.11 continued Queries That Locate Various Network Devices

Network Device	Query
Seyeon FlexWATCH Camera	*intitle:flexwatch intext:"Home page ver"*
Sony Network Camera	*intitle:snc-z20 inurl:home/*
webcamXP	*"powered by webcamXP" "Pro|Broadcast"*
Canon ImageReady	*intitle:"remote ui:top page"*
Fiery Printer Interface	*("Fiery WebTools" inurl:index2.html) | "WebTools enable * * observe, *, * * * flow * print jobs"*
Konica Printers	*intitle:"network administration" inurl:"nic"*
RICOH Copier	*inurl:sts_index.cgi*
RICOH Printers	*intitle:RICOH intitle:"Network Administration"*
Tektronix Phaser Printer	*intitle:"View and Configure PhaserLink"*
Xerox Phaser (generic)	*inurl:live_status.html*
Xerox Phaser 6250 Printer	*"Phaser 6250" "Printer Neighborhood" "XEROX CORPORATION"*
Xerox Phaser 740 Printer phaserlink	*"Phaser® 740 Color Printer" "printer named: "*
Xerox Phaser 8200 Printer	*"Phaser 8200" "© Xerox" "refresh" " Email Alerts"*
Xerox Phaser 840 Printer	*Phaser® 840 Color Printer*
Xerox Centreware Printers	*intext:centreware inurl:status*
XEROX WorkCentre	*intitle:"XEROX WorkCentre PRO - Index"*

Summary

Attackers use Google for a variety of reasons. An attacker might have access to an exploit for a particular version of Web software and may be on the prowl for vulnerable targets. Other times the attacker might have decided on a target and is using Google to locate information about other devices on the network. In some cases, an attacker could simply be looking for Web devices that are poorly configured with default pages and programs, indicating that the security around the device is soft.

Directory listings provide information about the software versions in use on a device. Server and application error messages can provide a wealth of information to an attacker and are perhaps the most underestimated of all information-gathering techniques. Default pages, programs, and documentation not only can be used to profile a target, but they serve as an indicator that the server is somewhat neglected and perhaps vulnerable to exploitation. Login portals, while serving as the "front door" of a Web server for regular users, can be used to profile a target, used to locate more information about services and procedures in use, and used as a virtual magnet for attackers armed with matching exploits. In some cases, login portals are set up by administrators to allow remote access to a server or network. This type of login portal, if compromised, can provide an entry point for an intruder as well.

Google can be used to locate or augment Web-based networking tools like NQT, which enables remote execution of various network-querying applications. Using creative queries, Google may even locate Web-enabled network devices in use by the target or output from network statistical packages. Whatever your goal during a network-based assessment, there's a good chance Google can be used to augment your existing tools and techniques.

Solutions Fast Track

Locating and Profiling Web Servers

☑ Directory listings and default server-generated error messages can provide details about the server. Even though this information could be obtained by connecting directly to the server, an attacker armed with an exploit for a particular version of software could find a target using a Google query designed to locate this information.

☑ Server and application error messages proved a great deal of information, ranging from software versions and patch level, to snippets of source code and information about system processes and programs. Error messages are one of the most underestimated forms of information leakage.

☑ Default pages, documentation, and programs speak volumes about the server that hosts them. They suggest that a server is not well maintained and is by extension vulnerable due to poor maintenance.

Locating Login Portals

☑ Login portals can draw attackers who are searching for specific types of software. In addition, they can serve as a starting point for information-gathering attacks, since most login portals are designed to be user friendly, providing links to help documents and procedures to aid new users. Administrative login portals and remote administration tools are sometimes even more dangerous, especially if they are poorly configured.

Locating Network Hardware

☑ All sorts of network devices can be located with Google queries. These devices are more than a passing technological curiosity for some attackers, since many devices linked from the Web are poorly configured, trusted devices often overlooked by typical security auditors. Web cameras are often overlooked devices that can provide insight for an attacker, even though an extremely small percentage of targets have Web cameras installed. Network printers, when compromised, can reveal a great deal of sensitive information, especially for an attacker capable of viewing print jobs and network information.

Using and Locating Various Web Utilities

☑ Web-enabled network devices can be located with simple Google queries.

☑ The information from these devices can be used to help build a network map.

Locating Various Network Reports

☑ Network statistic reports can be located with simple Google queries.

☑ The information from these reports can be used to help build a network map.

Frequently Asked Questions

The following Frequently Asked Questions, answered by the authors of this book, are designed to both measure your understanding of the concepts presented in this chapter and to assist you with real-life implementation of these concepts. To have your questions about this chapter answered by the author, browse to **www.syngress.com/solutions** and click on the **"Ask the Author"** form.

Q: I run an IIS 6.0 server, and I don't like the idea of those static HTTP 1.1 error pages hanging around my site, luring potential malicious interest in my server. How can I enable the customized error messages?

A: If you aren't in the habit of just asking Google by now, you should be! Seriously, try a Google search for *site:microsoft.com "Configuring Custom Error Messages" IIS 6.0*. At the time of this writing, the article describing this procedure is the first hit. The procedure involves firing up the IIS Manager, double-clicking **My Computer**, right-clicking the **Web Sites** folder, and selecting **Properties**. See the **Custom Errors** tab.

Q: I run an Apache server, and I don't like the idea of those server tags on error messages and directory listings. How can I turn these off?

A: To remove the tags, locate the section in your *httpd.conf* file (usually in */etc/httpd/conf/httpd.conf*) that contains the following:

```
#
# Optionally add a line containing the server version and virtual host
# name to server-generated pages (error documents, FTP directory listings,
# mod_status and mod_info output etc., but not CGI generated documents).
# Set to "EMail" to also include a mailto: link to the ServerAdmin.
# Set to one of:  On | Off | EMail
#
ServerSignature On
```

The *ServerSignature* setting can be changed to *Off* to remove the tag altogether or to *Email*, which presents an e-mail link with the *ServerAdmin* e-mail address as it appears in the *httpd.conf* file.

Q: I've got an idea for a search that's not listed here. If you're so smart about Google, why isn't my search listed in this book?

A: This book serves as more of a primer than a reference book. There are so many possible Google searches out there that it's impossible to include them all in one book. Most searches listed in this book are the result of a community of people working together to come up with as many effective searches as possible. Fortunately, this community of individuals has created a unique and extensive database that is open to the public for the purposes of adequately defending against this unique threat. The Search Engine Hacking forum and the GHDB are both available at http://johnny.ihackstuff.com. If you've got a new search, first search the database to make sure it's unique. If you think it is, submit it to the forums, and your search could be the newest addition to the database. But beware, Google searcher. Google hacking is fun and addictive. If you submit one search, I think you'll find it's hard to stop. Just ask any of the individuals on the Google Master's list. Some of them found it hard to stop at 10 or 20 unique submitted searches! Check out the Acknowledgments page for a list of users who have made a significant contribution to the Google hacking community.

Q: The NQT tool can only scan one port at a time. Could this behavior be modified?

A: Without modifying the code on the remote NQT server, this task would require the coding of a PHP loop that feeds the requests one at a time to the NQT server. Remember, though, that even single ports can play a critical role when it comes time to perform an actual network port scan. For many different types of scans, it's always advantageous to have a list of ports that are known to be open.

Q: Aren't there any Web-based tools besides NQT with a larger port scan range?

A: If you're interested in scanning lots of ports, you might be better off with a standard scanner like nmap. However, to flex those Google muscles, try a query like *inurl:portscan.php ("from Port" | "Port Range")* suggested by Jimmy Neutron on the Google Hacking Forums. Although there aren't many results, who knows what the future holds for this search!

Q: So Web interfaces on network devices are a bad idea?

A: They don't have to be, but statistically they are for a few reasons. First, they are often excessive when you consider that the same task could be more securely accomplished via serial port connection or via a dedicated admin network connection. Second, small devices require small servers, so some exotic Web servers are used that are not as well tested as Apache, for example (consider the vulnerabilities on Axis cams at security focus). Third, as we've seen in this chapter, the pages can be found with (or submitted to) Google if the admins are not careful. This opens the floodgates for all the fledgling Google hackers out there.

Q: Our network devices (routers) can't be accessed by anyone from the outside. Does that mean we are safe?

A: Even though it is not accessible from the wide area network (WAN), it may be accessible from a compromised host on your LAN. Posting information about it on usenet or tech forums is a risk. For an example, try searching for *intext:"enable secret 5 $"* as suggested by hevnsnt on the Google Hacking Forums. Then try the same on Google Groups. It's a good thing Cisco implemented strong encryption on those passwords, since these searches often reveal sensitive information about these devices.

## Chapter 9

Usernames, Passwords, and Secret Stuff, Oh My!

Solutions in this chapter:

- Searching for Usernames
- Searching for Passwords
- Searching for Credit Card Numbers, Social Security Numbers, and More
- Searching for Other Juicy Info
- List of Sites

☑ Summary

☑ Solutions Fast Track

☑ Frequently Asked Questions

Introduction

This chapter is not about finding sensitive data during an assessment as much as it is about what the "bad guys" might do to troll for the data. The examples presented in this chapter generally represent the lowest-hanging fruit on the security tree. Hackers target this information on a daily basis. To protect against this type of attacker, we need to be fairly candid about the worst-case possibilities. We won't be *overly* candid, however. We don't want to give the bad guys any ideas they don't already have.

We start by looking at some queries that can be used to uncover usernames, the less important half of most authentication systems. The value of a username is often overlooked, but as we've already discussed, an entire multimillion-dollar security system can be shattered through skillful crafting of even the smallest, most innocuous bit of information.

Next, we will take a look at queries that are designed to uncover passwords. Some of the queries we look at reveal encrypted or encoded passwords, which will take a bit of work on the part of an attacker to use to his or her advantage. We also take a look at queries that can uncover *cleartext* passwords. These queries are some of the most dangerous in the hands of even the most novice attacker. What could make an attack easier than handing a username and cleartext password to an attacker?

We wrap up this chapter by discussing the *very real* possibility of uncovering highly sensitive data such as credit card information and information used to commit identity theft, such as Social Security numbers. Our goal here is to explore ways of protecting against this very real threat. To that end, we don't go into details about uncovering financial information and the like. If you're a "dark side" hacker, you'll need to figure these things out on your own, or make the wise decision to turn to the light side of the force.

Searching for Usernames

Most authentication mechanisms use a username and password to protect information. To get through the "front door" of this type of protection, you'll need to determine usernames as well as passwords. Usernames also can be used for social engineering efforts, as we discussed earlier.

Many methods can be used to determine usernames. In the "Database Digging" chapter, we explored ways of gathering usernames via database error messages. In the "Tracking Down Web Servers" chapter, we explored Web server and application error messages that can reveal various information, including usernames. These indirect methods of locating usernames are helpful, but an attacker could target a usernames directory with a simple query like *"your username is"*. This phrase can locate help pages that describe the username creation process, as shown in Figure 9.1.

Figure 9.1 Help Documents Can Reveal Username Creation Processes

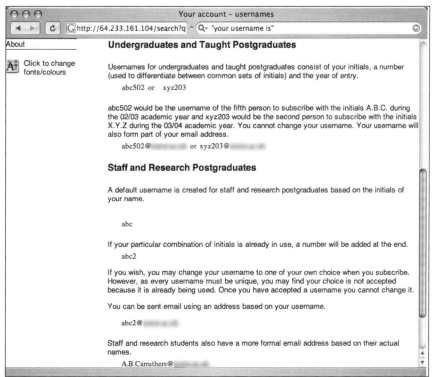

An attacker could use this information to postulate a username based on information gleaned from other sources, such as Google Groups posts or phone listings. The usernames could then be recycled into various other phases of the attack, such as a worm-based spam campaign or a social-engineering attempt. An attacker can gather usernames from a variety of sources, as shown in the sample queries listed in Table 9.1.

Table 9.1 Sample Queries That Locate Usernames

Query	Description
inurl:admin inurl:userlist	Generic userlist files
inurl:admin filetype:asp inurl:userlist	Generic userlist files
inurl:php inurl:hlstats intext: Server Username	Half-life statistics file, lists username and other information
filetype:ctl inurl:haccess.ctl Basic	Microsoft FrontPage equivalent(?)of htaccess shows Web user credentials
filetype:reg reg intext:"internet account manager"	Microsoft Internet Account Manager can reveal usernames and more

Continued

Table 9.1 continued Sample Queries That Locate Usernames

Query	Description
filetype:wab wab	Microsoft Outlook Express Mail address books
filetype:mdb inurl:profiles	Microsoft Access databases containing (user) profiles.
index.of perform.ini	mIRC IRC ini file can list IRC usernames and other information
inurl:root.asp?acs=anon	Outlook Mail Web Access directory can be used to discover usernames
filetype:conf inurl:proftpd.conf –sample	PROFTP FTP server configuration file reveals username and server information
filetype:log username putty	PUTTY SSH client logs can reveal user-names and server information
filetype:rdp rdp	Remote Desktop Connection files reveal user credentials
intitle:index.of .bash_history	UNIX bash shell history reveals com-mands typed at a bash command prompt; usernames are often typed as argument strings
intitle:index.of .sh_history	UNIX shell history reveals commands typed at a shell command prompt; user-names are often typed as argument strings
"index of " lck	Various lock files list the user currently using a file
+intext:webalizer +intext:Total Usernames +intext:"Usage Statistics for"	Webalizer Web statistics page lists Web usernames and statistical information
filetype:reg reg HKEY_CURRENT_ USER username	Windows Registry exports can reveal usernames and other information

Underground Googling

Searching for a Known Filename

Remember that there are several ways to search for a known filename. One way relies on locating the file in a directory listing, like *intitle:index.of install.log*. Another, often better, method relies on the *filetype* operator, as in *filetype:log inurl:install.log*. Directory listings are not all that common. Google will crawl a link to a file in a directory listing, meaning that the *filetype* method will find *both* directory listing entries as well as files crawled in other ways.

In some cases, usernames can be gathered from Web-based statistical programs that check Web activity. The Webalizer program shows all sorts of information about a Web server's usage. Output files for the Webalizer program can be located with a query such as *+intext:webalizer +intext:"Total Usernames" +intext:"Usage Statistics for"*. Among the information displayed is the username that was used to connect to the Web server, as shown in Figure 9.2. In some cases, however, the usernames displayed are not valid or current, but the "Visits" column lists the number of times a user account was used during the capture period. This enables an attacker to easily determine which accounts are more likely to be valid.

Figure 9.2 The Webalizer Output Page Lists Web Usernames

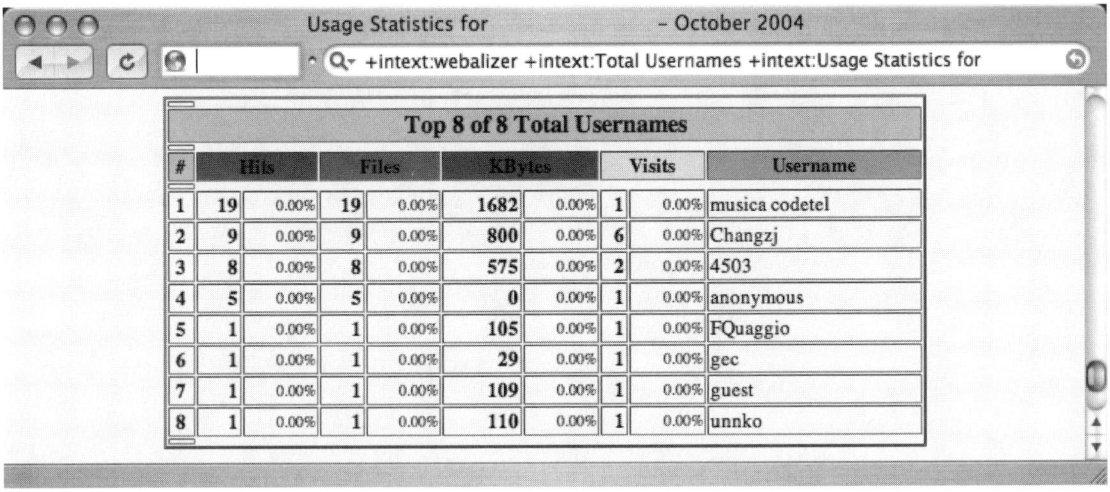

Usage Statistics for   – October 2004

Q▾ +intext:webalizer +intext:Total Usernames +intext:Usage Statistics for

Top 8 of 8 Total Usernames

#	Hits		Files		KBytes		Visits		Username
1	19	0.00%	19	0.00%	1682	0.00%	1	0.00%	musica codetel
2	9	0.00%	9	0.00%	800	0.00%	6	0.00%	Changzj
3	8	0.00%	8	0.00%	575	0.00%	2	0.00%	4503
4	5	0.00%	5	0.00%	0	0.00%	1	0.00%	anonymous
5	1	0.00%	1	0.00%	105	0.00%	1	0.00%	FQuaggio
6	1	0.00%	1	0.00%	29	0.00%	1	0.00%	gec
7	1	0.00%	1	0.00%	109	0.00%	1	0.00%	guest
8	1	0.00%	1	0.00%	110	0.00%	1	0.00%	unnko

The Windows registry holds all sorts of authentication information, including usernames and passwords. Though it is unlikely (and fairly uncommon) to locate live, exported Windows registry files on the Web, at the time of this writing there are nearly 200 hits on the query *filetype:reg HKEY_CURRENT_USER username,* which locates Windows registry files that contain the word *username* and in some cases passwords, as shown in Figure 9.3.

Figure 9.3 Generic Windows Registry Files Can Reveal Usernames and Passwords

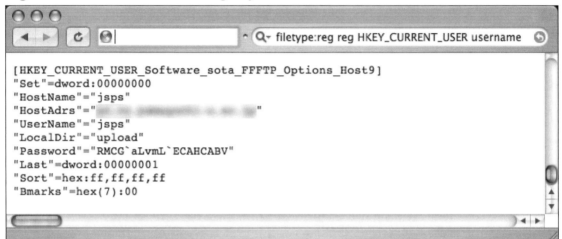

As any talented attacker or security person will tell you, it's rare to get information served to you on a silver platter. Most decent finds take a bit of persistence, creativity, intelligence, and just a bit of good luck. For example, consider the Microsoft Outlook Web Access portal, which can be located with a query like *inurl:root.asp?acs=anon.* There are few hits for this query, even though there lots of sites run the Microsoft Web-based mail portal. Regardless of how you might locate a site running this e-mail gateway, it's not uncommon for the site to host a public directory (denoted "Find Names," by default), as shown in Figure 9.4.

Figure 9.4 Microsoft Outlook Web Access Hosts a Public Directory

The public directory allows access to a search page that can be used to find users by name. In most cases, wildcard searching is not allowed, meaning that a search for ⋆ will not return a list of all users, as might be expected. Entering a search for a space is an interesting idea, since most user descriptions contain a space, but most large directories will return an error message reading "This query would return too many addresses!" Applying a bit of creativity, an attacker could begin searching for individual common letters, such as the "Wheel of Fortune letters" *R, S, T, L, N, and E*. Eventually one of these searches will most likely reveal a list of user information like the one shown in Figure 9.5.

Figure 9.5 Public Outlook Directory Searching for Usernames

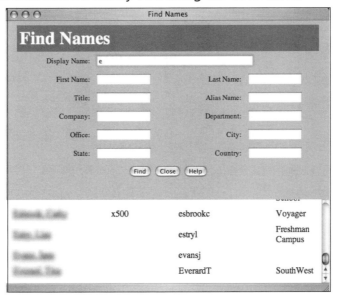

Once a list of user information is returned, the attacker can then recycle the search with words contained in the user list, searching for the words *Voyager, Freshmen, or Campus*, for example. Those results can then be recycled, eventually resulting in a nearly complete list of user information.

Searching for Passwords

Password data, one of the "Holy Grails" during a penetration test, should be protected. Unfortunately, many examples of Google queries can be used to locate passwords on the Web, as shown in Table 9.2.

Table 9.2 Queries That Locate Password Information

Query	Description
filetype:config config intext: appSettings "User ID"	.Net Web Application configuration may contain authentication information
filetype:netrc password	.netrc file may contain cleartext passwords
intitle:"Index of" passwords modified	"Password" directories
inurl:/db/main.mdb	ASP-Nuke database files often contain passwords
filetype:bak inurl:"htaccess|passwd|shadow|htusers"	BAK files referring to passwords or usernames
filetype:log "See `ipsec —copyright"	BARF log files reveal ipsec data
inurl:"calendarscript/users.txt"	CalenderScript passwords
inurl:ccbill filetype:log data	CCBill log files may contain authentication
inurl:cgi-bin inurl:calendar.cfg	CGI Calendar (Perl) configuration file reveals information including passwords for the program.
inurl:chap-secrets -cvs	chap-secrets file may list usernames and passwords
enable password | secret "current configuration" -intext:the	Cisco "secret 5" and "password 7" passwords
intext:"enable secret 5 $"	Cisco enable secrets
intext:"enable password 7"	Cisco router config files
[WFClient] Password= filetype:ica	Citrix WinFrame-Client may contain login information
inurl:passlist.txt	Cleartext passwords. No decryption required!

Continued

Table 9.2 continued Queries That Locate Password Information

Query	Description
filetype:cfm "cfapplication name" password	ColdFusion source code mentioning "passwords"
intitle:index.of config.php	Config.php files
inurl:config.php dbuname dbpass	config.php files
inurl:server.cfg rcon password	Counter strike rcon passwords
ext:inc "pwd=" "UID="	Database connection strings
ext:asa | ext:bak intext:uid intext:pwd -"uid..pwd" database | server | dsn	Database credentials in ASA and BAK files
filetype:ldb admin	Database lock files may contain credential info
filetype:properties inurl:db intext: password	db.properties file contains usernames, decrypted passwords
filetype:inc dbconn	Dbconn.inc files contain the username and password a website uses to connect to a database.
filetype:pass pass intext:userid	dbman password files
allinurl:auth_user_file.txt	DCForum's password file
"powered by ducalendar" -site:duware.com	ducalendar database may reveal password data
"Powered by Duclassified" -site:duware.com	Duclassified database may reveal password data
"powered by duclassmate" -site:duware.com	duclassmate database may reveal password data
"Powered by Dudirectory" -site:duware.com	dudirectory database may reveal password data
"powered by dudownload" -site:duware.com	dudownload database may reveal password data
"Powered by DUpaypal" -site:duware.com	Dupaypal database may reveal password data.
intitle:dupics inurl:(add.asp | default.asp | view.asp | voting.asp) -site:duware.com	dupics database may reveal password data
eggdrop filetype:user user	Eggdrop config files
"Powered By Elite Forum Version *.*"	Elite forums database contains authentication information

Continued

Table 9.2 continued Queries That Locate Password Information

Query	Description
intitle:"Index of" pwd.db	Encrypted pwd.db passwords
ext:ini eudora.ini	Eudora INI file may contain usernames and encrypted passwords
inurl:filezilla.xml -cvs	filezilla.xml contains passwords data
filetype:ini inurl:flashFXP.ini	FlashFXP configuration file may contain FTP passwords
filetype:dat inurl:Sites.dat	FlashFXP FTP passwords
inurl:"Sites.dat"+"PASS="	FlashFXP Sites.dat server configuration file
ext:pwd inurl:(service | authors | administrators | users) "# -FrontPage-"	Frontpage sensitive authentication-related files
filetype:url +inurl:"ftp://" +inurl:"@"	FTP bookmarks, some of which contain plaintext login names and passwords
intitle:index.of passwd passwd.bak	Generic PASSWD files
inurl:zebra.conf intext:password -sample -test -tutorial -download	GNU Zebra enable passwords (plain text or encrypted)
intext:"powered by EZGuestbook"	HTMLJunction EZGuestbook database reveals authentication data
intitle:"Index of" ".htpasswd" htpasswd.bak	htpasswd password files
intitle:"Index of" ".htpasswd" "htgroup" -intitle:"dist" -apache -htpasswd.c	htpasswd password files
filetype:htpasswd htpasswd	htpasswd password files
"http://*:*@www" bob:bob	HTTP web authentication information
"liveice configuration file" ext:cfg -site:sourceforge.net	Icecast liveice.cfg file which may contain passwords
"sets mode: +k"	IRC channel keys
signin filetype:url	Javascript user validation mechanisms may contain cleartext usernames and passwords
LeapFTP intitle:"index.of./" sites.ini modified	LeapFTP client configuration file may reveal authentication information
inurl:lilo.conf filetype:conf password -tatercounter2000 -bootpwd -man	LILO boot passwords
"Powered by Link Department"	Link management script contains encrypted admin passwords and session data

Continued

Table 9.2 continued Queries That Locate Password Information

Query	Description
"your password is" filetype:log	log files containing the phrase (Your password is).
"admin account info" filetype:log	logs containing admin server account information
intitle:index.of master.passwd	master.passwd files
allinurl: admin mdb	Microsoft Access "admin" databases
filetype:mdb inurl:users.mdb	Microsoft Access "user databases"
filetype:xls username password email	Microsoft Excel spreadsheets containing the words username, password and email
intitle:index.of administrators.pwd	Microsoft Front Page administrative usernames and passwords.
filetype:pwd service	Microsoft Frontpage service info
inurl:perform.ini filetype:ini	mIRC IRC passwords
inurl:perform filetype:ini	mIRC potential connection data
filetype:cfg mrtg "target[*]" -sample -cvs -example	Mrtg.cfg SNMP configuration file may reveal public and private community strings
intitle:"index of" intext:connect.inc	MySQL database connection information
intitle:"Index of" .mysql_history	mysql history files
intitle:"index of" intext:globals.inc	MySQL user/password information
"Your password is * Remember this for later use"	NickServ registration passwords
filetype:conf oekakibbs	Oekakibss configuration files may reveal passwords
filetype:conf slapd.conf	OpenLDAP slapd.conf file contains configuration data including the root password
inurl:"slapd.conf" intext:"credentials" -manpage -"Manual Page" -man: -sample	OpenLDAP slapd.conf file contains configuration data including the root password
filetype:dat wand.dat	Opera web browser "magic wand" stored cerdentials
inurl:pap-secrets -cvs	pap-secrets file may list usernames and passwords
filetype:dat inurl:pass.dat	Pass.dat files may reveal passwords
index.of passlist	Passlist password files

Continued

Table 9.2 continued Queries That Locate Password Information

Query	Description
filetype:dat "password.dat"	Password.dat files can contain plaintext usernames and passwords
filetype:log inurl:"password.log"	Password.log files can contain cleartext usernames and passwords
filetype:pem intext:private	PEM private key files
intitle:index.of people.lst	people.lst files
intitle:index.of intext:"secring.skr"|"secring.pgp"|"secring.bak"	PGP secret keyrings
inurl:secring ext:skr | ext:pgp | ext:bak	PGP secret keyrings
filetype:inc mysql_connect OR mysql_pconnect	PHP .inc files contain authentication information
filetype:inc intext:mysql_connect	PHP .inc files contain usernames, passwords
ext:php intext:"$dbms""$dbhost""$dbuser""$dbpasswd""$table_prefix""phpbb_installed"	phpBB mySQL connection information
intitle:"phpinfo()" +"mysql.default_password" +"Zend Scripting Language Engine"	phpinfo files may contain default mysql passwords
inurl:nuke filetype:sql	PHP-Nuke or Postnuke database dumps may contain authentication data
"parent directory" +proftpdpasswd	ProFTPd User names and password hashes from web server backups
filetype:conf inurl:psybnc.conf "USER.PASS="	psyBNC configuration files may contain authentication info
intitle:rapidshare intext:login	Rapidshare login passwords.
inurl:"editor/list.asp" | inurl:"database_editor.asp" | inurl:"login.asa" "are set"	Results Database Editor usernames/passwords
ext:yml database inurl:config	Ruby on Rails database link file
ext:ini Version=4.0.0.4 password	servU FTP Daemon ini file may contain usernames and passwords
filetype:ini ServUDaemon	servU FTP Daemon INI files may contains setting, session and authentication data
filetype:ini inurl:"serv-u.ini"	Serv-U INI file may contain username and password data

Continued

Table 9.2 continued Queries That Locate Password Information

Query	Description
intitle:"Index of" sc_serv.conf sc_serv content	Shoutcast sc_serv.conf files often contain cleartext passwords
intitle:"Index of" spwd.db passwd -pam.conf	spwd.db password files
filetype:sql "insert into" (pass|passwd|password)	SQL dumps containing cleartext or encrypted passwords
filetype:sql ("passwd values" | "password values" | "pass values")	SQL file password references
filetype:sql ("values * MD5" | "values * password" | "values * encrypt")	SQL files may contain encrypted passwords
filetype:sql +"IDENTIFIED BY" -cvs	SQL files mentioning authentication info
filetype:sql password	SQL files mentioning authentication info
filetype:reg reg HKEY_CURRENT_USER SSHHOSTKEYS	SSH host keys stored in Windows Registry
inurl:"GRC.DAT" intext:"password"	Symantec Norton Anti-Virus Corporate Edition data file contains encrypted passwords
filetype:inf sysprep	Sysprep.inf files contain all information for a Windows information including administrative passwords, IP addresses and product IDs
server-dbs "intitle:index of"	teamspeak server admin files
filetype:ini wcx_ftp	Total commander FTP passwords
intitle:index.of trillian.ini	Trillian INI files contain passwords.
ext:txt inurl:unattend.txt	unattend.txt files contain all information for a Windows information including administrative passwords, IP addresses and product IDs
index.of.etc	Unix /etc directories
intitle:"Index of..etc" passwd	Unix /etc/passwd files
intitle:Index.of etc shadow	UNIX /etc/shadow password files
ext:passwd -intext:the -sample -example	Various passwords
filetype:bak createobject sa	VBScript database connection backups
inurl:ventrilo_srv.ini adminpassword	ventrilo passwords for many servers

Continued

Table 9.2 continued Queries That Locate Password Information

Query	Description
filetype:reg reg +intext: WINVNC3	vnc passwords
!Host=*.* intext:enc_UserPassword= * ext:pcf	VPN profiles often contain authentication data
inurl:vtund.conf intext:pass -cvs	vtund configuration files can contain usernames and passwords
filetype:mdb wwforum	Web Wiz Forums database contains authentication information
intext:"powered by Web Wiz Journal"	Web Wiz Journal ASP Blog database contains administrative information
"AutoCreate=TRUE password=*"	Website Access Analyzer passwords
filetype:pwl pwl	Windows Password List files
filetype:reg reg +intext: "defaultusername" +intext: "defaultpassword"	Windows registry keys which reveal passwords
filetype:ini ws_ftp pwd	WS_FTP.ini file contains weakly encrypted passwords
"index of/" "ws_ftp.ini" "parent directory"	WS_FTP.ini file contains weakly encrypted passwords
inurl:"wvdial.conf" intext: "password"	wvdial.conf may contain phone numbers, usernames and passwords
inurl:/wwwboard	WWWBoard "passwd.txt" authentication configuration files
wwwboard WebAdmin inurl: passwd.txt wwwboard|webadmin	WWWBoard password files
"login: *" "password= *" filetype:xls	xls files containing login names and passwords
inurl:/yabb/Members/Admin.dat	YaBB forums Administrator password

In most cases, passwords discovered on the Web are either encrypted or encoded in some way. In most cases, these passwords can be fed into a password cracker such as John the Ripper from www.openwall.com/john to produce plaintext passwords that can be used in an attack. Figure 9.6 shows the results of the search *ext:pwd inurl:_vti_pvt inurl:(Service | authors | administrators)*, which combines a search for some common Microsoft FrontPage support files.

Figure 9.6 Encrypted or Encoded Passwords

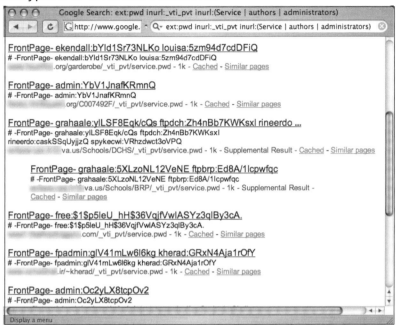

Exported Windows registry files often contain encrypted or encoded passwords as well. If a user exports the Windows registry to a file and Google subsequently crawls that file, a query like *filetype:reg intext:"internet account manager"* could reveal interesting keys containing password data, as shown in Figure 9.7.

Figure 9.7 Specific Windows Registry Entries Can Reveal Passwords

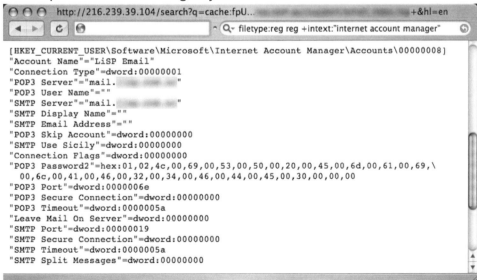

Note that live, exported Windows registry files are not very common, but it's not uncommon for an attacker to target a site simply because of one exceptionally insecure file. It's also possible for a Google query to uncover cleartext passwords. These passwords can be used as is without having to employ a password-cracking utility. In these extreme cases, the only challenge is determining the username as well as the host on which the password can be used. As shown in Figure 9.8, certain queries will locate all the following information: usernames, cleartext passwords, and the host that uses that authentication!

Figure 9.8 The Holy Grail: Usernames, Cleartext Passwords, and Hostnames!

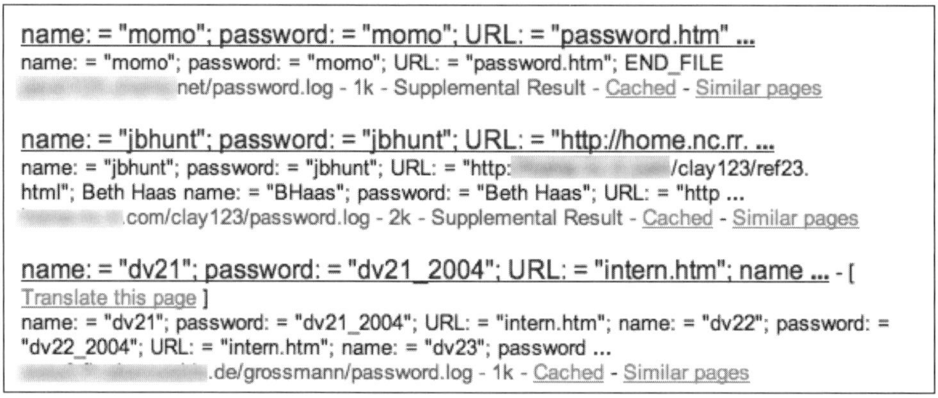

name: = "momo"; password: = "momo"; URL: = "password.htm" ...
name: = "momo"; password: = "momo"; URL: = "password.htm"; END_FILE
net/password.log - 1k - Supplemental Result - Cached - Similar pages

name: = "jbhunt"; password: = "jbhunt"; URL: = "http://home.nc.rr. ...
name: = "jbhunt"; password: = "jbhunt"; URL: = "http: /clay123/ref23.
html"; Beth Haas name: = "BHaas"; password: = "Beth Haas"; URL: = "http ...
.com/clay123/password.log - 2k - Supplemental Result - Cached - Similar pages

name: = "dv21"; password: = "dv21_2004"; URL: = "intern.htm"; name ... - [Translate this page]
name: = "dv21"; password: = "dv21_2004"; URL: = "intern.htm"; name: = "dv22"; password: = "dv22_2004"; URL: = "intern.htm"; name: = "dv23"; password ...
.de/grossmann/password.log - 1k - Cached - Similar pages

There is no magic query for locating passwords, but during an assessment, remember that the simplest queries directed at a site can have amazing results, as we discussed in the "Top Ten Searches" chapter. For example, a query like *"Your password" forgot* would locate pages that provide a forgotten password recovery mechanism. The information from this type of query can be used to formulate any of a number of attacks against a password. As always, effective social engineering is a terrific nontechnical solution to "forgotten" passwords.

Another generic search for password information, *intext:(password | passcode | pass) intext:(username | userid | user)*, combines common words for passwords and user IDs into one query. This query returns a lot of results, but the vast majority of the top hits refer to pages that list forgotten password information, including either links or contact information. Using Google's translate feature, found at http://translate.google.com/translate_t, we could also create multilingual password searches. Table 9.3 lists common translations for the word *password*. Note that the terms *username* and *userid* in most languages translate to *username* and *userid*, respectively.

Table 9.3 English Translations of the Word *Password*

Language	Word	Translation
German	password	Kennwort
Spanish	password	contraseña
French	password	mot de passe
Italian	password	parola d'accesso
Portuguese	password	senha
Dutch	password	Paswoord

Searching for Credit Card Numbers, Social Security Numbers, and More

Most people have heard news stories about Web hackers making off with customer credit card information. With so many fly-by night retailers popping up on the Internet, it's no wonder that credit card fraud is so prolific. These mom-and-pop retailers are not the only ones successfully compromised by hackers. Corporate giants by the hundreds have had financial database compromises over the years, victims of sometimes very technical, highly focused attackers. What might surprise you is that it doesn't take a rocket scientist to uncover live credit card numbers on the Internet, thanks to search engines like Google. Everything from credit information to banking data or supersensitive classified government documents can be found on the Web. Consider the (highly edited) Web page shown in Figure 9.9.

Figure 9.9 Google Stores Piles and Piles of Previously Pilfered Personal Data

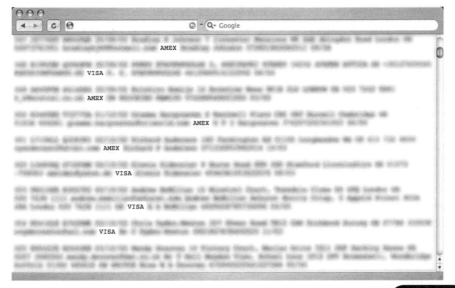

This document, found using Google, lists hundreds and hundreds of credit card numbers (including expiration date and card validation numbers) as well as the owners' names, addresses, and phone numbers. This particular document also included phone card (calling card) numbers. Notice the scroll bar on the right-hand side of Figure 9.9, an indicator that the displayed page is only a small part of this huge document—like many other documents of its kind. In most cases, pages that contain these numbers are not "leaked" from online retailers or e-commerce sites but rather are most likely the fruits of a scam known as *phishing*, in which users are solicited via telephone or e-mail for personal information. Several Web sites, including MillerSmiles.co.uk, document these scams and hoaxes. Figure 9.10 shows a screen shot of a popular eBay phishing scam that encourages users to update their eBay profile information.

Figure 9.10 Screenshot of an eBay Phishing Scam

Once a user fills out this form, all the information is sent via e-mail to the attacker, who can use it for just about anything. Sometimes this data is stored on a web server used by the attacker. In some cases I've seen online "phishing investigators" post reports which link to the phisher's cache of pilfered personal data. When a search engine crawls those links, all that personal data is suddenly available to even the most amateur Google hacker.

Tools and Traps...

Catching Online Scammers

In some cases, you might be able to use Google to help nab the bad guys. Phishing scams are effective because the fake page looks like an official page. To create an official-looking page, the bad guys must have examples to work from, meaning that they must have visited a few legitimate companies' Web sites. If the fishing scam was created using text from several companies' existing pages, you can key in on specific phrases from the fake page, creating Google queries designed to round up the servers that hosted some of the original content. Once you've located the servers that contained the pilfered text, you can work with the companies involved to extract correlating connection data from their log files. If the scammer visited each company's Web page, collecting bits of realistic text, his IP should appear in each of the log files. Auditors at SensePost (www.sensepost.com) have successfully used this technique to nab online scam artists. Unfortunately, if the scammer uses an exact copy of a page from only one company, this task becomes much more difficult to accomplish.

Social Security Numbers

Attackers can use similar techniques to home in on Social Security numbers (SSNs) and other sensitive data. For a variety of reasons, SSNs might appear online—for example, educational facilities are notorious for using an SSN as a student ID, then posting grades to a public Web site with the "student ID" displayed next to the grade. A creative attacker can do quite a bit with just an SSN, but in many cases it helps to also have a name associated with that SSN. Again, educational facilities have been found exposing this information via Excel spreadsheets listing student's names, grades, and SSNs, despite the fact that the student ID number is often used to help protect the privacy of the student! Although I've never revealed how to locate SSN's, several media outlets have done just that—irresponsibly posting the search details online. Although the blame lies with the sites that are leaking this information, in my opinion it's still not right to draw attention to how exactly the information can be located.

Personal Financial Data

In some cases, phishing scams are responsible for publicizing personal information; in other cases, hackers attacking online retails are to blame for this breach of privacy. Sadly, there are many instances where an individual is *personally* responsible for his own lack of privacy. Such is the case with personal financial information. With the explosion of personal computers in today's society, users have literally *hundreds* of personal finance programs to choose from. Many of these programs create data files with specific file extensions that can be searched with Google. It's hard to imagine why anyone would post personal financial information to a public Web site (which subsequently gets crawled by Google), but it must happen quite a bit, judging by the number of hits for program files generated by Quicken and Microsoft Money, for example. Although it would be somewhat irresponsible to provide queries here that would unearth personal financial data, it's important to understand the types of data that could potentially be uncovered by an attacker. To that end, Table 9.4 shows file extensions for various financial, accounting, and tax return programs.

Table 9.4 File Extensions for Various Financial Programs

File Extension	Description
afm	Abassis Finance Manager
ab4	Accounting and Business File
mmw	AceMoney File
lqd	AmeriCalc Mutual Fund Tax Report
et2	Electronic Tax Return Security File (Australia)
tax	Intuit TurboTax Tax Return
t98-t04	Kiplinger Tax Cut File (extension based on two-digit return year)
mny	Microsoft Money 2004 Money Data Files
mbf	Microsoft Money Backup Files
inv	MSN Money Investor File
ptdb	Peachtree Accounting Database
qbb	QuickBooks Backup Files reveal financial data
qdf	Quicken personal finance data
soa	Sage MAS 90 accounting software
sdb	Simply Accounting
stx	Simply Tax Form
tmd	Time and Expense Tracking
tls	Timeless Time & Expense
fec	U.S. Federal Campaign Expense Submission
wow	Wings Accounting File

Searching for Other Juicy Info

As we've seen, Google can be used to locate all sorts of sensitive information. In this section we take a look at some of the data that Google can find that's harder to categorize. From address books to chat log files and network vulnerability reports, there's no shortage of sensitive data online. Table 9.5 shows some queries that can be used to uncover various types of sensitive data.

Table 9.5 Queries That Locate Various Sensitive Information

Query	Description
intext:"Session Start * * * *:*:* *" filetype:log	AIM and IRC log files
filetype:blt blt +intext:screenname	AIM buddy lists
buddylist.blt	AIM buddy lists
intitle:index.of cgiirc.config	CGIIRC (Web-based IRC client) config file, shows IRC servers and user credentials
inurl:cgiirc.config	CGIIRC (Web-based IRC client) config file, shows IRC servers and user credentials
"Index of" / "chat/logs"	Chat logs
intitle:"Index Of" cookies.txt "size"	cookies.txt file reveals user information
"phone * * *" "address *" "e-mail" intitle:"curriculum vitae"	Curriculum vitae (resumes) reveal names and address information
ext:ini intext:env.ini	Generic environment data
intitle:index.of inbox	Generic mailbox files
"Running in Child mode"	Gnutella client data and statistics
":8080" ":3128" ":80" filetype:txt	HTTP Proxy lists
intitle:"Index of" dbconvert.exe chats	ICQ chat logs
"sets mode: +p"	IRC private channel information
"sets mode: +s"	IRC secret channel information
"Host Vulnerability Summary Report"	ISS vulnerability scanner reports, reveal potential vulnerabilities on hosts and networks
"Network Vulnerability Assessment Report"	ISS vulnerability scanner reports, reveal potential vulnerabilities on hosts and networks

Continued

www.syngress.com

Table 9.5 continued Queries That Locate Various Sensitive Information

Query	Description
filetype:pot inurl:john.pot	John the Ripper password cracker results
intitle:"Index Of" -inurl:maillog maillog size	Maillog files reveals e-mail traffic information
ext:mdb inurl:.mdb inurl:fpdb shop.mdb*	Microsoft FrontPage database folders
filetype:xls inurl:contact	Microsoft Excel sheets containing contact information.
intitle:index.of haccess.ctl	Microsoft FrontPage equivalent(?)of htaccess shows Web authentication info
*ext:log "Software: Microsoft Internet Information Services *.*"*	Microsoft Internet Information Services (IIS) log files
filetype:pst inurl:"outlook.pst"	Microsoft Outlook e-mail and calendar backup files
intitle:index.of mt-db-pass.cgi	Movable Type default file
filetype:ctt ctt messenger	MSN Messenger contact lists
"This file was generated by Nessus"	Nessus vulnerability scanner reports, reveal potential vulnerabilities on hosts and networks
inurl:"newsletter/admin/"	Newsletter administration information
inurl:"newsletter/admin/" intitle:"newsletter admin"	Newsletter administration information
filetype:eml eml intext:"Subject" +From	Outlook Express e-mail files
intitle:index.of inbox dbx	Outlook Express Mailbox files
intitle:index.of inbox dbx	Outlook Express Mailbox files
filetype:mbx mbx intext:Subject	Outlook v1–v4 or Eudora mailbox files
inurl:/public/?Cmd=contents	Outlook Web Access public folders or appointments
filetype:pdb pdb backup (Pilot | Pluckerdb)	Palm Pilot Hotsync database files
"This is a Shareaza Node"	Shareaza client data and statistics
inurl:/_layouts/settings	Sharepoint configuration information
inurl:ssl.conf filetype:conf	SSL configuration files, reveal various configuration information
site:edu admin grades	Student grades
intitle:index.of mystuff.xml	Trillian user Web links

Continued

Table 9.5 continued Queries That Locate Various Sensitive Information

Query	Description
inurl:forward filetype:forward –cvs	UNIX mail forward files reveal e-mail addresses
intitle:index.of dead.letter	UNIX unfinished e-mails
filetype:conf inurl:unrealircd.conf -cvs -gentoo	UnreallRCd config file reveals configuration information
filetype:bkf bkf	Windows XP/2000 backup files

Some of this information is fairly benign—for example, MSN Messenger contact list files that can be found with a query like *filetype:ctt messenger,* or AOL Instant Messenger (AIM) buddy lists that can be located with a query such as *filetype:blt blt +intext:screenname,* as shown in Figure 9.11.

Figure 9.11 AIM Buddy Lists Reveal Personal Relationships

This screen shows a list of "buddies," or acquaintances an individual has entered into his or her AIM client. An attacker often uses personal information like this in a social-engineering attack, attempting to convince the target that they are a friend or an acquaintance. This practice is akin to pilfering a Rolodex or address book from a target. For a seasoned attacker, information like this can lead to a successful compromise. However, in some cases, data found with a Google query reveals sensitive security-related information that even the most novice attacker could use to compromise a system.

For example, consider the output of the Nessus security scanner available from www.nessus.org. This excellent open-source tool conducts a series of security tests against a target, reporting on any potential vulnerability. The report generated by Nessus can then be used as a guide to help system administrators lock down any affected systems. An attacker could also use a report like this to uncover a target's potential vulnerabilities. Using a Google query such as *"This file was generated by Nessus",* an attacker could locate reports generated by the Nessus tool, as shown in Figure 9.12. This report lists the IP address of each tested machine as well as the ports opened and any vulnerabilities that were detected.

Figure 9.12 Nessus Vulnerability Reports Found Online

In most cases, reports found in this manner are samples, or test reports, but in a few cases, the reports are live and the tested systems *are,* in fact, exploitable as listed. One can only hope that the reported systems are honeypots—machines created for the sole purpose of luring and tracing the activities of hackers. In the next chapter, we'll talk more about "document-grinding" techniques, which are also useful for digging up this type of information. This chapter focused on locating the information based on the name of the file, whereas the next chapter focuses on the actual *content* of a document rather than the name.

Summary

Make no mistake—there's sensitive data on the Web, and Google can find it. There's hardly any limit to the scope of information that can be located, if only you can figure out the right query. From usernames to passwords, credit card and Social Security numbers, and personal financial information, it's all out there. As a purveyor of the "dark arts," you can relish in the stupidity of others, but as a professional tasked with securing a customer's site from this dangerous form of information leakage, you could be overwhelmed by the sheer scale of your defensive duties.

As droll as it might sound, a solid, enforced security policy is a great way to keep sensitive data from leaking to the Web. If users understand the risks associated with information leakage and understand the penalties that come with violating policy, they will be more willing to cooperate in what should be a security partnership.

In the meantime, it certainly doesn't hurt to understand the tactics an adversary might employ in attacking a Web server. One thing that should become clear as you read this book is that any attacker has an overwhelming number of files to go after. One way to prevent dangerous Web information leakage is by denying requests for unknown file types. Whether your Web server normally serves up CFM, ASP, PHP, or HTML, it's infinitely easier to manage what *should* be served by the Web server instead of focusing on what should *not* be served. Adjust your servers or your border protection devices to allow only specific content or file types.

Solutions Fast Track

Searching for Usernames

☑ Usernames can be found in a variety of locations.

☑ In some cases, digging through documents or e-mail directories might be required.

☑ A simple query such as *"your username is"* can be very effective in locating usernames.

Searching for Passwords

☑ Passwords can also be found in a variety locations.

☑ A query such as *"Your password" forgot* can locate pages that provide a forgotten-password recovery mechanism.

☑ *intext:(password | passcode | pass) intext:(username | userid | user)* is another generic search for locating password information.

Searching for Credit Cards Numbers, Social Security Numbers, and More

☑ Documents containing credit card and Social Security number information do exist and are relatively prolific.

☑ Some irresponsible news outlets have revealed functional queries that locate this information.

☑ There are relatively few examples of personal financial data online, but there is a great deal of variety.

☑ In most cases, specific file extensions can be searched for.

Searching for Other Juicy Info

☑ From address books and chat log files to network vulnerability reports, there's no shortage of sensitive data online.

Frequently Asked Questions

The following Frequently Asked Questions, answered by the authors of this book, are designed to both measure your understanding of the concepts presented in this chapter and to assist you with real-life implementation of these concepts. To have your questions about this chapter answered by the author, browse to **www. syngress.com/solutions** and click on the **"Ask the Author"** form.

Q: I'm concerned about phishing schemes. Are there resources to help me understand the risks and learn some safeguards?

A: There's an excellent Web site dedicated to the topic of phishing at www.antiphishing.org. You can also read a great white paper by Next Generation Security Software Ltd., *The Phishing Guide: Understanding and Preventing Phishing Attacks*, available from www.ngssoftware.com/papers/NISR-WP-Phishing.pdf.

Q: Why don't you give more details about locating information such as credit card numbers and Social Security numbers?

A: To be honest, neither the authors nor the publisher is willing to take personal responsibility for encouraging potential illegal activity. Most individuals interested in this kind of information will use it for illegal purposes. If you are interested in scanning for your own personal information online, simply enter your information into Google. If you get some hits, you should be worried. Of course entering *all* of your personal information such as credit card numbers and social security numbers isn't a great idea either, as an interloper could easily capture that information. It's better instead to enter pieces of that information. Be creative, but don't open yourself to exposure while trying to protect yourself!

Q: Many passwords grant access to meaningless services. Why should I be worried about the password for a useless service leaking out to the Web?

A: Studies have shown that the majority of people often opt for the easiest path to completing a task. In the world of security, this means that many people share passwords (or password cues) across many different applications on many different servers. So, you can see that one compromised password can provide clues about passwords used on other systems. Most policies forbid this type of password sharing, but this restriction is often hard to enforce.

## Chapter 10

Hacking Google Services

Solutions in this chapter:

- AJAX Search API
- Calendar
- Blogger and Google's Blog Search
- Signaling Alerts
- Google Co-op
- Google Code

AJAX Search API

AJAX Search API is one of the leading Google services on the AJAX front. This service is meant as a replacement of the older SOAP search service which support was discontinued some time ago. AJAX Search API is considered to be more powerful then the SOAP service and easier to work with. The primary goal of the service is to enable external websites to host Google supplied gadgets which provide searching facilities within or outside of the hosting website and also among video clips, maps, blogs, custom search engines, etc.

The default interface of the service looks like as shown on Figure 10.1.

Figure 10.1 Google AJAX Search API Dialog

The search dialog in Figure 10.1 is divided into several sections. Each section represents a search category: Local, Web, Video, Blog, News and Book. Having all results on a single place in particular is very useful since we can perform interesting queries and get instant feedback across the entire Google platform. This is where the Search API shines best. Let's try a query fir *firefox*, as shown in Figure 10.2.

Simply visit http://www.google.com/uds/samples/apidocs/helloworld.html demonstration application and type the query.

Figure 10.2 AJAX Search for "firefox"

Notice that the AJAX API result set contains also Image search section with the most relevant results. In the following section we are going to have more detailed look at the AJAX API Search service.

Embedding Google AJAX Search API

The Google AJAX Search API was designed to be embedded within external pages. This makes the service rather useful, since we can construct custom interfaces for better accessing the Google infrastructure. In order to start using the AJAX Search API you need to have some understanding of JavaScript and AJAX programming and an API key which you can generate yourself. Assuming basic understanding of AJAX, we will concentrate on the interesting stuff around the service itself.

In order to generate an API key, simply Visit the AJAX Search API Home page at http://code.google.com/apis/ajaxsearch. After clicking *Start using the Google AJAX Search API*, you will be presented with a page similar to the one shown in Figure 10.3.

Figure 10.3 AJAX Search API Key Generation

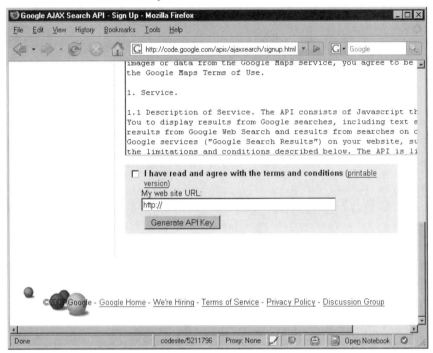

You need to provide a URL where the service will be accessed from. If you are planning to host the application from a simple page on your desktop, you can input just about anything you choose. In fact, this option seems to be largely irrelevant. For the purpose of this demonstration, we will use http://dummy as this URL. Most applications work with the internal Google key which is used across all API demo applications.

After accepting Google's term and conditions you will be provided a page that will present you with the actual Google API key which is specifically generated for the previously supplied URL. This page also gives you an example of how to use the AJAX Search box. This is the code was generated for us:

```
<!DOCTYPE html PUBLIC "-//W3C//DTD XHTML 1.0 Strict//EN"
"http://www.w3.org/TR/xhtml1/DTD/xhtml1-strict.dtd">
<html xmlns="http://www.w3.org/1999/xhtml">
  <head>
    <meta http-equiv="content-type" content="text/html; charset=utf-8"/>
    <title>My Google AJAX Search API Application</title>
    <link href="http://www.google.com/uds/css/gsearch.css" type="text/css"
rel="stylesheet"/>
    <script
src="http://www.google.com/uds/api?file=uds.js&amp;v=1.0&amp;key=ABQIAAAAsFym1Ew5o48
```

zXESOPhV4ExSFOvRczLyAyj57qAvViVrKq19E6hSZhJSVQBi2HRSzsW1XyZzxdffdfQ"
type="text/javascript"></script>

```
    <script language="Javascript" type="text/javascript">
    //<![CDATA[
    function OnLoad() {
      // Create a search control
      var searchControl = new GSearchControl();
      // Add in a full set of searchers
      var localSearch = new GlocalSearch();
      searchControl.addSearcher(localSearch);
      searchControl.addSearcher(new GwebSearch());
      searchControl.addSearcher(new GvideoSearch());
      searchControl.addSearcher(new GblogSearch());
      // Set the Local Search center point
      localSearch.setCenterPoint("New York, NY");
      // Tell the searcher to draw itself and tell it where to attach
      searchControl.draw(document.getElementById("searchcontrol"));
      // Execute an inital search
      searchControl.execute("Google");
    }
    GSearch.setOnLoadCallback(OnLoad);
    //]]>
    </script>
  </head>
  <body>
    <div id="searchcontrol">Loading...</div>
  </body>
</html>
```

Copy the code and paste it inside a new file named test.html, for example. Now open the file in your browser. You should be able to see a page similar to the one shown in Figure 10.4.

Figure 10.4 Test AJAX Search Page

Let's take a look at what we have done so far. The generated HTML code reveals some of the basic characteristics of the API. First, the code loads the AJAX Search API default style sheet (CSS), followed by a JavaScript script reference:

```
<script
src="http://www.google.com/uds/api?file=uds.js&amp;v=1.0&amp;key=ABQIAAAsFym1Ew5o48
zXESOPhV4ExSFOvRczLyAyj57qAvViVrKq19E6hSZhJSVQBi2HRSzsW1XyZzxdffdfQ"
type="text/javascript"></script>
```

This script loads a couple of JavaScript wrapper classes, which are used as a more convenient way to access the API. As we are going to learn from the following sections, we don't really need them since we can access the API directly (i.e. raw accesses).

Next, another script block is defined, which initializes the environment and configures the AJAX Search control box. This is done within the *OnLoad* function which is called after Google finishes with loading all dependencies required to render the graphical environment:

```
function OnLoad() {
    // Create a search control
    var searchControl = new GSearchControl();
    // Add in a full set of searchers
```

```
    var localSearch = new GlocalSearch();
    searchControl.addSearcher(localSearch);
    searchControl.addSearcher(new GwebSearch());
    searchControl.addSearcher(new GvideoSearch());
    searchControl.addSearcher(new GblogSearch());
    // Set the Local Search center point
    localSearch.setCenterPoint("New York, NY");
    // Tell the searcher to draw itself and tell it where to attach
    searchControl.draw(document.getElementById("searchcontrol"));
    // Execute an inital search
    searchControl.execute("Google");
}
```

The second line in the *OnLoad* function initializes a Google Search control object. The search control object can reference as many search engines as we need. We can even define our own, but in this example we will set the default ones which are *GwebSearch*, *GvideoSearch*, *GblogSearch* and the *GlobalSearch* (i.e. Google Local Search). At the end of this block, the controller is rendered on the current page with the *draw* function, which takes as a parameter an element from the DOM tree which will hold the Search box.

This search box can be customized in many different ways. For example, we can change the colors, re-order the search section and even supply custom search engines which we will discuss later in this chapter.

For more basic information refer to the Google AJAX Search API documentation which can be found from the following URL http://code.google.com/apis/ajaxsearch.

Deeper into the AJAX Search

Now that we have seen how to embed the AJAX Search box, it is time to come up with something more interesting. As you probably noticed, the AJAX Search form is a good place to start with experimenting with the service but it does not provide the level of flexibility hackers usually work with. For that reason we need to dig deeper into the AJAX Search API and discover the more interesting characteristics of the service. For the next step we are going to make use of a HTTP request listener. We are going to use Firefox as our primary tool for development.

There are a couple of prerequisites. Most of all you'll need Firefox, which can be downloaded from www.mozilla.com/firefox. We'll also make use of a Firefox Extension known as "LiveHTTP Headers", which can be downloaded from https://addons.mozilla.org/en-US/firefox/addon/3829. After installing the extension, restart Firefox.

The LiveHTTPHeaders extension allows us to analyze and replay HTTP requests. In case you want to monitor traffic, you can simply open the extension window in your browser sidebar by selecting *View | Sidebar | LiveHTTPHeaders*. On the other hand, in case you need to use the request reply feature you may want to open it in a separate window, by selecting *Tools | LiveHTTPHeaders*, as shown in Figure 10.5.

Figure 10.5 LiveHttpHeaders Main Window

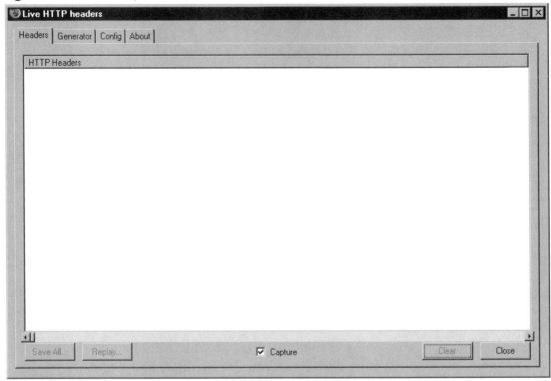

Traffic monitoring tools such as the LiveHTTPHeaders extension are essential to web application security testers. Theses tools reveal what is happing in the background and provide features for disassembling and reassembling the generated requests, easily exposing fundamental application vulnerabilities and insights of the tested application inner workings.

Once the environment is ready, we are able to start with hacking into the AJAX search logic. The plan is to set the LiveHTTP Headers extension to listen for all the traffic, while we are making subsequent queries to the service. Then we are going to look at the generated output and figure out what request needs to be made in order to mimic the AJAX form behavior. We are going to use that in the next section of this chapter where are going to talk about writing custom search engines for good or malicious purposes. But first, let's dig.

From within Firefox, enable the LiveHTTPHeaders extension and visit a page that contains an AJAX Search dialog, such as www.google.com/uds/samples/apidocs/helloworld.html. After submitting a query, LiveHTTPHeaders will reveal what happens behind the scenes. From within the results page, be sure to enable the *show all results* button located at the right of each section as shown on Figure 10.6. It is essential to do that for the

Web section so we get the complete query. Notice that many of the results point to .jpg, .gif or png images. There are quite a few going to the Ad Indicator service provided by Google, but the most interesting ones are those that point to GwebSearch service. Figure 10.7 shows what the live capture might look like.

Figure 10.6 Show all Results Button

Figure 10.7 LiveHTTP Headers Capture

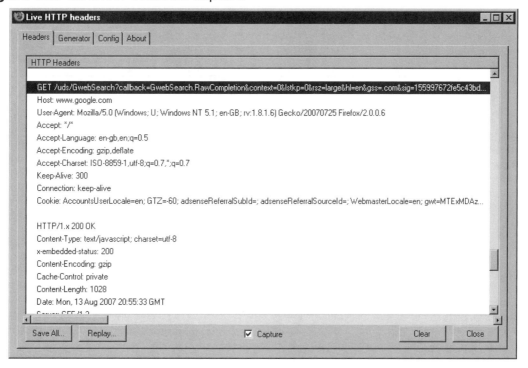

Figure 10.7 shows the format of the URL that is used to retrieve the queries. Here is an example:

```
http://www.google.com/uds/GwebSearch?callback=GwebSearch.RawCompletion&context=0&ls
tkp=0&rsz=large&hl=en&gss=.com&sig=51248261809d756101be2fa94e0ce277&q=VW%20Beetle&k
ey=internal&v=1.0
```

Table 10.1 lists each of the GET parameters and describes what they do.

Table 10.1 GET Parameters

parameter	value	description
callback	GwebSearch.RawCompletion	the callback JavaScript function the results
context	0	-
lstkp	0	-
rsz	large	the size of the query
hl	en	language preferences
gss	.com	-
sig	51248261809d756101be2fa94e0ce277	-
q	VW%20Beetle	the actual query/search
key	internal	the key (use the internal key)
v	1.0	version of the API

As an exercise, we can build a URL from these parameters, providing different values that we think are suitable for the task. For example:

```
www.google.com/uds/GwebSearch?callback=our_callback&context=0&rsz=large&q=GHDB&key=
internal&v=1.0
```

Notice that we have changed the callback parameter from "GwebSearch.Raw Completion" to "our_callback", and we are executing a search for *GHDB*. Executing this URL inside your browser will result in a JavaScript return call. This technique is also known as JavaScript on Demand or JavaScript remoting, and the results of this are shown below.

```
our_callback('0',{"results":[{"GsearchResultClass":"GwebSearch","unescapedUrl":"htt
p://johnny.ihackstuff.com/index.php?module\u003Dprodreviews","url":"http://johnny.i
hackstuff.com/index.php%3Fmodule%3Dprodreviews","visibleUrl":"johnny.ihackstuff.com
","cacheUrl":"http://www.google.com/search?q\u003Dcache:IS5G5YGJmHIJ:johnny.ihackst
uff.com","title":"johnny.ihackstuff.com -
Home","titleNoFormatting":"johnny.ihackstuff.com - Home","content":"Latest
Downloads. File Icon \u0026quot;No-Tech Hacking\u0026quot; Sample Chapter
\u0026middot; File Icon Yo Yo  SKillz #1 \u0026middot; File Icon Aggressive
Network Self-Defense Sample Chapter
\u003Cb\u003E...\u003C/b\u003E"},{"GsearchResultClass":"GwebSearch","unescapedUrl":
"http://johnny.ihackstuff.com/ghdb.php","url":"http://johnny.ihackstuff.com/ghdb.ph
p","visibleUrl":"johnny.ihackstuff.com","cacheUrl":"http://www.google.com/search?q\
u003Dcache:MxfbWg9ik-MJ:johnny.ihackstuff.com","title":"Google Hacking
```

Database","titleNoFormatting":"Google Hacking Database","content":"Welcome to the Google Hacking Database (\u003Cb\u003EGHDB\u003C/b\u003E)! We call them \u0026#39;googledorks\u0026#39;: Inept   or foolish people as revealed by Google. Whatever you call these fools, \u003Cb\u003E...\u003C/b\u003E"},{"GsearchResultClass":"GwebSearch","unescapedUrl": "http://ghh.sourceforge.net/","url":"http://ghh.sourceforge.net/","visibleUrl":"ghh .sourceforge.net","cacheUrl":"http://www.google.com/search?q\u003Dcache:WbkSIUl0UtM J:ghh.sourceforge.net","title":"GHH - The \u0026quot;Google Hack\u0026quot; Honeypot","titleNoFormatting":"GHH - The \u0026quot;Google Hack\u0026quot; Honeypot","content":"\u003Cb\u003EGHDB\u003C/b\u003E Signature #734 (\u0026quot;File Upload Manager v1.3\u0026quot; \u0026quot;rename to\u0026quot;) \u003Cb\u003E...\u003C/b\u003E \u003Cb\u003EGHDB\u003C/b\u003E Signatures   are maintained by the johnny.ihackstuff.com community. \u003Cb\u003E...\u003C/b\u003E"},{"GsearchResultClass":"GwebSearch","unescapedUrl": "http://thebillygoatcurse.com/11/","url":"http://thebillygoatcurse.com/11/","visibl eUrl":"thebillygoatcurse.com","cacheUrl":"http://www.google.com/search?q\u003Dcache :O30uZ81QVCcJ:thebillygoatcurse.com","title":"TheBillyGoatCurse.com \u00BB Blog Archive \u00BB Convert \u003Cb\u003EGHDB\u003C/b\u003E","titleNoFormatting":"TheBillyGoatCurse.com \u00BB Blog Archive \u00BB Convert GHDB","content":"The Google Hacking Database (\u003Cb\u003EGHDB\u003C/b\u003E) has one problem\u2026 it only uses the Google search   index. The trouble is that advanced search syntax can differ between \u003Cb\u003E...\u003C/b\u003E"},{"GsearchResultClass":"GwebSearch","unescapedUrl": "http://www.ethicalhacker.net/index.php?option\u003Dcom_smf\u0026Itemid\u003D35\u00 26topic\u003D184.msg328;topicseen","url":"http://www.ethicalhacker.net/index.php%3F option%3Dcom_smf%26Itemid%3D35%26topic%3D184.msg328%3Btopicseen","visibleUrl":"www. ethicalhacker.net","cacheUrl":"http://www.google.com/search?q\u003Dcache:EsO7aMyCR6 wJ:www.ethicalhacker.net","title":"The Ethical Hacker Network - Google Hacking Database (\u003Cb\u003EGHDB\u003C/b\u003E)","titleNoFormatting":"The Ethical Hacker Network - Google Hacking Database (GHDB)","content":"The Ethical Hacker Network - Your educational authority on penetration testing   and incident response., Google Hacking Database (\u003Cb\u003EGHDB\u003C/b\u003E)"},{"GsearchResultClass":"GwebSearch","unescapedUr l":"http://snakeoillabs.com/downloads/GHDB.xml","url":"http://snakeoillabs.com/down loads/GHDB.xml","visibleUrl":"snakeoillabs.com","cacheUrl":"http://www.google.com/s earch?q\u003Dcache:5nsf_DfjX4YJ:snakeoillabs.com","title":"\u003Cb\u003Eghdb\u003C/ b\u003E xml","titleNoFormatting":"ghdb xml","content":"PS: this vulnerability was found early this year (search google for the full   report), but was never added to the \u003Cb\u003EGHDB\u003C/b\u003E for some reason. \u003Cb\u003E...\u003C/b\u003E"},{"GsearchResultClass":"GwebSearch","unescapedUrl": "http://www.gnucitizen.org/projects/ghdb","url":"http://www.gnucitizen.org/projects /ghdb","visibleUrl":"www.gnucitizen.org","cacheUrl":"http://www.google.com/search?q \u003Dcache:dPVtU_3tmnMJ:www.gnucitizen.org","title":"\u003Cb\u003EGHDB\u003C/b\u00 3E | GNUCITIZEN","titleNoFormatting":"GHDB | GNUCITIZEN","content":"\u003Cb\u003EGHDB\u003C/b\u003E (aka Google Hacking Database) is HTML/JavaScript wrapper application that   uses advance JavaScript techniques to scrape information from Johnny\u0026#39;s Google \u003Cb\u003E...\u003C/b\u003E"},{"GsearchResultClass":"GwebSearch","unescapedUrl": "http://www.ghdb.org/","url":"http://www.ghdb.org/","visibleUrl":"www.ghdb.org","ca cheUrl":"http://www.google.com/search?q\u003Dcache:Y6lwVyfCQw8J:www.ghdb.org","titl e":"Menu","titleNoFormatting":"Menu","content":"\u003Cb\u003E...\u003C/b\u003E to contact us for any reason, or maybe just leave a comment (good, bad or   ugly, but not offensive) in our guestbook. Best regards The team at \u0026#39;\u003Cb\u003EGHDB\u003C/b\u003E\u0026#39; \u003Cb\u003E...\u003C/b\u003E"}],"adResults":[]}, 200, null, 200)

Hacking into the AJAX Search Engine

Now that we know how to query Google through their AJAX interface, let's see how we can access the data. We will begin with the following HTML, which can be pasted into a blank *html* file and opened with a browser:

```html
<html>
    <head>
        <title>Hacking AJAX API</title>
    </head>
    <body>
        <script>
            function our_callback(a, b, c, d, e) {
                for (var i = 0; i < b.results.length; i++) {
                    var link = document.createElement('a');
                    link.href = b.results[i].url;
                    link.innerHTML = b.results[i].url;

                    document.body.appendChild(link);

                    var br = document.createElement('br');

                    document.body.appendChild(br);
                }
            }
        </script>
        <script type="text/javascript"
src="http://www.google.com/uds/GwebSearch?callback=our_callback&context=0&rsz=large
&q=GHDB&key=internal&v=1.0"></script>
    </body>
</html>
```

This code will make submit a request for *GHDB* to Google's GwebSearch service. Notice that the callback parameter points back to *our_callback*, which is defined early in the code. The function simply grabs that data and presents it inside the page DOM (Document Object Model) in the form of links.

Although this looks interesting, there is a lot more that we can do. Let's have a look at the following example which dynamically grabs all entries from a particular category from the Google Hacking Database, performs test queries and lists the results within a single page:

```
<html>
    <head>
        <title>GHDB Lister</title>
    </head>
    <body>
        <script>
            function get_json(url, callback) {
                var name = '__json_' + (new Date).getTime();

                var s = document.createElement('script');
                s.src = url.replace('{callback}', name);

                window[name] = callback;

                document.body.appendChild(s);
            }


get_json('http://www.dapper.net/transform.php?dappName=GoogleHackingDatabaseReader&
transformer=JSON&extraArg_callbackFunctionWrapper={callback}&applyToUrl=http%3A//jo
hnny.ihackstuff.com/ghdb.php%3Ffunction%3Dsummary%26cat%3D19',
                function (data) {
                    console.log(data);
                    for (var i = 0; i < data.groups.entry.length; i++) {
                        var query = data.groups.entry[i].query[0].value;
                        var description =
data.groups.entry[i].description[0].value;


get_json('http://www.google.com/uds/GwebSearch?callback={callback}&context=0&rsz=la
rge&q=' + escape(query) + '&key=internal&v=1.0',
                            function (a, b, c, d, e) {
                                if (!b) {
                                    return;
                                }


                                  for (var i = 0; i < b.results.length; i++)
{
```

```
                                    var link = document.createElement('a');

                                    link.href = b.results[i].url;

                                    link.innerHTML = b.results[i].url;


                                    document.body.appendChild(link);


                                    var br = document.createElement('br');


                                    document.body.appendChild(br);
                                }
                            });
                        }
                    });
            </script>
        </body>
</html>
```

After running the example, you will be provided with a page similar to the one shown on Figure 10.8.

Figure 10.8 Result Page

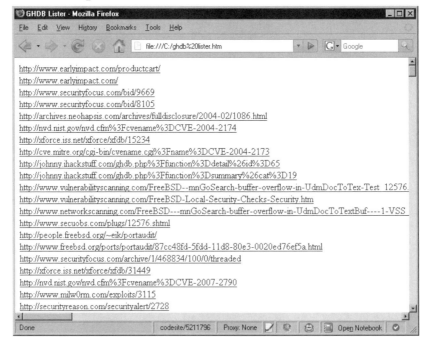

Let's examine the file. As you can see the page has only one script block. This block is responsible for obtaining a list of queries from the GHDB via the Dapper (http://dapper.net) screen scraping service. We scrape the URL http://johnny.ihackstuff.com/ghdb.php?function=summary&cat=19 which corresponds to GHDB entry 19 also known as "Advisories and Vulnerabilities". The scraper obtains several other interesting things that we are not interested for now.

Notes from the Underground…

Screen Scraping with Dapper

Using Dapper to screen scrape various security related databases and using the information as part of a well planned client-side oriented attack vector was discussed for the first time in OWASP, Italy 2007 by the author, Petko D. Petkov, also known as pdp (architect). For more information on the topic you can visit http://www.gnucitizen.org and http://www.gnucitizen.org/projects/6th-owasp-conference.

Once the list is retrieved, we enumerate each entry and build the custom Google AJAX API queries:

```
get_json('http://www.google.com/uds/GwebSearch?callback={callback}&context=0
&rsz=large&q=' + escape(query) + '&key=internal&v=1.0',
```

As you can see, instead of a static string, we actually supply a query that is taken from the information obtained from GHDB. The subsequent request to Google AJAX Search API will retrieve the sample results and the callback functions will render them inside the page DOM.

It is important to understand the purpose of the function get_json. This function is just a helper that saves us a lot of time writing the same procedures over and over again. The get_json function simply generates a unique name for the callback parameter and assigns it at the global scope. Then, it supplies the name to the callback field marked with the placeholder {callback} and calls the external script.

This technique was successfully implemented as part of the GHDB Proof of Concept application hosted at http://www.gnucitizen.org/ghdb (Figure 10.9).

Figure 10.9 GNUCITIZEN GHDB

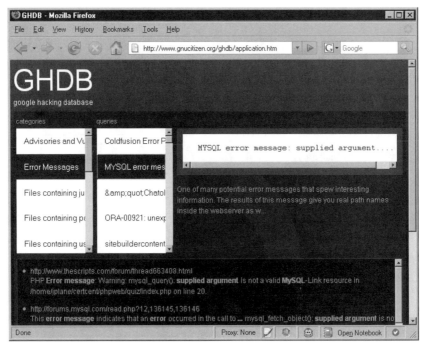

The application scrapes all the information from Johnny Long's Google Hacking Database at http://johnny.ihackstuff.com, dynamically and presents it to the user in a nice graphical form. You can browse through each vector by selecting a category and then selecting the query that you are interested in. Notice that the application provides a live feedback every time we select a query. The bottom part of the window contains the top searches, obtained by Google's AJAX Search API interface.

Notes from the Underground...

XSS and AJAX Worms

This technique can be implemented by XSS/AJAX worms to locate targets and exploit them, thus ensuring future generations. XSS/AJAX worms usually propagate within the domain of origin. This is due to inability of JavaScript to perform cross-site requests. The technique presented in this chapter allows worms to bypass the JavaScript restrictions and access other resources on-line. For more information on the subject please check the following resources: http://www.gnucitizen.org/blog/google-search-api-worms, http://www.gnucitizen.org/projects/ghdb and http://www.gnucitizen.org/blog/the-web-has-betrayed-us.

Calendar

Google Calendar is powerful calendar management application which supports features like calendar sharing, creation of invitations, search and calendar publishing. The service is also integrated with Google Mail (GMail) and can be accessed via a Mobile device. All in all, Google Calendar is very useful addition to our day-to-day work.

Calendar sharing in particular is a very useful feature since individual users can maintain event lists and calendars to which others may be interested in as well. Usually in order to share a calendar you have to explicitly do so from the calendar management interface as shown in Figure 10.10.

Figure 10.10 Calendar Management Interface

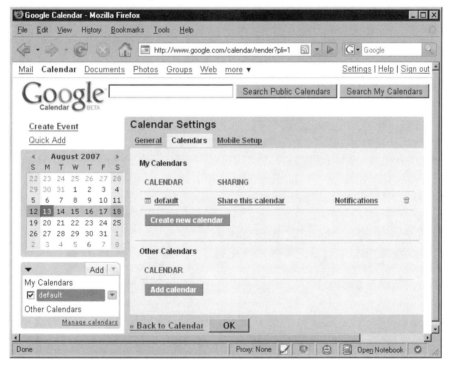

Once the calendar is shared, everyone will be able to look at it or even subscribe to the events that are inside. This can be done via the Calendar application or any RSS feed reader.

As a security expert, these shared calendars are especially interesting. Very often, even when performing the most basic searches, it is entirely possible to stumble across sensitive information that can be used for malicious purposes. For example, logging into Calendar and searching for the term "password" returns many results as shown in Figure 10.11.

Figure 10.11 Calendar Search for "password"

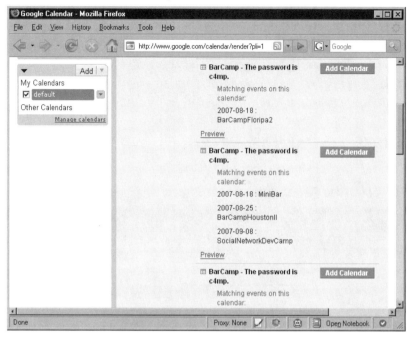

As you can see, there are several calendar entries that meet our search criteria. Among them, there are a few that are quite interesting and worth our attention. Another interesting query that brings a lot of juicy information is "passcode", as shown in Figure 10.12.

Figure 10.12 Calendar Search for "passcode"

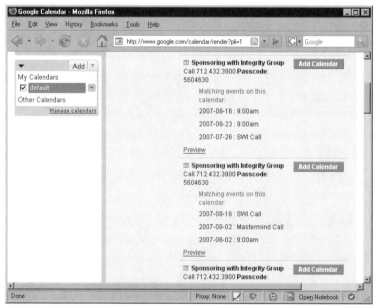

Figure 10.12 reveals several scheduled telephone conferences. Notice that the conference phone number and access code are also listed. An attacker could easily join the telephone conference at the scheduled time and silently eavesdrop on the conference. Mission accomplished. There is a lot attackers can learn from the conversation, like corporate secrets, technical details about systems in operations, etc.

Of course we can try variations of the above quires and even space them up with more keywords so we can get a better picture. For example the query *"username password"* returns results about people who may stored sensitive login information within their calendar, as shown in Figure 10.13.

Figure 10.13 Calendar Search for "username password"

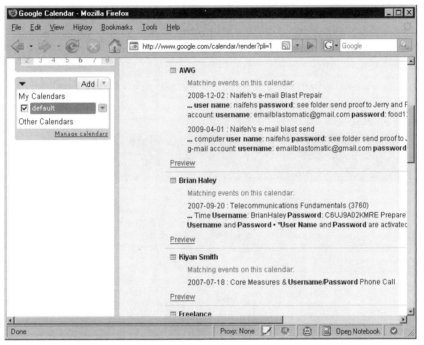

This is just the beginning though, how about looking for birthdays, pet's names, etc. As you probably know, a lot of password reminder facilities have a secret question. The secrets answer is usually something that we choose from our daily life so there is no chance that we can forget. However, the Calendar application may also contain our daily activities. When we mash both, we might be able to crack into the targeted user account by simply reading their calendar.

There are many different ways; the Calendar service can be abused. The main and most important security consideration that we, as users, need to make is whether the information that is enclosed within the Google's shiny event cells is sensitive and can be used to harm us.

Blogger and Google's Blog Search

Blogger is Google's blogging software hosted at blogger.com and blogspot.com. Blogger is one of the most widely used blogging platforms. It allows almost instant creations of multiple blogs and has some great features for collaborating with others and preventing comment and trackback spam.

When speaking about blogs, there are a several points that we need to take into consideration. The first and most important one is that blogs are public and are meant to be read by the Internet community. Saying that, it is important that you do not publish information about yourself which later may have serious consequences on your life. What is born on the Web stays on the web. Blog feeds are aggregated by numerous online services. It is almost impossible to remove what you once have said. The information on your blog will most probably be used by your future employer as part of the standard background checks (See Figure 10.14), when applying for a job. We have already proved that a few simple queries can reveal a lot of interesting information. Google simplifies to a great extent the process of looking into interesting information in blogs. Meat Google's Blog Search (see Figure 10.14).

Figure 10.14 Google Blog Search

Despite the fact that Google's Blogger service effectively blocks content and trackback SPAM, there's one loophole: what happens when SPAM originates from blogs posts themselves?

Enter the SPLOG. Splogs, or Spam Blogs, are normal blogs that reflect content consumed/aggregated from external entities but also provide additional information to accommodate their owner's purpose.

There are a number of reasons why splogs are interesting to malicious minds. The first reason is that attackers do not have to write the blog, a task that is very time consuming, and yet make people subscribe or attend their content. As a splog's search engine ranking increases, it attracts more visitors. If an attacker stands up an exploit on the splog's page targeted at popular web browsers he may be able to take over hundreds of machines in mere moments.

In addition, splogs may contain ads which can generate income for the owner. The more popular the splog is, the more money it will make. If a single splog can make $20 a day, multiple splogs can make much more. Splogging is a 24/7 business that earns big money.

No matter whether malicious minds will use splogging techniques to attract victims or make money, it is interesting to see what's behind the scenes. In the following section we are going to take a detailed look at how splogging works. We will examine a splog generation script which makes use of Google's Blogger service.

Google Splogger

Google has excellent application programming interfaces (APIs). One of the most famous Google Services is known as GData, from Google Data. GData allows developers to perform programmatic operations on Google's services. For example, GData can be used to programmatically update Google Calendar instances. GData can also be used to create, delete and manage Blogger entries and also manage our submissions to Google Base. The stage then seems to be set for Google's blogging service to be used as a base for splogging. In this section we'll show how this could be accomplished, but please note that we're not in the business of educating criminals. If you intend to use this information for malicious purposes, be advised that Google has every right to block your access to their service. They may even have the right to pursue legal action if you persist in performing malicious actions using their services.

In the following example we are going to make use of GData's Blogger interface. The following script allows us to programmatically login into Blogger and submit a new post. Effectively we can use a similar approach to automatically harvest RSS feeds and then upload them to a particular Blogger account which could then be used for splogging purposes.

```
#    GoogleSplogger
#    Copyright (C) 2007  Petko D. Petkov (GNUCITIZEN)
#
#    This program is free software; you can redistribute it and/or modify
#    it under the terms of the GNU General Public License as published by
#    the Free Software Foundation; either version 2 of the License, or
```

```
#     (at your option) any later version.
#
#     This program is distributed in the hope that it will be useful,
#     but WITHOUT ANY WARRANTY; without even the implied warranty of
#     MERCHANTABILITY or FITNESS FOR A PARTICULAR PURPOSE.  See the
#     GNU General Public License for more details.
#
#     You should have received a copy of the GNU General Public License
#     along with this program; if not, write to the Free Software
#     Foundation, Inc., 51 Franklin St, Fifth Floor, Boston, MA  02110-1301  USA

__version__ = '1.0'
__author__ = 'Petko D. Petkov; pdp (architect)'


__doc__ = """
GoogleSplogger (GNUCITIZEN) http://www.gnucitizen.org
by Petko D. Petkov; pdp (arhictect)
"""


import atom
import gdata.service


class GoogleSplogger:
    """

    GoogleSplogger

    The power of Blogger in a single object
    """
    def __init__(self, email, password):
        self.client = gdata.service.GDataService(email, password)
        self.client.source = 'Splogger ' + __version__
        self.client.service = 'blogger'
        self.client.server = 'www.blogger.com'

        self.client.ProgrammaticLogin()

        self.available_blogs = self.get_blogs()

    def get_blogs(self):
        """
```

```
        get_blogs -> Dict

        Get a dictionary of available blogs.
        """
        blogs = {}

        feed = self.client.Get('/feeds/default/blogs')

        for i in feed.entry:
            title = i.title.text
            for a in i.link:
                if a.rel == 'self':
                    blogs[title] = a.href.split('/')[-1]

        return blogs

    def post(self, blog_name, title, content, author_name):
        """
        post(blog_name, title, content, author_name) -> ?

        Post a new entry to blog
        """
        if blog_name not in self.available_blogs:
            raise 'blog name not found'

        entry = gdata.GDataEntry()
        entry.author.append(atom.Author(atom.Name(text=author_name)))
        entry.title = atom.Title('xhtml', title)
        entry.content = atom.Content('html', '', content)

        return self.client.Post(entry, '/feeds/' \
            + self.available_blogs[blog_name] + '/posts/default')

def usage(prog):
    print 'usage: ' + prog + ' -u username -p [password] -P blog ' \
        '-t title -c [content] -a author'
    print '       ' + prog + ' -u username -p [password] -l'
    print '-u username     username for the login'
    print '-p [password]   password for the login'
    print '-P blog         post to blog'
```

```
    print '-t title        title for the new post'
    print '-c [content]    content for the new post'
    print '-a author       author for the new post'
    print '-l              list available blogs'
    print '-h              print this page'


if __name__ == '__main__':
    import sys
    import getopt
    import getpass

    try:
        opts, args = getopt.gnu_getopt(sys.argv[1:], 'hlcpu:p:P:t:c:a:')

    except Exception, e:
        print e
        print

        usage(sys.argv[0])
        sys.exit()

    username = None
    password = None
    action = None

    post_blog = None
    post_title = None
    post_author = None
    post_content = None

    for key, val in opts:
        if key == '-h':
            usage(sys.argv[0]);
            sys.exit();

        elif key == '-l':
            action = 'list'

        elif key == '-P':
            action = 'post'
```

```
                post_blog = val

        elif key == '-u':
            username = val

        elif key == '-p':
            password = val

        elif key == '-t':
            post_title = val

        elif key == '-a':
            post_author = val

        elif key == '-c':
            post_content = val

if not action or not username:
    usage(sys.argv[0])
    sys.exit()

if action == 'post' and \
    (not post_blog or not post_title or not post_author):
    usage(sys.argv[0])
    sys.exit()

if not password:
    password = getpass.getpass('password: ')

try:
    gs = GoogleSplogger(username, password)

except Exception, e:
    print e
    sys.exit()

if action == 'post' and post_blog not in gs.available_blogs:
    print 'blog not found within the user profile'
    sys.exit()
```

```
if action == 'post' and not post_content:
    post_content = sys.stdin.read()


if action == 'list':
    for i in gs.available_blogs:
        print i


elif action == 'post':
    gs.post(post_blog, post_title, post_content, post_author)
```

NOTE

GoogleSplogger.py requires the presence of Google's GData API library for Python. The library can be obtained from the following URL: http://code.google.com/p/gdata-python-client/. Once the library is downloaded, extract the content of the archive and enter into that folder via the command line. Make sure that you have the permissions required to install Python module and type: **python setup.py**.

The setup.py script should install the rest of the API without any problems.

There are several ways you can run the script that we've listed here. For example, in order to list the names of the blogs that are currently registered under our profile, type the following command:

```
python GoogleSplogger.py -l -u username -p password
```

Keep in mind that if you do not provide the value for the -p (password) flag, you will be asked to enter it at run time. This method is preferred since you may not want to leave traces of your password in the system and command log files. Sample output from the command is shown on Figure 10.15.

Figure 10.15 Enumerating Current Blogs

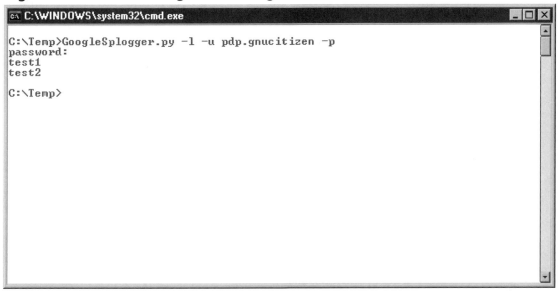

Once we have the blog names, we can post to them. For example:

```
python GoogleSplogger.py -u username -p -P blog_name_here -t title_for_the_post -a
author -c
```

After executing the command you will be asked to enter your password, followed by the post content. When you are done entering the post, simply terminate the input by pressing CTRL+Z within Windows or CTRL+D from within Unix. See Figure 10.16.

Figure 10.16 Command line Posting to Blogger

```
C:\WINDOWS\system32\cmd.exe                                    _ □ ×

C:\Temp>GoogleSplogger.py -l -u pdp.gnucitizen -p
password:
test1
test2

C:\Temp>GoogleSplogger.py -u pdp.gnucitizen -p -P test1 -t TestMe -a pdp -c
password:
This is the content of my post!
^Z

C:\Temp>
```

Figure 10.17 Result

This is simple enough, but the process can be streamlined further. Here's another way to post a new blog entry, this time with the password inline:

```
python GoogleSplogger.py -u username -p password -P blog_name_here -t
title_for_the_post -a author -c << EOF
```

Once you are done writing the post type **EOF** on a new line. A post can also be submitted from a file:

```
python GoogleSplogger.py -u username -p password -P blog_name_here -t
title_for_the_post -a author -c < file.txt
```

Programmatically inserting new posts into Blogger is not that useful. But the following example shows how easy it is to grab someone else's blog data and inject it into our blog. For that purpose, we are going to need another python utility which is based on a library called *FeedParser* from http://cheeseshop.python.org/pypi/FeedParser/4.1. The installation procedure for this package is the one used for all python packages.

Start python from the command line and make sure that the GoogleSplogger.py script is within your current working directory. Type the following commands:

```
import feedparser
import GoogleSplogger
```

```
gs = GoogleSplogger.GoogleSplogger('username', 'password')
feed = feedparser.parse('http://www.gnucitizen.org/feed') # we are going to import
this feed into our blog


for e in feed.entries:
    gs.post('my blog name', e.title, e.content[0].value, 'author')
```

Figure 10.18 - Import Blog Entries

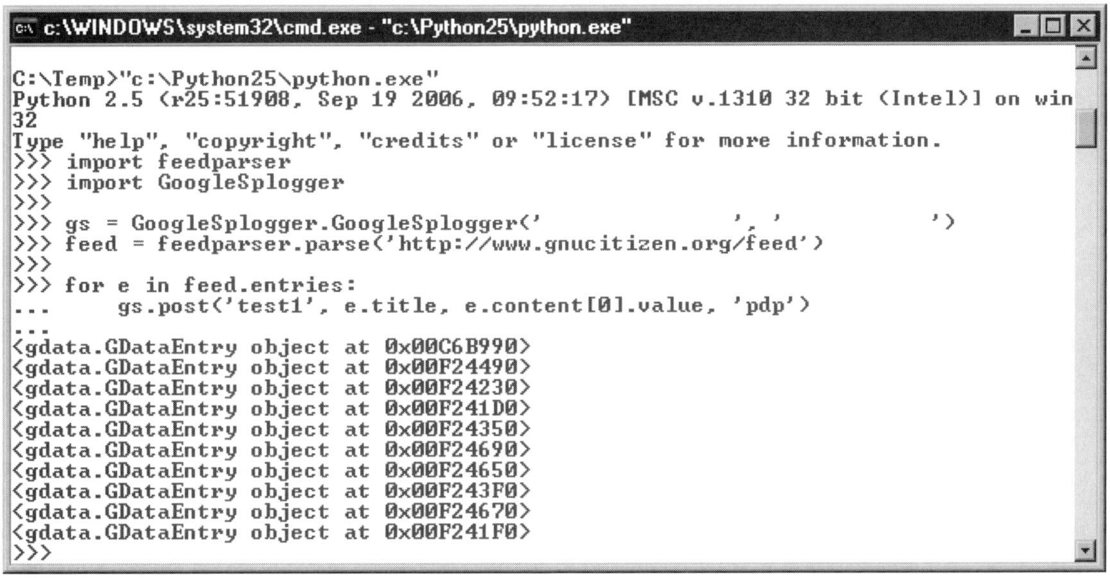

This script, entered as shown in Figure 10.18, will import all feed entries from GNUCITIZEN's blog into your blog, effectively creating a spam blog as shown in Figure 10.19.

Figure 10.19 The new Splog

Notice how quickly we created a new blog with content.

There are completely different set of strategies that can be undertaken to make the splog achieve its purposes however due to the size of this topic we can't really cover all of them in this book. It is important to understand the security and ethical implications that are related to splogging. Again, remember that spamming Google or any other service is totally prohibited by the terms of service. You can potentially damage your account and all data that it holds.

Signaling Alerts

Very often we need to track changes in Google's result set. For example, let's say that we want to monitor a certain site for vulnerabilities. How can we do that? We can simply run scanners every once in a while but this is a noisy exercise and will definitely take loads of time. Instead, being dedicated Google hackers, we can use Google itself and use a few powerful Google dorks to locate the things that we are interested in without the need for automated scanning software. Then we can setup a *cron* task to monitor the results returned by Google and when a change is detected email us the result.

Then again, we could simply use Google Alerts as shown in see Figure 10.20.

Figure 10.20 Google Alerts

Google Alerts is a powerful system that detects when a query's result set changes. The system can be modified to send updates once a day, once a week, or as they happen. Keep in mind that only the first 10 entries (the first page) are taken into consideration. Nevertheless, the Alert system does a good job when optimized.

This is a great tool, but it can be used for more interesting purposes. Let's say that we know that a target is using MsSQL as database backend. We could use Google alerts to poll the target, searching for error messages as they pop up. That search might look something like this:

```
"[SQL Server Driver][SQL Server]Line 1: Incorrect syntax near" -forum -thread -
showthread site:example.com
```

For the type of alert select **Web**, usually default option. Select the frequency of the alert, and your email address and click **Create Alert**.

Notice that the query that we use for this alert is domain restricted
(site:example.com). Also pay attention to the actual Google dork. Obviously we look for messages that look like being generated failures in the SQL queries sent to backend. These types of messages are sign for SQL Injection vulnerable resources.

A malicious user can use this service to alert whenever a vulnerability or interesting message appears on a target site. This is very low-profile, and does not alert the target; the transaction happens between the user and Google. An attacker could even enter alerts for every entry in the Google Hacking Database. Although this would be overkill, some of the entries in the database reveal extremely sensitive information, which could be harvested with very little further effort.

Google Co-op

Google Co-op (www.google.com/coop) is a powerful service that allows you to create powerful custom search engines. You do not need to be registered Google user in order to *use* the service but if you want to create an engine, it is required. In the following section, we'll guide you through some of the most interesting features of this service and we'll show you how to create your own search engines.

Let's start with the simplest of search engines. Browse the Google Go-op page and click **Create a Custom Search Engine**, or simply browse to www.google.com/coop/cse. From the Custom Engine configuration page (Figure 10.21), we need define the characteristics we need.

Figure 10.21 Google Custom Search Engine Creation page

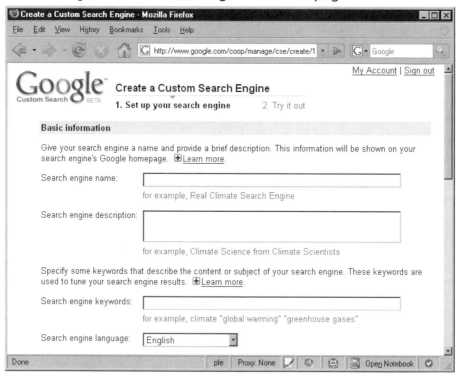

First enter a search engine name. We'll call ours the "Google Hacking Database Search". Enter a description and some basic search keywords, both of which are optional. The key-words are primary used by Google to find the most relevant results. This means that our query will be mingled with these keywords. For now, we'll leave this alone. Moving forward, to the field titled *What do you want to search*, we will define the scope of the search queries. For this example, we are going to use the default option entitled *Only sites that I select*.

Now, the interesting part- we need to supply the URLs Google will look into when performing the queries. Since our search engine will do stuff around the Google Hacking Database located at http://johnny.ihackstuff.com/ghdb.php, we'll simply drop that URL into this field. We'll customize this entry option further with the use of wildcards, in order to search URLs that match a specific syntax. Here are a few examples taken from Cop-op's documentation:

```
www.mysite.com/mypage.html - look for information within mypage.html part of the
www.mysite.com domain
www.mysite.com/* - look for information within the entire context of www.mysite.com
www.mysite.com/*about* - look for information within URLs from www.mysite.com that
has the about keyword
*.mydomain.com - look for information within sub-domains of mysite.com.
```

For our example, the main page is located at http://johnny.ihackstuff.com/ghdb.php, but in order to make Co-op go a couple of levels down from that location, we must change the site URL to http://johnny.ihackstuff.com/ghdb.php* (note the star at the end). This is because the URL for an individual database entry contains parameters tacked onto the data after the name of the *ghdb.php* script the following format:

```
http://johnny.ihackstuff.com/ghdb.php?function=detail&id=64
```

The rest of the options from the Go-op Custom engine creation page are irrelevant at this point. Agree to Google's terms of service and click on the next button. You must see something similar to Figure 10.22.

Figure 10.22 2nd Stage of Google's Custom Engine Creation Process

No we'll test how the search engine works. Type a few queries like "index" or "secret", and you'll see some sample results. If everything works as expected, click *finish*, and the custom search engine will be displayed as shown in Figure 10.234.

Figure 10.23 GHDB Custom Search Engine

The purpose of our search engine is find interesting queries within Johnny Long's excellent Google dorks collection which does not (at the time of this writing) support searching. For example, a query for *passwd* will return results similar to those in Figure 10.24.

Figure 10.24 Search Results

It's simple to create other customized search engines as well. For example, we could search Phenoelit's database of default passwords found at www.phenoelit-us.org/dpl/dpl.html. It normally takes ages to load the file and most browsers cannot handle its enormous size. Let's create a custom search engine to search this excellent page.

Following the same process as before, we will use a site restriction of www.phenoelit-us.org/dpl/dpl.htmlinstead of http://johnny.ihackstuff.com/ghdb.php*. Bake the engine and give it a try. Figure 10.25 shows the result of query for cisco.

Figure 10.25 Default Password List Search Engine

Notice that the resulting page contains all the details that we need, including the default username and password. We can improve this engine by adding more default password lists.

Notes from the Underground…

Google's Custom Search Engine

The GNUCITIZEN group http://www.gnucitizen.org has discovered that Google's Custom Search Engine platform can be used for many other useful things such as fingerprinting and enumerating hidden web servers. It is well known fact that not all Web resources are exposed to the Internet. We call that part of the network the Hidden Web. By using Custom Search Engines we can recover them and enumerate their content. Among the gathered information, we may find Intranet interfaces, Administrative panels and other types of sensitive information.

Google AJAX Search API Integration

Earlier in this chapter we discussed how to use the AJAX API to embed search engine facilities in your own applications and even do automated queries. Here we will do the same but this time we are going to use the Google Hacking Database custom search engine that we have created.

The first most important thing is to locate the unique identifier of your search engine. Just access the engine page and have a look at the URL bar. It should be similar to the following:

```
http://www.google.com/coop/cse?cx=016629205230705557969%3Assouol31jqq
```

The **cx** parameter is the unique identifier for that engine. Remember that value and substitute it for the placeholder in the following example:

```html
<html>
    <head>
        <title>Hacking AJAX API</title>
    </head>
    <body>
        <script>
            function our_callback(a, b, c, d, e) {
                for (var i = 0; i < b.results.length; i++) {
                    var link = document.createElement('a');
                    link.href = b.results[i].url;
                    link.innerHTML = b.results[i].url;

                    document.body.appendChild(link);

                    var br = document.createElement('br');

                    document.body.appendChild(br);
                }
            }
        </script>
        <script type="text/javascript"
src="http://www.google.com/uds/GwebSearch?callback=our_callback&context=0&rsz=large
&q=test&key=internal&v=1.0&cx=016629205230705557969%3Assouol31jqq"></script>
    </body>
</html>
```

There are tones of interesting and quite valuable things that can be accomplished with the AJAX Search API and Google Co-op. It is just a matter of imagination, something that hackers and computer security experts has quite a lot.

Google Code

Google Code is an offering to the open source community allowing for free-for-all project hosting. Feature-wise, the service is very much like the well the known Sourceforge. Developers are provided with a Wiki for hosting the project documentation, Bug tracking system and version control through SVN. At the time of this writing, each user is restricted by the number of projects they can spawn. However, this logical restriction can be easily bypassed.

Google Code is more then just a development environment – it is a free hosting provider. We can use the system to stash all sorts of stuff in there.

In order to open a Google Code project, you'll first need a Google account. Simply visit http://code.google.com/hosting/createProject, fill in the necessary details and you are ready to upload your content as shown in Figure 10.26.

Figure 10.26 Google Code Project Registration

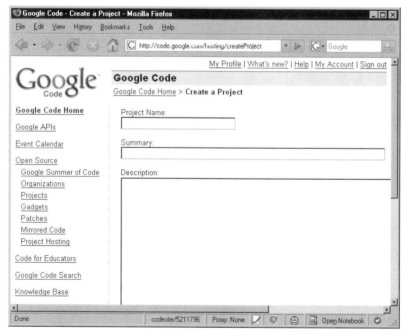

As we mentioned earlier, Google Code operates on the top of SVN (Subversion). In order to upload content, you will need the *svn* client which comes bundled with most Linux/Unix distributions. Windows users can obtain the *svn* client from http://tortoisesvn.net/downloads or by installing *Cygwin* (www.cygwin.com) and selecting the *svn* package. For the rest of this section, we are going to operate from the console via the command line *svn* util.

Brief Introduction to SVN

Before we continue, let's take a brief look at the subversion version management system.

Once you are ready to release your project, log into Google Code and click on the Source tab. You will be taken to your project source page. This page displays instructions on how to checkout your project folder as shown in Figure 10.27.

Figure 10.27 Google Code Source Page

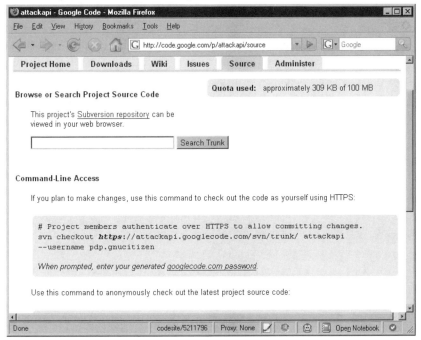

The following *svn* command will checkout a project:

```
svn checkout https://projectname.googlecode.com/svn/trunk/ projectname --username
username
```

Substitute *projectname* and *username* placeholders with your project name and your Google username. You will be prompted for your Google Code password (which is different than your Google account password). Your Google Code password can be found at http://code.google.com/hosting/settings.

This svn command will create a new folder within your current working directory with the name of your project. To add files, change to the project directory and create a file. Get back to command line mode and add the file in the repository like this:

```
svn add filename
```

Once you are happy with all changes and new file additions, you need to commit the project. This is achieved via the following line:

```
svn ci -m 'description of the commit'
```

Supply a different message (-m) for the commit message - something that is more descriptive and outlines the changes that you've made.

Getting the files online

Once your project is committed into the source repository, you can access its content online. Your project is available at http://**projectname**.googlecode.com/svn/trunk. Keep in mind that the committed files are served as Content-type text/plain or Content-Type application/octet-stream (see Figure 10.28) which prevents them from being rendered within the browser. This means that in theory you should not be able to see/preview uploaded image or html files.

Figure 10.28 Live HTTP Headers for output for Google's Subversion

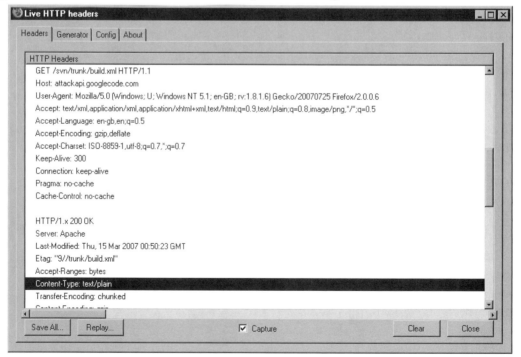

Despite this, an attacker could still host malicious scripts which could exploit vulnerable browsers, allowing them system control of a visitor's browser. This is where we start to see the true potentials of the Google Code development platform. There is nothing that prevents attackers from hosting their malicious files online and using them to attack their victims. This type of scenario is quite concerning since ISPs (Internet Service Providers) cannot simply block Google in order to stop a malware propagation, for example. Many users will stay unhappy.

Those familiar with IDS (Intrusion Detection Systems) and IPS (Intrusion Prevention Systems) may object that malware can be also detected by using signatures as the ones found in popular firewall products and open source projects such as Snort. Although, this is true, an attack may stay undetected for most its time, due to Google Code's encryption options. As we all know, encrypted traffic ensures privacy. Google provides SSL connection for hosted projects. Here is an example:

https://**projectname**.googlecode.com/svn/trunk/**path/to/file**

By substituting *https* for *http* within the URL, we engage the https protocol which encrypts our session, hiding the data in that session from the gaze of IDS and IPS systems. Because the *https* interface was meant to be used by developers, Google will prompt for authentication as shown in Figure 10.29.

Figure 10.29 Google Code Basic Authentication dialog

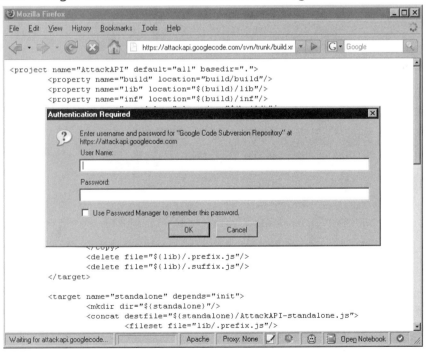

This is not the best scenario for an attacker wanting to host browser exploitation code, but a bit of HTTP trickery will help resolve that. The following URL will pre-supply the credentials:

https://**username:password@projectname**.googlecode.com/svn/trunk/**path/to/file**

Once the attack is discovered, anyone can use the supplied credentials to enter the subversion repository and revert the files back to a non-malicious state. However, given the fact that most of today's AJAX/XSS worms spread across millions of users within a couple of hours, the proposed setup is a compromise that most attackers will be willing to make.

> **NOTE**
>
> Keep in mind that all files stored within the source code repository will be in the public domain. Do not store any files that may contain sensitive information.

Searching the Code

So far in this book, we've learned a few good tricks how to recover interesting information from Google's vast indexes. We've also seen that the search facility is quite fuzzy and we often need to refine our queries in order to get better results. Wouldn't it be nice to be able to use regular expressions to find those pieces of information that are most interesting to us? Although Google Search cannot provide us with that, Google Code can. Enter Google's Code Search service http://www.google.com/codesearch (Figure 10.30).

Figure 10.30 Google Code Search

Code search is extremely useful in situations where we want to look for code snippets to borrow or just enumerate common vulnerabilities. Let's see how.

Open the Google Code Search interface and type of the following query:

```
echo\s*.*?PHP_SELF lang:php
```

Notice that the syntax is a bit different from what we usually see. This is known as a regular expression (regex) which you can learn more about from the following URL: http://en.wikipedia.org/wiki/Regular_expression. This regex search returns results similar to those found in Figure 10.31.

Figure 10.31 Searching for PHP_SELF vulnerabilities

Let's take a closer look at what the regex does. The first part of the query looks for the keyword echo. Then we specify that there may or may not be a couple of spaces (\s*). The part that follows specify that we are looking for an undefined number of characters until we reach the final delimiter (.*?). At the end we finish with the keyword PHP_SELF. Notice the special parameter lang. We specify that we are looking for PHP scripts only. In general, the query looks for something that may look like the following:

```
echo $PHP_SELF
echo($PHP_SELF)
echo ($PHP_SELF)
echo $_SERVER['PHP_SELF']
echo($_SERVER['PHP_SELF'])
```

The improper use of PHP_SELF results in a very well known XSS (Cross-site scripting) hole. This mistake is quite common in PHP applications. Most developers assume that PHP_SELF is not controlled by the user. In fact, it is controlled by the user and can be very easily exploited. Here is an example:

```
http://target/path/to/script.php/"><script>alert('xss')</script><!--
```

Notice that we append additional path to script.php which contains the characters **"><script>alert('xss')</script><!—**. Due to the fact that PHP_SELF is usually used to find the URL of the current script, it is very likely that it is going to be used as part of an element attribute. This is the reason why we use **">** character combination, to break out of the enclosed element. We end with **<!—**, to fix whatever it is left broken.

Let's try another query but this time, we are going too look for SQL Injection holes (SQLI):

```
mysql_query.*?_GET lang:php
```

The result of this query is as shown in Figure 10.32.

Figure 10.32 Looking for SQL Injection

The query starts with the keyword **mysql_query** which is a standard function in PHP. Then we look for undefined number of characters with the sequence **.*?**. Finally, we look for the keyword _GET which denotes HTTP GET parameter. In general, we are looking for SQL queries that can be controlled by $_GET. A similar tactic can be applied to $_POST based SQL Injection attacks. Keep in mind that the examples shown in this chapter are just a few of the many variations that we can try. Google Code Search is a very useful tool that can be used to locate vulnerabilities in many languages.

> ## NOTE
>
> We can use Google Code Search to locate strings within our own projects. If we have a large dataset to analyze, we can simply upload it to code and wait until the Google crawler finds it out. Then we can use standard regular expression queries to locate the data that we are most interested in.

Chapter 11

Google Hacking Showcase

Introduction

A self-respecting Google hacker spends hours trolling the Internet for juicy stuff. Firing off search after search, they thrive on the thrill of finding clean, mean, streamlined queries and get a real rush from sharing those queries and trading screenshots of their findings. I know because I've seen it with my own eyes. As the founder of the Google Hacking Database (GHDB) and the Search engine hacking forums at http://johnny.ihackstuff.com, I am constantly amazed at what the Google hacking community comes up with. It turns out the rumors are true—creative Google searches can reveal medical, financial, proprietary and even classified information. Despite government edicts, regulation and protection acts like HIPPA and the constant barking of security watchdogs, this problem still persists. Stuff still makes it out onto the web, and Google hackers snatch it right up.

In my quest to shine a spotlight on the threat, I began speaking on the topic of Google hacking at security conferences like Blackhat and Defcon. In addition, I was approached to write my first book, the first edition of the book you're holding. After months of writing, I assumed our cause would finally catch the eye of the community at large and that change would be on the horizon. I just knew people would be talking about Google hacking and that awareness about the problem would increase.

Google Hacking, first edition, has made a difference. But nothing made waves like the "Google Hacking Showcase," the fun part of my infamous Google hacking conference talks. The showcase wasn't a big deal to me—it consisted of nothing more than screenshots of wild Google hacks I had witnessed. Borrowing from the pool of interesting Google queries I had created, along with scores of queries from the community; I snagged screenshots and presented them one at a time, making smarmy comments along the way. Every time I presented the showcase, I managed to whip the audience into a frenzy of laughter at the absurd effectiveness of a hacker armed only with a browser and a search engine. It was fun, and it was effective. People talked about those screenshots for months after each talk. They were, after all, the fruits of a Google hacker's labor. Those photos represented the white-hot center of the Google hacking threat.

It made sense then to include the showcase in this edition of *Google Hacking*. In keeping with the original format of the showcase, this chapter will be heavy on photos and light on gab because the photos speak for themselves. Some of the screenshots in this chapter are dated, and some no longer exist on the web, but this is great news. It means that somewhere in the world, someone (perhaps inadvertently) graduated from the level of *googledork* and has taken a step closer to a better security posture.

Regardless, I left in many outdated photos as a stark reminder to those charge with protecting online resources. They serve as proof that this threat is pervasive— it can happen to anyone, and history has shown that it has happened to just about everyone.

So without further ado, enjoy this print version of the Google Hacking Showcase, brought to you by myself and the contributions of the Google Hacking community.

Geek Stuff

This section is about computer stuff. It's about technical stuff, the stuff of geeks. We will take a look at some of the more interesting technical finds uncovered by Google hackers. We'll begin by looking at various utilities that really have no business being online, unless of course your goal is to aid hackers. Then we'll look at open network devices and open applications, neither of which requires any real hacking to gain access to.

Utilities

Any self-respecting hacker has a war chest of tools at his disposal, but the thing that's interesting about the tools in this section is that they are online—they run on a web server and allow an attacker to effectively bounce his reconnaissance efforts off of that hosting web server. To make matters worse, these application-hosting servers were each located with clever Google queries. We'll begin with the handy PHP script shown in Figure 11.1 which allows a web visitor to *ping* any target on the Internet. A *ping* isn't necessarily a bad thing, but why offer the service to anonymous visitors?

Figure 11.1 Php-ping.cgi Provides Free Ping Bounces

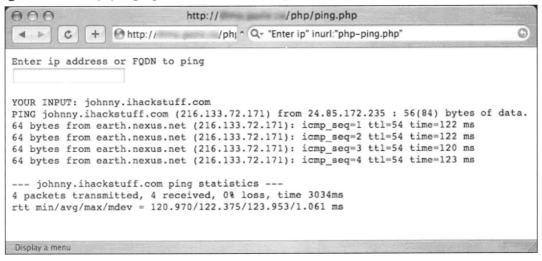

Unlike the *ping* tool, the *finger* tool has been out of commission for quite a long time. This annoying service allowed attackers to query users on a UNIX machine, allowing enumeration of all sorts of information such as user connect times, home directory, full name and more. Enter the *finger* CGI script, an awkward attempt to "webify" this irritating service. As shown in Figure 11.2, a well-placed Google query locates installations of this script, providing web visitors with a *finger* client that allows them to query the service on remote machines.

Figure 11.2 Finger CGI Script Allows Remote Fingering

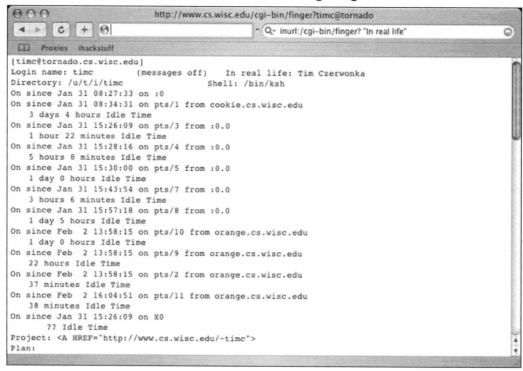

Pings and *finger* lookups are relatively benign; most system administrators won't even notice them traversing their networks. *Port scans*, on the other hand, are hardly ever considered benign, and a paranoid administrator (or piece of defense software) will take note of the source of a port scan. Although most modern port scanners provide options which allow for covert operation, a little Google hacking can go a long way. Figure 11.3 reveals a Google search submitted by Jimmy Neutron which locates sites that will allow a web visitor to portscan a target.

Remember, scans performed in this way will originate from the web server, not from the attacker. Even the most paranoid system administrator will struggle to trace a scan launched in this way. Of course, most attackers won't stop at a portscan. They will most likely opt to continue probing the target with any number of network utilities which could reveal their true location. However, if an attacker locates a web page like the one shown in Figure 11.4 (submitted by Jimmy Neutron), he can channel various network probes through the *WebUtil* Perl script hosted on that remote server. Once again, the probes will appear to come from the web server, not from the attacker.

Figure 11.3 PHPPort Scanner- A Nifty Web-Based Portscanner

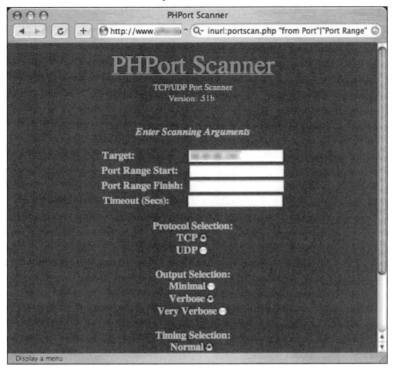

Figure 11.4 WebUtil Lets An Attacker Do Just About Anything

The web page listed in Figure 11.5 (submitted by Golfo) lists the name, address and device information for a school's "student enrollment" systems. Clicking through the interface reveals more information about the architecture of the network, and the devices connected to it. Consolidated into one easy-to-read interface and located with a Google search, this page makes short work of an attacker's reconnaissance run.

Figure 11.5 WhatsUp Status Screen Provides Guests with a Wealth of Information

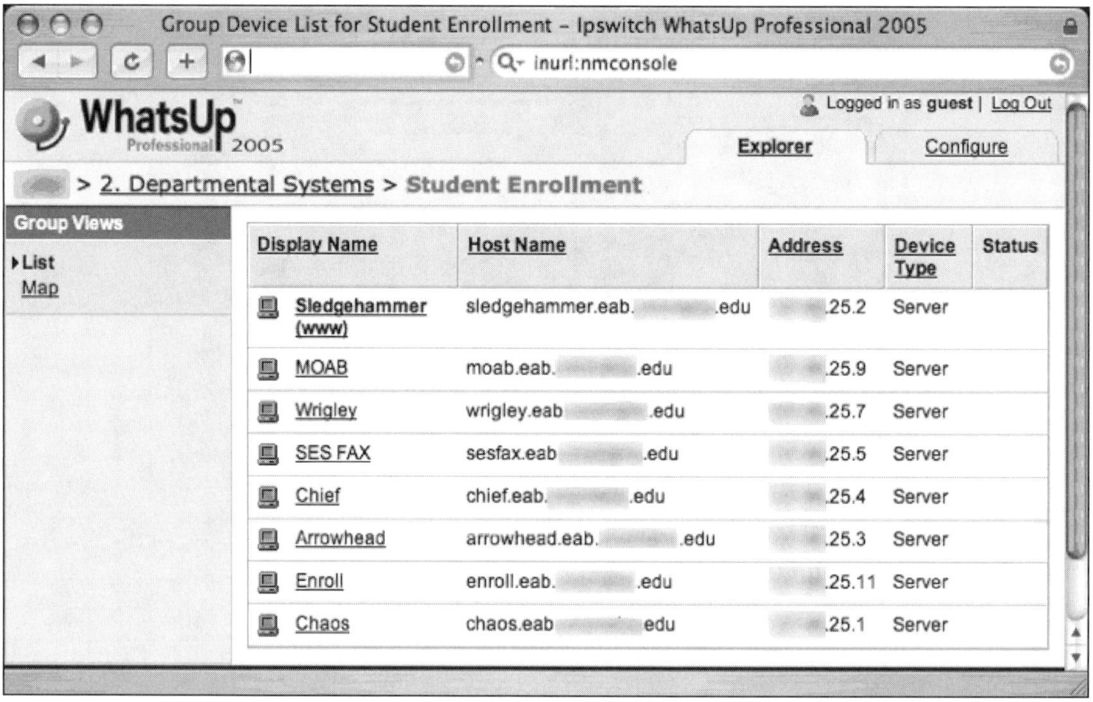

Open Network Devices

Why hack into a network server or device when you can just point and click your way into an *open* network device? Management devices, like the one submitted by Jimmy Neutron in Figure 11.6, often list all sorts of information about a variety of devices.

Figure 11.6 Open APC Management Device

When m00d submitted the query shown in Figure 11.7, I honestly didn't think much of it. The SpeedStream router is a decidedly lightweight device installed by home users, but I was startled to find them sitting wide-open on the Internet. I personally like the button in the point-to-point summary listing. Who do you want to disconnect today?

Figure 11.7 Open SpeedStream DSL Router Allows Remote Disconnects

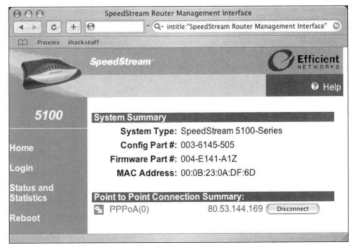

Belkin is a household name in home network gear. With their easy-to-use web-based administrative interfaces, it makes sense that eventually pages like the one in Figure 11.8 would get crawled by Google. Even without login credentials, this page reveals a ton of information that could be interesting to a potential attacker. I got a real laugh out of the *Features* section of the page. The firewall is enabled, but the wireless interface is wide open and unencrypted. As a hacker with a social conscience, my first instinct is to enable encryption on this access point—in an attempt to protect this poor home user from themselves.

Figure 11.8 Belkin Router Needs Hacker Help

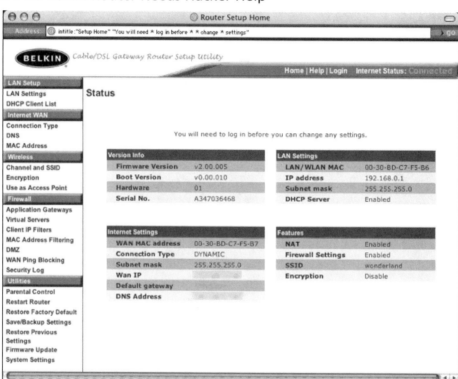

Milkman brings us the query shown in Figure 11.9, which digs up the configuration interface for Smoothwall personal firewalls. There's something just wrong about Google hacking someone's firewall.

Figure 11.9 Smoothwall Firewall Needs Updating

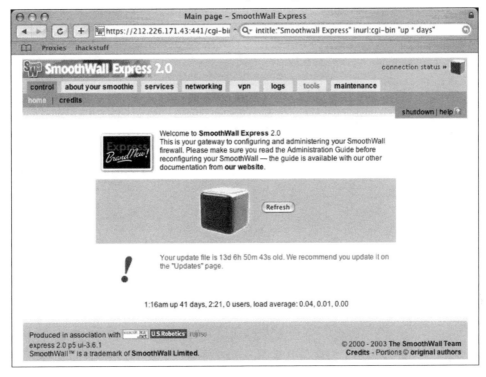

As Jimmy Neutron reveals in the next two figures, even big-name gear like Cisco shows up in the recesses of Google's cache every now and again. Although it's not much to look at, the switch interface shown in Figure 11.10 leaves little to the imagination—all the configuration and diagnostic tools are listed right on the main page.

Figure 11.10 Open Cisco Switch

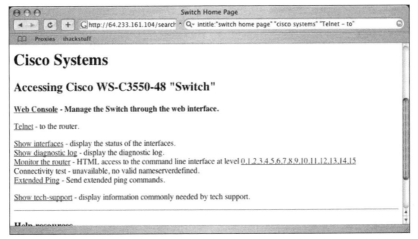

This second Cisco screenshot should look familiar to Cisco geeks. I don't know why, but the Cisco nomenclature reminds me of a bad Hollywood flick. I can almost hear the grating voice of an over-synthesized computer beckoning, "Welcome to Level 15."

Figure 11.11 Welcome to Cisco Level 15

The search shown in Figure 11.12 (submitted by Murfie) locates interfaces for an Axis network print server. Most printer interfaces are really boring, but this one in particular piqued my interest. First, there's the button named *configuration wizard*, which I'm pretty sure launches a configuration wizard. Then there's the handy link labeled *Print Jobs*, which lists the print jobs. In case you haven't already guessed, Google hacking sometimes leaves little to the imagination.

Printers aren't entirely boring things. Consider the *Web Image Monitor* shown in Figure 11.13. I particularly like the document on *Recent Religion Work*. That's quite an honorable pursuit, except when combined with the document about *Aphrodisiacs*. I really hope the two documents are unrelated. Then again, nothing surprises me these days.

Figure 11.12 Axis Print Server with Obscure Buttonage

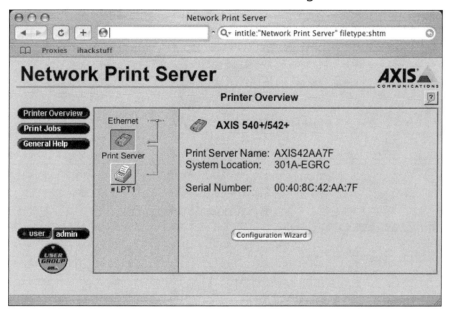

Figure 11.13 Ricoh Print Server Mixes Religion and Aphrodisiacs

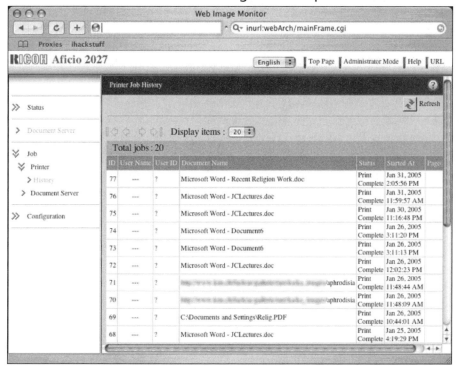

CP has a way of finding Google hacks that make me laugh, and Figure 11.14 is no exception. Yes, this is the web-based interface to a municipal water fountain.

Figure 11.14 Hacking Water Fountains For Fun and Profit

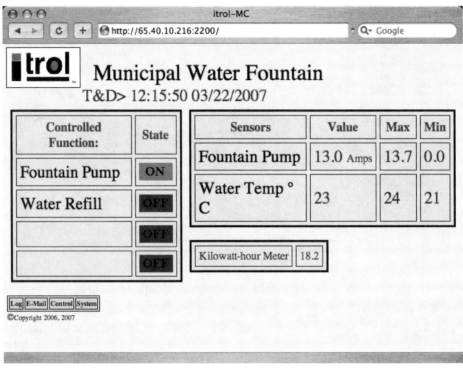

After watching the water temperature fluctuate for a few intensely boring seconds, it's only logical to click on the *Control* link to see if it's possible to actually control the municipal water fountain. As Figure 11.15 reveals, yes it is possible to remotely control the municipal water fountain.

One bit of advice though—if you happen to bump into one of these, be nice. Don't go rerouting the power into the water storage system. I think that would definitely constitute an act of terrorism.

Figure 11.15 More Water Fountain Fun

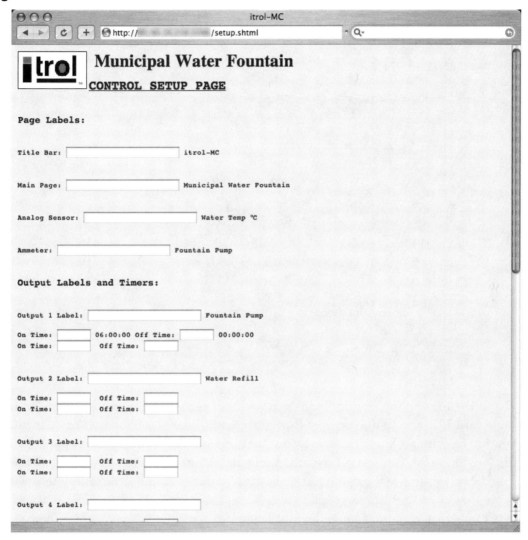

Moving along to a more traditional network fixture, consider the screenshot captured in Figure 11.16.

Figure 11.16 An IDS Manager on Acid

Now, I've been in the security business for a lot of years, and I'm not exactly brilliant in any one particular area of the industry. But I do know a little bit about a lot of different things, and one thing I know for sure is that security products are designed to protect stuff. It's the way of things. But when I see something like the log shown in Figure 11.16, I get all confused. See, this is a web-based interfaced for the Snort intrusion detection system. The last time I checked, this data was supposed to be kept away from the eyes of an attacker, but I guess I missed an email or something. But I suppose there's logic to this somewhere. Maybe if the attacker sees his screw-ups on a public webpage, he'll be too ashamed to ever hack again, and he'll go on to lead a normal productive life. Then again, maybe he and his hacker buddies will just get a good laugh out of his good fortune. It's hard to tell.

Open Applications

Many mainstream web applications are relatively idiot-proof, designed for the point-and-click masses that know little about security. Even still, the Google hacking community has discovered hundreds of online apps that are wide open, just waiting for a point-and-click script kiddy to come along and own them. The first in this section was submitted by Shadowsliv and is shown in Figure 11.17.

Figure 11.17 Tricky Pivot Hack Requires Five Correct Field Fills

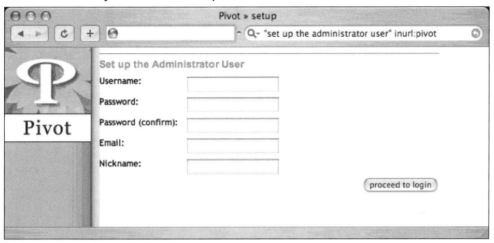

The bad news is that if a hacker can figure out what to type in those confusing fields, he'll have his very own Pivot web log. The good news is that most skilled attackers will leave this site alone, figuring that any software left this unprotected *must* be a honeypot. It's really sad that hacking (not *real* hacking mind you) can be reduced to a point-and-click affair, but as Arrested's search reveals in Figure 11.18, owning an entire website can be a relatively simple affair.

Figure 11.18 PHP-Nuke Ownage in Four Correct Field Fills

Sporting one less field than the open Pivot install, this configuration page will create a PHP-Nuke Administrator account, and allow any visitor to start uploading content to the page as if it were their own. Of course, this takes a bit of malicious intent on behalf of the web visitor. There's no mistaking the fact that he or she is creating an Administrator account on a site that does not belong to them. However, the text of the page in Figure 11.19 is a bit more ambiguous.

Figure 11.19 Hack This PHP-Nuke Install "For Security Reasons"

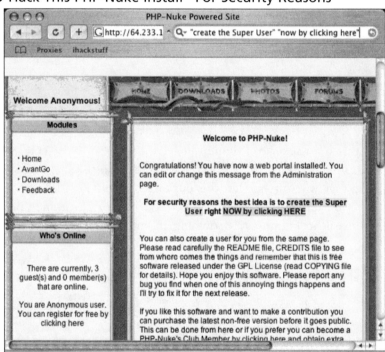

The bold text in the middle of the page really cracks me up. I can just imagine somebody's poor Grandma running into this page and reading it aloud. "For security reasons, the best idea is to create the Super User right NOW by clicking HERE." I mean who in their right mind would avoid doing something that was for *security reasons*? For all Grandma knows, she may be saving the world from evil hackers... by hacking into some poor fool's PHP-Nuke install.

And as if owning a website isn't cool enough, Figure 11.20 (submitted by Quadster) reveals a phpMyAdmin installation logged in as root, providing unfettered access to a MySQL database.

Figure 11.20 Open phpMyAdmin - MySQL Ownage for Dummies

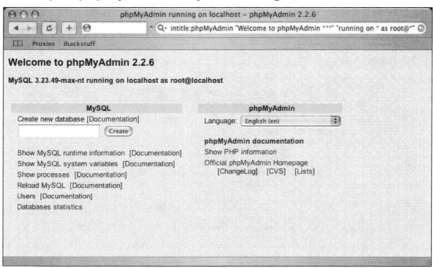

With a website install and an SQL database under his belt, it's a natural progression for a Google hacker to want the ultimate control of a system. VNC installations provide remote control of a system's keyboard and mouse. Figure 11.21, submitted by Lester, shows a query that locates RealVNC's Java-based client.

Figure 11.21 Hack A VNC, Grab A Remote Keyboard

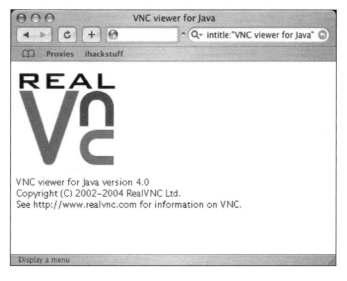

Locating a client is only part of the equation, however. An attacker will still need to know the address, port and (optional) password for a VNC server. As Figure 11.22 reveals, the Java client itself often provide two-thirds of that equation in a handy popup window.

Figure 11.22 VNC Options Handed Up With a Side of Fries

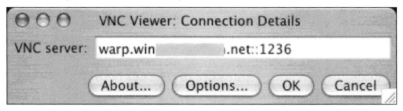

If the hacker really lucks out and stumbles on a server that's not password protected, he's faced with the daunting task of figuring out which of the four buttons to click in the above connection window. Here's a hint for the script kiddie looking to make his way in the world: it's not the *Cancel* button.

Of course running without a password is just plain silly. But passwords can be so difficult to remember and software vendors obviously realize this as evidenced by the password prompt shown in Figure 11.23.

Figure 11.23 Handy Password Reminder, In Case The Hacker Forgot

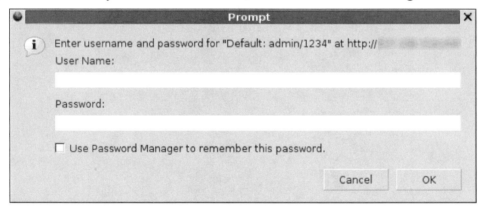

Posting the default username/password combination on a login popup is just craziness. Unfortunately it's not an isolated event. Check out Figure 11.24, submitted by Jimmy Neutron. Can you guess the default password?

Figure 11.24 You Suck If You Can't Guess This Default Password

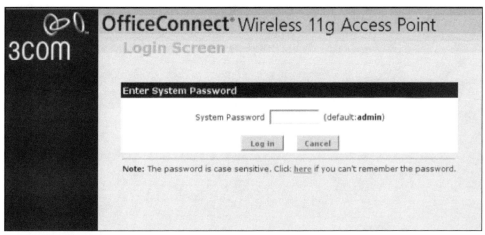

Graduating to the next level of hacker leetness requires a bit of work. Check out the user screen shown in Figure 11.25, which was submitted by Dan Kaminsky.

Figure 11.25 Welcome To Guest Access

If you look carefully, you'll notice that the URL contains a special field called *ADMIN*, which is set to *False*. Think like a hacker for a moment and imagine how you might gain administrative access to the page. The spoiler is listed in Figure 11.26.

Figure 11.26 Admin Access through URL Tinkering

Check out the shiny new *Exit Administrative Access* button. By Changing the *ADMIN* field to *True*, the application drops us into Administrative access mode. Hacking really is hard, I promise.

Cameras

I've got to be honest and admit that like printer queries, I'm really sick of webcam queries. For a while there, every other addition to the GHDB was a webcam query. Still, some webcam finds are pretty interesting and worth mentioning in the showcase. I'll start with a cell phone camera dump, submitted by Vipsta as shown in Figure 11.27.

Not only is this an interesting photo of some pretty serious-looking vehicular carnage, but the idea that Google trolls camera phone picture sites is interesting. Who knows what kind of blackmail fodder lurks in the world's camera phones. Not that anyone would ever use that kind of information for sensationalistic or economically lucrative purposes. Ahem.

Figure 11.27 Google Crawled Vehicular Carnage

Moving on, check out the office-mounted open web camera submitted by Klouw as shown in Figure 11.28.

Figure 11.28 Remote Shoulder Surfing 101

This is really an interesting web cam. Not only does it reveal all the activity in the office, but it seems especially designed to allow remote shoulder surfing. Hackers used to have to get out of the house to participate in this classic sport. These days all they have to do is fire off a few Google searches.

Figure 11.29, submitted by Jimmy Neutron, shows the I.T. infrastructure of a tactical US nuclear submarine.

Figure 11.29 Not Really A Tactical US Nuclear Submarine

OK, so not really. It's probably just a nuclear reactor or power grid control center or even a drug lord's warehouse in Columbia (Maryland). Or maybe I've been reading too many *Stealing The Network* books. Either way, it's a cool find none the less.

Figure 11.30, however (submitted by JBrashars) is unmistakable. It's definitely a parking lot camera. I'm not sure why, exactly, a camera is pointed at a handicapped parking space, but my guess is that there have been reports of handicapped parking spot abuse. Imagine the joy of being the guard that gets to witness the CIO parking in the spot, leaping out of his convertible and running into the building. Those are the stories of security guard legends.

Figure 11.30 Handicapped Parking Spot Gestapo Cam

WarriorClown sent me the search used for the capture shown in Figure 11.31. It shows what appears to be a loading dock, and a field of white explosive containers.

Figure 11.31 Remote Exploding Container Fun

Although it looks pretty boring at first, this webcam is really a lot of fun. Check out the interesting button in the upper right of the capture. I'm pretty sure that clicking on that button fires a laser beam at the explosive white containers, which creates maximum carnage, but can only be done once—unless you set them to respawn, which will bring them back automatically. Oh, wait. That only works in Halo 3's Forge mode. OK, all these webcams are starting to make me loopy. In an attempt to get my imagination in check, I present pretty straightforward security camera view shown in Figure 11.32.

Figure 11.32 Open Web "Security" Cameras

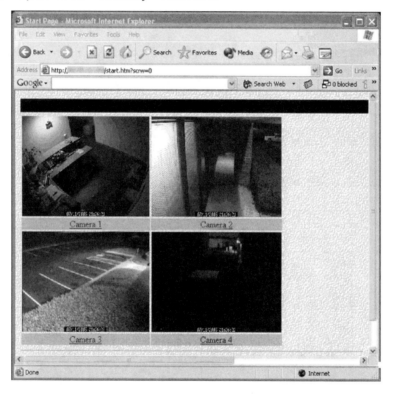

I can't be the only one that thinks it's insane to put open security camera feeds on the Internet. Of course it happens in Hollywood movies all the time. It seems the first job for the hired hacker is to tap into the video surveillance feeds. But the movies make it look all complicated and technical. I've never once seen a Hollywood hacker use Google to hack the security system. Then again, that wouldn't look nearly as cool as using fiber optic cameras, wire cutters and alligator clips.

Moving on, the search shown in Figure 11.33 (submitted by JBrashars) returns quite a few hits for open Everfocus EDSR applets.

Figure 11.33 EDSR Sounds Tame Enough

The Everfocus EDSR is a multi-channel digital video recording system with a web-based interface. It's a decent surveillance product, and as such it is password protected by default, as shown in Figure 11.34.

Figure 11.34 Password Protection: The Gold Standard of Security

Unfortunately, as revealed by an anonymous contributor, the factory-default administrative username and password provides access to many of these systems, as shown in Figure 11.35.

Figure 11.35 Welcome to Surveillance Central

Once inside, the EDSR applet provides access to multiple live video feeds and a historic record of any previously recorded activity. Again, just like the magic of Hollywood without all the hacker smarts.

The EDSR isn't the only multi-channel video system that is targeted by Google hackers. As Murfie reveals, a search for I-catcher CCTV returns many systems like the one shown in Figure 11.36.

Although the interface may look simple, it provides access to multiple live camera views, including one called "Woodie" which I was personally afraid to click on.

Figure 11.36 Housekeeper Needed. Apply Within.

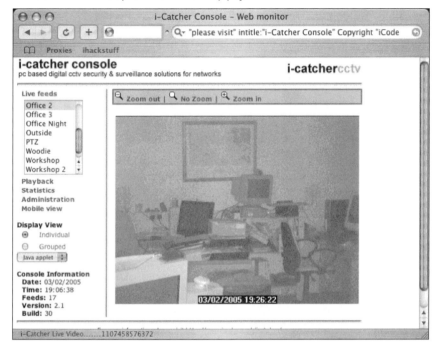

These cameras are all interesting, but I've saved my favorite for last. Check out Figure 11.37.

Figure 11.37 Shoulder Surfing Meets Webcam Meets Password Stickers

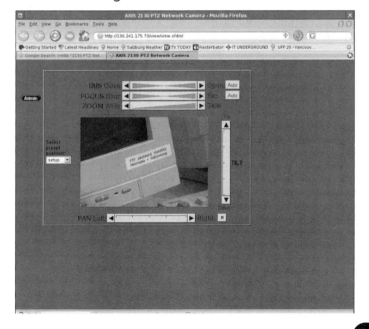

This camera provides open access to web visitors. Located in a computer lab, the camera's remote control capability allows anonymous visitors to peer around, panning and zooming to their hearts content. Not only does this allow for some great shoulder surfing, but the sticker in the above screen capture had me practically falling out of my chair. It lists a user-name and password for the lab's online FTP server. Stickers listing usernames and passwords are bad enough, but I wonder whose bright idea it was to point an open webcam at them?

Telco Gear

I've never been much of a phreaker (phone hacker), but thanks to the depth of Google's searching capabilities, I wouldn't need to have much experience to get into this shady line of work. As JBrashar's search reveals in Figure 11.38, the surge of Voice over IP (VOIP) service has resulted in a host of new web-based phone interfaces.

Figure 11.38 Google Hacking Residential Phone Systems

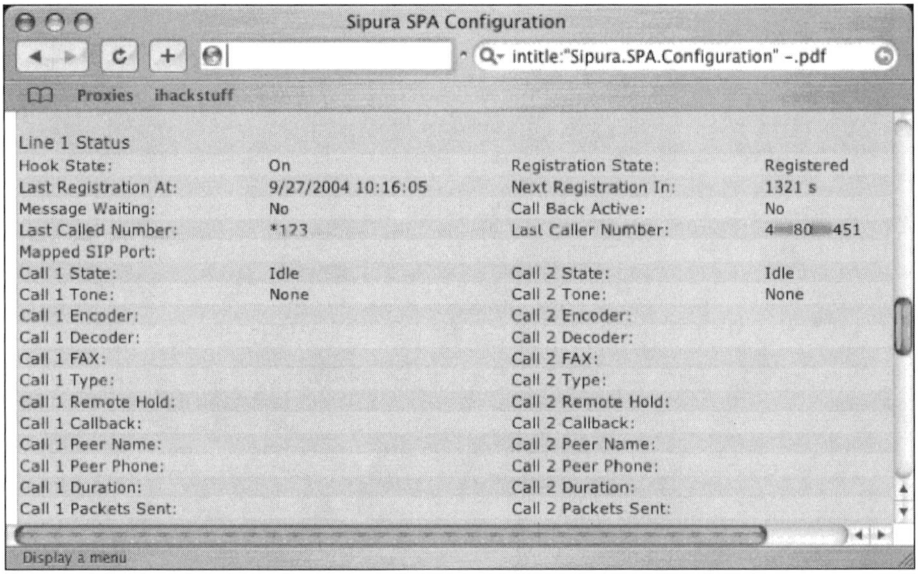

It's interesting to me that by just using Google, an attacker could get phone history information such as last called number and last caller number. Normally, the Sipura SPA software does a better job of protecting this information, but this particular installation is improperly configured. Other, more technical information can also be uncovered by clicking through the links on the web interface, as shown in Figure 11.39.

Figure 11.39 Redux

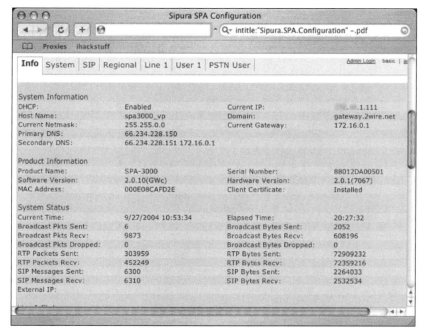

There are so many VOIP devices that it's impossible to cover them all, but the new kid on the VOIP server block is definitely Asterisk. After checking out the documentation for the Asterisk management portal, Jimmy Neutron uncovered the interesting search shown in Figure 11.40.

Figure 11.40 Asterisk, King of the VOIP

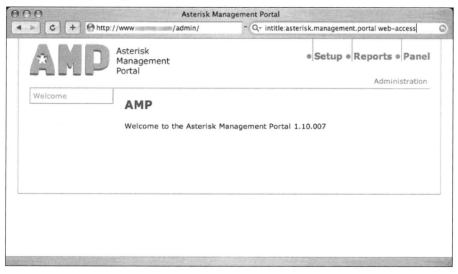

From this open, an attacker can make changes to the Asterisk server, including for-warding incoming calls, as shown in Figure 11.41.

Figure 11.41 Google Hacking Asterisk Management Portals

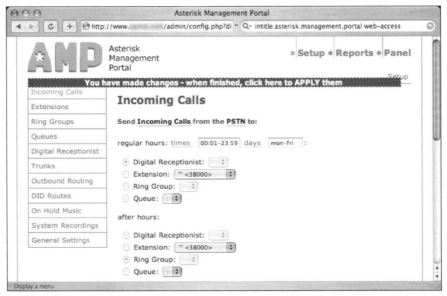

Unfortunately, a hacker's fun wouldn't necessarily stop there. It's simple to re-route extensions, monitor or re-route voicemail, enable or disable digital receptionists and even upload disturbing on-hold music. But Jimmy's Asterisk VOIP digging didn't stop there; he later submitted the search shown in Figure 11.42.

Figure 11.42 Redux. HackenBush. Heh.

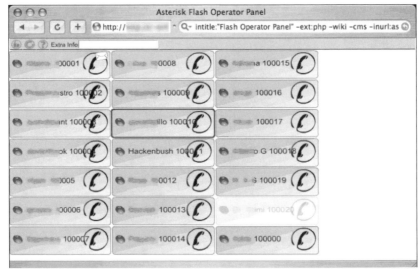

This flash-based operator panel provides access to similar capabilities, and once again, the interface was found open to any Internet visitor.

Moving along, Yeseins serves up the interesting search shown in Figure 11.43, which locates videoconferencing management systems.

Figure 11.43 Hacking Videoconference Systems?

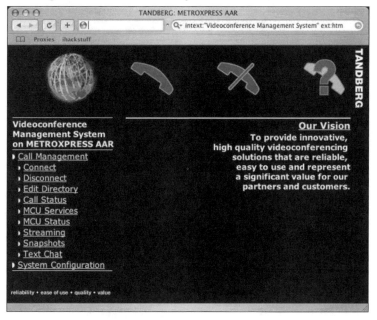

This management system allows a web visitor to connect, disconnect and monitor conference calls, take snapshots of conference participants, and even change line settings as shown in Figure 11.44.

Figure 11.44 Redirecting Videoconference Lines

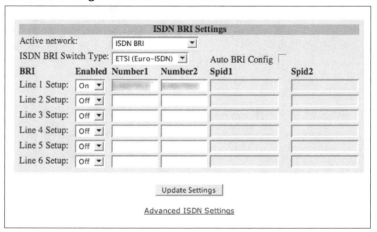

A malicious hacker could even change the system name and password, locking legitimate administrators out of their own system, as shown in Figure 11.45.

Figure 11.45 Videoconference System Ownage

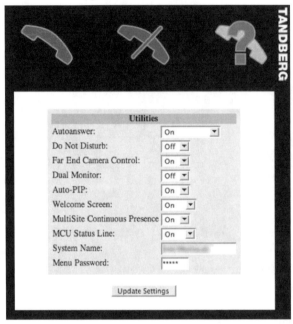

Despite all the new-fangled web interfaces we've looked at, Google hacking bridges the gap to older systems as well, as shown in Figure 11.46.

Figure 11.46 Google Phreaking Old School Style

This front-end was designed to put a new face on an older PBX product, but client security seems to have been an afterthought. Notice that the interface asks the user to "Logout" of the interface, indicating that the user is already logged in. Also, notice that cryptic button labeled *Start Managing the Device.* After firing off a Google search, all a malicious hacker has to do is figure out which button to press. What an unbelievably daunting task.

Power

I get a lot of raised eyebrows when I talk about using Google to hack power systems. Most people think I'm talking about UPS systems like the one submitted by Yeseins in Figure 11.47.

Figure 11.47 Whazzups?

This is a clever Google query, but it's only an uninterruptible power system (UPS) monitoring page. This can be amusing, but as Jimmy Neutron shows in Figure 11.48, there are more interesting power hacking opportunities available.

Figure 11.48 Bedroom Hacking For Dummies

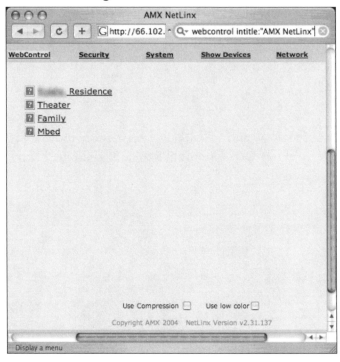

AMX NetLinx systems are designed to allow control of power systems. The figure above seems to suggest that a web visitor could control power in a theater, a family room and the master bedroom of a residence. The problem is that the Google search turns up a scarce number of results, most of which are password protected. As an alternative, Jimmy offers the search shown in Figure 11.49.

Figure 11.49 Passwords Are Nifty, Especially Default Ones

Although this query results in a long list of password-protected sites, many sites still use the default password, providing access to the control panel shown in Figure 11.50.

Figure 11.50 Google Hacking Light Sockets? Uh oh.

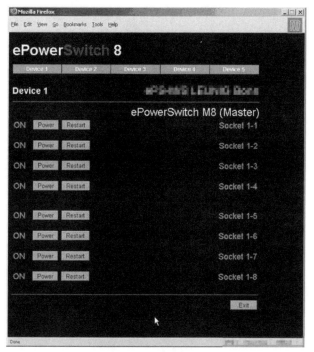

This control panel lists power sockets alongside interesting buttons named *Power* and *Restart*, which even the dimmest of hackers will undoubtedly be able to figure out. The problem with this interface is that it's just not much fun. A hacker will definitely get bored flipping unnamed power switches—unless of course he also finds an open webcam so he can watch the fun. The search shown in Figure 11.51 seems to address this, naming each of the devices for easy reference.

Figure 11.51 Step Away From The Christmas Lights

Of course even the most vicious hackers would probably consider it rude to nail someone's Christmas lights, but no hacker in their right mind could resist the open HomeSeer control panel shown in Figure 11.52.

Figure 11.52 Bong Hacking. BONG Hacking.

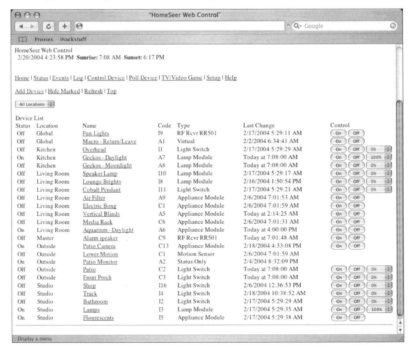

The HomeSeer control panel puts the fun back into power hacking, listing descriptions for each control, as well as an *On, Off* and slider switch for applicable elements. Some of the elements in this list are quite interesting, including *Lower Motion* and *Bathroom.* The best though is definitely *Electric Bong.* If you're a member of the Secret Service looking to bust the owner of this system, I would suggest a preemptive Google strike before barging into the home. Start by dimming the lights, and then nail the motion sensors. Last but not least, turn on the electric bong in case your other charges don't stick.

Sensitive Info

Sensitive info is such a generic term, but that's what this section includes: a hodgepodge of sensitive info discovered while surfing Google. We'll begin with the VCalendar search submitted by Jorokin as shown in Figure 11.53.

Figure 11.53 Let Me Check Their Calendar

There's at least a decent possibility that these calendar files were made public on purpose, but the Netscape history file submitted by Digital_Revolution in Figure 11.54 shouldn't be public.

Figure 11.54 Hot Chicks at IBM? Nah.

For starters, the file contains the user's POP email username and encoded password. Then there's the issue of his URL history, which contains not only the very respectable *IBM.com*, but also the not-so-respectable *hotchicks.com,* which I'm pretty sure is *NSFW*.

Next up is an MSN contact list submitted by Harry-AAC, which is shown in Figure 11.55.

Figure 11.55 Want To Steal My Friends?

This file lists the contact names and email addresses found in someone's contact list. At best, this file is spam fodder. There's really no shortage of email address lists, phone number lists and more on the Web, but what's surprising is how many documents containing this type of information were created with the express intention of sharing that information. Consider the screen shown in Figure 11.56, which was submitted by CP.

Figure 11.56 Call and Email the Entire Staff and Wish Them Happy Birthday

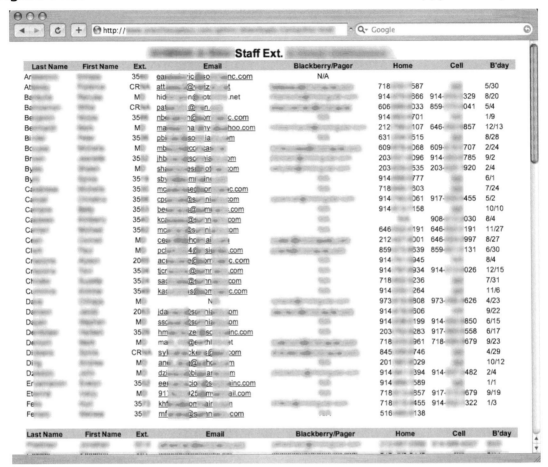

This document is a staff directory, which was created for internal use only. The only problem is that it was found on a public web site. While this doesn't seem to constitute seriously private information, the search shown in Figure 11.57 (submitted by Maerim) reveals slightly more sensitive information: passwords.

Figure 11.57 I Think This RCON Password is Written In Greek

This file lists the cleartext passwords for the Ghost Squad's *private* Counterstrike remote administration console. Ask any CS gamer how embarrassing this could be. But hacking a game server is fairly tame. Consider, however, Figure 11.58 which was submitted by Barabas.

Figure 11.58 Encoded VPN Passwords

This file lists information and encoded passwords for a Cisco Virtual LAN (VLAN). About the only thing worse than revealing your VLAN's encoded passwords is revealing your VLAN's *cleartext* passwords. Ask and you shall receive. Check out Figure 11.59, again from Barabas.

Figure 11.59 Plaintext VPN Passwords

Yup, that's a cleartext password nestled inside a University's configuration file. But interesting passwords can be found in all sorts of places, such as inside Windows unattended installation files, as shown in Figure 11.60, which was submitted by MBaldwin.

Figure 11.60 Owning a Windows Install before It's Installed. Leet.

This file also reveals the product key of the installed software, which could be re-used to install the software illegally. Last but not least, check out Figure 11.61, submitted by CP.

Figure 11.61 Hey, Can I Get All Your Web Passwords?

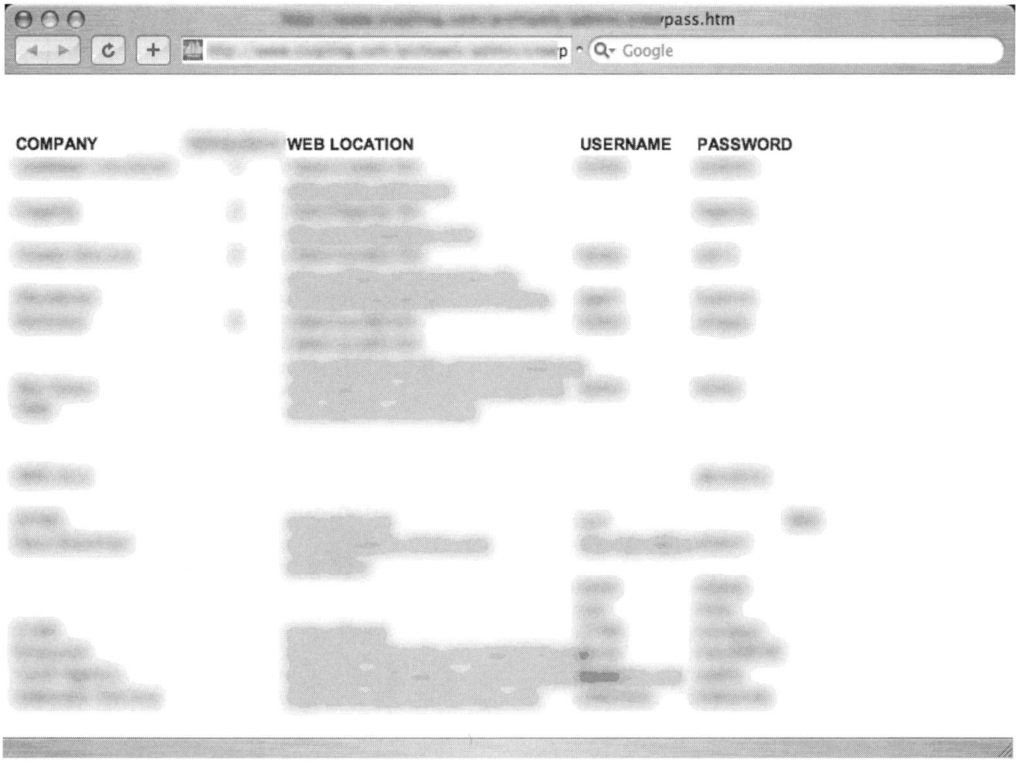

This document lists usernames and passwords for various websites. The document was stored on a website, presumably to allow the owner easy remote access to it. However, at some point the document's location was made public, and Google dutifully crawled it. Remember, public websites are generally just that—public. Don't combine public and private data without a great deal of forethought.

Police Reports

From what I understand, most police records are a matter of public record. So it doesn't surprise me when I see police reports like the one shown in Figure 11.62.

Figure 11.62 Police Reports Are Public Record. Okay.

However, when I find a police report like the one shown in Figure 11.63, I begin to question the sanity of posting unfiltered police records.

Figure 11.63 That Means Your Victoria's Secret Account Info Is Too

This police report records the details of a theft of a woman's purse. The problem is that the contents of the woman's purse are listed in great detail, including the account number of her Victoria's Secret card! This is not the only occurrence of such a detailed police report found on the web. Figure 11.64 shows another more revealing report.

Figure 11.64 Robbed Twice, Thanks To Open Police Reports

This report details another petty theft, this time listing the account numbers of the Visa and MasterCard credit cards that were stolen. It's very likely that the cards were cancelled immediately after they were reported stolen, but the police report shown in Figure 11.65 lists personal numbers that are not as easy to replace.

Figure 11.65 Police Report Triple Robbery or "Mom, I have bad news".

In this case, not only is the victim's driver's license number posted, but their social security number is listed alongside their mother's driver's license number—all of this posted on a public website, ripe for an identity thief's picking.[1].

Social Security Numbers

The Social Security Number (SSN) is the most sensitive piece of information a United States citizen possesses. Even an inexperienced criminal can use a pilfered SSN to establish a bank account, open a line of credit or more—all under the victim's name. In this section, we'll take a look at some of the ways an individual's SSN may end up online. Be advised that like the other sensitive searches in this book, every effort has been taken to obfuscate the selected documents and obscure the Google search that was used to locate them.

In most educational facilities, it is common to assign an identification number to students in order to keep their grades and personal information private. However, as shown in Figure 11.66, the identification number most often used is the student's social security number.

Figure 11.66 Social Security Numbers as Student ID Numbers

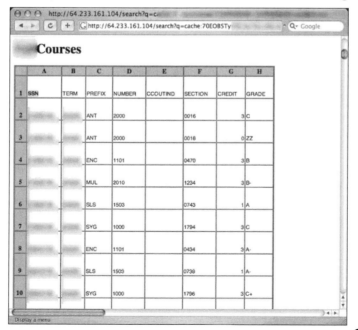

The SSN by itself is not necessarily a big deal, and when posted alongside student's grades (as shown in Figure 11.67) the system works well to keep student's progress private.

Figure 11.67 "Anonymous" Student Numbers and Grade Postings

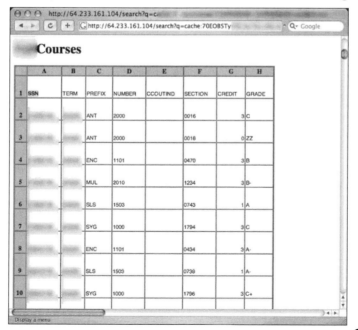

However, in many cases, student's names are posted right alongside their Social Security Number, as shown in Figure 11.68. This of course destroys the anonymity gained by using an identification number instead of a name.

Figure 11.68 Names and Social Security Numbers Together Again

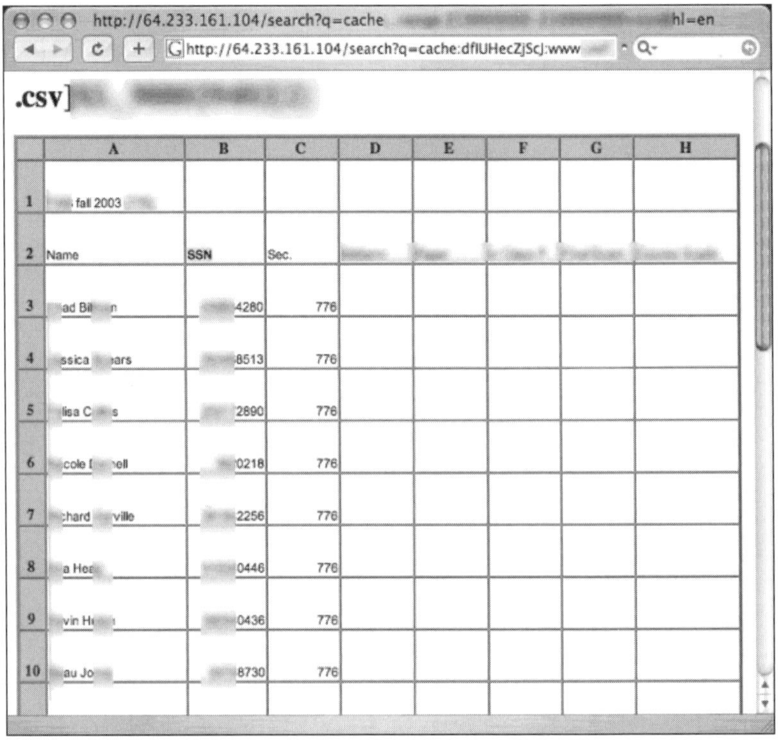

In some cases, these documents are not intended for public viewing, but somehow end up on Internet-facing websites. This is, of course, an unsafe handling practice and the documents end up in Google's cache. The document shown in Figure 11.69 was discovered sitting in an open directory by an anonymous Google hacker. Notice that it lists student's names, SSN and more. To make matters worse, this document was found on a US Government training facility website. The document has since been removed.

Figure 11.69 SSN and Names, an ID Thief's Birthday Present

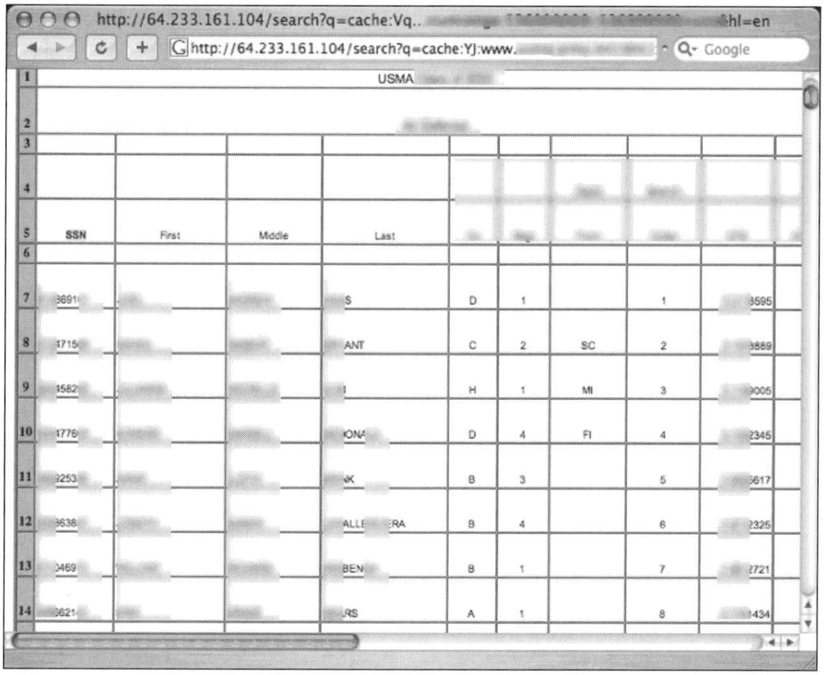

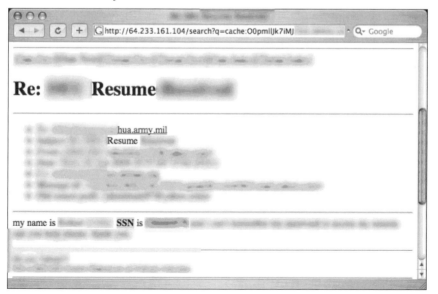

Social Security numbers appear on the web in other ways, most notably through user ignorance. The resume request shown in Figure 11.70 lists an individual's SSN in a message group post.

Figure 11.70 Hire This Guy. Here's His SSN.

The document shown in Figure 11.71 is known as curriculum vitae, or a CV. I wasn't sure what a CV was, but after a bit of research I discovered it is a sort of résumé for really smart people.

Figure 11.71 I'm Smart. Want to See My CV?

As for me, I think I'll keep my plain old résumé, especially if maintaining a CV means that I have to publicly expose my birthday and social security number. Finally, check out the spreadsheet shown in Figure 11.72 which lists the name, date of birth, sex, date of hire and SSN of a company's employees.

Figure 11.72 Employee Out Of the Closet Day

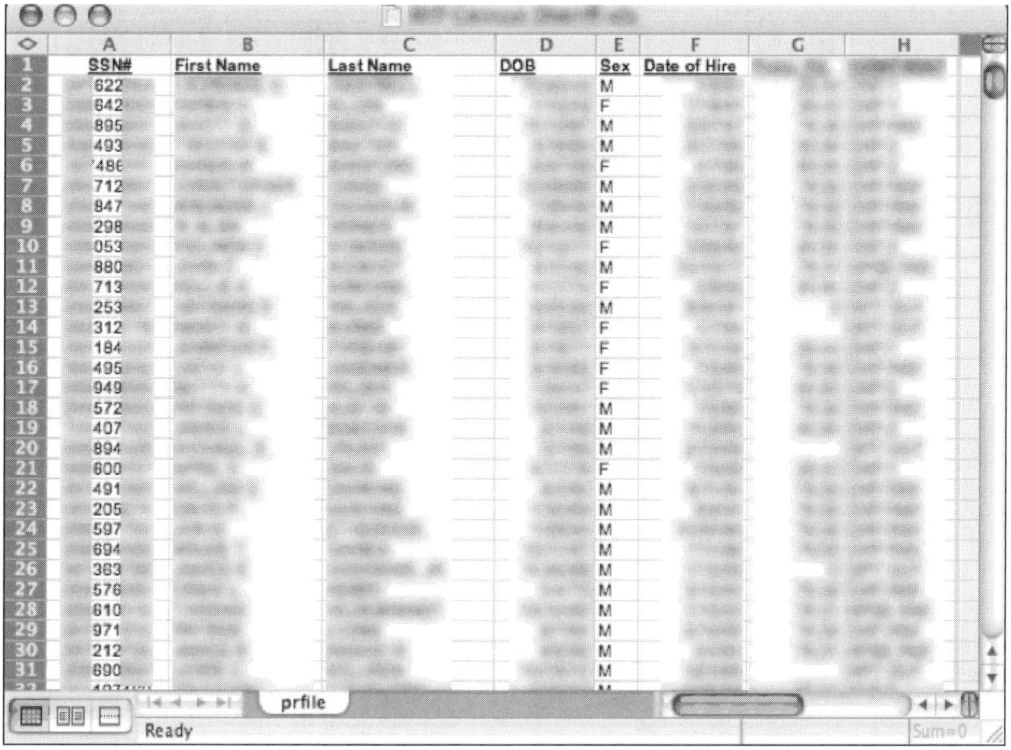

Credit Card Information

Credit card numbers are obviously very valuable, and should be kept well protected. However, as we'll see in this section, those numbers can be found on the web with very little effort. Figure 11.73 shows a relatively small document that lists a Visa credit card number alongside the associated expiration date.

Figure 11.73 Google Hacking Credit Card Info

Figure 11.74 shows a larger document that lists no only credit card numbers and their associated expiration dates, but also the card certification value (CVV) number which is often used to validate that the card is in the hands of a legitimate bearer.

Figure 11.74 Google Hacking More Credit Card Info

Figure 11.75 shows an extremely large document that contains hundreds of bits of personal information about victims including name, address, phone numbers, credit card information, CVV codes and expiration dates.

Figure 11.75 Google Hacking Lots of Credit Card Info

However, credit card numbers and expiration dates aren't the only financially sensitive bits of information on the web, as shown in Figure 11.76.

NOTE

Most often, information like this is collected by *phishers*—criminals using electronic communication to solicit personal information—and kept in an online list or database. In many cases, investigators locate these lists or databases and post links to them in online discussion groups. When Google's crawlers follow the link, the captured data is exposed to Google Hackers. In other cases, carders (credit card number traders) post this data on the web in open-air web discussions, which Google then crawls and caches. For more information about phishing, see *Phishing Exposed* from Syngress Publishing.

Figure 11.76 Is Nothing Sacred?

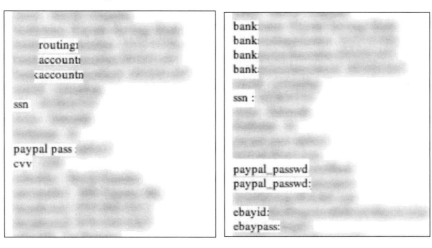

These samples were collected from various web sites, and include bank routing numbers, PayPal usernames and passwords, eBay usernames and passwords, bank account and routing numbers and more, most likely collected by phishers.

Beyond Google

In some cases, Google is the first step in a longer hacking chain. Decent hackers will often take the next step beyond Google. In this section, we'll take a quick look at some interesting Google hacks that took an extra few steps to pull off. Still simple in execution, these examples show the creative lengths hackers will go to.

This first screenshot, shown in Figure 11.77 (submitted by CP) reports that a staff directory has been removed from the web for privacy purposes.

Figure 11.77 Staff Contact List Removed?

This isn't a bad idea, but the problem is that the old document must also be removed from the website, or sites like archive.org will hold onto the document's link indefinitely. Figure 11.78 shows the staff contact document pulled from the original website, thanks to a link from archive.org.

Figure 11.78 Staff Contact List Recovered

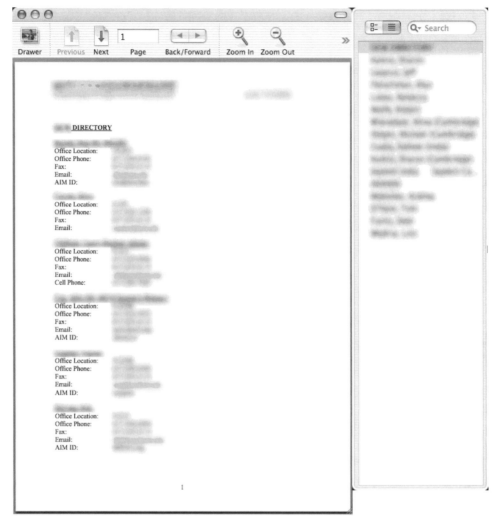

In this next example, a Google hacker noticed a password reference sitting in a PDF document, as shown in Figure 11.79.

Figure 11.79 A PDF File Password Reference

When downloaded, the PDF file does indeed contain a password reference. In this case, it comes in the form of a link to a password-protected PDF document as shown in Figure 11.80.

Figure 11.80 A Link to a Protected Document, And the Associated Password

As seen in Figure 11.81, the referenced PDF file is indeed password protected.

Figure 11.81 Password Protected PDF Document

Entering the password opens the document, as shown in Figure 11.82.

Figure 11.82 Sensitive Document Open with Pilfered Password

It makes no sense to password a document and give out the password, but in this case the problem occurred because the original document containing the password reference was not meant to be public. In this case, the blunder lead to the revelation of a sensitive Government document.

Summary

This chapter is all about what can go drastically wrong when the Google hacking threat is ignoredUse this chapter whenever you have trouble conveying the seriousness of the threat. Help spread the word, and become part of the solution and not part of the problem. And before you go sending cease and desist papers to Google, remember—it's not Google's fault if your sensitive data makes it online.

---

[1] We're obviously in tricky water here, as these are dangerous searches indeed. All identifying information in these and following searches has been blurred out, and any information that could lead to the recreation of the Google query has been removed as well. Additionally, most of the sensitive documents found in this chapter have since been removed from the web.

## Chapter 12

Protecting Yourself from Google Hackers

Solutions in this chapter:

- A Good, Solid Security Policy
- Web Server Safeguards
- Hacking Your Own Site
- Getting Help from Google
- Links to Sites

☑ Summary

☑ Solutions Fast Track

☑ Frequently Asked Questions

Introduction

The purpose of this book is to help you understand the tactics a Google hacker might employ so that you can properly protect yourself and your customers from this seemingly innocuous threat. The best way to do this, in my opinion, is to show you exactly what an attacker armed with a search engine like Google is capable of. There is a point at which we must discuss in no uncertain terms *exactly* how to prevent this type of information exposure or how to remedy an existing exposure. This chapter is all about protecting your site (or your customer's site) from this type of attack.

We'll look at this topic from several perspectives. First, it's important that you understand the value of strong policy with regard to posting data on the Internet. This is not a technical topic and could very easily put the techie in you fast asleep, but a sound security policy is absolutely necessary when it comes to properly securing any site. Second, we'll look at slightly more technical topics that describe how to secure your Web site from Google's (and other search engine's) crawlers. We'll then look at some tools that can be used to help check a Web site's Google exposure, and we'll spend some time talking about ways Google can help you shore up your defenses.

Underground Googling

Where Are the Details?

There are too many types of servers and configurations to show how to lock them all down. A discussion on Web server security could easily span an entire book series. We'll look at server security at a high level here, focusing on strategies you can employ to specifically protect you from the Google hacker threat. For more details, please check the references in the "Links to Sites" section.

A Good, Solid Security Policy

The best hardware and software configuration money can buy can't protect your resources if you don't have an effective security policy. Before implementing any software assurances, take the time to review your security policy. A good security policy, properly enforced, out- lines the assets you're trying to protect, how the protection mechanisms are installed, the acceptable level of operational risk, and what to do in the event of a compromise or disaster. Without a solid, enforced security policy, you're fighting a losing battle.

Web Server Safeguards

There are several ways to keep the prying eyes of a Web crawler from digging too deeply into your site. However, bear in mind that a Web server is designed to store data that is meant for public consumption. Despite all the best protections, information leaks happen. If you're really concerned about keeping your sensitive information private, keep it away from your public Web server. Move that data to an intranet or onto a specialized server that is dedicated to serving that information in a safe, responsible, policy-enforced manner.

Don't get in the habit of splitting a public Web server into distinct roles based on access levels. It's too easy for a user to copy data from one file to another, which could render some directory-based protection mechanisms useless. Likewise, consider the implications of a public Web server system compromise. In a well thought out, properly constructed environment, the compromise of a public Web server only results in the compromise of public information. Proper access restrictions would prevent the attacker from bouncing from the Web server to any other machine, making further infiltration of more sensitive information all the more difficult for the attacker. If sensitive information were stored alongside public information on a public Web server, the compromise of that server could potentially compromise the more sensitive information as well.

We'll begin by taking a look at some fairly simple measures that can be taken to lock down a Web server from within. These are general principles; they're not meant to provide a complete solution but rather to highlight some of the common key areas of defense. We will not focus on any specific type of server but will look at suggestions that should be universal to any Web server. We will not delve into the specifics of protecting a Web *application*, but rather we'll explore more common methods that have proven especially and specifically effective against Web crawlers.

Directory Listings and Missing Index Files

We've already seen the risks associated with directory listings. Although minor information leaks, directory listings allow the Web user to see most (if not all) of the files in a directory, as well as any lower-level subdirectories. As opposed to the "guided" experience of surfing through a series of prepared pages, directory listings provide much more unfettered access. Depending on many factors, such as the permissions of the files and directories as well as the server's settings for allowed files, even a casual Web browser could get access to files that should not be public.

Figure 12.1 demonstrates an example of a directory listing that reveals the location of an htaccess file. Normally, this file (which should be called *.htaccess*, not *htaccess*) serves to protect the directory contents from unauthorized viewing. However, a server misconfiguration allows this file to be seen in a directory listing and even read.

Figure 12.1 Directory Listings Provide Road Maps to Nonpublic Files

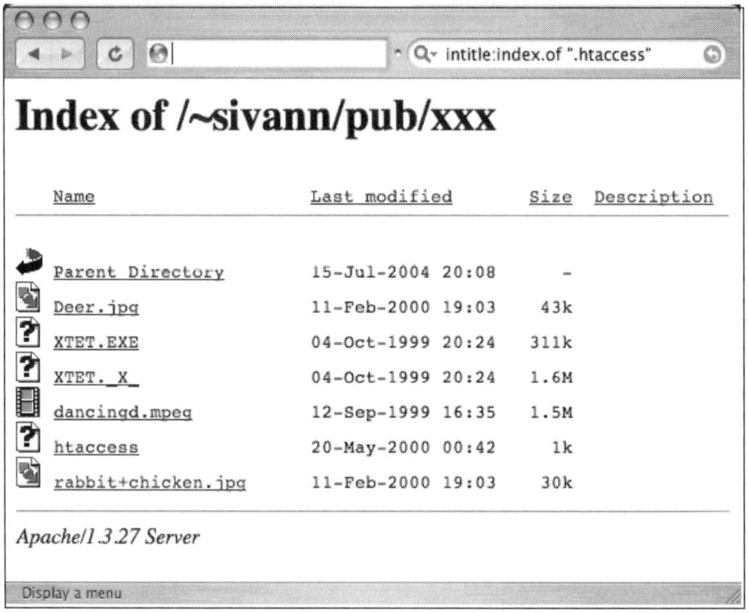

Directory listings should be disabled unless you intend to allow visitors to peruse files in an FTP-style fashion. On some servers, a directory listing will appear if an index file (as defined by your server configuration) is missing. These files, such as index.html, index.htm, or default.asp, should appear in each and every directory that should present a page to the user. On an Apache Web server, you can disable directory listings by placing a dash or minus sign before the word *Indexes* in the httpd.conf file. The line might look something like this if directory listings (or "indexes," as Apache calls them) are disabled:

```
Options -Indexes FollowSymLinks MultiViews
```

Robots.txt: Preventing Caching

The robots.txt file provides a list of instructions for automated Web crawlers, also called *robots* or *bots*. Standardized at www.robotstxt.org/wc/norobots.html, this file allows you to define, with a great deal of precision, which files and directories are off-limits to Web robots. The robots.txt file must be placed in the root of the Web server with permissions that allow the Web server to read the file. Lines in the file beginning with a # sign are considered comments and are ignored. Each line not beginning with a # should begin with either a *User-agent* or a *disallow* statement, followed by a colon and an optional space. These lines are written to disallow certain crawlers from accessing certain directories or files. Each Web crawler should send a *user-agent* field, which lists the name or type of the crawler. The value of Google's *user-agent* field is *Googlebot*. To address a *disallow* to Google, the *user-agent* line should read:

```
User-agent: Googlebot
```

According to the original specification, the wildcard character * can be used in the *user-agent* field to indicate all crawlers. The *disallow* line describes what, exactly; the crawler should *not* look at. The original specifications for this file were fairly inflexible, stating that a disallow line could only address a full or partial URL. According to that original specification, the crawler would ignore any URL *starting with* the specified string. For example, a line like *Disallow: /foo* would instruct the crawler to ignore not only */foo* but */foo/index.html,* whereas a line like *Disallow: /foo/* would instruct the crawler to ignore */foo/index.html* but *not /foo,* since the slash trailing *foo* must exist. For example, a valid robots.txt file is shown here:

```
#abandon hope all ye who enter
User-Agent: *
Disallow: /
```

This file indicates that no crawler is allowed on any part of the site—the ultimate exclude for Web crawlers. The robots.txt file is read from top to bottom as ordered rules. There is no *allow* line in a robots.txt file. To include a particular crawler, disallow it access to *nothing.* This might seem like backward logic, but the following robots.txt file indicates that all crawlers are to be sent away *except* for the crawler named *Palookaville*:

```
#Bring on Palookaville
User-Agent: *
Disallow: /
User-Agent: Palookaville
Disallow:
```

Notice that there is no slash after Palookaville's *disallow.* (Norman Cook fans will be delighted to notice the absence of both slashes *and* dots from anywhere near Palookaville.) Saying that there's no *disallow* is like saying that user agent is *allowed*—sloppy and confusing, but that's the way it is.

Google allows for extensions to the robots.txt standard. A disallow pattern may include * to match any number of characters. In addition, a $ indicates the end of a name. For example, to prevent the Googlebot from crawling all your PDF documents, you can use the following robots.txt file:

```
#Away from my PDF files, Google!
User-Agent: Googlebot
Disallow: /*.PDF$
```

Once you've gotten a robots.txt file in place, you can check its validity by visiting the Robots.txt Validator at www.sxw.org.uk/computing/robots/check.html.

Underground Googling

Web Crawlers and Robots.txt

Hackers don't have to obey your robots.txt file. In fact, Web crawlers really don't have to, either, although most of the big-name Web crawlers will, if only for the "CYA" factor. One fairly common hacker trick is to view a site's robots.txt file first to get an idea of how files and directories are mapped on the server. In fact, as shown in Figure 12.2, a quick Google query can reveal lots of sites that have had their robots.txt files *crawled*. This, of course, is a misconfiguration, because the robots.txt file is meant to stay behind the scenes.

Figure 12.2 Robots.txt Should Not Be Crawled

NOARCHIVE: The Cache "Killer"

The robots.txt file keeps Google away from certain areas of your site. However, there could be cases where you want Google to crawl a page, but you don't want Google to cache a copy of the page or present a "cached" link in its search results. This is accomplished with a *META* tag. To prevent all (cooperating) crawlers from archiving or caching a document, place the following *META* tag in the *HEAD* section of the document:

```
<META NAME="ROBOTS" CONTENT="NOARCHIVE">
```

If you prefer to keep *only* Google from caching the document, use this *META* tag in the *HEAD* section of the document:

```
<META NAME="GOOGLEBOT" CONTENT="NOINDEX, NOFOLLOW">
```

Any cooperating crawler can be addressed in this way by inserting its name as the *META NAME*. Understand that this rule only addresses crawlers. Web visitors (and hackers) can still access these pages.

NOSNIPPET: Getting Rid of Snippets

A *snippet* is the text listed below the title of a document on the Google results page. Providing insight into the returned document, snippets are convenient when you're blowing through piles of results. However, in some cases, snippets should be removed. Consider the case of a subscription-based news service. Although this type of site would like to have the kind of exposure that Google can offer, it needs to protect its content (including snippets of content) from nonpaying subscribers. Such a site can accomplish this goal by combining the *NOSNIPPET META* tag with IP-based filters that allow Google's crawlers to browse content unmolested. To keep Google from displaying snippets, insert this code into the document:

```
<META NAME="GOOGLEBOT" CONTENT="NOSNIPPET">
```

An interesting side effect of the *NOSNIPPET* tag is that Google will not cache the document. *NOSNIPPET* removes both the snippet and the cached page.

Password-Protection Mechanisms

Google does not fill in user authentication forms. When presented with a typical password form, Google seems to simply back away from that page, keeping nothing but the page's URL in its database. Although it was once rumored that Google bypasses or somehow magically side-steps security checks, those rumors have never been substantiated. These incidents are more likely an issue of timing.

If Google crawls a password-protected page either before the page is protected or while the password protection is down, Google will cache an image of the protected page. Clicking the original page will show the password dialog, but the cached page does not—

providing the illusion that Google has bypassed that page's security. In other cases, a Google news search will provide a snippet of a news story from a subscription site (shown in Figure 12.3), but clicking the link to the story presents a registration screen, as shown in Figure 12.4. This also creates the illusion that Google somehow magically bypasses pesky password dialogs and registration screens.

Figure 12.3 Google Grabs Information from the Protected Site

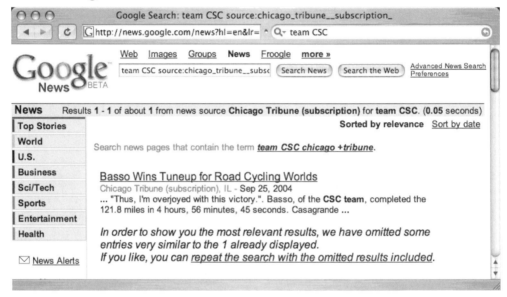

Figure 12.4 A Password-Protected News Site

If you're really serious about keeping the general public (and crawlers like Google) away from your data, consider a password authentication mechanism. A basic password authentication mechanism, htaccess, exists for Apache. An htaccess file, combined with an htpasswd file, allows you to define a list of username/password combinations that can access specific directories. You'll find an Apache htaccess tutorial at http://httpd.apache.org/docs/howto/htaccess.html, or try a Google search for *htaccess howto*.

Software Default Settings and Programs

As we've seen throughout this book, even the most basic Google hacker can home in on default pages, phrases, page titles, programs, and documentation with very little effort. Keep this in mind and remove these items from any Web software you install. It's also good security practice to ensure that default accounts and passwords are removed as well as any installation scripts or programs that were supplied with the software. Since the topic of Web server security is so vast, we'll take a look at some of the highlights you should consider for a few common servers.

First, for Microsoft IIS 6.0, consider the *IIS 6.0 Security Best Practices* document listed in the *Links* section at the end of this chapter.

For IIS 5, the *Microsoft IIS 5.0 Security Checklist* (see the "Links to Sites" section at the end of this chapter) lists quite a few tasks that can help lock down an IIS 5.0 server in this manner:

- Remove the \IISSamples directory (usually from c:\inetpub\iissamples).

- Remove the \IISHelp directory (usually from c:\winnt\help\iishelp).

- Remove the \MSADC directory (usually from c:\program files\common files\system\msadc).

- Remove the IISADMPWD virtual directory (found in c:\winnt\system32\inetsrv\iisadmpwd directory and the ISM.dll file).

- Remove unused script extensions:

  - Web-based password change: .htr

  - Internet database connector: .idc

  - Server-side includes: .stm, .shtm and .shtml

  - Internet printing: .printer

  - Index server: .htw, .ida and .idq

The Apache 1.3 series comes with fewer default pages and directories, but keep an eye out for the following:

- The /manual directory from the Web root contains the default documentation.

- Several language files in the Web root beginning with index.html. These default language files can be removed if unused.

For more information about securing Apache, see the *Security Tips* document at http://httpd.apache.org/docs/2.0/misc/security_tips.html.

Underground Googling

Patch That System

It certainly sounds like a cliché in today's security circles, but it can't be stressed enough: If you choose to do only one thing to secure any of your systems, it should be to keep up with and install all the latest software security patches. Misconfigurations make for a close second, but without a firm foundation, your server doesn't stand a chance.

Hacking Your Own Site

Hacking into your own site is a great way to get an idea of its potential security risks. Obviously, no single person can know everything there is to know about hacking, meaning that hacking your own site is no replacement for having a real penetration test performed by a professional. Even if you are a pen tester by trade, it never hurts to have another perspective on your security posture. In the realm of Google hacking, there are several automated tools and techniques you can use to give yourself another perspective on how Google sees your site. We'll start by looking at some manual methods, and we'll finish by discussing some automated alternatives.

> **WARNING**
>
> As we'll see in this chapter, there are several ways a Google search can be automated. Google frowns on any method that does not use its supplied Application Programming Interface (API) along with a Google license key. Assume that any program that does not ask you for your license key is running in violation of Google's terms of service and could result in banishment from Google. Check out www.google.com/accounts/TOS for more information. Be nice to Google and Google will be nice to you!

Site Yourself

We've talked about the *site* operator throughout the book, but remember that *site* allows you to narrow a search to a particular domain or server. If you're sullo, the author of the (most impressive) NIKTO tool and administrator of cirt.net, a query like *site:cirt.net* will list all Google's cached pages from your cirt.net server, as shown in Figure 12.5.

Figure 12.5 A Site Search is One Way to Test Your Google Exposure

You could certainly click each and every one of these links or simply browse through the list of results to determine if those pages are indeed supposed to be public, but this exercise could be very time consuming, especially if the number of results is more than a few hundred. Obviously, you need to automate this process. Let's take a look at some automation tools.

Gooscan

Gooscan, written by Johnny Long, is a Linux-based tool that enables bulk Google searches. The tool was not written with the Google API and therefore violates Google's Terms of Service (TOS). It's a judgment call as to whether or not you want to knowingly violate Google's TOS to scan Google for information leaks originating from your site. If you decide to use a non-API-based tool, remember that Google can (though very rarely does) block certain IP ranges from using its search engine. Also keep in mind that this tool was designed for securing your site, not breaking into other people's sites. Play nice with the other children, and unless you're accustomed to living on the legal edge, use the Gooscan code as a learning tool and don't actually run it!

Gooscan is available from http://johnny.ihackstuff.com. Don't expect much in the way of a fancy interface or point-and-click functionality. This tool is command-line only and requires a smidge of technical knowledge to install and run. The benefit is that Gooscan is lean and mean and a good alternative to some Windows-only tools.

Installing Gooscan

To install Gooscan, first download the tar file, decompressing it with the *tar* command. Gooscan comes with one C program, a README file, and a directory filled with data files, as shown in Figure 12.6.

Figure 12.6 Gooscan Extraction and Installation

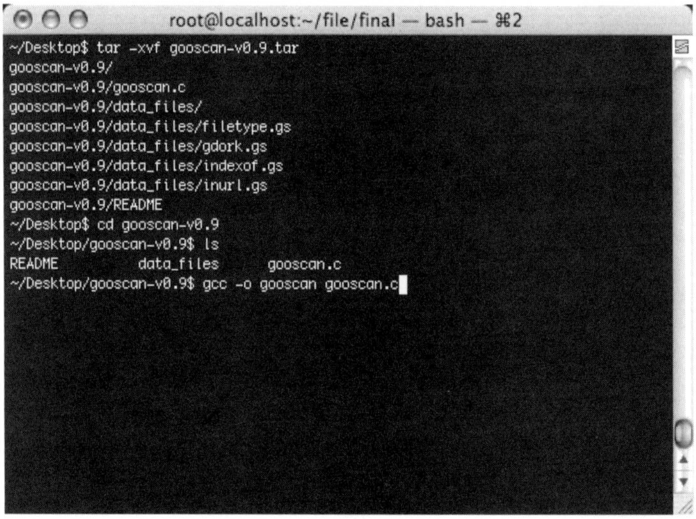

Once the files have been extracted from the tar file, you must compile Gooscan with a compiler such as GCC. Mac users should first install the XCode package from the Apple Developers Connection Web site, http://connect.apple.com/. Windows users should consider a more "graphical" alternative such as Athena or SiteDigger, because Gooscan does not currently compile under environments like CYGWIN.

Gooscan's Options

Gooscan's usage can be listed by running the tool with no options (or a combination of bad options), as shown in Figure 12.7.

Figure 12.7 Gooscan's Usage

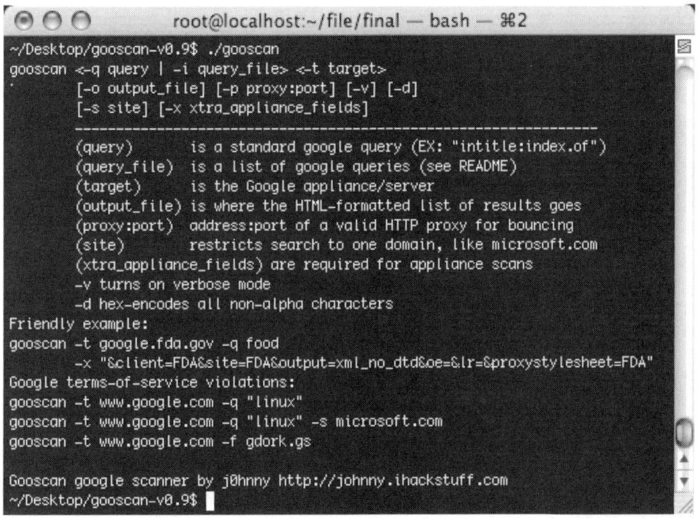

Gooscan's most commonly used options are outlined in the included README file. Let's take a look at how the various options work:

- **<-t target> (required argument)** This is the Google appliance or server to scan. An IP address or host name can be used here. Caution: Entering *www.google.com* here violates Google's terms of service and is neither recommended nor condoned by the author.

- **<-q query | -i query_file> (required argument)** The query or query file to send. Gooscan can be used to send an individual query or a series of queries read from a file. The *-q* option takes one argument, which can be any valid Google query. For example, these are valid options:

```
-q googledorks
-q "microsoft sucks"
-q "intitle:index.of secret"
```

- **[-i input_file] (optional argument)** The *-i* option takes one argument—the name of a Gooscan data file. Using a data file allows you to perform multiple queries with Gooscan. See the following list for information about the included Gooscan data files.

- **[-o output_file] (optional argument)** Gooscan can create a nice HTML output file. This file includes links to the actual Google search results pages for each query.

- **[-p proxy:port] (optional argument)** This is the address and port of an HTML proxy server. Queries will be sent here and bounced off to the appliance indicated with the *-t* argument. The format can be similar to 10.1.1.150:80 or *proxy.validcompany.com:8080.*

- **[-v] (optional argument)** Verbose mode. Every program needs a verbose mode, especially when the author sucks with a command-line debugger.

- **[-s site] (optional argument)** This filters only results from a certain site, adding the *site* operator to each query Gooscan submits. This argument has absolutely no meaning when used against Google appliances, since Google appliances are already site filtered. For example, consider the following Google queries:

```
site:microsoft.com linux
site:apple.com microsoft
site:linux.org microsoft
```

- **With advanced express permission from Google** (you do have advanced permission from Google, don't you?) you could run the following with Gooscan to achieve the same results:

```
$ ./gooscan -t www.google.com -s microsoft.com linux
$ ./gooscan -t www.google.com -s apple.com microsoft
$ ./gooscan -t www.google.com -s linux.org microsoft
```

The *[-x]* and *[-d]* options are used with the Google appliance. We don't talk too much about the Google appliance in this book. Suffice it to say that the vast majority of the techniques that work against Google.com will work against a Google appliance as well.

Gooscan's Data Files

Used in multiple query mode, Gooscan reads queries from a data file. The format of the data files is as follows:

```
search_type | search_string | count | description
```

search_type can be one of the following:

- **intitle** Finds *search_string* in the title of the page. If requested on the command line, Gooscan will append the site query. Example:

```
intitle|error||
```

This will find the word *error* in the title of a page.

- **inurl** Finds *search_string* in the URL of the page. If requested on the command line, Gooscan will append the site query. Example:

```
inurl|admin||
```

This will find the word *admin* in the URL of a page.

- **indexof** Finds *search_string* in a directory listing. If requested on the command line, Gooscan will append the site query. Directory listings often will have the term *index of* in the title of the page. Gooscan will generate a Google query that looks something like this:

```
intitle:index.of search_string
```

NOTE

When using the site switch, Gooscan automatically performs a generic search for directory listings. That query looks like this: intitle:index.of site:site_name. If this generic query returns no results, Gooscan will skip any subsequent indexof searches. It is a logical conclusion to skip specific indexof searches if the most generic of indexof searches returns nothing.

- **filetype** Finds *search_string* as a filename, inserting the site query if requested on the command line. For example:

```
filetype|cgi cgi||
```

This search will find files that have an extension of .cgi.

- **raw** This *search_type* allows the user to build custom queries. The query is passed to Google unmodified, adding a site query if requested in the command line. For example:

```
raw|filetype:xls email username password||
```

This example will find Excel spreadsheets with the words *email*, *username*, and *password* inside the document.

- **search string** The *search_string* is fairly straightforward. Any string is allowed here except chars \n and |. This string is *HTML-ized* before sending to Google. The *A* character is converted to *%65*, and so on. There are some exceptions, such as the fact that spaces are converted to the + character.

- **count** This field records the approximate number of hits found when a similar query is run against all of Google. *Site* is not applied. This value is somewhat arbitrary in that it is based on the rounded numbers supplied by Google and that this number can vary widely based on when and how the search is performed. Still, this number can provide a valuable watermark for sorting data files and creating custom

data files. For example, zero count records could safely be eliminated before running a large search. (This field is currently not used by Gooscan.)

- **description** This field describes the search type. Currently, only the filetype.gs data
  file populates this field. Keep reading for more information on the filetype.gs data
  file.

Several data files are included with Gooscan, each with a distinct purpose:

- **gdork.gs** This file includes excerpts from the Google Hacking Database (GHDB)
  hosted at http://johnny.ihackstuff.com. The GHDB is the Internet's largest database
  of Google hacking queries maintained by thousands of members who make up the
  Search Engine Hacking Forums, also hosted at http://johnny.ihackstuff.com.
  Updated many times a week, the GHDB currently sits at around 1500 unique
  queries.

- **filetype.gs** This *huge* file contains every known filetype in existence, according to
  www.filext.com. By selecting interesting lines from this file, you can quickly determine the types of files that exist on a server that might warrant further investigation. We suggest creating a subset of this file (with a Linux command such as:

  ```
  head -50 filetype.gs > short_filetype.gs
  ```

  for use in the field. Do not run this file as is. It's too big. With over 8,000
  queries, this search would certainly take quite a while and burn precious
  resources on the target server. Instead, rely on the numbers in the *count* field to
  tell you how many (approximate) sites contain these files in Google, selecting
  only those that are the most common or relevant to your site. The filetypes.gs
  file lists the most commonly found extensions at the top.

- **inurl.gs** This *very large* data file contains strings from the most popular CGI scanners, which excel at locating programs on Web servers. Sorted by the approximate
  number of Google hits, this file lists the most common strings at the top, with very
  esoteric CGI vulnerability strings listed near the bottom. This data file locates the
  strings in the URL of a page. This is another file that shouldn't be run in its
  entirety.

- **indexof.gs** Nearly identical to the inurl.gs file, this data file finds the strings in a
  directory listing. Run portions of this file, not all of it!

Using Gooscan

Gooscan can be used in two distinct ways: single-query mode or multiple-query mode.
Single-query mode is little better than using Google's Web search feature, with the exception
that Gooscan will provide you with Google's number of results in a more portable format.

As shown in Figure 12.8, a search for the term *daemon9* returns 2440 results from *all of Google*. To narrow this search to a specific site, such as phrack.org, add the *[-s]* option. For example:

```
gooscan -q "daemon9" -t www.google.com -s phrack.org.
```

Figure 12.8 Gooscan's Single-Query Mode

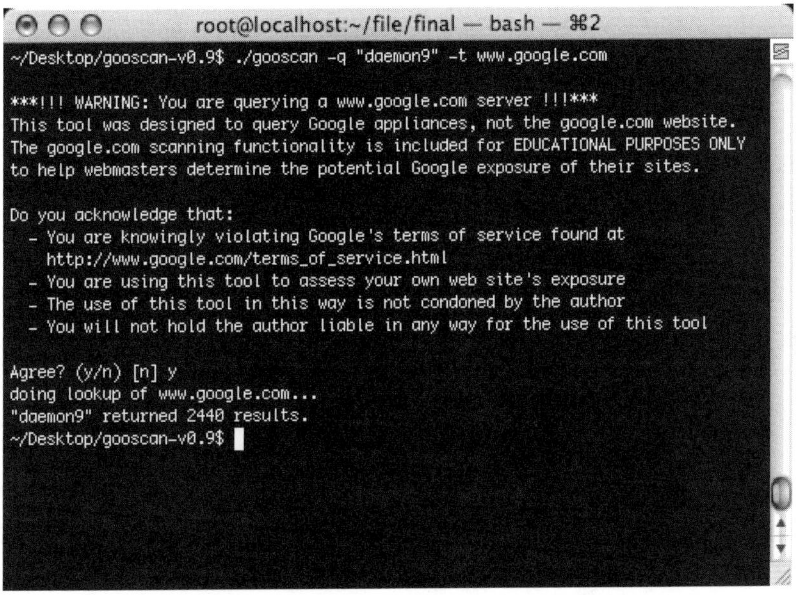

Notice that Gooscan presents a very lengthy disclaimer when you select www.google.com as the target server. This disclaimer is only presented when you submit a search that potentially violates Google TOS. The output from a standard Gooscan run is fairly paltry, listing only the number of hits from the Google search. You can apply the *[-o]* option to create a nicer HTML output format. To run the *daemon9* query with nicer output, run:

```
gooscan -q "daemon9" -t www.google.com -o daemon9.html
```

As shown in Figure 12.9, the HTML output lists the options that were applied to the Gooscan run, the date the scan was performed, a list of the queries, a link to the actual Google search, and the number of results.

Figure 12.9 Gooscan's HTML Output in Single-Query Mode

The link in the HTML output points to Google. Clicking the link will perform the Google search for you. Don't be too surprised if the numbers on Google's page differ from what is shown in the Gooscan output; Google's search results are sometimes only approximations.

Running Google in multiple-query mode is a blatant violation of Google's TOS but shouldn't cause too much of a Google-stink if it's done judiciously. One way to keep Google on your good side is to respect the spirit of its TOS by sending small batches of queries and not pounding the server with huge data files. As shown in Figure 12.10, you can create a small data file using the *head* command. A command such as:

```
head -5 data_files/gdork.gs > data_files/little_gdork.gs
```

will create a four-query data file, since the gdork.gs file has a commented header line.

Figure 12.10 Running Small Data Files Could Keep Google from Frowning at You

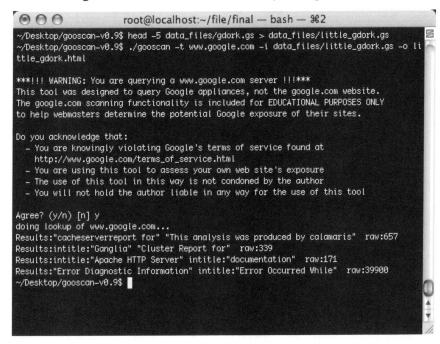

The output from the multiple-query run of Gooscan is still paltry, so let's take a look at the HTML output shown in Figure 12.11.

Figure 12.11 Gooscan's HTML Output in Multiple-Query Mode

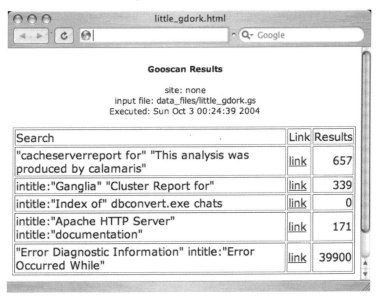

Using Gooscan with the *[-s]* switch we can narrow our results to one particular site, in this case http://johnny.ihackstuff.com, with a command such as:

```
Gooscan -t www.google.com -i data_files/little_gdork.gs -o ihackstuff.html -s
johnny.ihackstuff.com
```

as shown in Figure 12.12. (Don't worry, that Johnny guy won't mind!)

Figure 12.12 A Site-Narrowed Gooscan Run

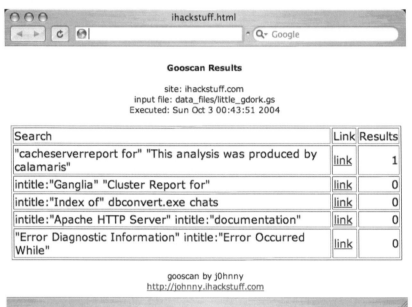

Most site-narrowed Gooscan runs should come back pretty clean, as this run did. If you see hits that look suspicious, click the link to see exactly what Google saw. Figure 12.13 shows the Google search in its entirety.

In this case, we managed to locate the Google Hacking Database itself, which included a reference that matched our Google query. The other searches didn't return any results, because they were a tad more specific than the Calamaris query, which didn't search titles, URLs, filetypes, and the like.

In summary, Gooscan is a great tool for checking your Web site's exposure, but it should be used cautiously since it does not use the Google API. Break your scans into small batches, unless you (unwisely) like thumbing your nose at the Establishment.

Figure 12.13 Linking to Google's Results from Gooscan

Windows Tools and the .NET Framework

The Windows tools we'll look at all require the Microsoft .NET framework, which can be located with a Google query of *.NET framework download*. The successful installation of the framework depends on a number of factors, but regardless of the version of Windows you're running, assume that you must be current on all the latest service packs and updates. If Windows Update is available on your version of Windows, run it. The Internet Explorer upgrade, available from the Microsoft Web site (Google query: *Internet Explorer upgrade*) is the most common required update for successful installation of the .NET Framework. Before downloading and installing Athena or Wikto, make sure you've got the .NET Framework (versions 1.1 or 2.0 respectively) properly installed.

> **NOTE**
>
> The only way Google will explicitly allow you to automate your queries is via the Google Application Programming Interface. Some of the API tools covered in this book rely on the SOAP API, which Google discontinued in favor of the AJAX API. If you have an old SOAP API key, you're in luck. That key will still work with API-based tools. However, if you don't have a SOAP key, you should consider using SensePost's Aura program (www.sensepost.com/research/aura) as an alternative to the old SOAP API.

Athena

Athena by Steve Lord (steve@buyukada.co.uk) is a Windows-based Google scanner that is not based on the Google API. As with Gooscan, the use of this tool is in violation of Google's TOS and that as a result, Google can block your IP range from using its search engine. Athena is potentially less intrusive than Gooscan, since Athena only allows you to perform one search at a time, but Google's TOS is clear: no automated scanning is allowed. Just as we discussed with Gooscan, use any non–API tool judiciously. History suggests that if you're nice to Google, Google will be nice to you.

Athena can be downloaded from http://snakeoillabs.com/. The download consists of a single MSI file. Assuming you've installed version 1.1 of the .NET Framework, the Athena installer is a simple wizard, much like most Windows-based software. Once installed and run, Athena presents the main screen, as shown in Figure 12.14.

Figure 12.14 Athena's Main Screen

As shown, this screen resembles a simple Web browser. The *Refine Search* field allows you to enter or refine an existing query. The Search button is similar to Google's Search button and executes a search, the results of which are shown in the browser window.

To perform basic searches with Athena, you need to load an XML file containing your desired search strings. Simply open the file from within Athena and all the searches will appear in the Select Query drop-down box. For example, loading the *digicams* XML file included with Athena will load a nice array of digital photo searches. Simply select a query from the list and click the **Search** button. For example, selecting *1st photo with a PENTAX cam* and clicking *Search* will deliver the Google results for that search, as shown in Figure 12.15.

Figure 12.15 Basic Search Results

Athena also allows you to add modifiers to the query using the *Refine Search* box. Using the previous query, entering **inurl:"buddylist.blt"** into the Refine Search box and clicking the **Search** button provides a much cleaner search (see Figure 12.16).

Figure 12.16 Athena's Refine Query Feature in Action

The results show that the image does not exist on the http://johnny.ihackstuff.com website. At this point, Athena might seem rather pointless. It functions just like a Web browser, submitting queries into Google and displaying the results. However, Athena's most powerful functionality lies in its XML-based configuration files.

Using Athena's Config Files

Two of these files are included with Athena: Athena.xml and digicams.xml. These files contain custom queries and descriptions of those queries. The digicams file contains sample queries for finding images and the Athena.xml file contains the queries found in the GHDB.

To load the GHDB, simply select **File | Open Config** and select the Athena.XML file.

Figure 12.17 Athena Loaded with Athena.XML

Jut as with the *digicams* image search, queries found in the GHDB can be modified and resubmitted through the *Refine Search* field.

Constructing Athena Config Files

Athena's XML-based config files, can be modified or even completely overhauled based on your needs. There are two main sections to the XML file: a *searchEngine* section and the *signature* section. The *searchEngine section* describes how a particular search engine's queries are constructed. A typical *searchEngine* section is shown in the following code examples.

```
<searchEngine>
        <searchEngineName>Google (UK)</searchEngineName>
        <searchEnginePrefixUrl>http://www.google.co.uk/search?q=
        </searchEnginePrefixUrl>
        <searchEnginePostfixUrl>%26ie=UTF-8%26hl=en%26meta=
        </searchEnginePostfixUrl>
</searchEngine>
```

This section is responsible for describing how the various search engines handle search requests. The *searchEngineName* field is simply a text-based field that describes the name of the search engine. This name will appear in Athena's drop-down box, allowing you to select from among different search engines. The *searchEnginePrefixUrl* field represents the first part of the search URL that is sent to the search engine. It is assumed that the query part of the search will be filled in after this prefix. The *searchEnginePostfixURL* field describes the part of the URL that will come after the prefix and the query. This usually describes various options such as output format (UTF-8). Note that Athena uses the *<searchEngine>* section, and SiteDigger does not. This section could be reworked to search the U.S.-based Google engine with the following *searchEngine* section:

```
<searchEngine>
        <searchEngineName>Google (US)</searchEngineName>
        <searchEnginePrefixUrl>http://www.google.com/search?q=
        </searchEnginePrefixUrl>
        <searchEnginePostfixUrl>%26ie=UTF-8%26hl=en%26meta=
        </searchEnginePostfixUrl>
</searchEngine>
```

The *signature* section describes the individual searches that are to be performed. A typical *signature* section is shown in the following code example:

```
<signature>
        <signatureReferenceNumber>22
        </signatureReferenceNumber>
        <categoryref>T1</categoryref>
        <category>TECHNOLOGY PROFILE</category>
        <querytype>DON</querytype>
        <querystring>intitle:"Index of" secring.bak
        </querystring>
        <shortDescription>PGP Secret KeyRing Backup
        </shortDescription>
        <textualDescription>This query looked for a backup of the PGP secret key
        ring. With this keyring an attacker could decrypt messages encrypted by the
        user. </textualDescription>
        <cveNumber>1000</cveNumber>
        <cveLocation>http://johnny.ihackstuff.com</cveLocation>
</signature>
```

The *signatureReferenceNumber* is a unique number assigned to each signature. The *categoryref* is a unique number that describes the signature in the context of its category, which is described in full by *category*. The *querystring* is the Google query that is to be performed. It is made HTML-friendly and inserted between the *searchEnginePrefixUrl* and the *searchEnginePostfixUrl* in the URL sent to Google. *shortDescription* and *textualDescription* are short and long descriptions of the search, respectively. The *cveNumber* and *cveLocation* refer to the www.cve.mitre.org Common Vulnerabilities and Exposures list.

The header of the XML file should contain these lines:

```
<?xml version="1.0" encoding="utf-8"?>
<searchEngineSignature>
```

and the file should be closed out with a *</searchEngineSignature>* line as well.

Using this format, it's fairly simple to create a file of custom queries. The file must conform to the UTF-8 character set and be strictly XML compliant. This means that HTML tags such as *<A HREF>* and *
* must not only be matched with closing tags but that each HTML tag be case sensitive. Microsoft's XML scanner will complain about an opening *
* tag followed by a closing *
* tag, since the case of the tags is different. The less-than and greater-than symbols (< and >) can also cause problems when used improperly. If your data contains the Internet shorthand for "grin," which is *<G>*, the MS XML scanner will complain.

Tools and Traps…

Current Config Files

The maintainers of the GHDB make available current config files for use with Athena. This file can be downloaded from http://johnny.ihackstuff.com.

Wikto

Wikto is an amazing web scanning tool written by Roloef Temmingh while he was with Sensepost (www.sensepost.com). Wikto does many different things, but since this book focuses on Google hacking, we'll take a look at the Google scanning portions of the tool. By default, Wikto launches a wizard interface as shown in Figure 11.18.

Figure 12.18 Wikto's Target Selection Panel

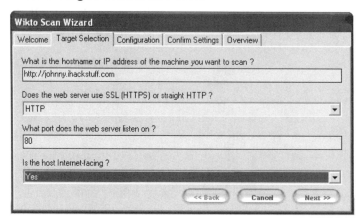

Wikto will first prompt for the target you wish to scan, as well as details about the target server. Clicking the *Next* button loads the *Configuration* panel *as shown in Figure 11.19*

Figure 12.19 Wikto's Configuration Panel

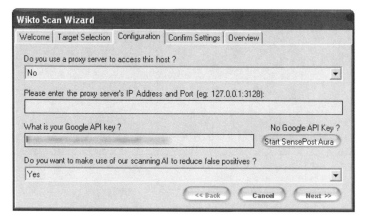

This panel prompts for proxy information and asks for your Google API key. The API issue is tricky, as Google is no longer giving out SOAP API keys. If you already have a SOAP API key (lucky you), enter it into the field and continue to the next panel. Otherwise, consider using Sensepost's Aura (www.sensepost.com/research/aura) tool to simulate Google SOAP API calls. Download and install Aura from the SensePost website, then click *Start SensePost Aura* to point Wikto at the Aura proxy. After entering an API key (or bypassing it with Aura), click through the rest of the wizard's confirmation screens. The main Wikto screen will be displayed. We will first concentrate on the *Googler* tab. Clicking *Start* will launch a Google scan against the target site, searching for the specific file types listed in

the *File Types* field. Figure 12.20 shows the result of a scan against
http://johnny.ihackstuff.com.

Figure 12.20 Wikto's Googler function

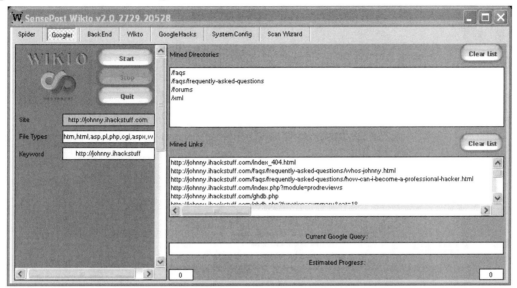

Notice that the output fields list files and directories that were located on the target site. All of this information was gathered through Google queries, meaning the transactions are transparent to the target. Wikto will use this directory and file information in later scanning stages.

Next, we'll take a look at the *GoogleHacks* tab, shown in Figure 12.21.

This scanning phase relies on the Google Hacking Database from http://johnny.ihack-stuff.com. Clicking the *Load Google Hacks Database* will load the most current version of the GHDB, providing Wikto with thousands of potentially malicious Google queries. Once the GHDB is loaded, pressing the *Start* button will begin the Google scan of the target site. What's basically happening here is Wikto is firing off tons of Google queries, each with a *site* operator which points to the target website. The GHDB is shown in the upper panel, and any results are presented in the lower panel. Clicking on a result in the lower panel will show the detailed information about that query (from the GHDB) in the middle panel. In this case, many results are returned, since the target website (http://johnny.ihackstuff.com) mentions each of these queries in great detail.

Figure 12.21 Wikto's GoogleHacks function

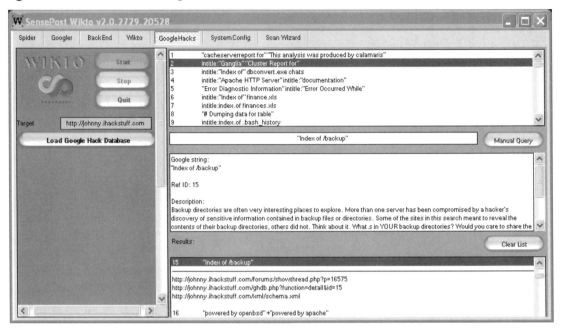

In addition to this automated scanning process, Wikto allows you to perform manual Google queries against the target through the use of the *Manual Query* button and the associated input field.

Wikto is an amazing tool with loads of features. Combined with GHDB compatibility, Wikto is definitely the best Google hacking tool currently available.

Google Rower

Google Rower is a Firefox extension (and also a stand–alone Windows program) that uses brute force lookup techniques to expand a search. Google Rower is a great tool to bypass the one thousand query lookup restriction. It accomplishes this by adding "padding digits" to a base query. It then harvests the results, removes duplicates, and displays the results. For example, Google Rower can obtain more results for the query *JeffBall5* by searching for *Jeffball55 a*, *Jeffball55 b*, *Jeffball55 c*, etc.

Google Rower can be downloaded from http://www.tankedgenius.com. Installation is a simple straightforward Firefox .xpi file installation. After installing Google Rower, open Firefox, select *Tools->Google Rower* and enter a query as shown in Figure 12.22.

Figure 12.22 GoogleRower Option Screen

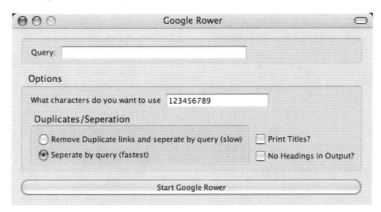

Entering a query of *ihackstuff* with the default options will query for the base term *ihack-stuff* followed by a series of characters, in this case the numbers one through nine. The results are sorted and displayed, as shown in Figure 12.23.

Figure 12.23 Google Rower Results

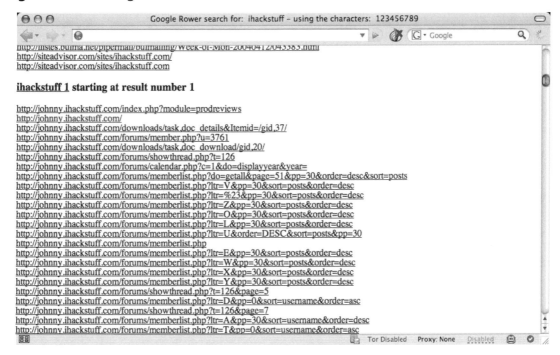

Alternatively you can right-click within Firefox and select *Google Rower*. In this case, Google Rower will launch with the query filled in based on the selected text.

Google Rower has several options to select from, as shown in Table 12.1.

Table 12.1 Google Rower Options

Google Rower Option	Description
Duplicates/Separation	Google Rower provides several different options for separating the links via query and removing the duplicate links. The different options affect speed and memory that the extension will use.
Print Titles	By default Google Rower outputs the links of the results returned by Google. Selecting this option allows the titles of the pages as reported by Google to be outputted.
No Headings in Output	By default Google Rower outputs some headings to show which links came from which query. Selecting this option turns off those Headings. This option is useful when the results will be piped into another program.

Google Site Indexer

Google Site Indexer (GSI) was written by Jeffball55 (Jeff Stewart) and CP. GSI uses some of Google's Advanced Operators, specifically *site and inurl* in order to create a file and directory map of a target web site. By sending Google queries such as site:tankedgenius.com, GSI can incrementally index all files Google has indexed. However, since Google only retrieves a maximum of a thousand results, GSI can mix the advanced operators (like site:tankedgenius.com inurl:cp) in order to get a better mix of unique results. GSI can be downloaded from www.tankedgenius.com.

Installation is a simple affair: clicking on the .xpi file from within Firefox will initiate the installation process. To run Google Site Indexer, open Firefox and select *Tools -> GSI*. The GSI interface will be displayed as shown in Figure 12.24.

Figure 12.24 GSI Options Screen

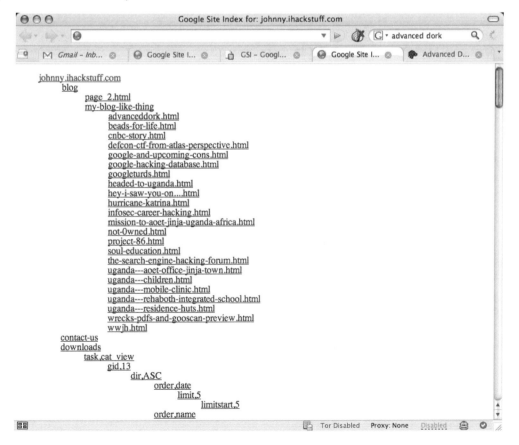

Execution is simple as well. Simply fill in the name of the target website, and click *Start GSI*. The results will be shown in a hierarchical format as shown in Figure 12.25.

Figure 12.25 GSI Output

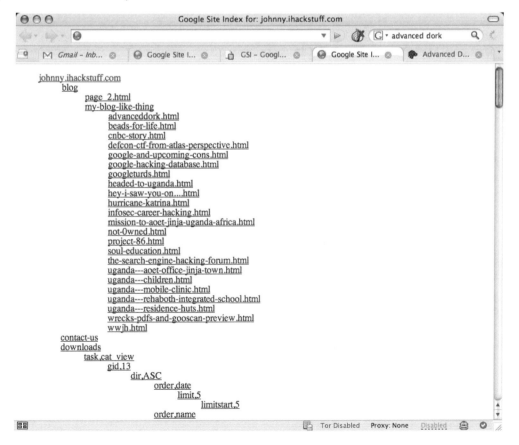

Notice that the results are presented in a hierarchical tree that represents the files and directories on the target site. Each link can be clicked on to browse to the appropriate page.

Alternatively you can right-click within Firefox and select *GSI*. In this case, GSI will launch with the query filled in based on the selected text, or if no text is selected, GSI will automatically fill in the name of the current website.

GSI has several options to select from, as shown in Table 12.2.

Table 12.2 GSI Options

GSI Option	Description
Recursive Search	If you choose to use a recursive search, GSI will use inurl searches. For example, if you choose to do a Google Site Index on tankedgenius.com. It would first send a query site:tankedgenius.com. The query would return a result of http://www.tankedgenius.com/blog/cp/index.html. If a recursive search is at level is at 1, then it would also send a query of site:tankedgenius.com inurl:blog. It would then add the results from that to the index. If the recursion level is set to 2, it would also send a query of site:tankedgenius.com inurl:cp and get the results.
Full website names	By default GSI displays an indented site index with only the directory name showing for each link. If you would prefer, you can set this option so that it shows the entire link

NOTE

Due to the nature of the Google queries that GSI sends, GSI may get 403 errors from Google. These errors are normal when sending queries with multiple operators.

Advanced Dork

Advanced Dork is an extension for Firefox and Mozilla browsers which provides Google Advanced Operators for use directly from the right-click context menu. Written by CP, the tool is available from https://addons.mozilla.org/en-US/firefox/addon/2144.

Like all Firefox extensions, installation is a snap: simply click the link to the .xpi file from within Firefox and the installation will launch.

Advanced Dork is context sensitive—Right licking will invoke Advanced Dork based on where the right-click was performed. For example, right-clicking on a link will invoke link-specific options as shown in Figure 12.26.

Figure 12.26 Advanced Dork Link Context

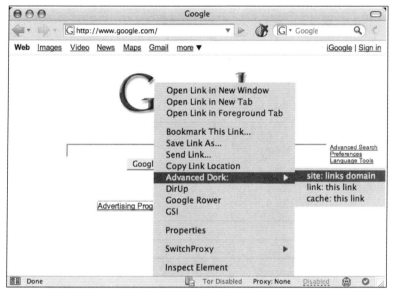

Right-clicking on a highlighted text will invoke the highlighted text search mode of Advanced Dork, as shown in Figure 12.27.

Figure 12.27

This mode will allow you to use the highlighted word in an *intitle, inurl, intext, site* or *ext* search. Several awesome options are available to Advanced Dork, as shown in Figures 12.28 and 12.29.

Figure 12.28

Figure 12.29

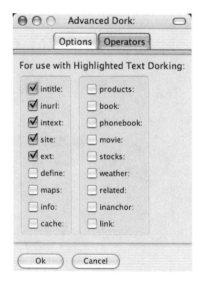

Some of these options are explained in Table 12.3.

Table 12.3 Advanced Dork Options

Option	Descriptions
Highlight Text Functions	Right click to choose from over 15 advanced Google operators. This function can be disabled in the options menu.
Right-Click HTML Page Info	Right click anywhere on a page with no text selected, and Advanced Dork will focus on the page's HTML title and ALT tags for searching using the intitle and allintext operators, respectively. This function can be disabled in the options menu.
Right-Click Links	Right click on a link to choose from site: links domain, link: this link, and cache: this link. Site: links domain will only search the domain name, not the full url.
Right Click URL Bar	Right click the URL Bar (Address Bar) and choose from site, inurl, link, and cache. Inurl works with the highlighted portion of text only. Site will only search the domain name, not the full url.

Advanced Dork is an amazing tool for any serious Google user. You should definitely add it to your arsenal.

Getting Help from Google

So far we've looked at various ways of checking your site for potential information leaks, but what can you do if you detect such leaks? First and foremost, you should remove the offending content from your site. This may be a fairly involved process, but to do it right, you should always figure out the source of the leak, to ensure that similar leaks don't happen in the future. Information leaks don't just happen; they are the result of some event that occurred. Figure out the event, resolve it, and you can begin to stem the source of the problem. Google makes a great Web page available that helps answer some of the most commonly asked questions from a Webmaster's perspective. The "Google Information for Webmasters" page, located at www.google.com/webmasters, lists all sorts of answers to commonly asked questions.

Solving the local problem is only half the battle. In some cases, Google has a cached copy of your information leak just waiting to be picked up by a Google hacker. There are two ways you can delete a cached version of a page. The first method involves the automatic URL removal system at http://www.google.com/webmasters/tools/removals. This page, shown in Figure 12.30, requires that you first verify your e-mail address. Although this appears to be a login for a Google account, Google accounts don't seem to provide you access. In most cases, you will have to reregister, even if you have a Google account. The exception seems to be Google Groups accounts, which appear to allow access to this page without a problem.

Figure 12.30 Google's Automatic URL Removal Tool

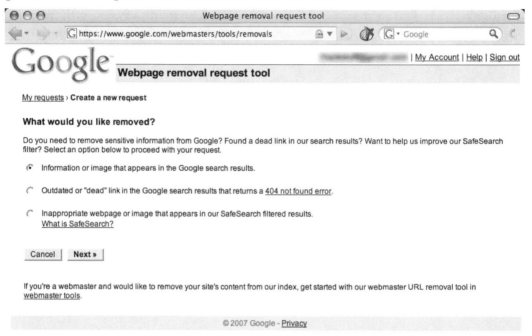

The URL removal tool will walk you through a series of questions that will verify your ownership of the content and determine what it is that you are trying to remove. Each of the options is fairly self-explanatory, but remember that the responsibility for content removal rests with you. You should ensure that your content is indeed removed from your site, and follow up the URL removal process with manual checks.

Summary

The subject of Web server security is too big for any one book. There are so many varied requirements combined with so many different types of Web server software, application software, and operating system software that no one book could do the topic justice. However, a few general principles can at least help you prevent the devastating effects a malicious Google hacker could inflict on a site you're charged with protecting.

First, understand how the Web server software operates in the event of an unexpected condition. Directory listings, missing index files, and specific error messages can all open up avenues for offensive information gathering. Robots.txt files, simple password authentication, and effective use of *META* tags can help steer Web crawlers away from specific areas of your site. Although Web data is generally considered public, remember that Google hackers might take interest in your site if it appears as a result of a malicious Google search. Default pages, directories and programs can serve as an indicator that there is a low level of technical know-how behind a site. Servers with this type of default information serve as targets for hackers. Get a handle on what, exactly; a search engine needs to know about your site to draw visitors without attracting undue attention as a result of too much exposure. Use any of the available tools, such as Gooscan, Athena, Wikto, GSI, Google Rower and Advanced Dork, to help you search Google for your site's information leaks. If you locate a page that shouldn't be public, use Google's removal tools to flush the page from Google's database.

Solutions Fast Track

A Good, Solid Security Policy

- An enforceable, solid security policy should serve as the foundation of any security effort.

- Without a policy, your safeguards could be inefficient or unenforceable.

Web Server Safeguards

- Directory listings, error messages, and misconfigurations can provide too much information.

- Robots.txt files and specialized *META* tags can help direct search engine crawlers away from specific pages or directories.

- Password mechanisms, even basic ones, keep crawlers away from protected content.

- Default pages and settings indicate that a server is not well maintained and can make that server a target.

Hacking Your Own Site

- Use the *site* operator to browse the servers you're charged with protecting. Keep an eye out for any pages that don't belong.

- Use a tool like Gooscan, Athena, GSI , Google Rower or Advanced Dork to assess your exposure. These tools do not use the Google API, so be aware that any blatant abuse or excessive activity could get your IP range cut off from Google.

- Use a tool like Wikto, which uses the Google API and should free you from fear of getting shut down.

- Use the Google Hacking Database to monitor the latest Google hacking queries. Use the GHDB exports with tools like Gooscan, Athena, or Wikto.

Getting Help from Google

- Use Google's Webmaster page for information specifically geared toward Webmasters.

- Use Google's URL removal tools to get sensitive data out of Google's databases.

Links to Sites

- **http://johnny.ihackstuff.com** The home of the Google Hacking Database (GHDB), the search engine hacking forums, the Gooscan tool, and the GHDB export files.

- **www.snakeoillabs.com** Home of Athena.

- http://www.seorank.com/robots-tutorial.htm A good tutorial on using the robots.txt file.

  http://googleblog.blogspot.com/2007/02/robots-exclusion-protocol.html Information about Google's Robots policy.

  http://www.microsoft.com/technet/archive/security/chklist/iis5cl.mspx The IIS 5.0 Security Checklist

  http://technet2.microsoft.com/windowsserver/en/library/ace052a0-a713-423e-8e8c-4bf198f597b81033.mspx The IIS 6.0 Security Best Practices

  http://httpd.apache.org/docs/2.0/misc/security_tips.html Apache Security Tips document

www.sensepost.com/research/aura Sensepost's AURA, which simulates Google SOAP API calls.

http://www.tankedgenius.com Home of JeffBall and Cp's GSI and Google Rower tools.

https://addons.mozilla.org/en-US/firefox/addon/2144 Home of Cp's Advanced Dork

Frequently Asked Questions

The following Frequently Asked Questions, answered by the authors of this book, are designed to both measure your understanding of the concepts presented in this chapter and to assist you with real-life implementation of these concepts. To have your questions about this chapter answered by the author, browse to **www. syngress.com/solutions** and click on the **"Ask the Author"** form.

Q: What is the no-cache pragma? Will it keep my pages from caching on Google's servers?

A: The no-cache pragma is a META tag that can be entered into a document to instruct the browser not to load the page into the browser's cache. This does not affect Google's caching feature; it is strictly an instruction to a client's browser. See www.htmlgoodies.com/beyond/nocache.html for more information.

Q: I'd like to know more about securing Web servers. Can you make any recommendations?

A:

Q: Can you provide any more details about securing IIS?

A: Microsoft makes available a very nice IIS Security Planning Tool. Try a Google search for *IIS Security Planning Tool*. Microsoft also makes available an IIS 5 security checklist; Google for *IIS 5 services checklist*. An excellent read pertaining to IIS 6 can be found with a query like *"elements of IIS security"*. Also, frequent the IIS Security Center. Try querying for *IIS security center*.

Q: Okay, enough about IIS. What about securing Apache servers?

A: Securityfocus.com has a great article, "Securing Apache: Step-by-Step," available from www.securityfocus.com/infocus/1694.

Q: Which is the best tool for checking my Google exposure?

A: That's a tough question, and the answer depends on your needs. The absolute most through way to check your Web site's exposure is to use the *site* operator. A query such as *site:gulftech.org* will show you all the pages on gulftech.org that Google knows about. By looking at each and every page, you'll absolutely know what Google has on you. Repeat this process once a week.

If this is too tedious, you'll need to consider an automation tool. A step above the *site* technique is Athena. Athena reads the full contents of the GHDB and allows you to step through each query, applying a *site* value to each search. This allows you to step through the comprehensive list of "bad searches" to see if your site is affected. Athena does not use the Google API but is not automated in the truest sense of the word. Gooscan is potentially the biggest Google automation offender when used improperly, since it is built on the GHDB and will crank through the entire GHDB in fairly short order. It does not use the Google API, and Google will most certainly notice you using it in its wide-open configuration. This type of usage is not recommended, since Google could make for a nasty enemy, but when Gooscan is used with discretion and respect for the spirit of Google's no-automation rule, it is a most thorough automated tool.

Index

Syngress: *The Definition of a Serious Security Library*

Syn·gress (sin‑gres): *noun, sing.* Freedom from risk or danger; safety. See *security.*

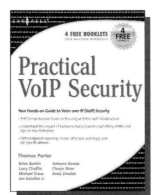

Syngress: *The Definition of a Serious Security Library*

Syn•gress (sin–gres): *noun, sing.* Freedom from risk or danger; safety. See *security*.

Syngress: *The Definition of a Serious Security Library*

Syn·gress (sin-gres): *noun, sing.* Freedom from risk or danger; safety. See *security*.

Phishing Exposed

Lance James, Secure Science Corporation,
Joe Stewart (Foreword)

If you have ever received a phish, become a victim of a phish, or manage the security of a major e-commerce or financial site, then you need to read this book. The author of this book delivers the unconcealed techniques of phishers including their evolving patterns, and how to gain the upper hand against the ever-accelerating attacks they deploy. Filled with elaborate and unprecedented forensics, Phishing Exposed details techniques that system administrators, law enforcement, and fraud investigators can exercise and learn more about their attacker and their specific attack methods, enabling risk mitigation in many cases before the attack occurs.

ISBN: 1-59749-030-X

Price: $49.95 US $69.95 CAN

Penetration Tester's Open Source Toolkit

Johnny Long, Chris Hurley, SensePost,
Mark Wolfgang, Mike Petruzzi

This is the first fully integrated Penetration Testing book and bootable Linux CD containing the "Auditor Security Collection," which includes over 300 of the most effective and commonly used open source attack and penetration testing tools. This powerful tool kit and authoritative reference is written by the security industry's foremost penetration testers including HD Moore, Jay Beale, and SensePost. This unique package provides you with a completely portable and bootable Linux attack distribution and authoritative reference to the toolset included and the required methodology.

ISBN: 1-59749-021-0

Price: $59.95 US $83.95 CAN

Google Hacking for Penetration Testers

Johnny Long, Foreword by Ed Skoudis

Google has been a strong force in Internet culture since its 1998 upstart. Since then, the engine has evolved from a simple search instrument to an innovative authority of information. As the sophistication of Google grows, so do the hacking hazards that the engine entertains. Approaches to hacking are forever changing, and this book covers the risks and precautions that administrators need to be aware of during this explosive phase of Google Hacking.

ISBN: 1-93183-636-1

Price: $44.95 U.S. $65.95 CAN

SYNGRESS®

Syngress: *The Definition of a Serious Security Library*

Syn·gress (sin–gres): *noun, sing.* Freedom from risk or danger; safety. See *security*.

Cisco PIX Firewalls:
Configure, Manage, & Troubleshoot

Charles Riley, Umer Khan, Michael Sweeney

Cisco PIX Firewall is the world's most used network firewall, protecting internal networks from unwanted intrusions and attacks. Virtual Private Networks (VPNs) are the means by which authorized users are allowed through PIX Firewalls. Network engineers and security specialists must constantly balance the need for air-tight security (Firewalls) with the need for on-demand access (VPNs). In this book, Umer Khan, author of the #1 best selling PIX Firewall book, provides a concise, to-the-point blueprint for fully integrating these two essential pieces of any enterprise network.

ISBN: 1-59749-004-0

Price: $49.95 US $69.95 CAN

Configuring Netscreen Firewalls

Rob Cameron

Configuring NetScreen Firewalls is the first book to deliver an in-depth look at the NetScreen firewall product line. It covers all of the aspects of the NetScreen product line from the SOHO devices to the Enterprise NetScreen firewalls. Advanced troubleshooting techniques and the NetScreen Security Manager are also covered..

ISBN: 1--93226-639-9

Price: $49.95 US $72.95 CAN

Configuring Check Point
NGX VPN-1/FireWall-1

Barry J. Stiefel, Simon Desmeules

Configuring Check Point NGX VPN-1/Firewall-1 is the perfect reference for anyone migrating from earlier versions of Check Point's flagship firewall/VPN product as well as those deploying VPN-1/Firewall-1 for the first time. NGX includes dramatic changes and new, enhanced features to secure the integrity of your network's data, communications, and applications from the plethora of blended threats that can breach your security through your network perimeter, Web access, and increasingly common internal threats.

ISBN: 1--59749-031-8

Price: $49.95 U.S. $69.95 CAN

SYNGRESS®

Syngress: *The Definition of a Serious Security Library*

Syn•gress (sin-gres): *noun, sing.* Freedom from risk or danger; safety. See *security.*